Java™ and XML

THE JAVA™ SERIES

Learning Java™
Java™ Threads
Java™ Network Programming
Java™ Virtual Machine
Java™ AWT Reference
Java™ Language Reference
Java™ Fundamental Classes Reference
Database Programming with JDBC™ and Java™
Java™ Distributed Computing
Developing Java Beans™
Java™ Security
Java™ Cryptography
Java™ Swing
Java™ Servlet Programming
Java™ I/O
Java™ 2D Graphics
Enterprise JavaBeans™
Creating Effective JavaHelp™
Java™ and XML

Also from O'Reilly

Java™ in a Nutshell
Java™ Examples in a Nutshell
Java™ Enterprise in a Nutshell
Java™ Foundation Classes in a Nutshell
Java™ Power Reference: A Complete Searchable Resource on CD-ROM

Java™ and XML

Brett McLaughlin

O'REILLY®

Beijing • Cambridge • Farnham • Köln • Paris • Sebastopol • Taipei • Tokyo

Java™ and XML
by Brett McLaughlin

Published by O'Reilly & Associates, Inc., 101 Morris Street, Sebastopol, CA 95472.

Editor: Mike Loukides

Production Editor: Madeleine Newell

Cover Designer: Hanna Dyer

Printing History:

June 2000: First Edition.

Library of Congress cataloging-in-publication data for this book can be found online at *http://www.oreilly.com/catalog/javaxml*

ISBN: 0-596-00016-2 [8/00]

[M]

Table of Contents

Preface ..... *ix*

1. ***Introduction*** *1*
   - What Is It? *2*
   - How Do I Use It? *12*
   - Why Should I Use It? *14*
   - What's Next? *31*

2. ***Creating XML*** *32*
   - An XML Document *33*
   - The Header *34*
   - The Content *36*
   - What's Next? *45*

3. ***Parsing XML*** *46*
   - Getting Prepared *47*
   - SAX Readers *49*
   - Content Handlers *54*
   - Error Handlers *74*
   - A Better Way to Load a Parser *81*
   - "Gotcha!" *84*
   - What's Next? *88*

4. *Constraining XML* 89
Why Constrain XML Data? 89
Document Type Definitions 93
XML Schema 108
What's Next? 124

5. *Validating XML* 125
Configuring the Parser 125
Output of XML Validation 130
The DTDHandler Interface 136
"Gotcha!" 139
What's Next? 141

6. *Transforming XML* 142
The Purpose 143
The Components 145
The Syntax 149
What's Next? 171

7. *Traversing XML* 173
Getting the Output 174
Getting the Input 176
The Document Object Model (DOM) 178
"Gotcha!" 197
What's Next? 199

8. *JDOM* 200
Parsers and the Java API for XML Parsing 200
JDOM: Another API? 205
Getting a Document 207
Using a Document 212
Outputting a Document 221
What's Next? 231

9. *Web Publishing Frameworks* 232
Selecting a Framework 234
Installation 236
Using a Publishing Framework 242
XSP 257
Cocoon 2.0 and Beyond 272
What's Next? 276

10. *XML-RPC* 277
RPC Versus RMI 278
Saying Hello 281
Putting the Load on the Server 294
The Real World 313
What's Next? 316

11. *XML for Configurations* 317
EJB Deployment Descriptors 318
Creating an XML Configuration File 321
Reading an XML Configuration File 328
The Real World 339
What's Next? 348

12. *Creating XML with Java* 349
Loading the Data 350
Modifying the Data 362
XML from Scratch 367
The Real World 370
What's Next? 378

13. *Business-to-Business* 379
The Foobar Public Library 380
mytechbooks.com 389
Push Versus Pull 399
The Real World 412
What's Next? 414

14. *XML Schema* 415
To DTD or Not To DTD 415
Java Parallels 418
What's Next? 427

A. *API Reference* 429

B. *SAX 2.0 Features and Properties* 463

Index 467

Preface

XML, XML, XML, XML. You can see it on hats and t-shirts, read about it on the cover of every technical magazine on the planet, and hear it on the radio or the occasional Gregorian chant album. . . . Well, maybe it hasn't gone quite that far yet, but don't be surprised if it does. XML, the Extensible Markup Language, has seemed to take over every aspect of technical life, particularly in the Java™ community. An application is no longer considered an enterprise-level product if XML isn't being used somewhere. Legacy systems are being accessed at a rate never before seen, and companies are saving millions and even billions of dollars on system integration, all because of three little letters. Java developers wake up with fever sweats wondering how they are going to absorb yet another technology, and the task seems even more daunting when embarked upon; the road to XML mastery is lined with acronyms: XML, XSL, XPath, RDF, XML Schema, DTD, PI, XSLT, XSP, JAXP™, SAX, DOM, and more. And there isn't a development manager in the world who doesn't want his or her team learning about XML today!

When XML became a formal specification at the World Wide Web Consortium in early 1998, relatively few were running in the streets claiming that the biggest thing since Java itself (arguably bigger!) had just made its way onto the technology stage. Barely two years later, XML and a barrage of related technologies for manipulating and constraining XML have become the mainstay of data representation for Java systems. XML promises to bring to a data format what Java brought to a programming language: complete portability. In fact, it is only with XML that the promise of Java is realized; Java's portability has been seriously compromised as proprietary data formats have been used for years, enabling an application to run on multiple platforms, but not across businesses in a standardized way. XML promises to fill this gap in complete interoperability for Java programs by removing these proprietary data formats and allowing systems to communicate using a standard means of data representation.

This is a book about XML, but it is geared specifically towards Java developers. While both XML and Java are powerful tools in their own right, it is their marriage that this book is concerned with, and that gives XML its true power. We will cover the various XML vocabularies, look at creating, constraining, and transforming XML, and examine all of the APIs for handling XML from Java code. Additionally, we cover the hot topics that have made XML such a popular solution for dynamic content, messaging, e-business, and data stores. Through it all, we take a very narrow view: that of the developer who has to put these tools to work. A candid look at the tools XML provides is given, and if something is not useful (even if it is popular!), we will address it and move on. If a particular facet of XML is a hidden gem, we will extract the value of the item and put it to use. *Java and XML* is meant to serve as a handbook to help you, and is neither a reference nor a book geared towards marketing XML.

Finally, the back half of this book is filled with working, practical code. Although available for download, the purpose of this code is to walk you through creating several XML applications, and you are encouraged to follow along with the examples rather than skimming the code. We introduce a new API for manipulating XML from Java as well, and complete coverage and examples are included. This book is for you, the Java developer, and it is about the real world; it is not a theoretical or fanciful flight through what is "cool" in the industry. We abandon buzzwords when possible, and define them clearly when not. All of the code and concepts within this book have been entered by hand into an editor, prodded and tested, and are intended to aid you on the path to mastering Java and XML.

Organization

This book is structured in a very particular way: the first half of the book (Chapters 1 through 7) focuses on getting you grounded in XML and the core Java APIs for handling XML. Although these chapters are not glamorous, they should be read in order, and at least skimmed even if you are familiar with XML. We cover the basics, from creating XML to transforming it. Chapter 8 serves as a halfway point in the book, covering an exciting new API for handling XML within Java, JDOM. This chapter is a must-read, as the API is being publicly released as this book goes to production, and this is *the* reference for JDOM 1.0 (as I wrote the API with Jason Hunter specifically for solving problems in using Java and XML!). The remainder of the book, Chapters 9 through 14, focuses on specific XML topics that continually are brought up at conferences and tutorials I am involved with, and seeks to get you neck-deep in using XML in your applications, now! Finally, there are two appendixes to wrap up the book. Here's a summary of the contents:

Chapter 1, Introduction
We look at what all the hype is about, examine the XML alphabet soup, and spend time discussing why XML is so important to the present and future of enterprise development.

Chapter 2, Creating XML
We start looking at XML by building an XML document from the ground up. Examination of the major XML constructs, such as elements, attributes, entities, and processing instructions is included.

Chapter 3, Parsing XML
The Simple API for XML (SAX), our first Java API for handling XML, is introduced and covered in this chapter. The parsing lifecycle is detailed, and the events that can be reported by SAX and used by developers are demonstrated.

Chapter 4, Constraining XML
In this chapter, we look at the two ways to impose constraints on XML documents: Document Type Definitions (DTDs) and XML Schema. We will dissect the differences and analyze when one should be used over the other.

Chapter 5, Validating XML
Complementing Chapter 4, this chapter looks at how to use the SAX skills previously learned to enforce validation constraints, as well as how to react when constraints are not met by XML documents.

Chapter 6, Transforming XML
In this chapter, the Extensible Stylesheet Language (XSL) and the other critical components for transforming XML from one format into another are introduced. We cover the various methods available for converting XML into other textual formats, and look at using formatting objects to convert XML into binary formats.

Chapter 7, Traversing XML
Continuing to look at transforming XML documents, we discuss XSL transformation processors and how they can be used to convert XML into other formats. We also examine the Document Object Model (DOM) and how it can be used for handling XML data.

Chapter 8, JDOM
We begin by looking at the Java API for XML Parsing (JAXP), and discuss the importance of vendor-independence when using XML. I then introduce the JDOM API, discuss the motivation behind its development, and detail its use, comparing it to SAX and DOM.

Chapter 9, Web Publishing Frameworks
This chapter looks at what a web publishing framework is, why it matters to you, and how to choose a good one. We then cover the Apache Cocoon

framework, taking an in-depth look at its feature set and how it can be used to serve highly dynamic content over the Web.

Chapter 10, XML-RPC
In this chapter, we cover Remote Procedure Calls (RPC), their relevance in distributed computing as compared to RMI, and how XML makes RPC a viable solution for some problems. We then look at using XML-RPC Java libraries and building XML-RPC clients and servers.

Chapter 11, XML for Configurations
In this chapter, we look at using configuration data in an XML format and why that format is so important to cross-platform applications, particularly as it relates to distributed systems.

Chapter 12, Creating XML with Java
Although this topic is covered in part in other chapters, here we look at the process of generating and mutating XML from Java and how to perform these modifications from server-side components such as Java servlets, and outline concerns when mutating XML.

Chapter 13, Business-to-Business
This chapter details a "case study" of creating inter- and intra-business communication channels using XML as a portable data format. Using multiple languages, we build several application components for different companies that all interact with each other using XML.

Chapter 14, XML Schema
We revisit XML Schema here, looking at why the XML Schema specification has garnered so much attention and how reality measures up to the promise of the XML Schema concept, and examining why Java and XML Schema are such complementary technologies.

Appendix A, API Reference
This appendix details all the classes, interfaces, and methods available for use in the SAX, DOM, JAXP, and JDOM APIs.

Appendix B, SAX 2.0 Features and Properties
This appendix details the features and properties available to SAX 2.0 parser implementations.

Who Should Read This Book?

This entire book is based on the premise that XML is quickly becoming an essential part of Java programming. The chapters are written to instruct you in the use of XML and Java, and other than in the introduction, they do not focus on *if* you should use XML. I believe that if you are a Java developer, you should use XML, without question. For this reason, if you are a Java programmer, want to be a Java programmer, manage Java programmers, or are responsible for or associated with a Java project, this book is for you. If you want to advance, want to become a better developer, want to write cleaner code, want to have projects succeed on time and under budget, need to access legacy data, need to distribute system components, or just want to know what the XML hype is about, this book is for you.

I tried to make as few assumptions about you as possible; I don't believe in setting the entry point for XML so high that it is impossible to get started. However, I also believe that if you spent your money on this book, you want more than the basics. For this reason, I assumed only that you know the Java language and understand some server-side programming concepts (such as Java servlets and Enterprise JavaBeans™). If you have never coded Java before or are just getting started with the language, you may want to read through *Learning Java*, by Pat Niemeyer and Jonathan Knudsen (O'Reilly & Associates), before starting this book. I do not assume that you know anything about XML, and so I start with the basics. However, I do assume that you are willing to work hard and learn quickly; for this reason, we move rapidly through the basics so that the bulk of the book can deal with advanced concepts. Material is not repeated unless appropriate, so you may need to re-read previous sections or be prepared to flip back and forth, as previously covered concepts are used in later chapters. If you want to learn XML, know some Java, and are prepared to enter some example code into your favorite editor, you should be able to get through this book without any real problem.

Software and Versions

This book covers XML 1.0 and the various XML vocabularies in their latest form as of April 2000. Because various XML specifications that are covered are not final, minor inconsistencies may be present between printed publications of this book and the current version of the specification in question.

All of the Java code used is based on the Java 1.1 platform, with the exception of the JDOM 1.0 coverage. This variance with regard to JDOM is noted in the text in Chapter 8, and addressed there. The Apache Xerces parser, Apache Xalan processor, and Apache FOP libraries were the latest stable versions available as of April 2000, and the Apache Cocoon web publishing framework used was Version 1.7.3. The XML-RPC Java libraries used were Version 1.0 beta 3. All software used is freely available and can be obtained online from *http://java.sun.com*, *http://xml.apache.org*, and *http://www.xml-rpc.com*.

The source code for the examples in this book, including the `com.oreilly.xml` utility classes, is contained completely within the book itself. Both source and binary forms of all examples (including extensive Javadoc not necessarily included in the text) are available online from *http://www.oreilly.com/catalog/javaxml* and *http://www.newInstance.com*. All of the examples that could run as servlets, or be converted to run as servlets, can be viewed and used online at *http://www.newInstance.com*.

The complete JDOM 1.0 distribution, including the specification, reference implementation, source code, API documentation, and binary release, is available for download online at *http://www.jdom.org*. Additionally, a CVS tree is being set up to host the JDOM code and allow community contribution and comment. See *http://www.jdom.org* for details on accessing JDOM from CVS.

Conventions Used in This Book

I use the following font conventions in this book.

Italic is used for:

- Unix pathnames, filenames, and program names
- Internet addresses, such as domain names and URLs
- New terms where they are defined

`Constant Width` is used for:

- Command lines and options that should be typed verbatim
- Names and keywords in Java programs, including method names, variable names, and class names
- XML element names and tags, attribute names, and other XML constructs that appear as they would within an XML document

`Constant Width Bold` is used for:

- Additions to code examples
- Parts of code examples that are discussed specifically in the text

Comments and Questions

Please address comments and questions concerning this book to the publisher:

O'Reilly & Associates, Inc.
101 Morris Street
Sebastopol, CA 95472
(800) 998-9938 (in the U.S. or Canada)
(707) 829-0515 (international or local)
(707) 829-0104 (fax)

You can also send us messages electronically. To be put on our mailing list or to request a catalog, send email to:

info@oreilly.com

To ask technical questions or comment on the book, send email to:

bookquestions@oreilly.com

We have a web site for the book, where we'll list errata and any plans for future editions. You can access this page at:

http://www.oreilly.com/catalog/javaxml

For more information about this book and others, see the O'Reilly web site at:

http://www.oreilly.com

Acknowledgments

As I look at the stack of pages that comprise the manuscript of this book, it seems absurd to try and thank all the people involved in making this book in only a few paragraphs. However, as this is arguably simpler than covering the entire realm of Java and XML in just under 500 pages, I am certainly willing to attempt it; for those of you I forget, please forgive me in advance!

This book was initiated by a call on Thanksgiving weekend, 1999, from my editor, Mike Loukides, which came as I was feverishly writing another book for O'Reilly. I was a bit dubious about putting a book I was very passionate about on hold for six months, but Mike was as adept at convincing me of the importance of this book as he has been at editing my words and making them useful. As I look back, this was easily the most enjoyable and exciting thing I have ever done in my technical career, and I owe much of that experience to Mike; he guided me through a very difficult first few chapters, allowed me to vent when I had to revise the XML Schema chapter three (yes, three!) times due to revisions of the specification coming out, and was also an all-around musical guy when I needed to take a break. Without him, this would certainly not be the high-quality book we both believe it is.

Additionally, I had a supporting cast of family and friends that made the amount of time and effort needed to make this book happen possible, and even enjoyable. My mom and dad, who corrected my grammar daily for eighteen years of my life; my aunt, who was always excited for me even when she didn't know what I was talking about; Jody Durrett, Carl Henry, and Pam Merryman, who spent more time making me a good writer than I had any right to expect; Gary and Shirley Greathouse, who always reminded me to never settle; and my grandparents, Dean and Gladys McLaughlin, who were always there in the wings supporting me.

I had an incredible group of technical reviewers, who made this book both accurate and relevant: Marc Loy, Don Weiss, George Reese (who managed to get an entire chapter added in response to his comments!), Matthew Merlo, and James Duncan Davidson. James in particular was helpful, as his willingness to correct minor errors and be brutally honest with me was instrumental in reminding me that I am a developer before I am a writer.

I also owe an incredible debt of gratitude to Jason Hunter, author of *Java Servlet Programming* (O'Reilly & Associates). This book, though started in November of 1999, experienced a rebirth in March of 2000 as Jason and I spent an entire afternoon sitting on a lawn in Santa Clara griping about the current Java API offerings for XML. The result of this discussion was twofold: first, we developed the JDOM API, covered in this book (with help and encouragement from James Davidson at Sun Microsystems). We believe that this API will be instrumental in bringing Java and XML more in line with each other, as well as keeping the focus of using XML on the Java programming language and usability, rather than on vague concepts and obscurity. Second, Jason has become an invaluable friend, and has helped me through the often confusing process of completing a book and being an O'Reilly author. We spent entirely too many evenings talking for hours into the night across the country about how to make JDOM and other code samples work in an intuitive way.

Most importantly, I owe everything in these pages to my wife, Leigh. Miraculously, she has managed to not kick me out of the house over the last six months, as I have been tired, inaccessible, and extremely busy almost constantly. The few moments I had with her away from writing and my full-time consulting job have been what made everything worthwhile. I have missed her terribly, and am anxious to return to spending time with her, my three basset hounds (Charlie, Molly, and Daisy), and my labs (Seth and Moses).

And to my grandfather, Robert Earl Burden, who didn't get to see this, you are everything that I have ever wanted to be; thanks for teaching me that other people's expectations were always lower than I should be satisfied with.

In this chapter:
- *What Is It?*
- *How Do I Use It?*
- *Why Should I Use It?*
- *What's Next?*

1

Introduction

XML. These three letters have brought shivers to almost every developer in the world today at some point in the last two years. While those shivers were often fear at another acronym to memorize, excitement at the promise of a new technology, or annoyance at another source of confusion for today's developer, they were shivers all the same. Surprisingly, almost every type of response was well merited with regard to XML. It is another acronym to memorize, and in fact brings with it a dizzying array of companions: XSL, XSLT, PI, DTD, XHTML, and more. It also brings with it a huge promise: what Java did for portability of code, XML claims to do for portability of data. Sun has even been touting the rather ambitious slogan "Java + XML = Portable Code + Portable Data" in recent months. And yes, XML does bring with it a significant amount of confusion. We will seek to unravel and demystify XML, without being so abstract and general as to be useless, and without diving in so deeply that this becomes just another droll specification to wade through. This is a book for you, the Java developer, who wants to understand the hype and use the tools that XML brings to the table.

Today's web application now faces a wealth of problems that were not even considered ten years ago. Systems that are distributed across thousands of miles must perform quickly and flawlessly. Data from heterogeneous systems, databases, directory services, and applications must be transferred without a single decimal place being lost. Applications must be able to communicate not only with other business components, but other business systems altogether, often across companies as well as technologies. Clients are no longer limited to thick clients, but can be web browsers that support HTML, mobile phones that support the Wireless Application Protocol (WAP), or handheld organizers with entirely different markup languages. Data, and the transformation of that data, has become the crucial centerpiece of every application being developed today.

XML offers a way for programmers to meet all of these requirements. In addition, Java developers have an arsenal of APIs that enable them to use XML and its many companions without ever leaving a Java Integrated Development Environment (IDE). If this sounds a little too good to be true, keep reading. You will walk through the pitfalls of the various Java APIs as well as look at some of the bleeding-edge developments in the XML specification and the Java APIs for XML. Through it all, we will take a developer's view. This is not a book about why you should use XML, but rather how you should use it. If there are offerings in the specification that are not of much use, details of why will be clearly given and we will move on; if something is of great value, we'll spend some extra time on it. Throughout, we will focus on using XML as a tool, not using it as a buzzword or for the sake of having the latest toy. With that in mind, let's begin to talk about what XML is.

What Is It?

XML is the *Extensible Markup Language.* Like its predecessor SGML, XML is a meta-language used to define other languages. However, XML is much simpler and more straightforward than SGML. XML is a markup language that specifies neither the tag set nor the grammar for that language. The *tag set* for a markup language defines the markup tags that have meaning to a language parser. For example, HTML has a strict set of tags that are allowed. You may use the tag `<TABLE>` but not the tag `<CHAIR>`. While the first tag has a specific meaning to an application using the data, and is used to signify the start of a table in HTML, the second tag has no specific meaning, and although most browsers will ignore it, unexpected things can happen when it appears. That is because when HTML was defined, the tag set of the language was defined with it. With each new version of HTML, new tags are defined. However, if a tag is not defined, it may not be used as part of the markup language without generating an error when the document is parsed. The *grammar* of a markup language defines the correct use of the language's tags. Again, let's use HTML as an example. When using the `<TABLE>` tag, several attributes may be included, such as the width, the background color, and the alignment. However, you cannot define the `TYPE` of the table because the grammar of HTML does not allow it.

XML, by defining neither the tags nor the grammar, is completely extensible; thus its name. If you choose to use the tag `<TABLE>` and then nest within that tag several `<CHAIR>` tags, you may do so. If you wish to define a `TYPE` attribute for the `<CHAIR>` tag, you may do that also. You could even use tags named after your children or co-workers if you so desired! To demonstrate, let's take a look at the XML file shown in Example 1-1.

Example 1-1. A Sample XML File

```
<?xml version="1.0"?>

<dining-room>
    <table type="round" wood="maple">
        <manufacturer>The Wood Shop</manufacturer>
        <price>$1999.99</price>
    </table>

    <chair wood="maple">
        <quantity>2</quantity>
        <quality>excellent</quality>
        <cushion included="true">
            <color>blue</color>
        </cushion>
    </chair>

    <chair wood="oak">
        <quantity>3</quantity>
        <quality>average</quality>
    </chair>
</dining-room>
```

If you have never looked at an XML file, but are familiar with HTML or another markup language, this may look a bit strange to you. That's because the tags and grammar being used are completely made up. No web page or specification defines the `<table>`, `<chair>`, or `<cushion>` tags (although one could, just as the XHTML specification defines HTML tags in XML); they are completely concocted. This is the power of XML: it allows you to define the content of your data in a variety of ways as long as you conform to the general structure that XML requires. Later we will go into detail on some additional constraints, but for now it is sufficient to realize that XML is built to allow flexibility of data formatting.

Although this flexibility is one of XML's strongest points, it also creates one of its greatest weaknesses: because XML documents can be processed in so many different ways and for so many different purposes, there are a large number of XML-related standards to handle translation and specification of data. These additional acronyms, and their constant pairing with XML itself, often confuse what XML is and what it is not. More often than not, when you hear "XML," the speaker is not referring specifically to the Extensible Markup Language, but to all or part of the suite of XML tools. Although sometimes these will be referred to separately, be aware that "XML" does not just mean XML; more often it means "XML and all the great ways there are to manipulate and use it." With those preliminaries out of the way, we are ready to define some of the most common XML acronyms and give short descriptions of each. These will be fundamental to everything else in the book, so keep this chapter marked for reference. These descriptions should start to help you understand how the XML suite of tools fits together, what XML is, and what it isn't. Discussion of publishing engines, applications, and tools for XML is avoided; these are discussed later when we talk about specific XML topics. Rather, this section only refers to specifications and recommendations in various stages of consideration. Most of these are initiatives of the W3C, the World Wide Web Consortium. This group defines standards for the XML community that help provide a common base of knowledge for this technology, much as Sun provides standards for Java and related APIs. For more on the W3C, visit *http://www.w3.org* on the Web.

XML

XML, of course, is the root of all these three- and four-letter acronyms. It defines the core language itself and provides a metadata-type framework. XML by itself is of limited value; it defines only that framework. However, all of the various technologies that rest upon XML provide developers and content managers unprecedented flexibility in data management and transmission. XML is currently a completed W3C Recommendation, meaning it is final and will not change until another version is released. For the complete XML 1.0 Specification, see *http://www.w3.org/TR/REC-xml/*. As this specification is tough to read through for even the XML-savvy, an excellent annotated version of the specification is available at *http://www.xml.com.*

As we will spend lots of time going into detail on this subject in future chapters, there are only two basic concepts you need to understand about XML documents right now. The first is that any XML document must be *well-formed* to be of any use and to be parsed correctly. A well-formed document is one that has every tag closed that is opened, has no tags nested out of order, and is syntactically correct in regard to the specification. You may be wondering: didn't we say that XML has no syntax rules? Not exactly; we said that it did not have any *grammatical* rules. While the document can define its own tags and attributes, it still must conform to a general set of principles. These principles are then used by XML-aware applications and parsers to make sense of the document and perform some action with the data, such as finding the price of a chair or creating a PDF file from the data within a document. We will discuss these details in greater depth in Chapter 2, *Creating XML.*

The second basic concept concerning XML documents is that they can be, but are not required to be, *valid.* A valid document is one that conforms to its document type definition (DTD), which we'll talk about in a moment. Simply put, a DTD defines the grammar and tag set for a specific XML formatting. If a document specifies a DTD and follows that DTD's rules, it is said to be a valid XML document. XML documents can also be constrained by a schema, a new way of dictating XML format that will replace DTDs. When a document conforms to a schema, it can be said to be *schema valid.* Don't worry if this isn't all clear yet; we have a long way to go, and we will look at each of these XML-related specifications. First, though, there are some acronyms and specifications that are used within an XML document. Let's take a look at these now.

PI

A PI in an XML document is a *processing instruction.* A processing instruction tells an application to perform some specific task. While PIs are a small portion of the XML specification, they are important enough to warrant a section in our discussion of XML acronyms. A PI is distinguished from other XML data because it represents a command to either the XML parser or a program that would use the XML document. For example, in our sample XML document in Example 1-1, the first line, which indicates the version of XML, is a processing instruction. It indicates to the parser what version of XML is being used. Processing instructions are of the form `<?target instructions?>`. Any PI that has the target `XML` is part of the XML standard set of PIs that parsers should recognize, often called *XML instructions,* but PIs can also specify information to be used by applications that may be wrapping the parsing behavior; in this case, the wrapping application might have a keyword (such as "cocoon") that could be used as the PI's target.

Processing instructions become extremely important when XML data is used in XML-aware applications. As a more salient example, consider the application that might process our sample XML file and then create advertisements for a furniture store based on what stock is available and listed in the XML document. A processing instruction could let the application know that some furniture is on a "want" list and must be routed to another application, such as an application that sends requests for more inventory, and should not be included in the advertisement, or other application-specific instructions. An XML parser will see PIs with external targets and pass them on unchanged to the external application.

DTD

A DTD is a *document type definition.* A DTD establishes a set of constraints for an XML document (or a set of documents). DTD is not a specification on its own, but is defined as part of the XML specification. Within an XML document, a document type declaration can both include markup constraints and refer to an external document with markup constraints. The sum of these two sets of constraints is the document type definition. A DTD defines the way an XML document should be constructed. Consider the XML document in Example 1-1 again. Although we were able to create our own tags, this document is useless to another application, or even another human, who does not understand what our tags mean. Although some common sense can help in determining what the tags mean, there are still ambiguities. Can the `<quantity>` tag tell us how many chairs are in stock? Can a wood attribute be specified within a <chair> tag? These questions must be answered for the XML document to be properly validated by an XML parser. A document is considered valid when it follows the constraints that the DTD lays out for the formatting of XML data. This is particularly important when trying to transfer data between applications, as there must be an agreed-upon formatting and syntax for different systems to understand each other.

Remember that earlier we said a DTD defined the constraints for a specific XML document or set of documents. A developer or content author also creates this DTD as an additional document referenced in his or her XML files, or includes it within the XML file itself, so it does not in any way limit the XML documents. In fact, the DTD is what gives XML data its portability. It might define that for the wood attribute, only "maple", "pine", "oak", and "mahogany" are acceptable values. This allows a parser to determine if the document is acceptable in its content, preventing data errors. A DTD also defines the order of nesting in tags. It might dictate that the <cushion> tag can only appear nested within the <chair> tag. This allows another application receiving our example XML file to know how to process and search within the received file. The DTD is what adds portability to an XML document's extensibility, resulting not only in flexible data, but data that can be processed and validated by any machine that can locate the document's DTD.

Namespaces

Namespaces is one of the few XML-related concepts that has not been converted into an acronym. It even has a name that describes its purpose! A *namespace* is a mapping between an element *prefix* and a URI. This mapping is used for handling namespace collisions and defining data structures that allow parsers to handle collisions. As an example of a possible namespace collision, consider an XML document that might include a <price> tag for a chair, between a <chair> and </chair> tag. However, we also include in the chair definition a <cushion> tag, which might also have a <price> tag. Also consider that the document may reference another XML document for copyright information. Both documents could reasonably have <date> or possibly <company> tags. Conflicting tags such as these result in ambiguity as to which tag means what. This ambiguity creates significant problems for an XML parser. Should the <price> tag be interpreted differently depending on which element is it within? Or did the content author make a mistake in using it in two contexts? Without additional namespace information, it is impossible to decide if this was an error in the XML document construction, and if not, how to use the data within the conflicting tags.

The XML namespace Recommendation defines a mechanism to qualify these names. This mechanism uses URIs to perform this task, although this is a little beyond what we need to know right now. In qualifying both the correct usage and placement of tags like the `<price>` tag in our example, an XML document is not forced to use rather foolish naming such as `<chair-price>` and `<cushion-price>`. Instead, a namespace is associated with a prefix to an XML element, and results in tags such as `<chair:price>` and `<cushion:price>`. An XML parser can then distinguish between these two namespaces without having to use entirely different element names. Namespaces are most often used within XML documents, but are also used in schemas and XSL stylesheets, as well as other XML-related specifications. The Recommendation for namespaces can be found at *http://www.w3.org/TR/REC-xml-names.*

XSL and XSLT

XSL is the *Extensible Stylesheet Language.* XSL transforms and translates XML data from one XML format into another. Consider, for example, that the same XML document may need to be displayed in HTML, PDF, and Postscript form. Without XSL, the XML document would have to be manually duplicated, and then converted into each of these three formats. Instead, XSL provides a mechanism of defining stylesheets to accomplish these types of tasks. Rather than having to change the data because of a different representation, XSL provides a complete separation of data, or content, and presentation. If an XML document needs to be mapped to another representation, then XSL is an excellent solution. It provides a method comparable to writing a Java program to translate data into a PDF or HTML document, but supplies a standard interface to accomplish the task.

To perform the translation, an XSL document can contain *formatting objects.* These formatting objects are specific named tags that can be replaced with appropriate content for the target document type. A common formatting object might define a tag that some processor uses in the transformation of an XML document into PDF; in this case, the tag would be replaced by PDF-specific information. Formatting objects are specific XSL instructions, and although we will lightly discuss them, they are largely beyond the scope of this book. Instead, we will focus more on XSLT, a completely text-based transformation process. Through the process of XSLT (*Extensible Stylesheet Language Transformation*), an XSL textual stylesheet and a textual XML document are "merged" together, and what results is the XML data formatted according to the XSL stylesheet. To help clarify this difficult concept further, let's look at another sample XML file, shown in Example 1-2.

Example 1-2. Another Sample XML File

```
<?xml version="1.0"?>
<?xml-stylesheet href="hello.xsl" type="text/xsl"?>

<!-- Here is a sample XML file -->
```

Example 1-2. Another Sample XML File (continued)

```
<page>
 <title>Test Page</title>
 <content>
  <paragraph>What you see is what you get!</paragraph>
 </content>
</page>
```

This document defines itself as XML version 1.0, and then defines the location of a corresponding XSL stylesheet, `hello.xsl`. This is similar to the way in which DTDs are used; just as a DTD can be referenced in XML to define how the data can be structured, an XSL file can be referenced to determine how the data is presented and displayed. Example 1-3 looks at the XSL stylesheet that is referred to.

Example 1-3. The Stylesheet for Example 1-2

```
<xsl:stylesheet xmlns:xsl="http://www.w3.org/1999/XSL/Transform">

  <xsl:template match="page">
   <html>
    <head>
     <title>
      <xsl:value-of select="title"/>
     </title>
    </head>
    <body bgcolor="#ffffff">
     <xsl:apply-templates/>
    </body>
   </html>
  </xsl:template>

  <xsl:template match="paragraph">
   <p align="center">
    <i>
     <xsl:apply-templates/>
    </i>
   </p>
  </xsl:template>

</xsl:stylesheet>
```

This stylesheet is designed to convert our basic XML document and its data into HTML suitable for a web browser. While most of these details are things we will discuss later, concentrate on the `<xsl:template match="[element name]">` tags. Any time this type of tag occurs, the element at the matching tag, for example, `paragraph`, is replaced by the contents of the XSL stylesheet, which in this case results in a <p> tag with italicized font encoding. What results from the transformation of the XML document by the XSL stylesheet is shown in Example 1-4.

Example 1-4. HTML Result from Examples 1-2 and 1-3

```
<html>
 <head>
  <title>
   Test Page
  </title>
 </head>
 <body bgcolor="#ffffff">
  <p align="center">
   <i>
    What you see is what you get!
   </i>
  </p>
 </body>
</html>
```

Don't worry about understanding all of the specifics of XSL and XSLT yet; just realize that using XML and XSL, highly flexible document formats can result from the same set of underlying XML data. We will spend more time on XSL in Chapter 6, *Transforming XML*. XSL is currently a W3C Working Draft. The Recommendations related to XSL may be viewed online at *http://www.w3.org/Style/XSL*.

XPath

XPath (XML Path Language) is a specification in its own right, but is used heavily by XSLT. The XPath specification defines how a specific item within an XML document can be located. This is accomplished through referencing specific *nodes* in the XML document; here, *node* refers to any piece of XML data, including elements, attributes, or textual data. In the XPath specification, an XML document is considered a tree of these nodes, where each node can be accessed by specifying the location in the tree at which it is located. We won't get into details about using XPath until we discuss XSL and XSLT more, but expect to use it anytime you must obtain a reference to a specific piece of data within an XML document. To let you know what to expect, here is a sample XPath expression:

```
*[not(self::JavaXML:Title)]
```

This particular expression evaluates to all child elements of the current element, where the child's name is not `JavaXML:Title`. For this document fragment:

```
<JavaXML:Book>
  <JavaXML:Title>Java and XML</JavaXML:Title>

  <JavaXML:Content>
    <!-- Chapters go here -->
  </JavaXML:Content>
```

```
    <JavaXML:Copyright>&OReillyCopyright;</JavaXML:Copyright>
  </JavaXML:Book>
```

evaluating the expression when the current node is the `JavaXML:Book` element would yield the `JavaXML:Content` and `JavaXML:Copyright` elements. The complete XPath specification is online at *http://www.w3.org/TR/xpath.*

XML Schema

XML Schema is designed to replace and amplify DTDs. XML Schema offers an XML-centric means to constrain XML documents. Though we have only looked briefly at DTDs so far, they have some rather critical limitations: they have no knowledge of hierarchy, they have difficulty handling namespace conflicts, and they have no means of specifying allowed relationships between XML documents. This is understandable, as the members of the working group who wrote the specification certainly had no idea that XML would be used in so many different ways! However, the limitations of DTDs have become constricting to XML authors and developers.

The most significant fact about XML Schema is that it brings DTDs back into line with XML itself. That may sound confusing; consider, though, that every acronym we have talked about uses XML documents to define its purpose. XSL stylesheets, namespaces, and the rest all use XML to define specific uses and properties of XML. But a DTD is entirely different. A DTD does not look like XML, it does not share XML's hierarchical structure, and it does not even represent data in the same way. This makes the DTD a bit of an oddball in the XML world, and because DTDs currently define how XML documents must be constructed, this has been causing some confusion. XML Schema corrects this problem by returning to using XML itself to define XML. We have been talking about "defining data about data" a lot, and XML Schema does this as well. The XML Schema specification moves XML a lot closer to having all of its constructs in the same language, rather than having DTDs as an aberration that has to be dealt with.

Wisely, the W3C and XML contributors realized that to refine DTD would be somewhat of a wasted effort. Instead, XML Schema is being developed to replace DTD, allowing these contributors to correct problems that DTD could not handle, as well as add enhancements in line with the various ways in which XML is currently being used. To learn more about this important W3C draft, visit *http://www.w3.org/TR/xmlschema-1/* and *http://www.w3.org/TR/xmlschema-2/*. A helpful primer on XML Schema is located at *http://www.w3.org/TR/xmlschema-0/*.

XQL

XQL is a query language designed to allow XML document formats to easily represent database queries. Although not yet formally adopted by the W3C, XQL's popularity and usefulness will almost certainly make it the *de facto* method for specifying access to data stored in a database from an XML document. The structure of a query is defined using XPath concepts, and the result set is defined using standard XML with XQL-specific tags. For example, the following XQL expression would search through the books table and return all records where the title contains "Java"; for each record, the author records (from the authors table) would be displayed:

```
//book[title contains "Java"] ( .//authors )
```

The result set from this query might look like the following:

```
<xql:result>
  <book>
    <author name="Richard Monson-Haefel" location="Minnesota" />
  </book>
  <book>
    <author name="Jason Hunter" location="California" />
    <author name="William Crawford" location="Massachusetts" />
  </book>
</xql:result>
```

There will most likely be quite a bit of change as the specification matures and is hopefully adopted by the W3C, but XQL is a technology worth keeping an eye on. The current proposal for XQL is at *http://metalab.unc.edu/xql/xql-proposal.html*. This proposal made its way to the W3C in January of 2000, and current requirements for the XML Query language can be found at *http://www.w3.org/TR/xmlquery-req*.

And All the Rest . . .

You have now been sped through a very brief introduction of some of the major XML-related specifications we will cover. You can probably think of one or two acronyms we didn't cover, if not more. We have selected only the particular acronyms that are especially relevant to our discussions on handling XML within Java. There are quite a few more, and they are listed here with the URLs for the appropriate recommendations or working drafts:

- Resource Description Framework (RDF): *http://www.w3.org/TR/PR-rdf-schema/*
- XML Link Language (XLL)
  - XLink: *http://www.w3.org/TR/xlink/*
  - XPointer: *http://www.w3.org/TR/xptr/*
- XHTML: *http://www.w3.org/TR/xhtml-basic/*

This list will probably be outdated by the time you read this chapter, as more XML-based ideas are being examined and proposed every day. Just because these are not given significant time or space in this book, it should not make you think they are somehow less important; they are just not as critical to our discussions on manipulating XML data within Java. A complete understanding and mastery of XML certainly would require these specifications to be absorbed as well as those we have discussed in more detail. We still are likely to run across some of the specifications we have listed here; when that occurs, a definition and discussion will be provided in the text to help you understand what we are talking about.

How Do I Use It?

All of the great ideas XML has brought to us are not much use without some tools to use these ideas within our familiar programming environments. Luckily, XML has been paired with Java since its inception, and Java boasts the most complete set of APIs available to allow use of XML directly within Java code. While C, C++, and Perl are quickly catching up, Java continues to set the standard on how to use XML from applications. There are two basic stages that occur in an XML document's lifecycle from an application point of view, as shown in Figure 1-1. First, the document is parsed, and then the data within it is manipulated.

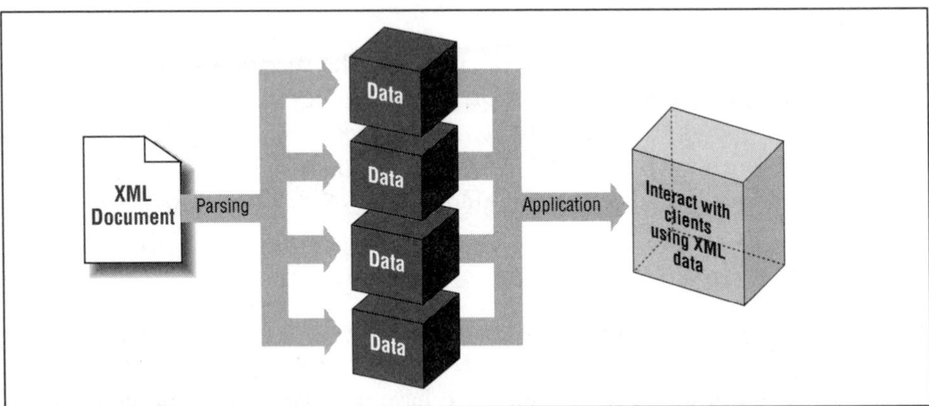

Figure 1-1. The application view of an XML document lifecycle

As Java developers, we are fortunate to have simple ways to handle these tasks and more.

SAX

SAX is the *Simple API for XML*. It provides an event-based framework for parsing XML data, which is the process of reading through the document and breaking down the data into usable parts; at each step of the way, SAX defines events that can occur. For example, SAX defines an `org.xml.sax.ContentHandler` interface that defines methods such as `startDocument()` and `endElement()`. Implementing this interface allows complete control over these portions of the XML parsing process. There is a similar interface for handling errors and lexical constructs. A set of errors and warnings is defined, allowing handling of the various situations that can occur in XML parsing, such as an invalid document, or one that is not well-formed. Behavior can be added to customize the parsing process, resulting in very application-specific tasks being available for definition, all with a standard interface into XML documents. For the SAX API documentation and other information on SAX, visit *http://www.megginson.com/SAX*.

Before continuing, it is important to clear up a common misconception about SAX. SAX is often mistaken for an XML parser. We even discuss SAX here as providing a means to parse XML data. However, SAX provides a *framework* for parsers to use, and defines events within the parsing process to monitor. A parser must be supplied to SAX to perform any XML parsing. This has resulted in many excellent parsers being made available in Java, such as Sun's Project X, the Apache Software Foundation's Xerces, Oracle's XML Parser, and IBM's XML4J. These can all be plugged into the SAX APIs and result in parsed XML data. SAX APIs provide the *means* to parse a document, not the XML parser itself.

DOM

DOM is an API for the *Document Object Model*. While SAX only provides *access* to the data within an XML document, DOM is designed to provide a means of manipulating that data. DOM provides a representation of an XML document as a tree. Because a tree is an age-old data representation, traversal and manipulation of tree structures are easy to accomplish in programming languages, Java being no exception. DOM also reads an entire XML document into memory, storing all the data in *nodes*, so the entire document is very fast to access; it is all in memory for the length of its existence in the DOM tree. Each node represents a piece of the data pulled from the original document.

There is a significant drawback to DOM, however. Because DOM reads an entire document into memory, resources can become very heavily taxed, often slowing down or even crippling an application. The larger and more complex the document, the more pronounced this performance degradation becomes. Keep in mind that while DOM is a good, prevalent means of manipulating XML data, it is not the only means of accomplishing this task. We will spend time using DOM, and we will also write code that manipulates data straight from SAX. Your application requirements will most likely define which solution is correct for your specific development project. To read the DOM recommendations at W3C, go to *http://www.w3.org/DOM* in your web browser.

JAXP

JAXP is Sun's *Java API for XML Parsing*. A relatively new addition to the XML developer's arsenal, it attempts to provide cohesiveness to the SAX and DOM APIs. While it does not compete with or replace either of these APIs, it does add some convenience methods to try to make the XML APIs easier to use for Java developers. It conforms to the SAX and DOM specifications, as well as adhering to the namespace Recommendation we discussed earlier. JAXP does not redefine SAX or DOM behavior, but ensures that all XML-conformant parsers can be accessed within Java applications through a standard pluggability layer.

It is expected that JAXP will continue to evolve as both SAX and DOM go through revision. It is also assumed that JAXP will eventually be part of other Sun specifications, as both the Tomcat servlet engine and the EJB 1.1 specification require XML-formatted configuration and deployment files. Although the J2EE™ 1.3 and J2SE™ 1.4 specifications do not mention JAXP explicitly, they are expected to have integrated JAXP support as well. For the complete JAXP specification, go to *http://java.sun.com/xml*.

These three APIs make up the Java developers toolkit for handling XML. While this is not a formal designation, these three APIs do provide us the mechanism to get XML data and manipulate it, all within normal Java code. These APIs will be our workhorses throughout the book, and we will learn to use every aspect of the classes that each provides.

Why Should I Use It?

So now you've managed to sort through the alphabet soup of XML-related technologies. You even have realized that there may be more to XML than just another way to build a presentation layer. But you aren't quite sure where XML fits in with the applications you are building at work. You aren't positive that you could convince your boss to let you spend time learning more about XML, because you don't know how it could help make a better application. You even are thinking about trying to evaluate some tools to use XML, but you aren't sure where to start.

If this is the situation you find yourself in, excited about a new technology but confused as to where to go next, then read on! In this section, we begin to cast XML in the light of real-world applications, and give you a reason to use XML in your applications today. We will first look at how XML is being used today in applications, and we'll give you the information to convince that boss of yours that "everybody's doing it." Next we will take a look at support for XML and related technologies, all in light of Java applications. In Java, there is a wealth of available parsers, transformers, publishing engines, and frameworks designed specifically for XML. Finally, we will spend some time looking at where XML is going and try to anticipate how it will affect applications six months and a year from now. This is the information to use to convince your boss's boss that XML can not only keep you even with your competitors, but give your company the leading edge in your industry, and help get you that next promotion!

Java and XML: A Perfect Match

Even if you have been convinced that XML is a great technology, and that it is taking the world by storm, we have yet to mention why this book is about *Java* and XML, rather than just XML alone. Java is, in fact, the ideal counterpart for XML, and the reason can be summed up in a single phrase: Java is portable code, and XML is portable data. Taken separately, both technologies are wonderful, but have limitations. Java requires the developer to dream up formats for network data and formats for presentation, and to use technologies like JavaServer Pages™ (JSP) that do not provide a real separation of content and presentation layers. XML is simply metadata, and without programs like parsers and XSL processors, is essentially "vapor-ware." However, Java and XML matched together fill in the gaps in the application development picture.

Writing Java code assures that any operating system and hardware with a Java™ Virtual Machine (JVM) can run your compiled bytecode. Add to this the ability to represent input and output to your applications with a system-independent, standards-based data layer, and your data is now portable. Your application is completely portable, and can communicate with any other application using the same (widely accepted) standards. If this isn't enough, we've already mentioned that Java provides the most robust set of APIs, parsers, processors, publishing frameworks, and tools for XML use of any programming language. With this synergy in mind, let's look at how these two technologies fit together, both today and tomorrow.

XML Today

Many developers and technology-driven companies are under the impression that while XML is certainly a hot topic, and has reached "buzzword" status, it is not yet ready for the mission-critical applications that companies rely on so heavily. Nothing could be further from the truth. XML and the related technologies we have been discussing have gained a firmer place in the application space in a shorter amount of time than even Java was able to achieve when it was announced several years ago. In fact, XML is possibly the only announcement in the development world to rival the impact of the Java platform. It is fortunate for us as developers that these are complementary technologies rather than competing ones. With Java and XML, portability of applications and data is at an all-time high, and is being used heavily, right now, as you read this chapter.

XML for presentation

The most popular use for XML is to create a separation of content and presentation. In this situation, we are defining application *content* as the data that needs to be displayed to a client, and application *presentation* as the formatting of that data. For example, a user's name and address in an administrative section of an ordering system would be content, while the HTML-formatted page with images and company branding would be the presentation. The primary distinction is that content is universal for an application, and no matter what type of client-specific formatting must occur, the same content is valid; however, presentation is specific to the type of client (web browser, Internet-ready phone, Java application) and that client's capabilities (HTML 4.0, the Wireless Markup Language, Java™ Swing) to view data. XML is being used to represent the content in this situation, while XSL and XSLT are used to provide a presentation suitable for the client.

One of the most significant challenges that applications face today, particularly web applications, is the variety of clients that might need to use the application. Ten years ago, users were almost always thick clients with software installed on their desktop computer to use an application; three years ago, application clients were almost always Internet web browsers that understood HTML. Clients today use web browsers on a multitude of operating system platforms, wireless mobile phones with Wireless Markup Language (WML) support, and handheld organizers that support a subset of HTML. This variety of client types often results in an application having numerous versions, one for each type of client it supports, and still not supporting all client variations. Although an application may not need to support a wireless phone, certainly there are advantages to allowing employees or customers the service if they have the equipment; and while a handheld organizer may not allow a user to perform all the operations that a web browser might, frequent travelers who could manage their accounts online would certainly be more likely to continue to use a service that a company provides. The shift from lots of functionality being offered to specific types of clients to a standard set of functionality being offered to an enormous variety of client types has left many companies and application developers scratching their heads. XML can resolve this confusion.

Although we said earlier that XML is not a presentation technology, it *can* be used to generate a presentation layer. If there doesn't seem to be much of a difference between the two, consider this: HTML is a presentation technology. It is a markup language designed specifically to allow graphical views of content for web browser clients. However, HTML is not by any means a good data representation. An

HTML document is not easy to parse, search, or manipulate. It follows only a loose format, and is at least one-half presentation information, if not more, while only a small percentage of the document is actual data. XML is substantially different, as it is a data-driven markup language. Nearly all of an XML document is data and data structure. Only instructions to an XML parser or wrapping application are not data-centric. XML is easily searchable and can be manipulated with APIs and tools due to the strict structure a DTD or schema can impose. This makes it very non-presentation-oriented. However, it can be used for presentation with its companion technologies, XSL and XSLT. XSL allows definition of presentation and formatting constructs and instructions on how to apply these constructs to the data within an XML document. And through XSLT, the original XML can be displayed to a client in a variety of ways, including very complex HTML. Still, the core XML document remains separate from any presentation-specific information and can just as easily be transformed into an entirely different style of presentation, such as a Swing user interface, with no change to the underlying content.

Perhaps the most powerful component offered by XML and XSL for presentation is the ability to specify multiple stylesheets to an XML document, or to impose XSL stylesheets on an XML document externally. This adds another layer of flexibility to presentation, as not only can the same XML document be used for multiple presentations, but the publishing framework performing transformation can determine what type of client is requesting the XML document and select the correct stylesheet to apply based on that information. While there is no standard way of performing this process, and no standard set of codes for various client types, an XML publishing framework can provide ways to accomplish this dynamic transformation. The process of specifying multiple XSL stylesheets within an XML document is not vendor-specific, so the only framework details your XML document should have to worry about may be an additional processing instruction or two. Because these are simply ignored if not supported by an application, the XML documents used remain completely portable and 100% standard XML.

XML for communication

In addition to these useful transformation capabilities, the same XML document and its data content can be used to transfer information between applications. This communication is easily achievable because the XML data is not tied to any type of client, or even to being used by a client. It also provides a very simple data representation easily transmissible over a network. It is this communication aspect of XML that is probably the most overlooked and undervalued feature of XML documents and data representations.

To understand the importance of XML for communications, you must first widen your concept of an application client. While talking about presentation, we made the common assumption that a client is a user that views a portion of an application. However, this is a fairly narrow assumption in today's applications, and we will now discard it. Instead, consider that a client is anything (yes, anything!) that accesses data or services within an application. Clients can be users with computers or mobile devices, other applications, data storage systems like databases or directory services, and even, at times, the application itself making callbacks. When the view of a client is widened like this, you will begin to see the impact that XML can have.

First, categorize these client types into two groups: one that requires a presentation layer and one that doesn't. When you begin to do this, you may find it a little difficult to draw such a distinction. While users certainly might view data as HTML or WML (Wireless Markup Language), data might need to be formatted a little differently for another application, possibly filtering out some secure content or using different element names. In fact, there will rarely be a time when a client does not need data formatted in a manner somewhat specific to the purpose the data is being used for.

This exercise should convince you that data is almost always transformed, often multiple times. Consider an XML document that is converted to a format usable for another application by an XSL stylesheet (see Figure 1-2). The result remains XML. That application may then use the data to gain a new result set, and create a new XML document. The original application then needs this information, so the new XML document is transformed back into the format used by the original application, although it now contains different data! This scenario is a very common one.

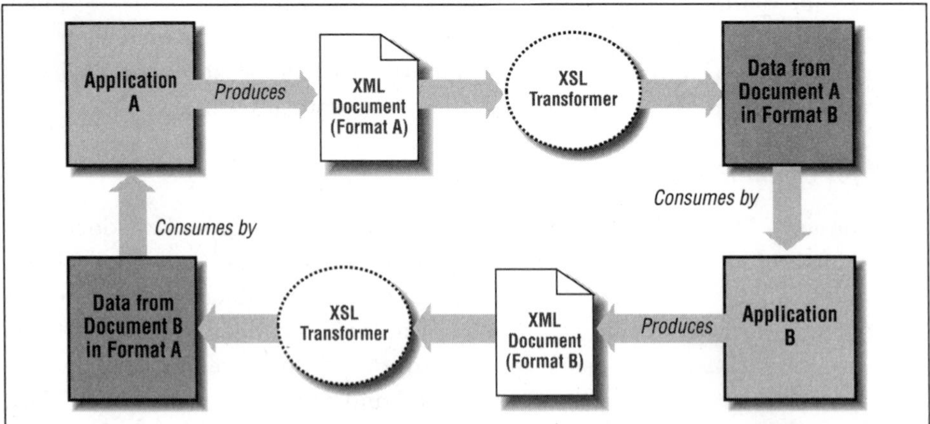

Figure 1-2. XML/XSL transformations between applications

This repeated process of transforming a document, and always generating a new XML result, is what makes XML such a powerful tool for communication. The same set of rules can be used at every step, always starting with XML, applying one or more XSL stylesheets over one or more transformations, and resulting in XML that is still usable with the same tools that initially created the original document.

Also consider that XML is a purely textual representation of data. Because text is such a lightweight and easily serialized data representation, XML provides a fast means of transmitting data across a network. Although some binary data formats can be transmitted very efficiently, textual network transmissions will typically average out as a faster means of communication.

XML-RPC

One specification concerned with using XML for communication is XML-RPC. XML-RPC is concerned with communication not between applications, but between components within an application, or to a shared set of services functioning across applications. RPC stands for Remote Procedure Calls, one of the primary predecessors of Remote Method Invocation (RMI). RPC is used for making procedural calls over a network, and receiving a response, also over the network. Note that this is significantly different than RMI, which actually allows a client to invoke methods on an object via stubs and skeletons loaded over the network. The primary difference is that RPC calls generate a remote response, and the response is returned over the network; the client never interacts directly with a remote object, but instead uses the RPC interfaces to request a method invocation. RMI allows a client to directly interact with a remote object, and no "proxying" of requests takes place. For a more complete discussion on exactly what XML-RPC is, you should visit *http://www.xml-rpc.com.*

The point worth noting about RPC, and XML-RPC in particular, is that it has now become a viable option for remote service calls. Because of the difficulty of providing a standard request and response model, RPC has become almost extinct in Java applications, and has been replaced by RMI. However, there are often times when rather than loading remote stubs and skeletons over a network, sending and receiving textual data results in higher performance. The historical problem of RPC has been trying to represent complex objects with nothing but textual information, both for requests and responses. XML has solved this problem, and RPC is again a possible solution for allowing disparate systems to communicate. With a standard in place for representing any type of data through textual documents, an XML-RPC engine can map an object instance's parameters to XML elements, and can easily decode this "graph" of the object on the server. A response can be generated, and again, can easily be "graphed" into XML and returned to the client (see Figure 1-3). We will look at XML-RPC in detail in Chapter 10, *XML-RPC.*

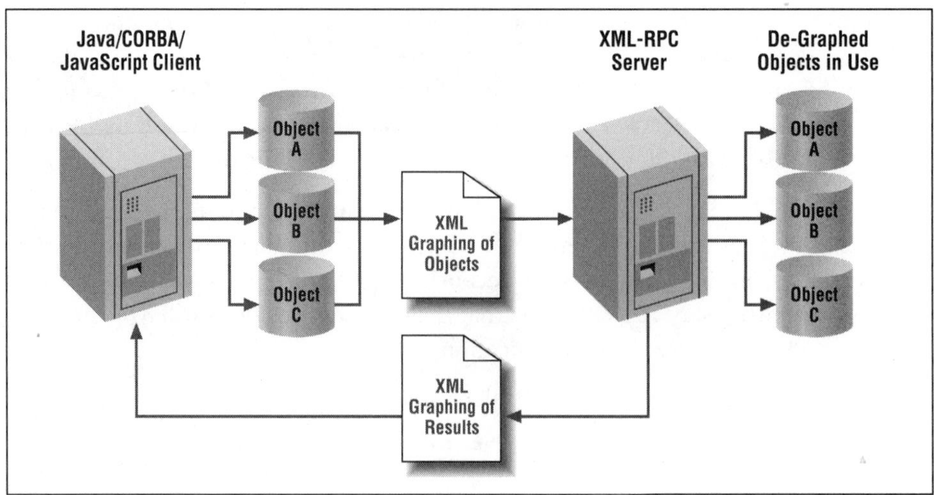

Figure 1-3. XML-RPC communication and messaging

Business-to-business

The last use of XML for communication is really not a different use or specification than those we have already talked about; however, the rise of the phrase "business-to-business" commerce and communication bears mentioning. Business-to business-communication generally refers to communication not just between differing applications, but across companies and sometimes industries. In these cases, XML is truly performing a significant service only available to extremely large companies in the past; it is allowing communication between closed systems. Consider a small- to medium-sized competitive local exchange carrier (CLEC), or a telecommunications company. When a network line, such as a DSL or T1, is sold to a customer, a variety of things must happen (see Figure 1-4). The provider of the line, such as UUNet, must be informed of the request for a new line. A router must be configured by the CLEC and the setup of the router must be coordinated with the Internet service provider. Then an installation must occur, which may involve another company if this process is outsourced. This relatively common and simple sale of a network line already involves three companies! Add to this the technical service group for the manufacturer of the router, the phone company for the customer's other communication services, and the Internic to register a domain, and the process becomes significant.

This rather intimidating process can be made extremely simple with the use of XML (as shown in Figure 1-5). Imagine that the initial request for a line is input into a system that converts the request into an XML document. This document is then transformed, via XSL, into a format that can be sent to the line provider, UUNet in our example. UUNet then adds line-specific information, transforming the request into yet another XML document, which is returned to the CLEC. This

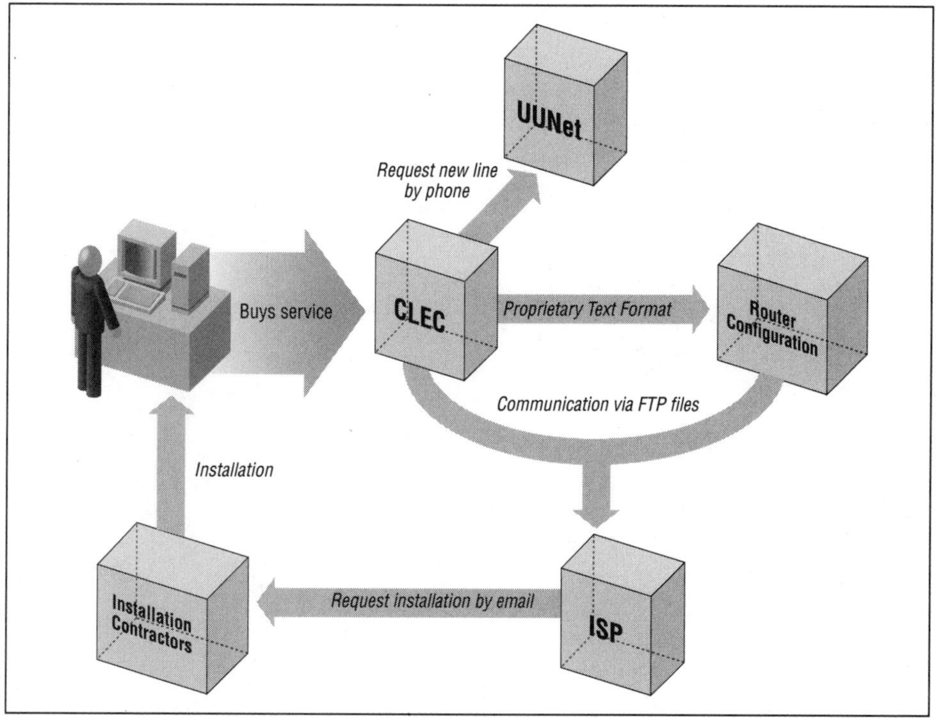

Figure 1-4. Setting up a customer network line using proprietary systems

new document is passed on to the installation company with additional information about where the client is located. Upon installation, notes detailing whether or not the installation was successful are added to the document, which is transformed again via XSL, and passed back to the original CLEC application. The beauty of this solution is that instead of multiple systems, each using vendor-specific formatting, the same set of XML APIs can be used at every step, allowing a standard interface for the XML data across applications, systems, and even businesses.

XML for configuration

One last significant use of XML in applications and Java technologies today is at the application server level. The Enterprise JavaBeans (EJB) 1.1 specification requires that deployment descriptors for Enterprise JavaBeans, which define the behavior and other information about EJBs, be XML based. This is a replacement for the previously used serialized deployment descriptors. In the EJB realm, this is a welcome change, as it removes vendor specificity from deployment descriptors. By requiring deployment descriptors to conform to a predefined DTD, vendors can all use the same XML deployment descriptors, increasing EJB portability.

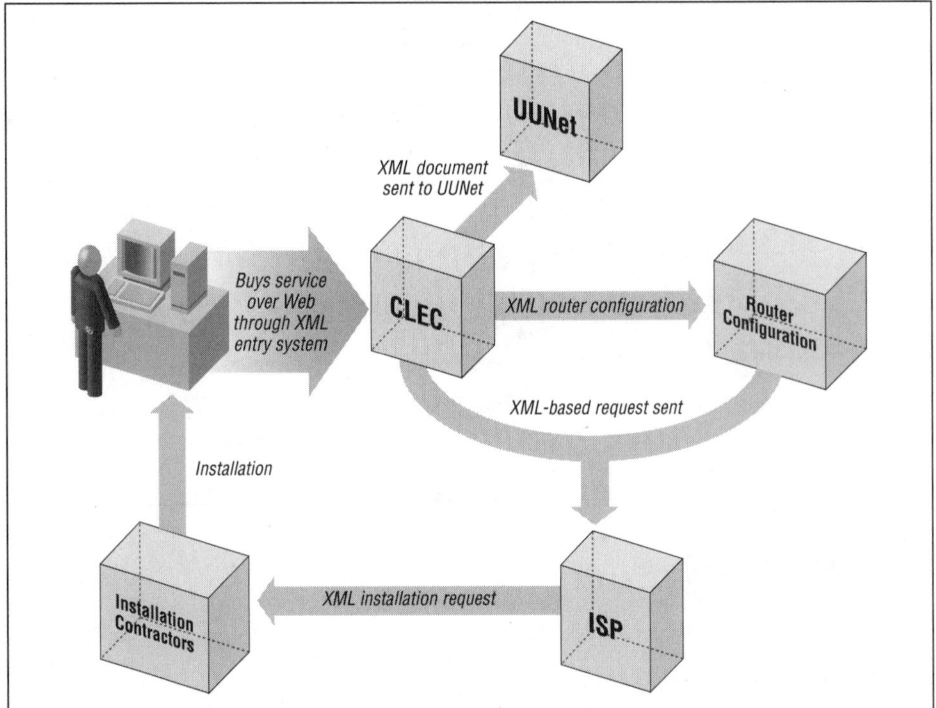

Figure 1-5. Setting up a customer network line using XML-based data

XML is also used for configuration of the servlet API, version 2.2. An XML file, which specifies the connector parameters to use, the servlet contexts to start up, and other engine-specific details, configures the servlet engine itself. XML configuration files are also used to configure individual servlets, allowing initial arguments, servlet aliasing, and URL matching to be accomplished for specific servlet contexts.

Although both the EJB 1.1 specification and the Tomcat servlet engine are fairly new to the Java world, their inclusion of XML as core to their configuration is indicative of Sun's intention to continue to use XML for these purposes. As XML parsers become increasingly common and marketable, XML-based configuration files are expected to increase across all server vendors and types, including non-Java-based servers, such as HTTP and database servers.

Support for XML

In the middle to late months of 1999, support for XML has blossomed, particularly for the Java platform. XML parsers, XSLT processors, publishing frameworks, XML editors and IDEs, and a wealth of related tools have become available and are even now becoming stable and extremely fast. Although the subject of this book is the Java APIs for directly manipulating XML, the parsers, processors, and other components are certainly a part of the overall process of using XML, so a reference on available components is included. Because the XML technology is changing so rapidly, and companies are devoting more time and energy to the platform than ever before, no versions are listed here; they would almost certainly be long out of date by the time this book gets into your hands. In addition, it is possible, even likely, that many more tools will be available than are listed here by the time you read this. You should consult your vendors to see if they have XML support or tools if you do not see them listed here.

Parsers

One of the most important layers to an XML-aware application is the XML parser. This component handles the extremely important task of taking a raw XML document as input and making sense of the document; it will ensure that the document is well-formed, and if a DTD or schema is referenced, it may be able to ensure that the document is valid. What results from an XML document being parsed is typically a data structure, in our case a Java-based one, that can easily be manipulated and handled by other XML tools or Java APIs. We will not detail these data structures now, as they are discussed in great depth in later chapters. For now, just realize that the parser is one of the core building blocks to using XML data.

Selecting an XML parser is not an easy task. There are no hard and fast rules, but two main criteria are typically used. The first is the speed of the parser. As XML documents are used more often and their complexity grows, the speed of an XML parser becomes extremely important to the overall performance of an application. The second factor is conformity to the XML specification. Because performance is often more of a priority than some of the obscure features in XML, some parsers may not conform to finer points of the XML specification in order to squeeze out additional speed. You must decide on the proper balance between the two factors based on your application's needs. In addition, some XML parsers are validating, which means they offer the option to validate your XML with a DTD, and some are not. Make sure you use a validating parser if that capability is needed in your applications.

Here's a list of the most commonly used XML parsers. The list does not show whether a parser is validating or not, as there are current efforts to add validation to several of the parsers that do not yet offer it. No overall ranking is given or suggested here, but there is a wealth of information on the web pages for each parser:

- Apache Xerces: *http://xml.apache.org*
- IBM XML4J: *http://alphaworks.ibm.com/tech/xml4j*

- James Clark's XP: *http://www.jclark.com/xml/xp*
- OpenXML: *http://www.openxml.org*
- Oracle XML Parser: *http://technet.oracle.com/tech/xml*
- Sun Microsystems Project X: *http://java.sun.com/products/xml*
- Tim Bray's Lark and Larval: *http://www.textuality.com/Lark*
- The W3C has stated that they intend to release an open source schema validating parser.

WARNING The Microsoft parser has been intentionally left out of this list; from all appearances, Microsoft does not now or in the future intend to conform to W3C standards. Instead, Microsoft seems to be developing their own flavor of XML. We have seen this before . . . be careful if you are forced to use Microsoft's parser, MSXML.

Processors

After an XML document is parsed, it is almost always transformed. This transformation, as we have discussed, is accomplished through XSLT. Similar to parsing, there are a wide variety of options for this component of the XML process. Again, the two primary considerations are speed of transformation and conformity to XSL and XSLT specifications. At the time of this writing, XSLT has just become a full W3C Recommendation, so the level of support for all XSL constructs and options is in great flux. The web site for each processor is the most informative location for determining conformance and for searching for performance benchmarks.

- Apache Xalan: *http://xml.apache.org*
- James Clark's XT: *http://www.jclark.com/xml/xt*
- Lotus XSL Processor: *http://www.alphaworks.ibm.com/tech/LotusXSL*
- Oracle XSL Processor: *http://technet.oracle.com/tech/xml*
- Keith Visco's XSL:P: *http://www.clc-marketing.com/xslp*
- Michael Kay's SAXON: *http://users.iclway.co.uk/mhkay/saxon*

Publishing frameworks

An XML *publishing framework* is a bit of a nebulous term, and certainly is not a formal definition. For the purposes of this book, a publishing framework for XML is considered to be a suite or set of XML tools that allow parsing, transformations, and possibly additional options for using XML within applications. Although the parsing and transforming is generally accomplished by using some of the tools we have already mentioned, a publishing framework ties these tools together with Java

APIs, and provides a standard interface for using the framework. More advanced frameworks allow for processing of both static XML documents and XML generated by Java applications, and some offer editors and component builders to ensure that generated XML fits the framework's constraints.

Because there is no specification for how an XML application or framework should behave, there is a tremendous amount of variety between the frameworks listed here. However, each has benefits that are significant enough to merit you spending some time looking at and using them. Additionally, several of these frameworks are open source software (OSS), and thus are not only accessible, but also open in that you can see exactly how things were accomplished. When we begin building application components later we will select a framework that best suits the examples, but for now, that decision is deferred so that you can do your own research based on your application's needs.

- Apache Cocoon: *http://xml.apache.org*
- Enhydra Application Server: *http://www.enhydra.org*
- Bluestone XML Server: *http://www.bluestone.com/xml*
- SAXON: *http://users.iclway.co.uk/mhkay/saxon*

XML editors and IDEs

Although there are many strong XML parsers and processors available, the same cannot be said for XML editors. Unfortunately, XML is in a similar situation to that of HTML several years ago; embraced by a small, highly technical group of developers, XML is most often created in text editors like vi, emacs, and notepad. Although there have been some recent offerings in the XML editor space, these offerings have been slow to mature, and are only now becoming usable. IBM does seem to be making significant strides towards providing editing tools for XML, and their latest offerings can be seen at *http://alphaworks.ibm.com/*. In addition, *http://www.xmlsoftware.com* provides an excellent, current listing of XML products, and should be consulted for the latest software offerings.

XML Tomorrow

To complete our look at how XML is being used, it seems only fair to try to anticipate where XML will be used tomorrow. XML is often referred to as the technology of the future. In fact, many companies and developers have held off using XML because they claim that it is not quite mature enough, but all admit that it will change the way applications are built in the next year. While the issue of XML's maturity is arguable, as evidenced by the many excellent uses for XML we have already discussed, the claim that it will revolutionize application development is not. Even those who do not use it heavily today are aware that they will have to use it eventually, and "eventually" gets closer every day.

Despite all the hype surrounding XML, and its massive promise, trying to anticipate where XML will be a year from now, or even six months from now, is almost impossible. It is a bit like trying to guess where a quirky OO language called Java that was great for building applets would go about four years ago: in other words, there is no telling! However, there are several trends in the use of XML that can help us anticipate what we may soon see on the horizon. Next, we take a look at some of the most significant of those ideas.

Configuration repositories

We have already discussed how XML is increasingly being used for server configuration. Because XML provides such an easy representation of data, it is ideal for configuration files; these files have historically been cryptic, difficult to use and modify, and very vendor-specific. For example, look at a portion of the configuration file for an Apache HTTP server, shown in Example 1-5.

Example 1-5. Apache HTTP Server Configuration File

```
ServerType standalone
ServerRoot "e:/java/server/apache/http"

PidFile logs/httpd.pid
ScoreBoardFile logs/apache_status

Timeout 300
KeepAlive On
MaxKeepAliveRequests 100
KeepAliveTimeout 15
MaxRequestsPerChild 0
ThreadsPerChild 50

Listen 80
Listen 85
```

While this is fairly straightforward, it is radically different from the configuration file for a Weblogic server, shown in Example 1-6.

Example 1-6. Weblogic Server Configuration File

```
weblogic.security.ssl.enable=true

weblogic.system.SSLListenPort=7002

weblogic.httpd.register.authenticated=
  weblogic.t3.srvr.ClientAuthenticationServlet
```

Example 1-6. Weblogic Server Configuration File (continued)

```
weblogic.security.certificateCacheSize=3

weblogic.httpd.register.T3AdminCaptureRootCA=admin.T3AdminCaptureRootCA

weblogic.security.clientRootCA=SecureServerCA.pem
weblogic.security.certificate.server=democert.pem
weblogic.security.key.server=demokey.pem
weblogic.security.certificate.authority=ca.pem

weblogic.httpd.register.Certificate=utils.certificate
weblogic.allow.execute.weblogic.servlet.Certificate=system

weblogic.httpd.enable=false
```

These two configuration files use entirely different syntax. Although different services will usually define their own DTDs and element names, XML allows formalization and standardization of file formatting, producing a universal configuration language. This can only help system and network administrators, as well as developers, over time.

You may be thinking that we have already covered configurations; why are we going through this again? Currently, each server has a local configuration file (or files). Although some servers are moving to using directory services for configuration, this has been slow in adoption, and requires knowledge of the directory service protocol, typically the Lightweight Directory Access Protocol (LDAP). A growing trend is the concept of creating an XML repository for configuration (see Figure 1-6). There is also growing support for a Java Naming and Directory Interface™ (JNDI) provider for XML, similar to a file provider. In this situation, XML could either function separately from a directory service or as an abstraction layer over a directory service, allowing applications to need only an XML parser to obtain configuration information. This is substantially easier and more powerful than providing LDAP libraries with servers. In addition, as more servers become XML aware, the ability to store configurations in a central location allows interoperability between components. HTTP servers can discover what servlet engines are available and self-configure connectors. Enterprise JavaBean containers can locate directory services on the network and register beans with those directories, as well as discover databases that can be used for object persistence. These are just a few of the options available when standalone servers are discarded for networked servers, all using a common XML repository for configuration information.

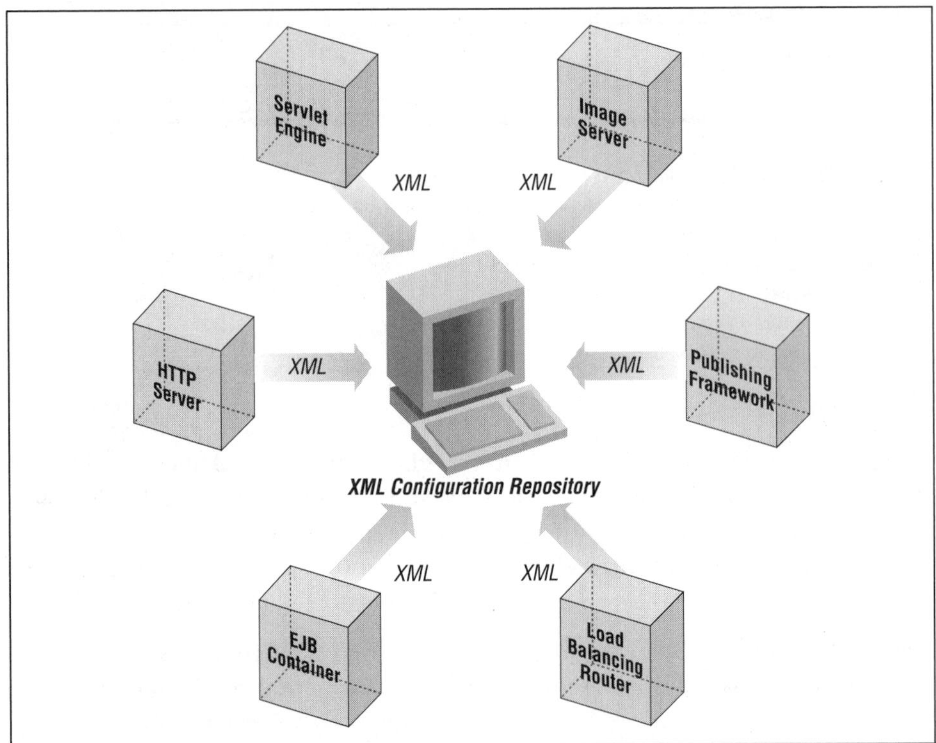

Figure 1-6. XML configuration repository

XSP

XSP stands for Extensible Server Pages, and is yet another XML-related acronym that has the potential to throw the Java community into excited action. XSP is currently a working draft authored by Ricardo Rocha and Stefano Mazzocchi, the lead developers on the Apache Cocoon project. Although not adopted by the W3C or any other formal organization at the time of this writing, it is possible that the XSP draft may make its way to one of those committees by the time you are reading this chapter. In a nutshell, XSP seeks to provide the frontend portion of an XML framework, providing dynamic XML pages that are parsed and transformed by the framework and allow application interoperability, yet are constructed and stored as static files on a filesystem.

To those of you familiar with Java server-side components, you probably realize that this sounds a lot like JSP, or at least an XML version of JSP. To some degree, you are right. XSP offers an XML, and therefore language-independent, alternative to a scripting language for building web pages and web sites. Much as enterprise applications in Java are aimed at providing a clear separation of content from application and business logic, XSP seeks to provide the same for XML-based applications. Although many of the currently available XML frameworks allow this separation of layers within compiled code, changes to the formatting of actual data in an XML document still require changes to Java code and a subsequent recompilation. This is in addition to any changes that might result from changing the actual presentation and related XSL stylesheet. In addition, XSP defines a process of allowing XSLT transformations to take place within the document, but allows programmatic transformations as well as presentation ones. For example, consider the sample XSP document (based on an example from the XSP working draft) shown in Example 1-7.

Example 1-7. A Simple XSP Page

```
<?xml version="1.0"?>

<xsp:page
  language="java"
  xmlns:xsp="http://www.apache.org/1999/XSP/Core"
>
  <title>A Simple XSL Page</title>
  <p>Hi, I've been hit <counter/> times.</p>
</xsp:page>
```

In addition to being well-formed and easily validated XML, there is no programming logic within the XSP page. This is where XSP diverges from JSP; logic, and therefore coding structures, are defined in an associated logicsheet (analogous to an XSL stylesheet) rather than within the XSP page itself. This allows complete language independence within XSP, and the abstraction of language-specific constructs in the logicsheet. The following logicsheet in Example 1-8 would handle the transformation of the `<counter/>` tag and the rest of the XSP page into actual content.

Example 1-8. XSP Logicsheet

```
<?xml version="1.0"?>
<xsl:transform
 xmlns:xsl="http://www.w3.org/1999/XSL/Tranform"
 xmlns:xsp="http://www.apache.org/1999/XSP/Core"
>

 <xsl:template match="xsp:page">
  <xsp:page language="java">

   <xsp:structure>
    <xsp:include>java.lang.*</xsp:include>
   </xsp:structure>

   <xsp:logic>
```

Example 1-8. XSP Logicsheet (continued)

```
    private static int counter = 0;

    private synchronized int currentCount() {
      return ++counter;
    }
   </xsp:logic>

   <xsp:content>
    <page>
     <xsl:apply-templates/>
    </page>
   </xsp:content>
  </xsp:page>
</xsl:template>

<xsl:template match="counter">
  <xsp:expr>currentCount()</xsp:expr>
</xsl:template>

<!-- Transcribe everything else verbatim -->
<xsl:template match="*|@*|comment()|pi()|text()">
  <xsl:copy>
   <xsl:apply-templates/>
  </xsl:copy>
</xsl:template>
</xsl:transform>
```

You should be able to understand what is happening here with very little explanation. Although XSP does offer some new constructs, such as `<xsp:structure>` and `<xsp:logic>`, the remainder of the document looks like a standard XSL stylesheet. The XSP tags are also very clear and understandable, allowing inline coding of Java in this example.

Although XSP is currently available only as part of the Apache Cocoon project, it is an extremely well thought out draft, and will very likely provide XML-aware applications with the ability to remain abstracted from presentation details much more efficiently than possible today. It also offers an easier entry path into XML, much as JSP has encouraged many developers not familiar with Java to learn JSP and then move on to more complex Java APIs. XSP may further the spread of XML in addition to offering the advantages we've already discussed. For more information on XSP and to view the complete Layer 1 Working Draft, visit *http://xml.apache.org/cocoon/xsp.html* on the Web.

What's Next?

With our whirlwind tour of XML technologies and the Java APIs to manipulate them complete, we are ready to dive into more detail. We will spend the next two chapters detailing XML syntax and how XML can be used in web applications. This will give us the understanding of XML data that we need in order to create, format, parse, and manipulate it within our applications. In the next chapter, creating an XML document will be detailed, and further definition will be given of what it means for an XML document to be well-formed.

One last important note before we begin; if you skimmed the rest of the chapter, please take a moment and read this paragraph carefully. XML has been surrounded with confusion and misinformation since its inception. This book proceeds with the assumption that you are taking XML at face value, and not carrying any of those assumptions around with you, particularly ones about XML being designed for presentation. In other words, we are going to focus on XML as data. We will not refer to XML documents as data that is about to be presented, or information we can transform, but rather as simple data. This important concept may surprise you a bit, as most people still think of presentation when they think of XML. However, as Java developers, we need to treat XML as data and nothing more. We will spend the larger portion of this book *not* formatting XML, but merely parsing and manipulating it. The power of XML is transmitting data from system to system, application to application, and business to business. Trying to remove any preconceptions about what XML can do for you can help make this book more enjoyable, as well as show you a few ways to use XML you may not have considered.

2

In this chapter:
- *An XML Document*
- *The Header*
- *The Content*
- *What's Next?*

Creating XML

Now that you have a greater understanding of XML, how it can be used, and some of the Java APIs available, it's time to turn concepts into practice. Although this book is not by any means a definitive guide to XML syntax, or even an XML reference, it would be impossible to discuss how to parse and manipulate XML documents without first being able to create those documents. In addition, the Java APIs for handling XML all assume a fair amount of familiarity with XML syntax and structure, as well as with the design patterns that go into creating an XML document, constraining it, and transforming it. Therefore we look at each of these tasks before discussing the corresponding Java APIs.

To begin, we will take a closer look at XML syntax in this chapter. Starting with the very basic XML constructs, we will discuss what a well-formed XML document is and how to create one. The various XML rules and syntactical "gotchas" will be covered to help you build XML documents that are not only legal, but can be used in realistic applications. All this work will set the stage for writing our first Java program in the next chapter to understand how parsing XML works, and how Java provides callbacks into the parsing process.

If you have ever read a chapter or even a book on a programming language's syntax, you probably realize it is usually pretty dry reading. To try and avoid this, we will look at syntax in a bit of a different light than you may be used to. Rather than starting with a simple one- or two-line XML file and adding to it, which typically makes for a lengthy, useless file at the end of the exercise, we will look at a complete, usable, relatively complex XML file. The file we will use is a portion of the actual XML document that represents the table of contents page for this book. We will walk through this document line by line, examining the different constructs. What a lot of syntactical discussions ignore is that in the real world, you almost never get to see the simple files that are so often used as examples; instead, you see complex files that don't make any sense to you, even after reading a book. You should get used to seeing an XML file with all its constructs, and begin to learn its structure through practical examples. Hopefully this makes the discussion at least a little more applicable for you, if not somewhat less dry.

Before we begin, one final observation: this chapter doesn't try to be a reference. In other words, it doesn't have each term with a definition, and it doesn't have a nutshell-type entry system. Instead, it is a progressive chapter. Definitions are given in context of the examples and what has already been said about other constructs, rather than each definition standing alone. You should have a good XML reference nearby for the rest of this book, as we will not explain constructs we go over in this chapter again in the latter part of the book, so we can get to more advanced topics. You might want to pick up the *XML Pocket Reference* by Robert Eckstein (O'Reilly & Associates) for this purpose.

An XML Document

As promised, we begin with a practical, real-world example of an XML document that represents a portion of this book's table of contents, shown in Example 2-1.

Example 2-1. An XML File

```
<?xml version="1.0"?>
<?xml-stylesheet href="XSL\JavaXML.html.xsl" type="text/xsl"?>
<?xml-stylesheet href="XSL\JavaXML.wml.xsl" type="text/xsl"
                 media="wap"?>
<?cocoon-process type="xslt"?>
<!DOCTYPE JavaXML:Book SYSTEM "DTD\JavaXML.dtd">

<!-- Java and XML -->
<JavaXML:Book xmlns:JavaXML="http://www.oreilly.com/catalog/javaxml/">
 <JavaXML:Title>Java and XML</JavaXML:Title>
 <JavaXML:Contents>

  <JavaXML:Chapter focus="XML">
   <JavaXML:Heading>Introduction</JavaXML:Heading>
   <JavaXML:Topic subSections="7">What Is It?</JavaXML:Topic>
   <JavaXML:Topic subSections="3">How Do I Use It?</JavaXML:Topic>
   <JavaXML:Topic subSections="4">Why Should I Use It?</JavaXML:Topic>
   <JavaXML:Topic subSections="0">What's Next?</JavaXML:Topic>
  </JavaXML:Chapter>

  <JavaXML:Chapter focus="XML">
   <JavaXML:Heading>Creating XML</JavaXML:Heading>
   <JavaXML:Topic subSections="0">An XML Document</JavaXML:Topic>
   <JavaXML:Topic subSections="2">The Header</JavaXML:Topic>
   <JavaXML:Topic subSections="6">The Content</JavaXML:Topic>
```

Example 2-1. An XML File (continued)

```
    <JavaXML:Topic subSections="1">What's Next?</JavaXML:Topic>
  </JavaXML:Chapter>

  <JavaXML:Chapter focus="Java">
    <JavaXML:Heading>Parsing XML</JavaXML:Heading>
    <JavaXML:Topic subSections="3">Getting Prepared</JavaXML:Topic>
    <JavaXML:Topic subSections="3">SAX Readers</JavaXML:Topic>
    <JavaXML:Topic subSections="9">Content Handlers</JavaXML:Topic>
    <JavaXML:Topic subSections="4">Error Handlers</JavaXML:Topic>
    <JavaXML:Topic subSections="0">
      A Better Way to Load a Parser
    </JavaXML:Topic>
    <JavaXML:Topic subSections="4">"Gotcha!"</JavaXML:Topic>
    <JavaXML:Topic subSections="0">What's Next?</JavaXML:Topic>
  </JavaXML:Chapter>

  <JavaXML:SectionBreak/>

  <JavaXML:Chapter focus="Java">
    <JavaXML:Heading>Web Publishing Frameworks</JavaXML:Heading>
    <JavaXML:Topic subSections="4">Selecting a Framework</JavaXML:Topic>
    <JavaXML:Topic subSections="4">Installation</JavaXML:Topic>
    <JavaXML:Topic subSections="3">
      Using a Publishing Framework
    </JavaXML:Topic>
    <JavaXML:Topic subSections="2">XSP</JavaXML:Topic>
    <JavaXML:Topic subSections="3">Cocoon 2.0 and Beyond</JavaXML:Topic>
    <JavaXML:Topic subSections="0">What's Next?</JavaXML:Topic>
  </JavaXML:Chapter>

 </JavaXML:Contents>

 <JavaXML:Copyright>&OReillyCopyright;</JavaXML:Copyright>

</JavaXML:Book>
```

The Header

The first syntax we look at is XML itself. An XML document can be broken into two basic pieces: the header, which gives an XML parser and XML applications information about how to handle the document, and the content, which is the XML data itself. Although this is a fairly loose division, it will help us differentiate the instructions to applications within an XML document from the XML content itself, and is an important distinction to understand. In our example, we will begin with the first several lines, which lead up to the `JavaXML:Book` element. These initial lines, excluding the `JavaXML:Book` element, make up the document header.

The term "header" is not a formal term defined in the XML specification, but is commonly used in the XML community, and we will use it in this book to denote these initial lines of an XML document.

XML Instructions

The first statement you will see in any XML document is an XML instruction. XML instructions are actually a specific subset of processing instructions (PIs), which we talked about in the last chapter. Remember that we said PIs are generally passed on from the parser to the calling application, and handled there. However, PIs that specify their target as `xml` are intended for the XML parser itself. They specify the version of XML being used, a stylesheet, or other information that a parser may need to know to properly parse XML data. Here is an XML instruction:

```
<?xml version="1.0" standalone="no"?>
```

Like any other PI, it is of the form `<?target instruction?>`, and in this case it specifies that XML Version 1.0 is being used and that the document is not a standalone XML document. Notice that the `instruction` is not necessarily a single keyword=value pair; in this case, both the version and whether the document needs to be paired with an external document or documents are specified. By specifying that it is not a standalone document, a parser knows that an external DTD must be used to determine if the XML document is valid. If this were set to `yes`, the document parser would not have to reference an external DTD. This initial instruction can also specify an encoding type.

Other variations on XML instructions are those that refer to stylesheets. Two of these references are present in our example:

```
<?xml-stylesheet href="XSL\JavaXML.html.xsl" type="text/xsl"?>
<?xml-stylesheet href="XSL\JavaXML.wml.xsl" type="text/xsl" media="wap"?>
```

Generally a PI that begins with `xml-[name]` refers to the XML-related technology given in `[name]`. In this case, an XSL stylesheet is being specified, and the XML instruction is passed to the XSLT engine rather than the XML parser. In the first line, a default stylesheet is being referenced, and the location of this stylesheet is specified, as well as the type. The second line specifies an alternate stylesheet. In this case, the `media` attribute is given, telling the processor which type of client media this stylesheet should be used for. When the publishing engine determines that the media being requested matches the specified type, the alternate stylesheet is used. We will look at publishing engines in Chapter 9, *Web Publishing Frameworks.*

Document Type Declarations

What often follows the initial XML Instructions is a DOCTYPE declaration. This declaration has its own unique syntax because it is used only for one specific purpose in a document, if at all: specifying a DTD to use for the XML document. Let's look at the DOCTYPE declaration in our example:

```
<!DOCTYPE JavaXML:Book SYSTEM "DTD\JavaXML.dtd">
```

In this example, we specify the file *JavaXML.dtd*, which is located on the local filesystem, as the DTD for this XML document. XML parsers typically allow either the forward or backward slash (Unix and Windows, respectively) to be used to accommodate cross-platform portability in local pathnames. The first parameter to DOCTYPE is the root element of the document, which we will talk about in a moment. For now, just understand that it identifies the current XML document. The second argument can be either SYSTEM or PUBLIC. Because we specified SYSTEM, the XML parser will expect the next argument to specify the location at which the DTD file can be loaded, identified by a given Uniform Resource Indicator (URI). However, using SYSTEM does not necessarily mean that the DTD has to be on the local system. We could also have specified our DTD like this:

```
<!DOCTYPE JavaXML:Book SYSTEM
          "http://www.oreilly.com/catalog/javaxml/DTD/JavaXML.dtd">
```

The XML specification allows any valid URI for this parameter, so a URL is perfectly acceptable. Using the PUBLIC variant specifies that the DTD being referenced is publicized and available for widespread use. In this case, before specifying the URI, a public name must be specified. You may see the following DOCTYPE declaration at the top of some HTML files, such as the W3C homepage at *http://www.w3c.org/*, when you view their source:

```
<!DOCTYPE html PUBLIC "-//W3C//DTD XHTML 1.0 Transitional//EN"
          "http://www.w3.org/TR/xhtml1/DTD/xhtml1-transitional.dtd">
```

Following the keyword PUBLIC is a name that identifies the public DTD being used. The XML parser will first try to use this name to locate and reference the DTD, and only if that fails will it use the additionally specified URI given. The semantics of the public name of a DTD are detailed in the XML specification, and are not something you need to worry about right now. In Chapter 4, *Constraining XML*, we will look at a DTD and go into detail on its format and how it is used.

The Content

With our header worked out, we now can move on to the actual data content in our XML document. This consists of all the elements, attributes, and textual data within these constructs.

The Root Element

The root element is the highest-level element in the XML document, and must be the first opening tag and the last closing tag within the document. It provides a reference point that enables an XML parser or XML-aware application to recognize a beginning and end to an XML document. In our example, the root element is `<JavaXML:Book>`:

```
<JavaXML:Book xmlns:JavaXML="http://www.oreilly.com/catalog/javaxml/">

  <!-- Content of XML Document -->

</JavaXML:Book>
```

This tag and its matching closing tag surround all other data content within the XML document. XML specifies that there may only be one root element in a document. In other words, the root element must enclose all other elements within the document. Aside from this requirement, a root element does not differ from any other XML element. It's important to understand this, because XML documents can reference and include other XML documents. In these cases, the root element of the referenced document becomes an enclosed element in the referring document, and must be handled normally by an XML parser. Defining root elements as standard XML elements without special properties or behavior allows document inclusion to work seamlessly.

Identifying XML with Namespaces

Although we will not delve deeply into XML namespaces here, you should note the use of a namespace in the root element. You probably observed that all of the XML elements' names are prefixed with `JavaXML`. In our XML example, it may be necessary later to include portions of other O'Reilly books. Because each of these books may also have `<Chapter>`, `<Heading>`, or `<Topic>` tags, the document must be designed and constructed in a way to avoid namespace collision problems with other documents. The XML namespaces specification nicely solves this problem. Because our XML document represents a specific book, and no other XML document should represent the same book, using a prefix like `JavaXML` can associate the element to a namespace. The namespace specification requires that a unique URI be associated with the prefix to distinguish the elements in the namespace from elements in other namespaces. A URL is recommended, which is what is supplied here (`http://www.oreilly.com/catalog/javaxml`, the web site for the book):

```
<JavaXML:Book xmlns:JavaXML="http://www.oreilly.com/catalog/javaxml/">
```

Once the namespace is defined like this, it can then be referenced by any other element within the XML document. In our case, we use it for all of the elements because they are all part of the book's namespace. The proper way to associate an element with a namespace is to prefix the name of the element with the namespace prefix and a colon:

```
<JavaXML:Chapter focus="XML">
 <JavaXML:Heading>Introduction</JavaXML:Heading>
 <JavaXML:Topic subSections="7">What Is It?</JavaXML:Topic>
 <JavaXML:Topic subSections="3">How Do I Use It?</JavaXML:Topic>
 <JavaXML:Topic subSections="4">Why Should I Use It?</JavaXML:Topic>
 <JavaXML:Topic subSections="0">What's Next?</JavaXML:Topic>
</JavaXML:Chapter>
```

Each of these elements is treated by the XML parser as part of the `http://www.oreilly.com/catalog/javaxml/` namespace, and will not result in collisions with any other elements named `Chapter`, `Heading`, or `Topic` within other namespaces. Multiple namespace declarations can be included in the same document, all within the same element:

```
<JavaXML:Book xmlns:JavaXML="http://www.oreilly.com/catalog/javaxml/"
              xmlns:Cocoon="http://xml.apache.org/cocoon/">
```

Although this is a legal declaration, be very careful when using multiple namespaces within one document. Often, the benefits of using namespaces can be outweighed by the additional clutter and textual data they add to the document. Generally, a single namespace for a single document provides a clear, clean XML document while still avoiding namespace collisions; the only notable exception is when another XML specification (such as XML Schema) is used and that namespace must be referenced.

A final interesting (and somewhat confusing) point: XML Schema, which we will talk about more in Chapter 4, requires the schema of an XML document to be specified in a manner that looks very similar to a set of namespace declarations; see Example 2-2.

Example 2-2. XML Document Using XML Schema

```
<?xml version="1.0"?>
<addressBook xmlns:xsi="http://www.w3.org/1999/XMLSchema/instance"
             xmlns="http://www.oreilly.com/catalog/javaxml"
             xsi:schemaLocation="http://www.oreilly.com/catalog/javaxml
                                 mySchema.xsd"
>
  <person>
    <name>
      <firstName>Brett</firstName>
      <lastName>McLaughlin</lastName>
```

Example 2-2. XML Document Using XML Schema (continued)

```
    </name>
    <email>brettmclaughlin@earthlink.net</email>
  </person>
  <person>
    <name>
      <firstName>Eddie</firstName>
      <lastName>Balucci</lastName>
    </name>
    <email>eddieb@freeworld.net</email>
  </person>
</addressBook>
```

Several things happen here, and it is important to understand each. First, the XML Schema instance namespace is defined and associated with a URL. This namespace, abbreviated `xsi`, is used for specifying information in XML documents about a schema, exactly as we are doing here. Thus, our first line makes the elements in the XML Schema instance available to our document for use. The next line defines the namespace for the XML document itself. Because the document does not use an explicit namespace, like `JavaXML` in earlier examples, the *default namespace* is declared. The XML namespaces specification dictates that every element in an XML document is in a namespace; the *default namespace* is the namespace that an element is associated with if no other namespace is specified. This means that all elements without an explicit namespace and associated prefix (all of them, in this example) will be associated with this default namespace.

With both the document and XML Schema instance namespaces defined like this, we can then actually do what we want, which is to associate a schema with this document. The `schemaLocation` attribute, which belongs to the XML Schema instance namespace, is used to accomplish this. We preface this attribute with its namespace (`xsi`), which we just defined. The argument to this attribute is actually *two* URIs: the first specifying the namespace being associated with a schema, and the second the URI of the schema to refer to. In our example, this results in the first URI being the default namespace we just declared, and the second a file on the local filesystem called *mySchema.xsd.* Like any other XML attribute, this entire pair is enclosed in a single set of quotation marks. And as simple as that, you have referenced a schema in your XML document!

Seriously, this is not simple, and is to date one of the most misunderstood portions of using namespaces and XML Schema. We will look more at the mechanics used here as we continue. For now, try to understand how namespaces allow elements from various groupings to be used, yet remain identified as a part of their specific grouping.

XML Data Elements

So far we have glossed over defining what an actual element is. Now we will take an in-depth look at elements, which are represented by arbitrary names and must be enclosed in angle brackets. There are several different variations of elements in the sample document, as shown here:

```
<!-- Standard element opening tag -->
<JavaXML:Contents>

 <!-- Standard element with attribute -->
 <JavaXML:Chapter focus="XML">

 <!-- Element with textual data -->
 <JavaXML:Heading>Web Publishing Frameworks</JavaXML:Heading>

 <!-- Empty element -->
 <JavaXML:SectionBreak/>

<!-- Standard element closing tag -->
</JavaXML:Contents>
```

The first rule in creating elements is that their names must start with a letter or underscore, and then may contain any number of letters, numbers, underscores, hyphens, or periods. They may not contain embedded spaces; the following is not well-formed XML:

```
<!-- Embedded spaces are not allowed -->
<my element name>
```

XML element names are also case-sensitive. Generally, using the same rules that govern Java variable naming will result in sound XML element naming. Using an element named `<tcbo>` to represent Telecommunications Business Object is not a good idea because it is cryptic, while an overly verbose tag name like `<beginningOfNewChapter>` just clutters up a document. Keep in mind that your XML documents will probably be seen by other developers and content authors, so self-documentation through good naming is essential.

Every opened element must in turn be closed. There are no exceptions to this rule as there are in many other markup languages, like HTML. An ending element tag consists of the forward slash and then the element name: `</JavaXML:Content>`. Between an opening and closing tag, there can be any number of additional elements or textual data. However, you cannot mix the order of nested tags: the first opened element must always be the last closed element. If any of the rules for XML syntax are not followed in an XML document, the document is not *well-formed*. A well-formed document is one in which all XML syntax rules are followed, and all elements and attributes are correctly positioned. However, a well-formed document is not necessarily *valid*, which means that it follows the constraints set upon a document by its DTD or schema. There is a significant difference between a well-formed document and a valid one; the rules we discuss in this chapter ensure that your document is well-formed, while the rules discussed in Chapter 4 allow your document to be valid.

As an example of a document that is not well-formed, consider this XML fragment:

```
<tag1>
 <tag2>
</tag1>
 </tag2>
```

The order of nesting of tags is incorrect, as the opened `<tag2>` is not followed by a closing `</tag2>` within the surrounding `tag1` element. However, if these syntax errors are corrected, there is no guarantee that the document will be valid. This is an important difference to understand, and we will revisit the subject in Chapter 4.

While this example of a document that is not well-formed may seem silly and trivial, remember that this would be acceptable HTML, and commonly occurs in large tables within an HTML document. In other words, HTML and many other markup languages do not require well-formed XML documents. XML's strict adherence to ordering and nesting rules allows data to be parsed and handled much more quickly than when using markup languages without these constraints.

The last rule we look at is the slightly odd case of empty elements. We already said that XML tags must always be paired; an opening tag and a closing tag constitute a complete XML element. There are cases where an element is used purely by itself, like a flag stating a chapter is incomplete, or where an element has attributes but no textual data, like an image declaration in HTML. These would have to be represented as:

```
<chapterIncomplete></chapterIncomplete>
<img src="/images/xml.gif"></img>
```

This is obviously a bit silly, and also adds more clutter to what can often be very large XML documents. The XML specification provides a means to signify both an opening and closing element tag within one element:

```
<chapterIncomplete/>
<img src="/images/xml.gif"/>
```

This nicely solves the problem of unnecessary clutter, and still follows the rule that every XML element must have a matching end tag; it simply consolidates both start and end tag into a single tag.

Element Attributes

In addition to text contained within an element's tags, an element can also have attributes. Attributes are included with their respective values within the element's opening declaration (which can also be its closing declaration!). For example, in the `JavaXML:Chapter` tag, the focus of the chapter was part of what was noted in an attribute:

```
<JavaXML:Chapter focus="XML">
 <!-- Chapter Information -->
</JavaXML:Chapter>

<JavaXML:Chapter focus="Java">
 <!-- Chapter Information -->
</JavaXML:Chapter>
```

In this example, `focus` is the attribute name; the value is the focus of the chapter, `XML` and `Java`, respectively. Attribute names must follow the same rules as XML element names, and attribute values must be within quotation marks. Although both single and double quotes are allowed, using double quotes is a widely used standard and results in XML documents that model Java programming practices. Additionally, single and double quotation marks may be used in attribute values; surrounding the value in double quotes allows single quotes to be used as part of the value, and surrounding the value in single quotes allows double quotes to be used as part of the value. This is not good practice, though, as XML parsers and processors often uniformly convert the quotes around an attribute's value to all double (or all single) quotes, possibly introducing unexpected results.

In addition to how to use attributes, there is an issue of when to use attributes. Because XML allows such a variety of data formatting, it is rare that an attribute cannot be represented by an element, or that an element could not easily be converted to an attribute. Although there is no specification or widely accepted standard for determining when to use an attribute and when to use an element, there is a good rule of thumb: use elements for presentable data and attributes for system data. If you have a piece of data that is going to be presented to a client, or an application, or used as part of a formula, the data most likely belongs in an element. It can then be treated primarily as application data, and is easily searchable and usable. Examples are the titles of a book's chapters, the price of a piece of furniture, or the URL of a company's web site. However, if the data is used as a grouping, or to let an application know how to handle a portion of data, or is never directly visible to a client or XML-aware application, it most likely belongs as an attribute. Examples of good candidates for attributes are the section of a chapter; while the section item itself might be an element and have its own title, the grouping of chapters within a section is easily represented by a `section` attribute within the `JavaXML:Chapter` element. This attribute would allow easy grouping and indexing of chapters, but would never be directly displayed to the user. Another good example of a piece of data that could be represented in XML as an attribute is if a particular table or chair is on layaway. This instruction could let an XML application used to generate a brochure or flyer know not to include items on layaway in current stock. Again, the application client would never directly see this information, but the data would be used in processing and handling the XML document. If after all of this analysis you are still unsure, you can always play it safe and use an element.

You may have already come up with alternate ways to represent these various examples, using different approaches. For example, rather than using a section attribute, it might make sense to nest `JavaXML:Chapter` elements within a `JavaXML:Section` element. Perhaps an empty tag, `<layaway/>`, might be more useful to mark furniture that is on layaway. In XML, there is rarely only one way to perform data representation, and often several good ways to accomplish the same task. Most often the application and use of the data dictates what makes the most sense. Rather than try to tell you how to write XML, which would be difficult, we will use XML, and in that use you will hopefully gain insight into how different data formats can be handled and used. This will then give you the knowledge to make your own decisions about formatting XML documents.

Referring to XML "Constants"

One item we have not discussed is escaping characters, or referring to other constant type data values. For example, a common way to represent a path to an installation directory is `<path-to-Cocoon>` or `<Cocoon-Root>`. In both these cases, the user would replace the text with the appropriate choice of installation directory. In our example, the chapter that discusses web applications needs to give some details on installing and using Apache Cocoon, and might need to represent this data within an element:

```
<JavaXML:Topic>
 <JavaXML:Heading>Installing Cocoon</JavaXML:Heading>
 <JavaXML:Content>
  Locate the Cocoon.properties file in the <path-to-Cocoon>/bin
  directory.
 </JavaXML:Content>
</JavaXML:Topic>
```

The problem with this is that XML parsers will attempt to handle this data as an XML tag, and then generate an error because there is no closing tag. This is a common problem, as any use of angle brackets results in this behavior. *Entity references* provide a way to overcome these problems. An entity reference is a special data type in XML that is used to refer to another piece of data. The entity reference consists of a unique name, preceded by an ampersand and followed by a semicolon: &[entity name];. When an XML parser sees an entity reference, the substitution value specified is inserted and no processing of that value occurs. XML defines five entities to address the problem discussed in the example: < for the less-than bracket, > for the greater-than bracket, & for the ampersand sign itself, " for a double quotation mark, and ' for a single quotation mark or apostrophe. Using these special references, we could then accurately represent our installation directory reference as:

```
<JavaXML:Topic>
 <JavaXML:Heading>Installing Cocoon</JavaXML:Heading>
 <JavaXML:Content>
  Locate the Cocoon.properties file in the
  &lt;path-to-Cocoon&gt;/bin directory.
 </JavaXML:Content>
</JavaXML:Topic>
```

Once this document is parsed, the data will be interpreted as <path-to-Cocoon> and the document will still be considered well-formed.

Also be aware that entity references are user-definable. This allows a sort of shortcut markup; in the XML example we have been walking through, we reference an external shared copyright text. Because the copyright is used for multiple O'Reilly books, we don't want to include the text within this XML document; however, if the copyright is changed, our document should reflect these changes. You may notice that the syntax used in the XML document looks like the predefined XML entity references:

```
<JavaXML:Copyright>&OReillyCopyright;</JavaXML:Copyright>
```

Although we won't see how the XML parser is told what to reference when it sees &OReillyCopyright; until our section on DTDs, you should see that there are more uses of entity references than just representing difficult or unusual characters within data.

Unparsed Data

The last XML construct to look at is the CDATA section marker. A CDATA section is used when a significant amount of data should be passed on to the calling application without any XML parsing. This can be used when an unusually large amount of characters would have to be escaped using entity references, or when spacing must be preserved. In an XML document, a CDATA section looks like this:

```
<unparsed-data>
  <![CDATA[Diagram:
       <Step 1>Install Cocoon to "/usr/lib/cocoon"
       <Step 2>Locate the correct properties file.
```

```
        <Step 3>Download Ant from "http://jakarta.apache.org"
                                    -----> Use CVS for this <----
   ]]>
</unparsed-data>
```

In this example, all of the information within the CDATA section does not have to use entity references or other mechanisms to alert the parser that reserved characters are being used; instead, the XML parser passes them unchanged to the wrapping program or application.

At this point, we have looked at the major components of XML documents. Although each has only been looked at somewhat in passing, this should give you enough comfort and familiarity to recognize XML tags when you see them and know their general purpose. As you use XML data and documents throughout this book, you will gain additional knowledge about these constructs through their use, which is a much more effective teacher than any amount of dry documentation.

What's Next?

With this primer on creating XML documents, we are ready to begin writing our first Java code. In the next chapter, we will take a look at using the Simple API for XML (SAX). Starting with a simple program to parse through our XML document, we will learn how PIs, elements, attributes, and other XML constructs are handled within the XML parsing process. Along with each step, we will provide Java code to perform specific actions, beginning with a simple program to print out our XML document. This will start the extensive process of learning how to manipulate all of the various components of an XML document, and how to use this information within Java applications.

3

In this chapter:

- *Getting Prepared*
- *SAX Readers*
- *Content Handlers*
- *Error Handlers*
- *A Better Way to Load a Parser*
- *"Gotcha!"*
- *What's Next?*

Parsing XML

With two solid chapters of introduction behind us, we are ready to code! By now you have seen the numerous acronyms that make up the world of XML, you have delved into the language itself, and you should be familiar with an XML document. This chapter takes the next step, and the first on our path of Java programming, by demonstrating how an XML document is parsed and how we can access the parsed data from within Java code.

One of the first things you will have to do when dealing with XML programmatically is take an XML document and parse it. As the document is parsed, the data in the document becomes available to the application using the parser, and suddenly we are within an XML-aware application! If this all sounds a little too simple to be true, it almost is. In this chapter, we will look closely at how an XML document is parsed. Using a parser within an application and how to feed that parser your document's data will be covered. Then we will look at the various callbacks that are available within the parsing lifecycle. These events are the points where application-specific code can be inserted and data manipulation can occur.

In addition to looking at how parsers work, we will also begin our exploration of the Simple API for XML (SAX) in this chapter. SAX is what makes these parsing callbacks available. The interfaces provided in the SAX package will become an important part of our toolkit for handling XML. Even though the SAX classes are small and few in number, everything else in our discussions of XML is based on these classes. A solid understanding of how they help us access XML data is critical to effectively leveraging XML in your Java programs.

Getting Prepared

There are several items that we should take care of before beginning to code. First, you must obtain an XML parser. Writing a parser for XML is a serious task, and there are several efforts going on to provide excellent XML parsers. We are not going to detail the process of actually writing an XML parser here; rather, we will discuss the applications that wrap this parsing behavior, focusing on using existing tools to manipulate XML data. This results in better and faster programs, as we do not seek to reinvent what is already available. After selecting a parser, we must ensure that a copy of the SAX classes is on hand. These are easy to locate, and are key to our Java code being able to process XML. Finally, we will need an XML document to parse. Then, on to the code!

Obtaining a Parser

The first step in getting ready to code Java that uses XML is locating and obtaining the parser you want to use. We briefly talked about this process in Chapter 1, *Introduction*, and listed various XML parsers that could be used. To ensure that your parser works with all of the examples in the book, you should verify your parser's compliance with the XML specification. Because of the variety of parsers available and the rapid pace of change within the XML community, all of the details about which parsers have what compliance levels are beyond the scope of this book. You should consult the parser's vendor and visit the web sites previously given for this information.

In the spirit of the open source community, all of the examples in this book will use the Apache Xerces parser. Freely available in binary and source form at *http://xml.apache.org*, this C- and Java-based parser is already one of the most widely contributed-to parsers available. In addition, using an open source parser such as Xerces allows you to send questions or bug reports to the parser's authors, resulting in a better product, as well as helping you use the software quickly and correctly. To subscribe to the general list and request help on the Xerces parser, send a blank email to *xerces-dev-subscribe@xml.apache.org*. The members of this list can help if you have questions or problems with a parser not specifically covered in this book. Of course, the examples in this book all run normally on any parser that uses the SAX implementation covered here.

Once you have selected and downloaded an XML parser, make sure that your Java environment, whether it be an IDE (Integrated Development Environment) or a command line, has the XML parser classes in its class path. This will be a basic requirement for all further examples.

Getting the SAX Classes and Interfaces

Once you have your parser, you need to locate the SAX classes. These classes are almost always included with a parser when downloaded, and Xerces is no exception. If this is the case with your parser, you should be sure not to download the SAX classes explicitly, as your parser is probably packaged with the latest version of SAX that is supported by the parser. At the time of this writing, SAX 2.0 had just gone final. The SAX 2.0 classes are used throughout this book, and should come bundled with the latest version of the Apache Xerces parser.

If you are not sure whether you have the SAX classes, look at the *jar* file or class structure used by your parser. The SAX classes are packaged in the `org.xml.sax` structure. The latest version of these includes 17 classes in this root directory, as well as 9 classes in `org.xml.sax.helpers` and 2 in `org.xml.sax.ext`. If you are missing any of these classes, you should try to contact your parser's vendor to see why the classes were not included with your distribution. It is possible that some classes may have been left out if they are not supported in whole.* These class counts are for SAX 2.0 as well; fewer classes may appear if only SAX 1.0 is supported.

Finally, you may want to either download or bookmark the SAX API Javadocs on the Web. This documentation is extremely helpful in using the SAX classes, and the Javadoc structure provides a standard, simple way to find out additional information about the classes and what they do. This documentation is located at *http://www.megginson.com/SAX/SAX2/javadoc/index.html*. You may also generate Javadoc from the SAX source if you wish, by using the source included with your parser, or by downloading the complete source from *http://www.megginson.com/SAX/SAX2*.

Have an XML Document on Hand

You should also make sure that you have an XML document to parse. The output shown in the examples is based on parsing the XML document we discussed in Chapter 2, *Creating XML*. Save this file as *contents.xml* somewhere on your local hard drive. We highly recommend that you follow what we're doing in this file. You can simply type the file in from the book, or you may download the XML file from the book's web site, *http://www.oreilly.com/catalog/javaxml*. You are encouraged to take the time to type in the example, though, as it will almost certainly familiarize you with XML syntax more than a quick download will.

---

* Supporting SAX in whole is a very important item for a parser. Although you are certainly welcome to use any parser you like, if your parser does not have complete SAX 2.0 support, many of the examples in this book will not work. In addition, your parser is not keeping up with the latest XML developments. For either or both reasons, you may want to consider at least trying the Xerces parser for the duration of this book.

In addition to downloading or creating the XML file, you need to make a couple of small modifications. Because we haven't covered or discussed how to constrain and transform documents, our programs only parse XML in this chapter. To prevent errors, we need to remove the references within the XML document to an external DTD, which constrains the XML, and the XSL stylesheets that transform it. You should comment out these two lines in the XML document, as well as the processing instruction to Cocoon requesting XSL transformation:

```
<?xml version="1.0"?>

<!-- We don't need these yet
  <?xml-stylesheet href="XSL\JavaXML.html.xsl" type="text/xsl"?>
  <?xml-stylesheet href="XSL\JavaXML.wml.xsl" type="text/xsl"
                   media="wap"?>
  <?cocoon-process type="xslt"?>
  <!DOCTYPE JavaXML:Book SYSTEM "DTD\JavaXML.dtd">
-->

<!-- Java and XML -->
<JavaXML:Book xmlns:JavaXML="http://www.oreilly.com/catalog/javaxml/">
```

Once these lines are commented, note the full path to the XML document. You will need to supply that path to our programs in this and later chapters.

Finally, we need to comment out our reference to the `OReillyCopyright` external entity that would be used to load a file from the filesystem with the needed copyright information. Without a DTD to define how to resolve this entity reference, we will receive unwanted errors. In the next chapter, we will look at how to resolve this reference for the XML document.

```
</JavaXML:Contents>

<!-- Leave out until DTD Section
 <JavaXML:Copyright>&OReillyCopyright;</JavaXML:Copyright>
-->

</JavaXML:Book>
```

SAX Readers

Without spending any further time on the preliminaries, let's begin to code. Our first program will be able to take an XML file as a command-line parameter, and parse that file. We will build document callbacks into the parsing process so that we can display events in the parsing process as they occur, which will give us a better idea of what exactly is going on "under the hood."

The first thing we need to do is get an instance of a class that conforms to the SAX `org.xml.sax.XMLReader` interface. This interface defines parsing behavior and allows us to set features and properties, which we will look at in Chapter 5, *Validating XML*. For those of you familiar with SAX 1.0, this interface replaces the `org.xml.sax.Parser` interface.

Instantiating a Reader

SAX provides an interface that all SAX-compliant XML parsers should implement. This allows SAX to know exactly what methods are available for callback and use within an application. For example, the Xerces main SAX parser class, `org.apache.xerces.parsers.SAXParser`, implements the `org.xml.sax.XMLReader` interface. If you have access to the source of your parser, you should see the same interface implemented in your parser's main SAX parser class. Each XML parser must have one class (sometimes more!) that implements this interface, and that is the class we need to instantiate to allow us to parse XML:

```
XMLReader parser =
  new SAXParser();

// Do something with the parser
parser.parse(uri);
```

For those of you new to SAX entirely, it may be a bit confusing not to see the instance variable we used named `reader` or `XMLReader`. While that would be a normal convention, the SAX 1.0 classes defined the main parsing interface as `Parser`, and a lot of legacy code has variables named `parser` because of that naming. This interface was deprecated because of the large number of changes required for namespace and feature and properties support, but the naming convention is still a good one, as `parser` does indicate the purpose of the instance variable.

With that in mind, let's look at a small program to start up and instantiate a SAX parser. This program, shown in Example 3-1, won't actually parse a document, but sets up the skeleton within which we can work for the rest of the chapter; we will add the actual parsing behavior in the next chapter.

Example 3-1. SAX Parser Example

```
import org.xml.sax.XMLReader;

// Import your vendor's XMLReader implementation here
import org.apache.xerces.parsers.SAXParser;

/**
 * <b><code>SAXParserDemo</code></b> will take an XML file and parse it
```

Example 3-1. SAX Parser Example (continued)

```
 *   using SAX, displaying the callbacks in the parsing lifecycle.
 *
 * @author
 *     <a href="mailto:brettmclaughlin@earthlink.net">Brett McLaughlin</a>
 * @version 1.0
 */
public class SAXParserDemo {

    /**
     * <p>
     * This parses the file, using registered SAX handlers, and outputs
     *   the events in the parsing process cycle.
     * </p>
     *
     * @param uri <code>String</code> URI of file to parse.
     */
    public void performDemo(String uri) {
        System.out.println("Parsing XML File: " + uri + "\n\n");

        // Instantiate a parser
        XMLReader parser =
            new SAXParser();
    }

    /**
     * <p>
     * This provides a command-line entry point for this demo.
     * </p>
     */
    public static void main(String[] args) {
        if (args.length != 1) {
            System.out.println("Usage: java SAXParserDemo [XML URI]");
            System.exit(0);
        }

        String uri = args[0];
        SAXParserDemo parserDemo = new SAXParserDemo();
        parserDemo.performDemo(uri);
    }
}
```

You should be able to load and compile this program if you made the preparations talked about earlier to ensure the SAX classes are in your class path. This simple program doesn't do much yet; in fact, if you run it and supply a bogus filename or URI as an argument, it should happily grind away and do nothing, other than print out the initial "Parsing XML file" message. That's because we have only instantiated a parser, not requested that our XML document be parsed.

NOTE If you have trouble compiling this source file, you most likely have problems with your IDE or system's class path. First, make sure you obtained the Apache Xerces parser (or your vendor's parser). For Xerces, this involves downloading a *jar* file. This archive can then be extracted, and will contain a *xerces.jar* file; it is this *jar* file that contains the compiled class files for the program. Add this archive to your class path. You should then be able to compile the source file listing.

Parsing the Document

Once a parser is loaded and ready for use, we can instruct it to parse our document. This is conveniently handled by the `parse()` method of `org.xml.sax.XMLReader`, and this method can accept either an `org.xml.sax.InputSource`, or a simple string URI. For now, we will defer talking about using an `InputSource` and look at passing in a simple URI. Although this URI could be a network-accessible address, we will use the full path to the XML document we prepared for this use earlier. If you did choose to use a URL for network-accessible XML documents, you should be aware that the application would have to resolve the URL before passing it to the parser (generally this requires only some form of network connectivity).

We need to add the `parse()` method to our program, as well as two exception handlers. Because the document must be loaded, either locally or remotely, a `java.io.IOException` can result, and must be caught. In addition, the `org.xml.sax.SAXException` can be thrown if problems occur while parsing the document. So we can add two more import statements and a few lines of code, and have an application that parses XML ready to use:

```
import java.io.IOException;

import org.xml.sax.SAXException;
import org.xml.sax.XMLReader;

// Import your vendor's XMLReader implementation here
import org.apache.xerces.parsers.SAXParser;

...

    /**
     * <p>
     * This parses the file, using registered SAX handlers, and outputs
     *   the events in the parsing process cycle.
     * </p>
     *
```

```
     * @param uri <code>String</code> URI of file to parse.
     */
    public void performDemo(String uri) {
        System.out.println("Parsing XML File: " + uri + "\n\n");

        try {
            // Instantiate a parser
            XMLReader parser =
                new SAXParser();

            // Parse the document
            parser.parse(uri);

        } catch (IOException e) {
            System.out.println("Error reading URI: " + e.getMessage());
        } catch (SAXException e) {
            System.out.println("Error in parsing: " + e.getMessage());
        }
    }
```

Compile these changes and you are ready to execute the parsing example. You should specify the full path to your file as the first argument to the program:

```
D:\prod\JavaXML> java SAXParserDemo
file:///d:/prod/JavaXML/contents/contents.xml
Parsing XML File: file:///d:/prod/JavaXML/contents/contents.xml
```

This rather uninteresting output may make you doubt that anything has happened. However, if you lean nice and close, you may hear your hard drive spin briefly (or you can just have faith in our bytecode). In fact, the XML document is parsed, and if you pass in an invalid file URI, the parser will throw an exception letting you know it couldn't locate a file to parse. However, we have not set up any callbacks to tell SAX to take action during the parsing process and let us know what is going on. Without these callbacks, a document is parsed quietly and without application intervention. Of course, we want to intervene in that process, so we must next look at creating some parser callback methods. This intervention is the most important part of using SAX. Parser callbacks let us insert action into the program flow, and turn our rather boring, quiet parsing of an XML document into an application that can react to the data, elements, attributes, and structure of the document being parsed, as well as interact with other programs and clients along the way.

Using an InputSource

Instead of using a full URI, the `parse()` method may also be invoked with an `org.xml.sax.InputSource` as an argument. There is actually remarkably little to comment on in regard to this class; it is used as a helper and wrapper class more than anything else. An `InputSource` simply encapsulates information about a single object. While this isn't very helpful in our example, in situations where a system identifier, public identifier, or a stream may all be tied to one URI, using an `InputSource` for encapsulation can become very handy. The class has accessor and mutator methods for its system ID and public ID, a character encoding, a byte stream (`java.io.InputStream`), and a character stream (`java.io.Reader`). Passed as an argument to the `parse()` method, SAX also guarantees that the parser will never modify the `InputSource`. This ensures that the original input to a parser is still available unchanged after its use by a parser or XML-aware application. While we do not spend any further time looking at this utility class here, many of the applications we look at later in the book use the `InputSource` class as input to SAX parsers rather than a specific URI.

Content Handlers

In order to let our application do something useful with XML data as it is being parsed, we must register *handlers* with the SAX parser. A handler is nothing more than a set of callbacks that SAX defines to let us interject application code at important events within a document's parsing. Realize that these events will take place as the document is parsed, not after the parsing has occurred. This is one of the reasons that SAX is such a powerful interface: it allows a document to be handled sequentially, without having to first read the entire document into memory. We will later look at the Document Object Model (DOM), which has this limitation.

There are four core handler interfaces defined by SAX 2.0: `org.xml.sax.ContentHandler`, `org.xml.sax.ErrorHandler`, `org.xml.sax.DTDHandler`, and `org.xml.sax.EntityResolver`. In this chapter, we discuss `ContentHandler`, which allows standard data-related events within an XML document to be handled, and take a first look at `ErrorHandler`, which receives notifications from the parser when errors in the XML data are found. `DTDHandler` will be examined in Chapter 5. We briefly discuss `EntityResolver` at various points in the text; it is enough for now to understand that `EntityResolver` works just like the other handlers, and is built specifically for resolving external entities specified within an XML document. Custom application classes that perform specific actions within the parsing process can implement each of these interfaces. These implementation classes can be registered with the parser with the methods `setContentHandler()`, `setErrorHandler()`, `setDTDHandler()`, and `setEntityResolver()`. Then the parser invokes the callback methods on the appropriate handlers during parsing.

For our example, we want to implement the `ContentHandler` interface. This interface defines several important methods within the parsing lifecycle that our application can react to. First we need to add the appropriate `import` statements to our source file (including the `org.xml.sax.Locator` and `org.xml.sax.Attributes` class and interface, which we will discuss in a moment), as well as a new class that will implement these callback methods. This new class can be added at the end of your source file, *SAXParserDemo.java*:

```
import java.io.IOException;

import org.xml.sax.Attributes;
import org.xml.sax.ContentHandler;
import org.xml.sax.Locator;
import org.xml.sax.SAXException;
import org.xml.sax.XMLReader;

// Import your vendor's XMLReader implementation here
import org.apache.xerces.parsers.SAXParser;

...

/**
 * <b><code>MyContentHandler</code></b> implements the SAX
 *   <code>ContentHandler</code> interface and defines callback
 *   behavior for the SAX callbacks associated with an XML
 *   document's content.
 */
class MyContentHandler implements ContentHandler {

    /** Hold onto the locator for location information */
    private Locator locator;

    /**
     * <p>
     * Provide reference to <code>Locator</code> which provides
     *   information about where in a document callbacks occur.
     * </p>
     *
     * @param locator <code>Locator</code> object tied to callback
     *                process
     */
    public void setDocumentLocator(Locator locator) {
    }

    /**
     * <p>
     * This indicates the start of a Document parse-this precedes
     *   all callbacks in all SAX Handlers with the sole exception
     *   of <code>{@link #setDocumentLocator}</code>.
     * </p>
     *
     * @throws <code>SAXException</code> when things go wrong
     */
    public void startDocument() throws SAXException {
    }
```

```
    /**
     * <p>
     * This indicates the end of a Document parse—this occurs after
     *   all callbacks in all SAX Handlers.</code>.
     * </p>
     *
     * @throws <code>SAXException</code> when things go wrong
     */
    public void endDocument() throws SAXException {
    }

    /**
     * <p>
     * This indicates that a processing instruction (other than
     *   the XML declaration) has been encountered.
     * </p>
     *
     * @param target <code>String</code> target of PI
     * @param data <code>String</code containing all data sent to the PI.
     *             This typically looks like one or more attribute value
     *             pairs.
     * @throws <code>SAXException</code> when things go wrong
     */
    public void processingInstruction(String target, String data)
        throws SAXException {
    }

    /**
     * <p>
     * This indicates the beginning of an XML Namespace prefix
     *   mapping.  Although this typically occurs within the root element
     *   of an XML document, it can occur at any point within the
     *   document.  Note that a prefix mapping on an element triggers
     *   this callback <i>before</i> the callback for the actual element
     *   itself (<code>{@link #startElement}</code>) occurs.
     * </p>
     *
     * @param prefix <code>String</code> prefix used for the namespace
     *               being reported
     * @param uri <code>String</code> URI for the namespace
     *               being reported
     * @throws <code>SAXException</code> when things go wrong
     */
    public void startPrefixMapping(String prefix, String uri) {
    }

    /**
     * <p>
     * This indicates the end of a prefix mapping, when the namespace
```

```
     *   reported in a <code>{@link #startPrefixMapping}</code> callback
     *   is no longer available.
     * </p>
     *
     * @param prefix <code>String</code> of namespace being reported
     * @throws <code>SAXException</code> when things go wrong
     */
    public void endPrefixMapping(String prefix) {
    }

    /**
     * <p>
     * This reports the occurrence of an actual element. It includes
     *   the element's attributes, with the exception of XML vocabulary
     *   specific attributes, such as
     *   <code>xmlns:[namespace prefix]</code> and
     *   <code>xsi:schemaLocation</code>.
     * </p>
     *
     * @param namespaceURI <code>String</code> namespace URI this element
     *                     is associated with, or an empty
     *                     <code>String</code>
     * @param localName <code>String</code> name of element (with no
     *                  namespace prefix, if one is present)
     * @param rawName <code>String</code> XML 1.0 version of element name:
     *                [namespace prefix]:[localName]
     * @param atts <code>Attributes</code> list for this element
     * @throws <code>SAXException</code> when things go wrong
     */
    public void startElement(String namespaceURI, String localName,
                             String rawName, Attributes atts)
        throws SAXException {
    }

    /**
     * <p>
     * Indicates the end of an element
     *   (<code>&lt;/[element name]&gt;</code>) is reached. Note that
     *   the parser does not distinguish between empty
     *   elements and non-empty elements, so this occurs uniformly.
     * </p>
     *
     * @param namespaceURI <code>String</code> URI of namespace this
     *                     element is associated with
     * @param localName <code>String</code> name of element without prefix
     * @param rawName <code>String</code> name of element in XML 1.0 form
     * @throws <code>SAXException</code> when things go wrong
     */
    public void endElement(String namespaceURI, String localName,
```

```
                              String rawName)
        throws SAXException {
    }

    /**
     * <p>
     * This reports character data (within an element).
     * </p>
     *
     * @param ch <code>char[]</code> character array with character data
     * @param start <code>int</code> index in array where data starts.
     * @param length <code>int</code> length of characters in array.
     * @throws <code>SAXException</code> when things go wrong
     */
    public void characters(char[] ch, int start, int length)
        throws SAXException {
    }

    /**
     * <p>
     * This reports whitespace that can be ignored in the
     *   originating document. This is typically invoked only when
     *   validation is ocurring in the parsing process.
     * </p>
     *
     * @param ch <code>char[]</code> character array with character data.
     * @param start <code>int</code> index in array where data starts.
     * @param length <code>int</code> length of characters in array.
     * @throws <code>SAXException</code> when things go wrong.
     */
    public void ignorableWhitespace(char[] ch, int start, int length)
        throws SAXException {
    }

    /**
     * <p>
     * This reports an entity that is skipped by the parser. This
     *   should only occur for non-validating parsers, and then is still
     *   implementation-dependent behavior.
     * </p>
     *
     * @param name <code>String</code> name of entity being skipped
     * @throws <code>SAXException</code> when things go wrong
     */
    public void skippedEntity(String name) throws SAXException {
    }
}
```

We have added empty implementations for all the methods defined in the ContentHandler interface, which allows our source file to compile. Of course, these empty implementations don't provide any feedback for us, so we will walk through each of these required methods now.

The Document Locator

The first method we need to define is one that sets an org.xml.sax.Locator for any SAX event. When a callback event occurs, a class that implements a handler often needs access to the location within an XML file of the SAX parser. This can then be used to help the application make decisions about the event and its location within the XML document. The Locator class has several useful methods such as getLineNumber() and getColumnNumber() that return the current location within an XML file when invoked. Because this location is only valid for the current parsing lifecycle, the Locator should only be used within the scope of the ContentHandler implementation. Since we may want to use this later, we save the provided Locator instance to a member variable, as well as printing out a message indicating that the callback has occurred. This will help outline the order and occurrence of SAX events:

```
/** Hold onto the locator for location information */
private Locator locator;

/**
 * <p>
 * Provide reference to <code>Locator</code>, which provides
 *   information about where in a document callbacks occur.
 * </p>
 *
 * @param locator <code>Locator</code> object tied to callback
 *                process
 */
public void setDocumentLocator(Locator locator) {
        System.out.println("    * setDocumentLocator() called");
        // We save this for later use if desired.
        this.locator = locator;
}
```

Later, we can add details to this method if we need to act upon information about the origin of events; in this example, we merely want to show information about what is occurring in the parsing process. However, if we wanted to show information about where in the document events were occurring, such as the line number an element appeared on, we would want to assign this Locator to a member variable for later use within the class.

The Start and the End of a Document

In any lifecycle process, there must always be a beginning and an end. These important events should both occur once, the former before all other events, and the latter after all other events. This obvious fact is critical to applications, as it allows them to know exactly when parsing begins and exactly when it ends. SAX provides callback methods for each of these events, `startDocument()` and `endDocument()`.

The first method, `startDocument()`, is called before any other callbacks, including the callback methods within other SAX handlers, such as `DTDHandler`. In other words, `startDocument()` is not only the first method called within `ContentHandler`, but also within the entire parsing process, aside from the `setDocumentLocator()` method we just discussed. This ensures a finite beginning to parsing, and lets the application perform any tasks it needs to before parsing takes place.

The second method, `endDocument()`, is always the last method called, again across all handlers. This includes situations in which errors occur that cause parsing to halt. We will discuss errors later, but there are both recoverable errors and unrecoverable errors. If an unrecoverable error occurs, the `ErrorHandler`'s callback method will be invoked, and then a final call to `endDocument()` completes the attempted parsing.

In our example, we want to output to the console when both these events occur to further illustrate the parsing lifecycle:

```
/**
 * <p>
 * This indicates the start of a Document parse—this precedes
 *   all callbacks in all SAX Handlers with the sole exception
 *   of <code>{@link #setDocumentLocator}</code>.
 * </p>
 *
 * @throws <code>SAXException</code> when things go wrong
 */
public void startDocument() throws SAXException {
        System.out.println("Parsing begins...");
}

/**
 * <p>
 * This indicates the end of a Document parse - this occurs after
 *   all callbacks in all SAX Handlers.</code>.
 * </p>
 *
 * @throws <code>SAXException</code> when things go wrong
```

```
    */
    public void endDocument() throws SAXException {
            System.out.println("...Parsing ends.");
    }
```

Both of these callback methods can throw SAXExceptions. These are the only types of exceptions that SAX events ever throw, and they provide another standard interface to the parsing behavior. However, these exceptions often wrap other exceptions that are indicative of what problems occur. For example, if an XML file was being parsed over the network via a URL, and the connection suddenly became invalid, an IOException would result. However, an application using the SAX classes should not have to catch this exception, because it should not have to know where the XML resource is located. Instead, the application can catch the single SAXException. Within the SAX parser, the original exception is caught and re-thrown as a SAXException, with the originating exception stuffed inside the new one. This allows applications to have one standard exception to trap for, while allowing specific details of what errors occurred within the parsing process to be wrapped and made available to the calling program through this standard exception. The SAXException class provides a method, getException(), which returns the underlying Exception.

Processing Instructions

You should recall that we talked about processing instructions (PIs) within XML as a bit of a special case. They were not considered XML elements, and were handled differently by being passed to the calling application. Because of these special characteristics, SAX defines a specific callback for handling processing instructions. This method receives the target of the processing instruction and any data sent to the PI. For our example, we want to echo this information to the screen to notify us when a callback is made:

```
    /**
     * <p>
     * This indicates that a processing instruction (other than
     *   the XML declaration) has been encountered.
     * </p>
     *
     * @param target <code>String</code> target of PI
     * @param data <code>String</code containing all data sent to the PI.
     *              This typically looks like one or more attribute-value
     *              pairs.
     * @throws <code>SAXException</code> when things go wrong
     */
    public void processingInstruction(String target, String data)
        throws SAXException {
```

```
        System.out.println("PI: Target:" + target + " and Data:" + data);
    }
```

In a real application that is using XML data, this is where an application could receive instructions and set variable values or execute methods to perform application-specific processing. For example, the Apache Cocoon publishing framework might set flags to perform transformations on the data once it is parsed, or to display the XML as a specific content type. This method, like the other SAX callbacks, throws a `SAXException` when errors occur.

You may also remember that in our discussion of PIs we mentioned the XML declaration. This special processing instruction gives the version and optional information about the encoding of the document and whether it is a standalone document:

```
<?xml version="1.0" encoding="UTF-8" standalone="yes"?>
```

This instruction is specifically for the XML parser, allowing the parser to report an error, like a version that is not supported, at the outset of parsing. Because this instruction is only intended to be used by the parser, it does not initiate a callback to `processingInstruction()`. Be sure not to build application code that expects this instruction or version information, because the application will never receive a callback for this PI. In fact, it is only the parser that should have much interest in the encoding and version of an XML document, as these items are used in parsing. Once the data is available to you through Java APIs, these details are generally irrelevant.

Namespace Callbacks

By the amount of discussion (and confusion) we have already encountered about namespaces in XML, you should be starting to realize their importance and impact on parsing and handling XML. Alongside XML Schema, XML Namespaces is easily the most significant concept added to XML since the original XML 1.0 Recommendation. With SAX 2.0, support for namespaces was introduced at the element level. This allows a distinction to be made between the namespace of an element, signified by an element prefix and an associated namespace URI, and the local name of an element. In this case, we use *local name* to refer to the unprefixed name of an element. For example, the local name of `JavaXML:Book` is simply `Book`. The namespace prefix is `JavaXML`, and the namespace URI (in our example) is declared as *http://www.oreilly.com/catalog/javaxml*.

There are two SAX callbacks specifically dealing with namespaces (although the element callbacks use them as well). These callbacks are invoked when the parser reaches the start and end of a *prefix mapping*. Although this is a new term, it is not a new concept; a prefix mapping is simply an element that uses the `xmlns` attribute to declare a namespace. This is often the root element (which may have multiple mappings), but can be any element within an XML document that declares an explicit namespace. For example:

```
<root>
  <element1>
    <myNamespace:element2 xmlns:myNamespace="http://myUrl.com">
      <myNamespace:element3>Here is some data</myNamespace:element3>
    </myNamespace:element2>
  </element1>
</root>
```

In this case, an explicit namespace is declared several element nestings deep within the document.

The `startPrefixMapping()` callback is given the namespace prefix as well as the URI associated with that prefix. The mapping is considered "closed" or "ended" when the element that declared the mapping is closed. The only twist to this callback is that it doesn't quite behave in the sequential manner in which SAX usually is structured; the prefix mapping callback occurs directly *before* the callback for the element that declares the namespace. We look at this callback now:

```
/**
 * <p>
 * This will indicate the beginning of an XML Namespace prefix
 *   mapping.  Although this typically occurs within the root element
 *   of an XML document, it can occur at any point within the
 *   document.  Note that a prefix mapping on an element triggers
 *   this callback <i>before</i> the callback for the actual element
 *   itself (<code>{@link #startElement}</code>) occurs.
 * </p>
 *
 * @param prefix <code>String</code> prefix used for the namespace
 *               being reported
 * @param uri <code>String</code> URI for the namespace
 *            being reported
 * @throws <code>SAXException</code> when things go wrong
 */
public void startPrefixMapping(String prefix, String uri) {
        System.out.println("Mapping starts for prefix " + prefix +
                           " mapped to URI " + uri);
}
```

In our document, the only mapping we have is declared as an attribute of the root element. That means we should expect to see this callback invoked before the first element callback (which we look at next), although still after the `startDocument()` callback as well as any PIs we have at the top of our document. The other half of this namespace pair of callbacks is invoked to signify the end of the mapping, and appears directly *after* the closing tag of the element declaring the mapping:

```
/**
 * <p>
 * This indicates the end of a prefix mapping, when the namespace
 *   reported in a <code>{@link #startPrefixMapping}</code> callback
 *   is no longer available.
 * </p>
 *
 * @param prefix <code>String</code> of namespace being reported
 * @throws <code>SAXException</code> when things go wrong
 */
public void endPrefixMapping(String prefix) {
        System.out.println("Mapping ends for prefix " + prefix);
}
```

For the XML document fragment above, we could then expect the following output when the `element2` element was reached:

```
Mapping starts for prefix myNamespace mapped to URI http://myUrl.com
```

This lets us know the prefix being mapped, and what URI that prefix is associated with.

Element Callbacks

By now you are probably ready to actually get to the data in our XML document. It is true that over half of the SAX callbacks have nothing to do with XML elements, attributes, and data. This is because the process of parsing XML is intended to do more than simply provide your application with the XML data; it should give the application instructions from XML PIs so your application can know what actions to take, let the application know when parsing starts and when it ends, and even tell it when there is whitespace that can be ignored! If some of these callbacks don't make much sense, keep reading. We'll explain more here, as well as in Chapter 5, when we look at how validation of XML fits into the picture.

Still, there certainly are SAX callbacks intended to give you access to the XML data within your documents. The three primary events you will concern yourself with to get that data are the start and end of elements and the `characters()` callback. These tell you when an element is parsed, the data within that element, and when the closing tag for that element is reached. The first of these, `startElement()`, gives an application information about an XML element and any attributes it may have. The parameters to this callback are the name of the element (in various forms), and an `org.xml.sax.Attributes` instance (remember our import statement earlier?). This helper class holds references to all of the attributes within an element. It allows easy iteration through the element's attributes in a form similar to a Vector. In addition to being able to reference an attribute by its index (used when iterating through all attributes), it is possible to reference an attribute by its name. Of course, by now you should be a bit cautious when you see the word "name" referring to an XML element or attribute, as it can mean various things. In this case, either the complete name of the attribute (with a namespace prefix, if any), called its "raw" name, can be used, or the combination of its local name and namespace URI if a namespace is used. There are also helper methods such as getURI(int index) and getLocalName(int index) that help give additional namespace information about an attribute. Used as a whole, the Attributes interface can be a comprehensive set of information about an element's attributes.

In addition to the element attributes, we mentioned you get several forms of the element's name. This again is in deference to XML namespaces. The namespace URI of the element is first supplied. This places the element in its correct context across the complete document's set of namespaces. Then the local name of the element is supplied, which we mentioned is the unprefixed element name. In addition (and for backwards compatibility), the "raw" name of the element is supplied. This is the unmodified, unchanged name of the element, which includes a namespace prefix if present. In other words, this is exactly what was in the XML document, and so it would be JavaXML:Book for our Book element. With these three types of names supplied, you should be able to describe an element with or without respect to its namespace.

Now that we've seen how an element and its attributes are made available, let's look at an implementation of the SAX callback that prints this information out to the screen when it is invoked. In this example, we see if the element name has a namespace URI associated with it; if so, we print out that namespace; if not, we print a message stating that the element has no namespace associated with it:

```
/**
 * <p>
 * This reports the occurrence of an actual element. It will include
 *   the element's attributes, with the exception of XML vocabulary
 *   specific attributes, such as
 *   <code>xmlns:[namespace prefix]</code> and
 *   <code>xsi:schemaLocation</code>.
 * </p>
 *
 * @param namespaceURI <code>String</code> namespace URI this element
 *                     is associated with, or an empty
 *                     <code>String</code>
 * @param localName <code>String</code> name of element (with no
 *                  namespace prefix, if one is present)
 * @param rawName <code>String</code> XML 1.0 version of element name:
 *                [namespace prefix]:[localName]
 * @param atts <code>Attributes</code> list for this element
```

```
     * @throws <code>SAXException</code> when things go wrong
     */
    public void startElement(String namespaceURI, String localName,
                             String rawName, Attributes atts)
        throws SAXException {

            System.out.print("startElement: " + localName);
            if (!namespaceURI.equals("")) {
                System.out.println(" in namespace " + namespaceURI +
                                   " (" + rawName + ")");
            } else {
                System.out.println(" has no associated namespace");
            }

            for (int i=0; i<atts.getLength(); i++)
                System.out.println("  Attribute: " + atts.getLocalName(i) +
                                   "=" + atts.getValue(i));
    }
```

SAX makes this process very simple and straightforward. One final thing to notice when looking at the `startElement()` callback and attributes in particular is that attributes do not remain ordered. When iterating through an `Attributes` implementation, the attributes will not necessarily be available in the order in which they were parsed, which is the order in which they were written. This means it is not a good idea to depend on the ordering of attributes, due to XML not requiring this ordering to be maintained by XML parsers. While there are some parsers that implement an ordering, it often is not included in a parser's feature set.

The closing half of an element callback is the `endElement()` method. This simple callback is fairly self-explanatory, and only the name of the element is sent to the callback, allowing that name to be matched with the appropriate element name passed earlier to a `startElement()` callback. The main purpose of this callback is to signify the close of an element, and let an application know that further characters are part of another scope, rather than the element now being closed. We make note of this in our example by printing out the name of an element when it is closed:

```
    /**
     * <p>
     * Indicates the end of an element
     *   (<code>&lt;/[element name]&gt;</code>) is reached. Note that
     *   the parser does not distinguish between empty
     *   elements and non-empty elements, so this will occur uniformly.
     * </p>
     *
     * @param namespaceURI <code>String</code> URI of namespace this
     *                     element is associated with
     * @param localName <code>String</code> name of element without prefix
```

```
     * @param rawName <code>String</code> name of element in XML 1.0 form
     * @throws <code>SAXException</code> when things go wrong
     */
    public void endElement(String namespaceURI, String localName,
                           String rawName)
        throws SAXException {

        System.out.println("endElement: " + localName + "\n");
    }
```

Element Data

Once the beginning and end of an element block are identified and the element's attributes are enumerated for an application, the next piece of important information is the actual data contained within the element itself. This generally consists of additional elements, textual data, or a combination of the two. When other elements appear, the callbacks for those elements are initiated, and a type of pseudo-recursion happens: elements nested within elements results in callbacks "nested" within callbacks. At some point, textual data will be encountered. This is typically the most important information to an XML client, as this data is usually either what is shown to the client or what is processed to generate a client response.

In XML, textual data within elements is sent to a wrapping application via the `characters()` callback. This method provides the wrapping application with an array of characters as well as a starting and ending index from which to read the relevant textual data:

```
    /**
     * <p>
     * This will report character data (within an element).
     * </p>
     *
     * @param ch <code>char[]</code> character array with character data
     * @param start <code>int</code> index in array where data starts.
     * @param length <code>int</code> length of characters in array.
     * @throws <code>SAXException</code> when things go wrong
     */
    public void characters(char[] ch, int start, int length)
        throws SAXException {

        String s = new String(ch, start, end);
        System.out.println("characters: " + s);
    }
```

Seemingly a simple callback, this method often results in a significant amount of confusion because the SAX interface and standards do not strictly define how this callback must be used for lengthy pieces of character data. In other words, a parser may choose to return all contiguous character data in one invocation, or split this data up into multiple method invocations. For any given element, this method will be called not at all (if no character data is present within the element) or one or more times. Different parsers will implement this behavior differently, often using algorithms designed to increase parsing speed. You should never count on having all the textual data for an element within one callback method; conversely, you should never assume that multiple callbacks would result for one element's contiguous character data.

As you are writing your SAX event handlers, you should also be sure to keep your mind in a hierarchical mode. In other words, you should not get in the habit of thinking that any element owns its data and *child elements*, but only that it serves as a parent. Also keep in mind that the parser is moving along, handling elements, attributes, and data as it comes across them. This can make for some surprising results. Consider the following XML document fragment:

```
<parent>This is<child>embedded text</child>more text</parent>
```

Forgetting that SAX parses sequentially, making callbacks as it sees elements and data, and forgetting that the XML is viewed as hierarchical, you might make the assumption that the output here would be something like:

```
startElement: parent has no associated namespace
characters: This is more text
startElement: child has no associated namespace
characters: embedded text
endElement: child
endElement: parent
```

This would seem logical, as the `parent` element completely "owns" the `child` element, right? Wrong. What actually occurs is that a callback is made at each SAX event-point, resulting in the following event-firing chain:

```
startElement: parent has no associated namespace
characters: This is
startElement: child has no associated namespace
characters: embedded text
endElement: child
characters: more text
endElement: parent
```

SAX does not do any reading ahead, so the result here is exactly what you would expect if you viewed the XML document as sequential data, without all the human assumptions that we tend to make. This is an important point to remember.

Finally, whitespace is often reported by the `characters()` method. This introduces additional confusion, as another SAX callback, `ignorableWhitespace()`, also reports whitespace. In our example, we are not validating our XML document; however, we may still be using a validating (capable) parser. This subtle detail is very important, as the way in which whitespace is reported is defined by whether the parser being used is a validating one or not. Validating parsers will report all whitespace through the `ignorableWhitespace()` method, due to some validation issues we will address in the next two chapters. Non-validating parsers can report whitespace either through the `ignorableWhitespace()` method or the `characters()` method. To determine the difference, you will need to consult your parser's documentation to determine if you are using a validating parser or not. Remember, just because you are not requesting validation of your document does not mean that your parser is non-validating; a parser that is *capable* of validating, even if not actively doing so, is a validating parser.

To add to this confusion, many parsers are actually made up of dual parser implementations: one for validation and one for parsing without validation. At runtime, the correct class is loaded dynamically, as a non-validating parser often performs much better than a validating one, even if validation is not occurring, due to the extra data structures that must be implemented to allow validation to be used. This is exactly the case with the Apache Xerces parser; our example will utilize an instance of a non-validating parser, although if a DTD or schema was specified and validation was requested, a different parser class would be loaded and validation could occur.

The best way to avoid this confusion altogether is to not make any assumptions at all about whitespace. You should rarely, if ever, be using whitespace as data within your XML document. If you are forced to use whitespace, such as several spaces, non-space data, and then several more spaces, and the number of spaces in this data is relevant to an application, a `CDATA` section should be used. This ensures that your space-specific data will not be parsed at all; instead, it will be handed to the XML wrapper application as a large "chunk" of character data. Other than that special case, whitespace should be avoided as a data representation, and assumptions about which document callback will report whitespace should not be made.

Whitespace, Just the Whitespace

We have already addressed most of the issues with whitespace. We simply need to add this last SAX callback to our `MyContentHandler` class. The `ignorableWhitespace()` method takes parameters in the exact same format as the `characters()` method, and should use the starting and ending indexes provided to read from the character array supplied:

```
/**
 * <p>
 * This will report whitespace that can be ignored in the
```

```
 *   originating document. This is typically only invoked when
 *   validation is occurring in the parsing process.
 * </p>
 *
 * @param ch <code>char[]</code> character array with character data
 * @param start <code>int</code> index in array where data starts.
 * @param length <code>int</code> length of characters in array.
 * @throws <code>SAXException</code> when things go wrong
 */
public void ignorableWhitespace(char[] ch, int start, int length)
    throws SAXException {

        String s = new String(ch, start, end);
        System.out.println("ignorableWhitespace: [" + s + "]");
}
```

Of course, our sample will not print out any visible content, as the `String` created from the character array will be made up completely of whitespace, so we enclose the output within brackets. Whitespace is reported in the same manner as character data; it can be handled with one callback, or a SAX parser may break up the whitespace and report it over several method invocations. In either case, the precautions we have already discussed about not making assumptions or counting on whitespace as textual data should be closely adhered to in order to avoid troublesome bugs in your applications.

Skipped Entities

As you recall, we had one entity reference in our document, the `OReillyCopyright` entity. When parsed and resolved, this results in another file being loaded, either from the local filesystem or some other URI. However, we are not requesting that validation occur in our document. An often overlooked facet of non-validating parsers is that they are not required to resolve entity references, and instead may skip them. This has caused some headaches before, as parser results may simply not include entity references that were expected. SAX 2.0 nicely accounts for this with a callback that is issued when an entity is skipped by a non-validating parser. The callback gives the name of the entity, which we will include in our output (although Apache Xerces does not exhibit this behavior, your parser may):

```
/**
 * <p>
 * This will report an entity that is skipped by the parser. This
 *   should only occur for non-validating parsers, and then is still
 *   implementation-dependent behavior.
 * </p>
 *
 * @param name <code>String</code> name of entity being skipped
```

```
     * @throws <code>SAXException</code> when things go wrong
     */
    public void skippedEntity(String name) throws SAXException {
            System.out.println("Skipping entity " + name);
    }
```

Before you go trying to recreate this behavior, you should note that most established parsers will not skip entities, even if they are not validating. Apache Xerces, for example, will never invoke this callback; instead, the entity reference will be expanded and the result will be included in the data available after parsing. In other words, this is there for parsers to use, but you will be hard-pressed to find a case where it crops up! If you do have a parser that exhibits this behavior, be aware that the parameter passed does not include the leading ampersand and trailing semicolon in the entity reference. For `&OReillyCopyright;`, only the name of the entity, `OReillyCopyright`, is passed to `skippedEntity()`.

The Results

Finally, we need to register our handler with the `XMLReader` we have instantiated. This is done with `setContentHandler()`, which takes a `ContentHandler` implementation as its single argument. Add the following lines to the `demo()` method of your parser example program:

```
    /**
     * <p>
     * This parses the file, using registered SAX handlers, and outputs
     *   the events in the parsing process cycle.
     * </p>
     *
     * @param uri <code>String</code> URI of file to parse.
     */
    public void performDemo(String uri) {
        System.out.println("Parsing XML File: " + uri + "\n\n");

            // Get instances of our handlers
            ContentHandler contentHandler = new MyContentHandler();

        try {
            // Instantiate a parser
            XMLReader parser =
                new SAXParser();

            // Register the content handler
            parser.setContentHandler(contentHandler);

            // Parse the document
            parser.parse(uri);
```

```
        } catch (IOException e) {
            System.out.println("Error reading URI: " + e.getMessage());
        } catch (SAXException e) {
            System.out.println("Error in parsing: " + e.getMessage());
        }
    }
```

If you have entered in all of the document callbacks as we have gone along, you should be able to compile the `MyContentHandler` class and the enclosing `SAXParserDemo` file. Once done, you may run the SAX parser demonstration on our XML sample file created earlier. The complete Java command should read:

```
D:\prod\JavaXML> java SAXParserDemo file:///d:/prod/JavaXML/contents.xml
```

This should result in a fairly long and verbose output. If you are on a Windows machine, you may need to increase the buffer size of your DOS window so you may scroll and view the complete command output. The output should look similar to that in Example 3-2.*

Example 3-2. SAXParserDemo Output

```
D:\prod\JavaXML> java SAXParserDemo file:///d:/prod/JavaXML/contents.xml
Parsing XML File: file:///d:/prod/JavaXML/contents.xml


    * setDocumentLocator() called
Parsing begins...
Mapping starts for prefix JavaXML mapped to URI
    http://www.oreilly.com/catalog/javaxml/
startElement: Book in namespace
    http://www.oreilly.com/catalog/javaxml/ (JavaXML:Book)
characters:

startElement: Title in namespace
    http://www.oreilly.com/catalog/javaxml/ (JavaXML:Title)
characters: Java and XML
endElement: Title

characters:

startElement: Contents in namespace
    http://www.oreilly.com/catalog/javaxml/ (JavaXML:Contents)
characters:
```

* In this and other output examples, note that carriage returns may have been inserted to ensure that the output is formatted correctly on the printed page. As long as the actual content is the same, you have got everything working correctly!

Example 3-2. SAXParserDemo Output (continued)

```
startElement: Chapter in namespace
    http://www.oreilly.com/catalog/javaxml/ (JavaXML:Chapter)
  Attribute: focus=XML
characters:

startElement: Heading in namespace
    http://www.oreilly.com/catalog/javaxml/ (JavaXML:Heading)
characters: Introduction
endElement: Heading

characters:

startElement: Topic in namespace
    http://www.oreilly.com/catalog/javaxml/ (JavaXML:Topic)
  Attribute: subSections=7
characters: What Is It?
endElement: Topic

characters:

startElement: Topic in namespace
    http://www.oreilly.com/catalog/javaxml/ (JavaXML:Topic)
  Attribute: subSections=3
characters: How Do I Use It?
endElement: Topic

characters:

startElement: Topic in namespace
    http://www.oreilly.com/catalog/javaxml/ (JavaXML:Topic)
  Attribute: subSections=4
characters: Why Should I Use It?
endElement: Topic

characters:

startElement: Topic in namespace
    http://www.oreilly.com/catalog/javaxml/ (JavaXML:Topic)
  Attribute: subSections=0
characters: What's Next?
endElement: Topic
...
```

This output should go on quite a while, as the XML document being parsed has a number of elements within it. You can clearly see exactly how the parser sequentially handles each element, the element's attributes, any data within the element, nested elements, and the element's end tag. This process repeats for each element within the document. In our example, a non-validating instance of the

Xerces parser was used (remember our rather confusing discussion on this?), so whitespace is being reported with the `characters()` callback; in the next two chapters we will discuss validation and see how this reporting changes.

You have now seen how a SAX-compliant parser handles a well-formed XML document. You should also be getting an understanding of the document callbacks that occur within the parsing process and how an application can use these callbacks to get information about an XML document as it is parsed. In the next two chapters, we will spend time looking at validating an XML document by using additional SAX classes designed for handling DTDs. Before moving on, though, we want to address the issue of what happens when your XML document is not valid, and the errors that can result from this condition.

Error Handlers

In addition to providing the `ContentHandler` interface for handling parsing events, SAX provides an `ErrorHandler` interface that can be implemented to treat various error conditions that may arise during parsing. This class works in the same manner as the document handler we have already constructed, but only defines three callback methods. Through these three methods, all possible error conditions are handled and reported by SAX parsers.

Each method receives information about the error or warning that has occurred through a `SAXParseException`. This object holds the line number that trouble was encountered on, the URI of the document being treated, which could be the parsed document or an external reference within that document, and normal exception details such as a message and a printable stack trace. In addition, each method can throw a `SAXException`. This may seem a bit odd at first; an exception handler that throws an exception? Keep in mind that what each handler receives is a parsing exception. This can be a warning that should not cause the parsing process to stop or an error that needs to be resolved for parsing to continue; however, the callback may need to perform system I/O or another operation that can throw an exception, and it needs to be able to bubble this exception up the application chain. It can do this through the `SAXException` the method is allowed to throw.

For example, consider an error handler that receives error notifications and writes those errors to an error log. This method needs to be able to either append to or create an error log on the local filesystem. If a warning were to occur within the process of parsing an XML document, the warning would be reported to this method. The intent of the warning would be to give information to the callback and then continue parsing the document. However, if the error handler could not write to the log file, it might need to notify the parser and application that all parsing should stop. This can be done by catching any I/O exceptions and re-throwing these to the calling application, thus causing any further document parsing to stop. This common scenario is why error handlers must be able to throw exceptions (see Example 3-3).

Example 3-3. Error Handler That May Throw a SAXException

```
public void warning(SAXParseException exception)
    throws SAXException {

    try {
        FileWriter fw = new FileWriter("error.log");
        BufferedWriter bw = new BufferedWriter(fw);
        bw.write("Warning: " + exception.getMessage() + "\n");
        bw.flush();
        bw.close();
        fw.close();
    } catch (Exception e) {
        throw new SAXException("Could not write to log file", e);
    }
}
```

We can now define the skeleton of our error handler and register it with our parser in the same way we registered our document handler. First we need to add the `SAXParseException` class and `ErrorHandler` interface to our import statements:

```
import java.io.IOException;
import org.xml.sax.Attributes;
import org.xml.sax.ContentHandler;
import org.xml.sax.ErrorHandler;
import org.xml.sax.Locator;
import org.xml.sax.SAXException;
import org.xml.sax.SAXParseException;
import org.xml.sax.XMLReader;
```

We should now create a class within the same Java file (again at the bottom, after the `MyContentHandler` class) to implement the `ErrorHandler` interface defined by SAX. Like our discussion of `ContentHandler`, empty implementations are provided here that we fill in the next section:

```
/**
 * <b><code>MyErrorHandler</code></b> implements the SAX
 *   <code>ErrorHandler</code> interface and defines callback
 *   behavior for the SAX callbacks associated with an XML
 *   document's errors.
 */
class MyErrorHandler implements ErrorHandler  {

    /**
     * <p>
     * This will report a warning that has occurred; this indicates
```

```
     *   that while no XML rules were broken, something appears
     *   to be incorrect or missing.
     * </p>
     *
     * @param exception <code>SAXParseException</code> that occurred.
     * @throws <code>SAXException</code> when things go wrong
     */
    public void warning(SAXParseException exception)
        throws SAXException {
    }

    /**
     * <p>
     * This will report an error that has occurred; this indicates
     *   that a rule was broken, typically in validation, but that
     *   parsing can reasonably continue.
     * </p>
     *
     * @param exception <code>SAXParseException</code> that occurred.
     * @throws <code>SAXException</code> when things go wrong
     */
    public void error(SAXParseException exception)
        throws SAXException {
    }

    /**
     * <p>
     * This will report a fatal error that has occurred; this indicates
     *   that a rule has been broken that makes continued parsing either
     *   impossible or an almost certain waste of time.
     * </p>
     *
     * @param exception <code>SAXParseException</code> that occurred.
     * @throws <code>SAXException</code> when things go wrong
     */
    public void fatalError(SAXParseException exception)
        throws SAXException {
    }
}
```

Finally, in preparation to use our custom error handler, we need to register this error handler with our SAX parser. This is done with the `setErrorHandler()` method of the `XMLReader` interface, and occurs in our example's `demo()` method. This method takes the `ErrorHandler` interface or an implementation of that interface as the single parameter:

```
    // Get instances of our handlers
    ContentHandler contentHandler = new MyContentHandler();
        ErrorHandler errorHandler = new MyErrorHandler();
```

```
        try {
            // Instantiate a parser
            XMLReader parser =
                new SAXParser();

            // Register the content handler
            parser.setContentHandler(contentHandler);

            // Register the error handler
            parser.setErrorHandler(errorHandler);

            // Parse the document
            parser.parse(uri);

        } catch (IOException e) {
            System.out.println("Error reaading URI: " + e.getMessage());
        } catch (SAXException e) {
            System.out.println("Error in parsing: " + e.getMessage());
        }
    ...
```

Now let's take a look at making these methods give us some feedback when they are invoked.

Warnings

Any time a warning (as defined by the XML 1.0 specification) occurs, this method is invoked in the registered error handler. There are several conditions that can generate a warning; however, all of them are related to the DTD and validity of a document, and we will discuss them in the next two chapters rather than here. For now, we need to define a simple method that prints out the line number, URI, and warning message when a warning occurs. Because we want any warnings to stop parsing, we throw a `SAXException` and let the wrapping application exit gracefully, cleaning up any used resources:

```
    /**
     * <p>
     * This will report a warning that has occurred; this indicates
     *   that while no XML rules were "broken", something appears
     *   to be incorrect or missing.
     * </p>
     *
     * @param exception <code>SAXParseException</code> that occurred.
     * @throws <code>SAXException</code> when things go wrong
     */
    public void warning(SAXParseException exception)
        throws SAXException {
```

```
        System.out.println("**Parsing Warning**\n" +
                           "  Line:    " +
                              exception.getLineNumber() + "\n" +
                           "  URI:     " +
                              exception.getSystemId() + "\n" +
                           "  Message: " +
                              exception.getMessage());
        throw new SAXException("Warning encountered");
    }
```

Non-Fatal Errors

Errors that occur within parsing that can be recovered from, but constitute a violation of some portion of the XML specification, are considered non-fatal errors. An error handler should always at least log these, as they are typically serious enough to merit informing the user or administrator of an application, if not so critical as to cause parsing to cease. Like warnings, most non-fatal errors are concerned with validation, and will be covered in the relevant chapters. Also like warnings, we want our simple error handler to report information sent to the callback method and exit the parsing process:

```
    /**
     * <p>
     * This will report an error that has occurred; this indicates
     *   that a rule was broken, typically in validation, but that
     *   parsing can reasonably continue.
     * </p>
     *
     * @param exception <code>SAXParseException</code> that occurred.
     * @throws <code>SAXException</code> when things go wrong
     */
    public void error(SAXParseException exception)
        throws SAXException {

        System.out.println("**Parsing Error**\n" +
                           "  Line:    " +
                              exception.getLineNumber() + "\n" +
                           "  URI:     " +
                              exception.getSystemId() + "\n" +
                           "  Message: " +
                              exception.getMessage());
        throw new SAXException("Error encountered");
    }
```

Fatal Errors

Fatal errors are those that necessitate stopping the parser. These are typically related to a document not being well-formed, and make further parsing either a complete waste of time or technically impossible. An error handler should almost always notify the user or application administrator when a fatal error occurs; without intervention, these can bring an application to a shuddering halt. For our example, we want to emulate the behavior of the other two callback methods and stop parsing and write an error message to the screen when a fatal error is encountered:

```
/**
 * <p>
 * This will report a fatal error that has occurred; this indicates
 *   that a rule has been broken that makes continued parsing either
 *   impossible or an almost certain waste of time.
 * </p>
 *
 * @param exception <code>SAXParseException</code> that occurred.
 * @throws <code>SAXException</code> when things go wrong
 */
public void fatalError(SAXParseException exception)
    throws SAXException {

        System.out.println("**Parsing Fatal Error**\n" +
                           "  Line:    " +
                              exception.getLineNumber() + "\n" +
                           "  URI:     " +
                              exception.getSystemId() + "\n" +
                           "  Message: " +
                              exception.getMessage());
        throw new SAXException("Fatal Error encountered");
}
```

With this third error handler coded, you should be able to compile the example source file successfully, and run it on our XML file once again. Your output should not be any different than it was earlier, as there are no reportable errors, in the XML. We will next demonstrate some errors in non-validated XML documents.

Breaking the Data

Now that we have some error handlers in place, it is possible to view some of these handlers in action. As mentioned several times, most warnings and non-fatal errors are associated with document validity issues, which we will address in the next few chapters. However, there is one non-fatal error that can result from a non-validated XML document. This involves the version of XML that a document reports. To view this error, make the following change to the XML table of contents example:

```
<?xml version="1.2"?>

<!-- We don't need these yet
  <?xml-stylesheet href="XSL\JavaXML.html.xsl" type="text/xsl"?>
  <?xml-stylesheet href="XSL\JavaXML.wml.xsl" type="text/xsl"
                   media="wap"?>
```

```
    <?cocoon-process type="xslt"?>
    <!DOCTYPE JavaXML:Book SYSTEM "DTD\JavaXML.dtd">
-->
```

You should now attempt to run the Java parser example program on the modified XML document. Your output should be similar to that in Example 3-4.

Example 3-4. SAXParserDemo Output Issuing an Error

```
D:\prod\JavaXML>java SAXParserDemo D:\prod\JavaXML\contents.xml
Parsing XML File: D:\prod\JavaXML\contents.xml


**Parsing Error**
  Line:    1
  URI:     file:/e:/prod/JavaXML/contents.xml
  Message: XML version "1.2" is not supported.
```

When an XML parser is operating upon a document that reports a version of XML greater than that supported by the parser, a non-fatal error is reported, in accordance with the XML 1.0 Specification. This allows an application to know that newer features expected to be utilized by the document may not be available within the parser and the version that it supports. Because parsing is still able to continue, this is a non-fatal error. However, because it signifies a major impact on the document (such as newer syntax possibly generating subsequent errors), it is considered more important than a warning. This is why our `error()` method is invoked and triggers the error message and parsing halt in the example program.

All other meaningful warnings and non-fatal errors will be discussed in the next two chapters; still, there are a variety of fatal errors that a non-validated XML document may have. These are related to an XML document not being well-formed. There is no logic built into XML parsers to try to resolve or estimate fixes to malformed XML, so an error in syntax results in the parsing process halting. The easiest way to demonstrate one of these errors is to introduce problems within our XML document. Reset the XML declaration to specify XML Version 1.0, and make the following change to the XML document:

```
<?xml version="1.0"?>

<!-- We don't need these yet
  <?xml-stylesheet href="XSL\JavaXML.html.xsl" type="text/xsl"?>
  <?xml-stylesheet href="XSL\JavaXML.wml.xsl" type="text/xsl"
                   media="wap"?>
  <?cocoon-process type="xslt"?>
  <!DOCTYPE JavaXML:Book SYSTEM "DTD\JavaXML.dtd">
-->
```

```
<!-- Java and XML -->
<JavaXML:Book xmlns:JavaXML="http://www.oreilly.com/catalog/javaxml/">
 </JavaXML:Title>Java and XML</JavaXML:Title>
 <!-- Note the incorrect slash before the JavaXML:Title element -->

 <JavaXML:Contents>
```

This is no longer a well-formed document. To see the fatal error that parsing this document generates, run the SAXParserDemo on this modified file (the output is shown in Example 3-5).

Example 3-5. SAXParserDemo Output Issuing a Fatal Error

```
D:\prod\JavaXML>java SAXParserDemo D:\prod\JavaXML\contents.xml
Parsing XML File: D:\prod\JavaXML\contents.xml


    * setDocumentLocator() called
Parsing begins...
startElement: Book in namespace
        http://www.oreilly.com/catalog/javaxml/ (JavaXML:Book)
  Attribute: xmlns:JavaXML=http://www.oreilly.com/catalog/javaxml/
characters:

**Parsing Fatal Error**
  Line:    12
  URI:     file:/e:/prod/xml-book/contents.xml
  Message: The element type "JavaXML:Book" must be terminated by the
           matching end-tag "</JavaXML:Book>".
```

The parser reports an incorrect ending to the JavaXML:Book element. This fatal error is exactly as we expected; parsing could not continue beyond this error. To understand the error message, you should realize that the parser sees the slash character before the JavaXML:Title element, and makes the assumption that the element that must be closed is the JavaXML:Book element, the current "open" element. When it finds a closing tag for the JavaXML:Title element, it reports that the tag is incorrect for the closing of the open element, JavaXML:Book.

With our error handler, we have begun to understand what can go wrong within the parsing process, as well as how to handle those events. In Chapter 5, we will revisit our error handlers and look at the problems that can be reported by the validating parser.

A Better Way to Load a Parser

Although we now have a successful demonstration of SAX parsing, there is a glaring problem with our code. Let's take a look again at how we obtain an instance of XMLReader:

```
    try {
        // Instantiate a parser
        XMLReader parser =
            new SAXParser();

        // Register the content handler
        parser.setContentHandler(contentHandler);

        // Register the error handler
        parser.setErrorHandler(errorHandler);

        // Parse the document
        parser.parse(uri);

    } catch (IOException e) {
        System.out.println("Error reading URI: " + e.getMessage());
    } catch (SAXException e) {
        System.out.println("Error in parsing: " + e.getMessage());
    }
```

Do you see anything that rubs you wrong? Let's look at another line of our code that may give you a hint:

```
// Import your vendor's XMLReader implementation here
import org.apache.xerces.parsers.SAXParser;
```

We have to explicitly import our vendor's `XMLReader` implementation, and then instantiate that implementation directly. The problem here is not the difficulty of this task, but that we have broken one of Java's biggest tenets: portability. Our code cannot run or even be compiled on a platform that does not use the Apache Xerces parser. In fact, it is conceivable that an updated version of Xerces might even change the name of the class used here! Our "portable" Java code is no longer very portable.

What is preferred is to request an instance of a class by the name of the implementation class. This allows a simple `String` parameter to be changed in your source code. Luckily, this facility is available in SAX 2.0. The `org.xml.sax.helpers.XMLReaderFactory` class provides the method you should be looking for:

```
/**
 * Attempt to create an XML reader from a class name.
 *
 * <p>Given a class name, this method attempts to load
 * and instantiate the class as an XML reader.</p>
 *
 * @return A new XML reader.
 * @exception org.xml.sax.SAXException If the class cannot be
 *            loaded, instantiated, and cast to XMLReader.
 * @see #createXMLReader()
 */
```

```
public static XMLReader createXMLReader (String className)
    throws SAXException {

    // Implementation
}
```

We can use this method in our code like this:

```
    try {
        // Instantiate a parser
        XMLReader parser =
            XMLReaderFactory.createXMLReader(
               "org.apache.xerces.parsers.SAXParser");

        // Register the content handler
        parser.setContentHandler(contentHandler);

        // Register the error handler
        parser.setErrorHandler(errorHandler);

        // Parse the document
        parser.parse(uri);

    } catch (IOException e) {
        System.out.println("Error reading URI: " + e.getMessage());
    } catch (SAXException e) {
        System.out.println("Error in parsing: " + e.getMessage());
    }
```

This static method takes in the name of the parser class to load and returns an instantiated version of the class, cast to the `XMLReader` interface (assuming that it actually does implement `XMLReader`). If any problems occur, they are all handled and then wrapped in a `SAXException` that is thrown to the calling program. Add in the additional import statement, remove the vendor-specific parser reference, make the changes noted above, and you should be able to recompile your source file:

```
import java.io.IOException;

import org.xml.sax.Attributes;
import org.xml.sax.ContentHandler;
import org.xml.sax.ErrorHandler;
import org.xml.sax.Locator;
import org.xml.sax.SAXException;
import org.xml.sax.SAXParseException;
import org.xml.sax.XMLReader;
import org.xml.sax.helpers.XMLReaderFactory;

// This goes away
// import org.apache.xerces.parsers.SAXParser;
```

Suddenly you are writing portable code again! To further portability, it makes sense to store the name of the parser class in a properties file. This allows easy loading of the class at runtime, and it means your code can be moved from platform to platform without recompilation based on the parser being used; instead, only the properties file could be changed. Although the code to read properties files is not provided here, take a look at some code that performs this behavior:

```
try {
    // Instantiate a parser
    XMLReader parser =
        XMLReaderFactory.createXMLReader(
            PropertiesReader().getInstance()
                                .getProperty("parserClass"));

    // Register the content handler
    parser.setContentHandler(contentHandler);

    // Register the error handler
    parser.setErrorHandler(errorHandler);

    // Parse the document
    parser.parse(uri);

} catch (IOException e) {
    System.out.println("Error reading URI: " + e.getMessage());
} catch (SAXException e) {
    System.out.println("Error in parsing: " + e.getMessage());
}
```

Here a utility class, `PropertiesReader`, is being used to read a properties file and return the value for the key "parserClass", which would contain the parser class name to use on the specific platform the code was being used for. In our examples, this would be our old friend `org.apache.xerces.parsers.SAXParser`. Of course, Java system properties could also be used, but they are not as appropriate for web-centric distributed applications like the ones we focus on in this book, as they must be specified on a command line. Often, distributed applications are started up in whole, rather than individually, making specification of a system property to one particular component difficult.

"Gotcha!"

Before leaving our introduction to parsing XML documents, there are a few pitfalls to make you aware of. These "gotchas" will help you avoid common programming mistakes when using SAX, and we will discuss more of these for other APIs in the appropriate sections.

My Parser Doesn't Support SAX 2.0: What Can I Do?

For those of you who are unlucky enough not to have a parser with SAX 2.0 support, don't despair. First, you always have the option of changing parsers; keeping current on SAX standards is an important part of an XML parser's responsibility, and if your vendor is not doing this, you may have other concerns to address with them as well. However, there are certainly cases where you are forced to use a parser because of legacy code or applications; in these situations, you are still not "left out in the cold."

SAX 2.0 includes a helper class, `org.xml.sax.helpers.ParserAdapter`, which can actually cause a SAX 1.0 `Parser` implementation to behave like a SAX 2.0 `XMLReader` implementation. This handy class takes in a 1.0 `Parser` implementation as an input parameter and then can be used in the stead of that implementation. It allows a `ContentHandler` to be set, and handles all namespace callbacks properly. The only feature loss you will see is that skipped entities will not be reported, as this capability was not available in a 1.0 implementation in any form, and cannot be emulated by a 2.0 adapter class. The sample class would be used as shown in Example 3-6.

Example 3-6. Using a SAX 1.0 Parser as a 2.0 XMLReader

```
try {
    // Register a parser with SAX
    Parser parser =
        ParserFactory.makeParser(
            "org.apache.xerces.parsers.SAXParser");

    ParserAdapter myParser = new ParserAdapter(parser);

    // Register the document handler
    myParser.setContentHandler(contentHandler);

    // Register the error handler
    myParser.setErrorHandler(errHandler);

    // Parse the document
    myParser.parse(uri);

} catch (ClassNotFoundException e) {
    System.out.println(
        "The parser class could not be found.");
} catch (IllegalAccessException e) {
    System.out.println(
        "Insufficient privileges to load the parser class.");
} catch (InstantiationException e) {
    System.out.println(
```

Example 3-6. Using a SAX 1.0 Parser as a 2.0 XMLReader (continued)

```
        "The parser class could not be instantiated.");
} catch (ClassCastException e) {
    System.out.println(
        "The parser does not implement org.xml.sax.Parser");
} catch (IOException e) {
    System.out.println("Error reaading URI: " + e.getMessage());
} catch (SAXException e) {
    System.out.println("Error in parsing: " + e.getMessage());
}
```

If SAX is new to you and this example doesn't make much sense, don't worry about it; you are using the latest and greatest version of SAX (2.0) and probably won't ever have to write code like this. Only in cases where a 1.0 parser must be used is this code helpful.

The SAX XMLReader: Reused and Reentrant

One of Java's nicest features is the ease of reuse of objects, and the memory advantages of this reuse. SAX parsers are no different. Once an `XMLReader` has been instantiated, it is possible to continue using that parser, parsing several or even hundreds of XML documents. Different documents or `InputSources` may be continually passed to a parser, allowing it to be used for a variety of different tasks. However, parsers are not reentrant. Once the parsing process has started, a parser may not be used until the parsing of the requested document or input has completed. For those of you who are prone to coding recursive methods, this is definitely a "gotcha!" The first time that you attempt to use a parser that is in the middle of processing another document, you will receive a rather nasty `SAXException` and all parsing will stop. What is the lesson learned? Parse one document at a time, or pay the price of instantiating multiple parser instances.

The Misplaced Locator

Another dangerous but seemingly innocuous feature of SAX events is the `Locator` instance that is made available through the `setDocumentLocator()` callback method. This gives the application the origin of a SAX event, and is useful for making decisions about the progress of parsing and how to react to events. However, this origin point is only valid for the duration of the life of the `ContentHandler` instance; once parsing is complete, the `Locator` is no longer valid, including in the case when another parse begins. A "gotcha" that many XML newcomers make is to hold a reference to the `Locator` object within a class member variable outside of the callback method:

```
public void setDocumentLocator(Locator locator) {
    // Saving the Locator to a class outside the ContentHandler
    myOtherClass.setLocator(locator);
```

```
}
...

public myOtherClassMethod() {
    // Trying to use this outside of the ContentHandler
    System.out.println(locator.getLineNumber());
}
```

This is an extremely bad idea, as this `Locator` becomes meaningless as soon as the scope of the `ContentHandler` implementation is left. Often, using the member variable resulting from this operation results in not only erroneous information being supplied to an application, but corruption of the XML document that was parsed. In other words, use this object locally, and not globally. In our `ContentHandler` implementation, we saved the supplied `Locator` to a member variable. It could then correctly be used (for example) to give you the line number of each element as it was encountered:

```
public void startElement(String namespaceURI, String localName,
                         String rawName, Attributes atts)
    throws SAXException {

        System.out.print("startElement: " + localName +
                         " at line " + locator.getLineNumber());

    if (!namespaceURI.equals("")) {
        System.out.println(" in namespace " + namespaceURI +
                           " (" + rawName + ")");
    } else {
        System.out.println(" has no associated namespace");
    }

    for (int i=0; i<atts.getLength(); i++)
        System.out.println("  Attribute: " + atts.getLocalName(i) +
                           "=" + atts.getValue(i));
}
```

Getting Ahead of the Data

The `characters()` callback method accepts a character array and `start` and `end` parameters to signify which index to start and end reading of that array from. This can cause some confusion; a common mistake is to include code like this example to read from the character array:

```
public void characters(char[] ch, int start, int end)
    throws SAXException {

    for (int i=0; i<ch.length; i++)
        System.out.print(i);
}
```

The mistake here is in reading from the beginning to the end of the character array. This natural "gotcha" results from years of iterating through arrays, either in Java, C, or another language. However, in the case of a SAX event, this can cause quite a bug. SAX parsers are required to pass in starting and ending boundaries on the character array which any loop constructs should use to read from the array. This allows lower-level manipulation of textual data to occur to optimize parser performance, such as reading data ahead of the current location as well as array reuse. This is all legal behavior within SAX, as the expectation is that a wrapping application will not try to "get ahead" of the `end` parameter sent to the callback.

Mistakes as in the example shown can result in gibberish data being output to the screen or used within the wrapping application, and are almost always problematic for applications. The loop construct looks very normal and compiles without a hitch, so this "gotcha" can be a very tricky problem to track down.

What's Next?

You should now have a solid understanding of the SAX interfaces and how they interact with an XML parser and the parsing process, with regard to a non-validated XML document. These interfaces are key to the rest of our discussions and Java code, as we will expand on our knowledge of SAX and add additional SAX classes to our example program. In the next chapter, we will look at how an XML document can be validated, and cover an XML document's DTD and schema. These will teach you how to constrain an XML document, and then in the chapter after that, we will look at implementing validation in our example parsing code.

In this chapter:

- *Why Constrain XML Data?*
- *Document Type Definitions*
- *XML Schema*
- *What's Next?*

4

Constraining XML

Learning to use XML, both for data representation and within Java applications, is an iterative process. In fact, almost every time you learn something about XML or one of its sister technologies, you will find that it gives you tools to learn yet another subset of the XML picture. Because there are so many XML-related projects and specifications, you will be hard-pressed to "know all there is to know" about XML; and just when you think you do, new versions of things you had down will come out, and you will get to start all over again! However, the more you do understand about the various components that make up the XML technology space, the better equipped you will be to add additional components to your programming toolkit. In keeping with this idea, we will now drop out of the Java programming language and return to XML-related specifications.

Chapters 2 and 3 should have given you the information and skills to create a well-formed XML document and then manipulate that document to a limited degree within Java. You also should begin to have a basic idea of how XML documents are parsed, and how the SAX Java classes aid in this process. In this chapter, we will discuss constraining the XML documents we have been creating. We will look at how Java can use these constraints in the parsing process in the next chapter.

Why Constrain XML Data?

Before assuming that you want to know about DTDs and XML Schema, it is only fair to help you understand why we should spend time on these specifications. There are some XML users and technologists who argue that there is never a need for constraining XML and ensuring document validity. Remember, we have already said that an XML document that is valid meets all the constraints that are set upon the document in the referenced DTD or schema. Also recall that a document can be well-formed, but still not be valid. So why go to the trouble to create a DTD or schema that does nothing but impose additional rules on your XML data?

Self-Documentation

As a Java developer, you have hopefully had lots of experience commenting your code, both with Javadoc and inline comments. At some point in your career, you were probably lectured on the importance of these comments; someone may have to read your code, someone may have to maintain your code, someone may actually have to understand your code. If you are involved in open source projects, the importance of commenting rises to even higher levels. And at some point, you probably rushed a project to completion to meet tight deadlines, and weren't exactly verbose in your comments. Then about three months later, another developer left with the task of supporting your project came to you and asked what this block of code did, or how that task was accomplished. Hopefully, you rattled off the correct explanation, but more likely you looked at him blankly and couldn't remember how you managed that particular feat of coding wizardry. At that point, you learned the value of documentation.

Now XML data is certainly not code, and simply because of the element nesting and other syntactical rules, it is almost always easier to understand than a snippet of complex Java code. However, don't be so sure that your outlook on data representation is the same outlook that other content authors may have. The simple XML file in Example 4-1 is an excellent example.

Example 4-1. An Ambiguous XML File

```
<?xml version="1.0"?>

<page>
  <screen>
    <name>Commerce</name>
    <trimColor>#CC9900</trimColor>
    <fontFace>Arial</fontFace>
  </screen>
  <content>
    <p>Lots of content would go here</p>
  </content>
</page>
```

The purpose of the file in Example 4-1 seems abundantly clear. It gives information to an application about a particular screen to render to a client. The color of the page trim is given, as well as the font to use, and then content for the screen is included. Where is the ambiguity? Well, it only shows up when another XML document used within the same application is seen, as in Example 4-2.

Example 4-2. A Less Ambiguous XML File

```
<?xml version="1.0"?>

<page>
  <screen>
    <name>Commerce</name>
    <trimColor>#CC9900</trimColor>
    <fontFace>Arial</fontFace>
  </screen>
  <screen>
    <name>Message Center</name>
    <trimColor>#9900FF</trimColor>
    <fontFace>Arial</fontFace>
  </screen>
  <screen>
    <name>News Center</name>
    <trimColor>#EECCEE</trimColor>
    <fontFace>Helvetica</fontFace>
  </screen>
  <content>
    <p>Lots of content would go here</p>
  </content>
</page>
```

Suddenly our interpretation of the first XML file would seem to be invalid. The `screen` element cannot represent the current screen, as the second example has three `screen` elements. In actuality, the application is rendering links to available screens at the top of the page, and the `screen` elements denote what each of these links should look like; the name of the link, the color of the section, and the font face of the link's title. The first example happened to have only one screen to link to, creating confusion. Only the content author or application developer could look at the first XML document and know this.

Constraining XML documents can aid in documenting these confusing situations. If we knew that there was only one allowed screen element within an XML page, we could safely make our first assumption at the use of the `screen` element. However, if we knew that multiple `screen` elements were allowed, then even with the first XML document, we could make a better estimation of the purpose of the data. To put it another way, a well-formed XML document contains words that are all found in the dictionary. The words have meaning, but can be used in meaningless ways: "Fox cat run happily smear bread jelly down." Validity ensures that these "words" (elements and attributes in XML) are put together in ways that make sense: "Foxes and cats happily run toward the bread smeared with jelly."

Documenting the "correct," or "valid," combinations of elements and attributes is the job of the DTD or schema. This is an important use of DTDs and schemas, in that they offer self-documentation of XML data in a meaningful way (and one that you can remember when your co-worker wants to know what your XML data means!).

Portability

In addition to helping viewers of your XML documents understand how and what data is being represented, constraining XML aids other applications in understanding XML data. We touched on this earlier; given any two arbitrary applications, the two cannot be assumed to have shared resources. In other words, the program that created an XML document for one application may not be available to the other application, hiding the logic by which data was generated in XML. This leaves the second application with the task of determining what type of data is being received in a transmitted XML document. Without any aid, the second application can only make assumptions about what is meant, often incorrectly.

This is somewhat similar to the problems that the C language has had, and that Java has tried to remedy. Because it defines a platform-independent programming language and relies on no native code, Java has become the most portable programming language available today. This is because there is a set of constraints put upon what Java can do, and these constraints are available to all platforms; while implementation details for tasks such as garbage collection and thread management are left to the specific platform, the interface to those tasks is always the same for the application developer.

Constraining XML documents with DTDs or schemas provides an analogous portability in XML. Consider our original example in this section: if the second application could access a resource that described the allowable formats of the data it is receiving, it could process that data with an XML-based set of utilities. Because the constraints of the document are not coded directly into the application (either the first or the second), there is no application logic that would have to be changed if the format of the document changed. The DTD or schema would change, but because this is simply a textual constraint file, neither application would have to be modified to immediately utilize the document structure changes. This allows XML data to be portable without having to resort to application-specific code, similar to the native code we try to avoid in Java programs.

Whether it is for documentation purposes, portability across applications and systems, or just because it allows a stricter checking of XML data, constraining XML is almost always a good idea. The only group whose view is not addressed here is the group that would say the performance hit taken for validating XML is greater than the gain from more structured data. This is a sound point; validating data does take additional processing time. However, many good publishing frameworks, such as the Apache Cocoon project, allow the specification of whether to validate a document or not. This means that development and testing can be performed with validation turned on. Then, once a document's structure is sound and tested, the framework can be told to not validate the document. Applications receiving this data can choose in a similar fashion if they want to validate the document or not, as the document will still contain a reference to a DTD or schema for which it is valid. In this way, the benefits of validation can be gained without additional processing time. Consult the vendor of any XML framework you consider using to see if this feature is supported.

In production systems, validation provides value in business-to-business applications; validation can ensure that data received from other applications, often ones you have no control over, is correctly formatted. This can help avoid errors in your application resulting from erroneous data input. For all of these purposes, DTDs and schemas are invaluable.

Document Type Definitions

As we have just discussed, an XML document is not very usable without an accompanying DTD. Just as XML can effectively describe data, the DTD makes this data usable in a variety of ways by many different programs by defining the structure of the data. In this section, we will look at the constructs for a DTD. We will again use as an example the XML representation of a portion of the table of contents for this book, and we will go through the process of constructing a DTD for the XML table of contents document.

The DTD's job is to define how data must be formatted. It must define each allowed element in an XML document, the allowed attributes, and possibly the acceptable attribute values for each element, the nesting and occurrences of each element, and any external entities. In fact, DTDs can specify quite a few other things about an XML document, but these basics are what we will focus on. We will learn the constructs that a DTD offers by applying them to and constraining our example XML file from Chapter 2, *Creating XML*. Because we will be referring to that file often throughout this chapter, it is reprinted here in Example 4-3.

Example 4-3. Table of Contents XML File

```
<?xml version="1.0"?>
<?xml-stylesheet href="XSL\JavaXML.html.xsl" type="text/xsl"?>
```

Example 4-3. Table of Contents XML File (continued)

```
<?xml-stylesheet href="XSL\JavaXML.wml.xsl" type="text/xsl"
                 media="wap"?>
<?cocoon-process type="xslt"?>
<!DOCTYPE JavaXML:Book SYSTEM "DTD\JavaXML.dtd">

<!-- Java and XML -->
<JavaXML:Book xmlns:JavaXML="http://www.oreilly.com/catalog/javaxml/">
 <JavaXML:Title>Java and XML</JavaXML:Title>
 <JavaXML:Contents>

  <JavaXML:Chapter focus="XML">
   <JavaXML:Heading>Introduction</JavaXML:Heading>
   <JavaXML:Topic subSections="7">What Is It?</JavaXML:Topic>
   <JavaXML:Topic subSections="3">How Do I Use It?</JavaXML:Topic>
   <JavaXML:Topic subSections="4">Why Should I Use It?</JavaXML:Topic>
   <JavaXML:Topic subSections="0">What's Next?</JavaXML:Topic>
  </JavaXML:Chapter>

  <JavaXML:Chapter focus="XML">
   <JavaXML:Heading>Creating XML</JavaXML:Heading>
   <JavaXML:Topic subSections="0">An XML Document</JavaXML:Topic>
   <JavaXML:Topic subSections="2">The Header</JavaXML:Topic>
   <JavaXML:Topic subSections="6">The Content</JavaXML:Topic>
   <JavaXML:Topic subSections="1">What's Next?</JavaXML:Topic>
  </JavaXML:Chapter>

  <JavaXML:Chapter focus="Java">
   <JavaXML:Heading>Parsing XML</JavaXML:Heading>
   <JavaXML:Topic subSections="3">Getting Prepared</JavaXML:Topic>
   <JavaXML:Topic subSections="3">SAX Readers</JavaXML:Topic>
   <JavaXML:Topic subSections="9">Content Handlers</JavaXML:Topic>
   <JavaXML:Topic subSections="4">Error Handlers</JavaXML:Topic>
   <JavaXML:Topic subSections="0">
     A Better Way to Load a Parser
   </JavaXML:Topic>
   <JavaXML:Topic subSections="4">"Gotcha!"</JavaXML:Topic>
   <JavaXML:Topic subSections="0">What's Next?</JavaXML:Topic>
  </JavaXML:Chapter>

  <JavaXML:SectionBreak/>

  <JavaXML:Chapter focus="Java">
   <JavaXML:Heading>Web Publishing Frameworks</JavaXML:Heading>
   <JavaXML:Topic subSections="4">Selecting a Framework</JavaXML:Topic>
   <JavaXML:Topic subSections="4">Installation</JavaXML:Topic>
   <JavaXML:Topic subSections="3">
```

Example 4-3. Table of Contents XML File (continued)

```
      Using a Publishing Framework
    </JavaXML:Topic>
    <JavaXML:Topic subSections="2">XSP</JavaXML:Topic>
    <JavaXML:Topic subSections="3">Cocoon 2.0 and Beyond</JavaXML:Topic>
    <JavaXML:Topic subSections="0">What's Next?</JavaXML:Topic>
   </JavaXML:Chapter>

  </JavaXML:Contents>

  <JavaXML:Copyright>&OReillyCopyright;</JavaXML:Copyright>

</JavaXML:Book>
```

Specifying Elements

Our first concern is specifying which elements are allowed within the document. We want content authors using this DTD to be able to use elements such as `JavaXML:Book` and `JavaXML:Contents`, but not to be able to use elements like `JavaXML:foo` and `JavaXML:bar`. When we decide on a set of allowed elements, we begin to give a semantic meaning to our XML document; in other words, we give it a context in which it is useful. First, then, we want to make a list of all allowed elements. The easiest way to make this list is to scan our XML document and make a note of each element being used. It also is a good idea to define the purpose of each tag. Although this is not something defined in the DTD unless by a comment (not a bad idea!), it helps you, the DTD author, keep things straight. Table 4-1 has a complete listing of the elements in the *contents.xml* document.

Table 4-1. Elements Allowed for Our XML Document

Element Name	Purpose
`JavaXML:Book`	Overall root element
`JavaXML:Title`	Title of the book being documented
`JavaXML:Contents`	Denotes the table of contents
`JavaXML:Chapter`	A chapter within the book
`JavaXML:Heading`	The heading (title) of a chapter
`JavaXML:Topic`	The main focus of a section within a chapter
`JavaXML:SectionBreak`	A break between chapters denoting a new section of the book
`JavaXML:Copyright`	The copyright for the book

With these elements defined, we can now specify each one in our DTD. This is done with the following notation:

```
<!ELEMENT [Element Name] [Element Definition/Type]>
```

The [Element Name] is the actual element from our table. This name, as in the table, should include the namespace prefix. Within the DTD, there is no idea of an element with a namespace prefix, and then a mapping from a namespace URI to that prefix. Within a DTD, the element name is either the name itself, when no namespace is used, or the namespace prefix and element name separated by a colon.

The [Element Definition/Type] is the most useful portion of the DTD. It allows the data within the element to be defined, giving a "type" to the element, whether it is pure data or a compound type consisting of data and other elements. The most unrestrictive element type is the keyword ANY. Using this keyword allows the element to contain textual data, nested elements, or any legal XML combination of the two. Thus, we can now define all the elements in our XML document within our DTD, albeit not in a very useful way. Example 4-4 shows the beginning of a DTD for our XML document.

Example 4-4. A "Bare-Bones" DTD with Element Definitions

```
<!ELEMENT JavaXML:Book ANY>
<!ELEMENT JavaXML:Title ANY>
<!ELEMENT JavaXML:Contents ANY>
<!ELEMENT JavaXML:Chapter ANY>
<!ELEMENT JavaXML:Heading ANY>
<!ELEMENT JavaXML:Topic ANY>
<!ELEMENT JavaXML:SectionBreak ANY>
<!ELEMENT JavaXML:Copyright ANY>
```

Of course, this simple DTD, in addition to not handling either attributes or entity references, doesn't help us much. Although it defines each allowed element, it says nothing about the types of those elements, or the nesting allowed. It would still be simple to create a nonsensical XML document that conformed to this DTD, as in Example 4-5.

Example 4-5. A Conformant XML Document That Is Useless

```
<?xml version="1.0"?>
<?xml-stylesheet href="XSL\JavaXML.html.xsl" type="text/xsl"?>
<?xml-stylesheet href="XSL\JavaXML.wml.xsl" type="text/xsl"
                 media="wap"?>
<?cocoon-process type="xslt"?>
<!DOCTYPE JavaXML:Book SYSTEM "DTD\JavaXML.dtd">

<JavaXML:Topic>
  <JavaXML:Book>Here's my Book</JavaXML:Book>
  <JavaXML:Copyright>
    <JavaXML:Chapter>Chapter One</JavaXML:Chapter>
```

Example 4-5. A Conformant XML Document That Is Useless (continued)

```
  </JavaXML:Copyright>
  <JavaXML:SectionBreak>Here's a Section</JavaXML:SectionBreak>
</JavaXML:Topic>
```

Although this document fragment uses only elements allowed by the DTD, its structure is incorrect. This is because the DTD gives no information about how elements are nested and which elements can contain textual data.

Nesting elements

One of the keys to XML document structure is the nesting of tags. We can expand on our original table of elements by adding the elements that can be nested within each structure. This will create our element hierarchy for us, which we can then define within our DTD. Table 4-2 summarizes the element hierarchy.

Table 4-2. Element Hierarchy

Element Name	Allowed Nested Elements	Purpose
JavaXML:Book	JavaXML:Title JavaXML:Contents JavaXML:Copyright	Overall root element
JavaXML:Title	None	Title of the book being documented
JavaXML:Contents	JavaXML:Chapter JavaXML:SectionBreak	Denotes the table of contents
JavaXML:Chapter	JavaXML:Heading JavaXML:Topic	A chapter within the book
JavaXML:Heading	None	The heading (title) of a chapter
JavaXML:Topic	None	The main focus of a section within a chapter
JavaXML:SectionBreak	None	A break between chapters denoting a new section of the book
JavaXML:Copyright	None	The copyright for the book

With this table complete, we are now ready to define the allowed element nestings within our DTD. The way to perform this is:

```
<!ELEMENT [Element Name] ([Nested Element][,Nested Element]...)>
```

In this case, a list of comma-separated elements within parentheses becomes the element type. The order of the elements is also important; this ordering is enforced as a validity constraint within the XML document. This adds additional constraints to our document, ensuring that a copyright element always comes at the end of a book, or that a title element appears before content elements. With this new notation, we can update our DTD to add the allowed nestings of elements, shown in Example 4-6.

Example 4-6. DTD with Element Hierarchy

```
<!ELEMENT JavaXML:Book (JavaXML:Title,
                        JavaXML:Contents,
                        JavaXML:Copyright)>
<!ELEMENT JavaXML:Title ANY>
<!ELEMENT JavaXML:Contents (JavaXML:Chapter, JavaXML:SectionBreak)>
<!ELEMENT JavaXML:Chapter (JavaXML:Heading, JavaXML:Topic)>
<!ELEMENT JavaXML:Heading ANY>
<!ELEMENT JavaXML:Topic ANY>
<!ELEMENT JavaXML:SectionBreak ANY>
<!ELEMENT JavaXML:Copyright ANY>
```

Although some elements, those that contain parsed data, are not changed, we have a hierarchy of elements that adds a lot of meaning to our XML document constraints. The earlier example that made no sense because of element ordering and nesting would now be invalid. However, there are still a lot of problems with allowing any type of data within the remaining elements.

Parsed data

The element type to use for textual data is `#PCDATA`. This keyword represents Parsed Character Data, and can be used for elements that contain character data that we want our XML parser to handle normally. Using the `#PCDATA` keyword limits the element to using only character data, though; nested elements are not allowed. We will discuss situations like this a little later. For now, we can modify our title, heading, and topic elements to reflect that textual data should be used within these elements, as in Example 4-7.

Example 4-7. DTD with Element Hierarchy and Character Data Elements

```
<!ELEMENT JavaXML:Book (JavaXML:Title,
                        JavaXML:Contents,
                        JavaXML:Copyright)>
<!ELEMENT JavaXML:Title (#PCDATA)>
<!ELEMENT JavaXML:Contents (JavaXML:Chapter, JavaXML:SectionBreak)>
<!ELEMENT JavaXML:Chapter (JavaXML:Heading, JavaXML:Topic)>
<!ELEMENT JavaXML:Heading (#PCDATA)>
<!ELEMENT JavaXML:Topic (#PCDATA)>
<!ELEMENT JavaXML:SectionBreak ANY>
<!ELEMENT JavaXML:Copyright ANY>
```

Empty elements

We are moving right along in our element definitions within DTDs. In addition to elements that contain textual data and elements that contain other elements, we have one element, `JavaXML:SectionBreak`, which should contain no data. In other words, the element should always be empty. Although it would be legal to specify that this element contained parsed character data and simply never insert any, this isn't a good use of our constraints. It is better to actually require that the element always be empty, preventing accidental misuse. The keyword `EMPTY` allows this constraint. This keyword does not need to appear within parentheses, as it denotes a type and cannot be grouped with any other elements, which, as we will soon see, the parentheses allow. We can update our section break element in our DTD now in Example 4-8.

Example 4-8. DTD with EMPTY Element Defined

```
<!ELEMENT JavaXML:Book (JavaXML:Title,
                        JavaXML:Contents,
                        JavaXML:Copyright)>
<!ELEMENT JavaXML:Title (#PCDATA)>
<!ELEMENT JavaXML:Contents (JavaXML:Chapter, JavaXML:SectionBreak)>
<!ELEMENT JavaXML:Chapter (JavaXML:Heading, JavaXML:Topic)>
<!ELEMENT JavaXML:Heading (#PCDATA)>
<!ELEMENT JavaXML:Topic (#PCDATA)>
<!ELEMENT JavaXML:SectionBreak EMPTY>
<!ELEMENT JavaXML:Copyright ANY>
```

Entity references

The last element we have to define more rigidly is the `JavaXML:Copyright` element. As you recall, this is actually a container for an entity reference to another file that should be included. When our XML sees `&OReillyCopyright;`, it will attempt to look up the `OReillyCopyright` entity within the DTD, which in our case should reference an external file. This external file should have a shared copyright for all books being documented in XML. The DTD has the job of specifying where the external file is located, and how it should be accessed. In our case, we assume that the copyright file is on the local filesystem, and we want to reference that file. Entity references are specified in DTDs with the notation:

```
<!ENTITY [Entity Name] "[Replacement Characters/Identifier]">
```

You will notice that the notation indicated that a set of replacement characters could be specified, allowing substitution similar to using an external file. In fact, this is how the "escape" characters within XML are handled:

```
<!ENTITY &amp; "&">
<!ENTITY &lt; "<">
```

```
<!ENTITY &gt; ">">
...
```

So if our copyright was a very short piece of text, we could use something like:

```
<!ENTITY OReillyCopyright
        "Copyright O&apos;Reilly and Associates, 2000">
```

However, the copyright we expect to use is a longer piece of text, more appropriately stored in an external file for easy modification. This also allows it to be used in multiple XML documents without duplication of the data within each document's DTD. This requires us to specify a system-level resource as the resolution for the entity reference. The notation for this type of reference is:

```
<!ENTITY [Entity Reference] SYSTEM "[URI]">
```

As in the case of parsing our XML document and our discussion on namespaces, the URI specified can be either a local resource or a network-accessible resource. In our case, we want to use a file located on an external server, so the entity would reference that file through a URL:

```
<!ENTITY OReillyCopyright SYSTEM
        "http://www.oreilly.com/catalog/javaxml/docs/copyright.xml">
```

With this reference set up, an XML parser could now handle the `OReillyCopyright` reference within an XML document and properly resolve it within the parsing process. This section of the XML had to be commented out in Chapter 3, *Parsing XML*, for this very reason, and in the next chapter, we will uncomment the reference and see how a validating parser handles the entity and uses a DTD to resolve it.

Finally, we need to let our containing element know it should expect parsed character data:

```
<!ELEMENT JavaXML:Copyright (#PCDATA)>
```

Say It Again One More Time

The last major construct in DTD element specifications we will look at is the variety of combinations of grouping, multiple occurrences, and choices within an element. In other words, the case where element X can appear once, or element Y can occur, followed by element Z. These structures are critical to DTDs; by default, an element can appear exactly once when specified without any modifiers in the DTD:

```
<!ELEMENT MyElement (NestedElement, AnotherElement)>
```

Here `NestedElement` must appear exactly once, and must always be followed by exactly one `AnotherElement`. If this were not the structure of the corresponding

XML document, the document would be invalid. A special set of modifiers must be applied to elements to change this default constraining behavior.

Zero, one, or more

The most common modifier applied to an element is a recurrence operator. These operators allow an element to appear zero or more times, one or more times, or optionally not at all, in addition to the default, which requires an element to appear exactly one time. Table 4-3 lists each of the recurrence operators and what recurrence they indicate.

Table 4-3. Recurrence Operators

Operator	Description
[Default]	Must appear exactly one time
?	Must appear once or not at all
+	Must appear at least once (1 ... N times)
*	May appear any number of times, or not at all (0 ... N times)

Each operator can be appended to the end of an element name. In our previous example, to allow `NestedElement` to appear one or more times, and then require that `AnotherElement` appear either once or not at all, we would use the following within the DTD:

```
<!ELEMENT MyElement (NestedElement+, AnotherElement?)>
```

This would make the following XML perfectly valid:

```
<MyElement>
  <NestedElement>One</NestedElement>
  <NestedElement>Two</NestedElement>
</MyElement>
```

In the DTD we have been building, we have a similar situation within the `JavaXML:Chapter` element. We would like to allow a chapter heading (`JavaXML:Heading`) to either appear once, or optionally be omitted, and to allow one or more `JavaXML:Topic` elements to appear. We can now make this change using our recurrence operators:

```
<!ELEMENT JavaXML:Chapter (JavaXML:Heading?,JavaXML:Topic+)>
```

This easy change makes our XML chapter representation much more realistic. We also need to make a change to the `JavaXML:Contents` element definition. A chapter or set of chapters should appear, and then possibly a section break. The section break must be optional, as a book may only contain chapters. We can define the recurrence of chapters and the section break elements like this:

```
<!ELEMENT JavaXML:Contents (JavaXML:Chapter+,JavaXML:SectionBreak?)>
```

However, we still have not let the DTD know that more chapters can appear after the `JavaXML:SectionBreak` element. In fact, if we look at the structure of the XML we would like to allow this structure to occur multiple times. Chapters followed by a section break can be followed by more chapters followed by another section break! We need a concept of grouping within our element.

Grouping

Grouping allows us to solve problems like the element nesting within `JavaXML:Contents`. Often, recurrence occurs for a block or group of elements, rather than a single element. For this reason, any of the recurrence operators can be applied to a group of elements. Enclosing a set of elements within parentheses signifies the group. If you are starting to remember your old LISP classes in college, don't worry; it stays fairly simple in our examples, and the parentheses don't get out of hand. Nested parentheses are, of course, acceptable. So to group a set of elements the following notation would be used:

```
<!ELEMENT GroupingExample ((Group1El1, Group1El2),
                           (Group2El1, Group2El2))>
```

An operator can then be applied to the group, rather than to a single element. In the scenario we are currently looking at, we need to apply the operator allowing multiple occurrences to the group containing our chapter and section break element. This would then allow repetition of the entire construct:

```
<!ELEMENT JavaXML:Contents (JavaXML:Chapter+,JavaXML:SectionBreak?)+>
```

This now accurately allows the various combinations: a set of chapters followed by one section break, and then the structure repeating multiple times or optionally not repeating at all. It also allows the case where only chapters are included, without any section breaks. However, this is not particularly clear from the DTD. What would be better is to specify that one or more chapters could occur, *or* this structure could occur. Although this is not going to result in different behavior, it certainly would make more sense to readers other than the DTD author. To accomplish this, though, we need to introduce an "or" function.

Either or

DTDs do conveniently offer an "or" function, signified by the pipe operator. This allows one thing or the other to occur, and the pipe is often used in conjunction with groupings. One common, although not necessarily good, use of the "or" operator is to allow a certain element or elements to appear within an enclosing element, or for textual data to appear:

```
<!ELEMENT AggregateElement (#PCDATA | Element1 | Element2)*>
```

For this DTD, both of the following XML document fragments would be valid:

```
<AggregateElement>
  <Element1>One</Element1>
  <Element2>Two</Element2>
</AggregateElement>

<AggregateElement>
  Textual Data
</AggregateElement>
```

Using this type of constraint is discouraged, though, as the meaning of the enclosing element becomes obscure. An element should typically include textual, parsed data, or other elements; it should not allow both.

We have now completely specified and constrained our XML elements. The DTD shown in Example 4-9 should function in regard to our elements, and only attribute definitions are left, which we will look at next.

Example 4-9. DTD with Elements Specified

```
<!ELEMENT JavaXML:Book (JavaXML:Title,
                        JavaXML:Contents,
                        JavaXML:Copyright)>
<!ELEMENT JavaXML:Title (#PCDATA)>
<!ELEMENT JavaXML:Contents (JavaXML:Chapter+, JavaXML:SectionBreak?)+)>
<!ELEMENT JavaXML:Chapter (JavaXML:Heading?,JavaXML:Topic+)>
<!ELEMENT JavaXML:Heading (#PCDATA)>
<!ELEMENT JavaXML:Topic (#PCDATA)>
<!ELEMENT JavaXML:SectionBreak EMPTY>
<!ELEMENT JavaXML:Copyright (#PCDATA)>
<!ENTITY OReillyCopyright SYSTEM
        "http://www.oreilly.com/catalog/javaxml/docs/copyright.xml">
```

Defining Attributes

With element specifications thoroughly covered, we can move on to defining attributes. Because there are not complicated nesting scenarios with attributes, defining them is somewhat simpler than dealing with element specifications. In addition, whether the presence of an attribute is required is specified by a keyword, so no recurrence operators are needed. Attribute definitions are in the following form:

```
<!ATTLIST [Enclosing Element]
          [Attribute Name] [type] [Modifer]
          ...
>
```

The first two parameters, the element name and the attribute name, are simple to define. For any element, the ATTLIST construct allows multiple attributes to be defined within the same structure. We can add this portion of the attribute definition for the attributes we are using within our XML document, creating placeholders for the rest of the definition. Best practice is to include the attribute definitions right after the element specification, again in the spirit of a DTD being as self-documenting as possible (see Example 4-10).

Example 4-10. DTD with Elements and Attribute Placeholders

```
<!ELEMENT JavaXML:Book (JavaXML:Title,
                       JavaXML:Contents,
                       JavaXML:Copyright)>
<!ATTLIST JavaXML:Book
      xmlns:JavaXML [type] [Modifier]
>
<!ELEMENT JavaXML:Title (#PCDATA)>
<!ELEMENT JavaXML:Contents (JavaXML:Chapter+, JavaXML:SectionBreak?)+)>
<!ELEMENT JavaXML:Chapter (JavaXML:Heading?,JavaXML:Topic+)>
<!ATTLIST JavaXML:Chapter
      focus [type] [Modifier]
>
<!ELEMENT JavaXML:Heading (#PCDATA)>
<!ELEMENT JavaXML:Topic (#PCDATA)>
<!ATTLIST JavaXML:Topic
      subSections [type] [Modifier]
>
<!ELEMENT JavaXML:SectionBreak EMPTY>
<!ELEMENT JavaXML:Copyright (#PCDATA)>
<!ENTITY copyright SYSTEM
        "http://www.oreilly.com/catalog/javaxml/docs/copyright.xml">
```

We now need to define the types allowed for each attribute.

Attribute types

For many attributes, the value can be any textual data. This is the simplest type of attribute value, but also the least constrained. This type is signified by the keyword CDATA, representing Character Data. And yes, this is the same CDATA construct used within XML documents themselves to represent "escaped" character data. This is the type generally used when an attribute can take on any value and may represent a comment or additional information about an element. We will soon see that a better solution is to define a set of values that are allowed for an attribute to take on. In our document, the xmlns attribute should be character data. You may wonder why we need to define this as an allowed attribute. Although the xmlns is an XML keyword that signifies a namespace declaration, it is still an attribute that must be validated. Therefore, we include it to ensure our document validity. The subSections attribute of JavaXML:Topic should be character data, as well:

```
<!ATTLIST JavaXML:Book
      xmlns:JavaXML CDATA [Modifier]
>
<!ELEMENT JavaXML:Title (#PCDATA)>
<!ELEMENT JavaXML:Contents (JavaXML:Chapter+, JavaXML:SectionBreak?)+)>
<!ELEMENT JavaXML:Chapter (JavaXML:Heading?,JavaXML:Topic+)>
<!ATTLIST JavaXML:Chapter
      focus [type] [Modifier]
>
<!ELEMENT JavaXML:Heading (#PCDATA)>
<!ELEMENT JavaXML:Topic (#PCDATA)>
<!ATTLIST JavaXML:Topic
      subSections CDATA [Modifier]
>
```

The next type of attribute, and one of the most commonly used, is an enumeration. This type allows any of the specified values to be used, but any other value for the attribute results in an invalid document. This is useful when the set of values for an attribute can be determined at authoring time, as it tightly constrains the XML document. This is the type our focus attribute should take on, as the only allowed foci for the book are "Java" and "XML." The allowed values are set within parenthetical notation, separated by the "or" operator, similar to the way element nestings can be specified:

```
<!ELEMENT JavaXML:Chapter (JavaXML:Heading?,JavaXML:Topic+)>
<!ATTLIST JavaXML:Chapter
      focus (XML|Java) [Modifier]
>
<!ELEMENT JavaXML:Heading (#PCDATA)>
```

To be or not to be

The final question that should be answered in defining an attribute is whether the attribute is required within an element. This is specified with one of three possible keywords: #IMPLIED, #REQUIRED, or #FIXED. An implied attribute can remain unspecified. We can make this modification to the subSections attribute, as it is not required for the document to remain valid:

```
<!ELEMENT JavaXML:Topic (#PCDATA)>
<!ATTLIST JavaXML:Topic
      subSections CDATA #IMPLIED
>
```

For our xmlns attribute, we want to ensure that a content author always specifies the namespace for the book. Otherwise, our namespace prefixes become useless.

In this case, we want to use the #REQUIRED keyword. If this attribute were not included within the JavaXML:Book element, the document would be invalid, as it doesn't specify a required attribute:

```
<!ELEMENT JavaXML:Book (JavaXML:Title,
                        JavaXML:Contents,
                        JavaXML:Copyright)>
<!ATTLIST JavaXML:Book
      xmlns:JavaXML CDATA #REQUIRED
>
```

The final keyword, #FIXED, is not frequently used for applications. Most common in backend systems, this keyword states that the user can never change the value of this attribute. The format of this type of notation is:

```
<!ATTLIST [Element Name]
          [Attribute Name] #FIXED [Fixed Value]
>
```

Because of its irrelevance in highly dynamic applications (an attribute whose value cannot change does not help us much in representing dynamic data!), we will not spend more time on it.

We have still not addressed the focus attribute. We have enumerated the possible values it can take on, but because the book is primarily focused on Java, we would like to allow the content author not to have to explicitly define the attribute as "Java" in chapters where that is the focus. In a book with twenty or thirty chapters, this becomes tedious. Imagine a listing of a science library's books where each book had to notate that its primary subject was "science"! This data duplication is not very efficient, so requiring the attribute is not a great solution. However, using the #IMPLIED keyword does not result in a value being assigned to the attribute, which is precisely what we want to happen if no value is specified. What we do want is to provide a default value; if no attribute value is given, we want the default to be passed on to the XML parser. Fortunately, this is an allowed construct within XML DTDs. Instead of one of the keyword modifiers, a default value can be given. This value should be in quotes, and if an enumeration is the type for the attribute, the default must be one of the enumerated values. We can now use this to define our focus attribute:

```
<!ELEMENT JavaXML:Chapter (JavaXML:Heading?,JavaXML:Topic+)>
<!ATTLIST JavaXML:Chapter
      focus (XML|Java) "Java"
>
```

With this attribute definition, we have completed our DTD! Although the syntax may have seemed awkward and a bit clumsy, hopefully you were able to easily follow along and understand how elements and attributes, as well as entities, are defined within DTDs. We certainly have not thoroughly covered DTDs, as this is primarily a book on Java and XML, not just XML; however, you should feel comfortable with our sample DTD and be able to create simple DTDs for your own XML documents. Before we move on to schemas, let's take a final look at our complete DTD in Example 4-11.

Example 4-11. Completed DTD

```
<!ELEMENT JavaXML:Book (JavaXML:Title,
                        JavaXML:Contents,
                        JavaXML:Copyright)>
<!ATTLIST JavaXML:Book
      xmlns:JavaXML CDATA #REQUIRED
>
<!ELEMENT JavaXML:Title (#PCDATA)>
<!ELEMENT JavaXML:Contents (JavaXML:Chapter+, JavaXML:SectionBreak?)+)>
<!ELEMENT JavaXML:Chapter (JavaXML:Heading?,JavaXML:Topic+)>
<!ATTLIST JavaXML:Chapter
      focus (XML|Java) "Java"
>
<!ELEMENT JavaXML:Heading (#PCDATA)>
<!ELEMENT JavaXML:Topic (#PCDATA)>
<!ATTLIST JavaXML:Topic
      subSections CDATA #IMPLIED
>
<!ELEMENT JavaXML:SectionBreak EMPTY>
<!ELEMENT JavaXML:Copyright (#PCDATA)>
<!ENTITY OReillyCopyright SYSTEM
         "http://www.oreilly.com/catalog/javaxml/docs/copyright.xml">
```

In comparing our example XML document to its DTD, you should start to notice some unnecessary complexities in the DTD's structure. The DTD that defines the organization of this XML file (and other XML files like it) has a structure completely unlike the XML file itself. You will also see that the DTD's structure is different from a schema, an XSL stylesheet, and nearly every other XML-related document. Unfortunately, XML DTDs were developed as part of the XML 1.0 specification, and some design decisions made in that specification still cause XML users and developers grief. Much of the basis for XML DTDs came from the way DTDs are used in SGML, a much older specification. However, the structure of an SGML DTD is not necessarily appropriate or in the spirit of the XML specification. The result is that DTDs are not one of the best design decisions made in the formation of the XML specification. Fortunately, XML Schema looks to correct these structural differences, making constraining XML more of an XML-centric process, rather than a break from XML format. We will discuss XML Schema next. Although XML Schema is likely to replace DTDs, the process will be a slow and cautious one, as many applications have already embraced XML in production systems, and those systems use documents constrained by DTDs. For this reason, understanding DTDs is important, even if they will be phased out of heavy use.

Things Left Out

Strangely enough, there is a need for a section on things left out of a DTD. Although all of the elements within an XML document must be specified, and their attributes defined, processing instructions do not have to be part of a DTD. In fact, there is no possible way to specify the PIs and XML declaration found at the top of XML files. The DTD begins with the first occurrence of the first element within an XML file. This probably seems quite natural to you; why specify that an XML document may have this processing instruction, but not that one? The rationale behind this decision is portability.

There are some good arguments for allowing the specification of PIs within a DTD. For example, it is plausible that a content author might want to make sure his XML document is always transformed, and require an `xml-stylesheet` PI. But which type of stylesheet is required? Well, this can be defined too. And what type of engine should be used for transformations? Cocoon? James Clark's Servlet? Another framework? Again, these items can be defined. However, by the time all of these details have been specified and constrained, the document has lost all its portability! It can only be used for one specific purpose on one specific framework, and can no longer be transformed iteratively and easily moved from one platform or framework or application to another. For this reason, PIs and initial XML declarations are left unconstrained within DTDs. We only have to consider the elements and attributes within the document, beginning with the root element.

XML Schema

XML Schema is a new working draft at the W3C that seeks to remedy many of the problems and limitations of DTDs. In addition to handling more accurate representations of XML structure constraints, XML Schema also seeks to provide an XML styling to the process of constraining data. Schemas are actually XML documents that are both well-formed and valid. This allows parsers and other XML-aware applications to handle XML Schema documents in a fashion similar to other XML documents, as opposed to employing special techniques as are needed for handling DTD documents.

Because XML Schema is both a new and young specification, as well as still incomplete, we will only lightly treat it here. In addition, details of the implementation of XML Schema are subject to change; if you have problems with some of the examples, you may want to consult the latest version of the XML Schema proposal at *http://www.w3.org/TR/xmlschema-1/* and *http://www.w3.org/TR/xmlschema-2/*. You should also be aware that many XML parsers do not support XML Schema, or support only portions of the specification. You should check with your vendor to verify the level of XML Schema support provided by your XML parser.

There is also a difference between a *valid* document and a *schema-valid* document. Because XML Schema is not part of the XML 1.0 specification, a document that conforms to a given schema is not said to be valid. Only an XML document conforming to a referenced DTD through a `DOCTYPE` declaration is considered a valid XML document. This has caused quite a bit of confusion in the XML community as to how to handle schema validation. In addition to the difference in terms of validity, an XML 1.0 parser or application does not have to perform schema validation, again because XML Schema is not in the 1.0 specification of XML. This means that even if your document has a schema reference, the document may not be validated against that schema, regardless of the parser's level of schema support. For these reasons, you should take care to determine when your parser will and will not validate, and specifically how it handles schema validation. For clarity, we will continue to use validity as the single term, representing either schema or DTD validity. It will be up to you to see whether a `DOCTYPE` declaration or a schema reference exists; in addition, the meaning of the word will be clear from the context in which it is used. Any possible ambiguities will be expressly defined and handled in the appropriate portion of the text.

The most significant aspect of creating a schema for your XML document is that you will actually be creating another XML document. Unlike DTDs, which use an entirely different format for specification of elements and definition of attributes, a schema is simply an XML document. For this reason, the syntax will be largely the same as we have already discussed in Chapter 2. Interestingly enough, XML Schema itself is constrained by a DTD. If this seems a little strange to you, consider that until XML Schema, DTDs were the only means of creating document constraints. For XML Schema to enforce validity, it must use a mechanism other than itself to define its own constraints. This other mechanism, then, must be a DTD. However, that initial DTD allows the creating of a schema, which allows all other XML documents to completely disregard DTDs. This rather odd flow of logic is not unusual in the world of specifications and evolving versions; new versions must be shaped by old versions.

The Schema Namespace

You should expect XML Schema documents to begin with a standard XML declaration, and then to refer to the XML Schema namespace. This is exactly correct. In addition, there are standards for the naming of the root element. The accepted practice is to always use schema as the root element of XML Schema documents, and we will not deviate from that standard here. When we specify the root element, we also need to make some namespace definitions, much as we did in our original XML document. The first thing needed is the default namespace declaration:

```
<schema xmlns:xsd="http://www.w3.org/1999/XMLSchema">
```

We briefly discussed this in Chapter 2; omitting an identifier after the xmlns attribute results in a *default namespace* being applied to the document. In our original XML document, our namespace definition was specifically for the JavaXML namespace:

```
<JavaXML:Book xmlns:JavaXML="http://www.w3.org/1999/XMLSchema">
```

This told the XML parser that all elements prefixed with JavaXML belonged to that namespace, associated with the given URL. In our XML document, that was all elements, as all elements had this namespace prefix. However, we could also have had additional elements within the document that were not prefixed with a namespace. Elements without a prefix don't simply disappear; they too must be assigned to a namespace. These would be considered part of the default namespace, which is not defined in the document. It could be defined with an additional namespace declaration in our root element:

```
<JavaXML:Book xmlns:JavaXML="http://www.oreilly.com/catalog/javaxml"
              xmlns="http://www.someOtherUrl.com"
>
```

This would result in any element not prefixed with JavaXML or another namespace prefix being associated with the default namespace, identified by the URL http://www.someOtherUrl.com. So in the following document fragment, Book, Contents, and Title are associated with the JavaXML namespace, while element1 and element2 are associated with the default namespace:

```
<JavaXML:Book xmlns:JavaXML="http://www.oreilly.com/catalog/javaxml"
              xmlns="http://www.someOtherUrl.com"
>
  <JavaXML:Title>My Title</JavaXML:Title>
  <JavaXML:Contents>
    <element1>
      <element2 />
    </element1>
  </JavaXML:Contents>

</JavaXML:Book>
```

Because our schema will be dealing with another document, all elements specifically related to XML Schema constructs should be part of the default namespace. For this reason, we included the default namespace definition. However, these element constructs are *acting* upon the namespace within the constrained XML document. In other words, although XML Schema constructs are part of the XML Schema namespace, they are used to constrain elements in other namespaces, namely those of the XML document or documents they operate upon. In our continuing example, that would be the JavaXML namespace. So we need to add this additional namespace definition to our schema element:

```
<schema xmlns="http://www.w3.org/1999/XMLSchema"
        xmlns:JavaXML="http://www.oreilly.com/catalog/javaxml"
>
```

Finally, we need to let our schema know that the target of its constraints is on this second namespace. To do that, the targetNamespace attribute is specified, which does exactly what it implies:

```
<schema targetNamespace="http://www.oreilly.com/catalog/javaxml"
        xmlns="http://www.w3.org/1999/XMLSchema"
        xmlns:JavaXML="http://www.oreilly.com/catalog/javaxml"
>
```

So we end up with two namespaces defined (the default and JavaXML), and the target of the constraints set forth in the document being associated with the latter namespace (JavaXML). And with our root element defined, we are ready to begin setting constraints on this namespace. Also keep in mind that it is possible, in the world of HTTP and web servers, that the URL referred to in a namespace might actually be a valid URL; in our example, you could type http://www.oreilly.com/catalog/javaxml into your web browser and get an HTML response. However, the document returned is not being used here; in fact, the URL itself does not have to be accessible, but instead is only used as an association for the declared namespace. This has caused quite a bit of confusion, so don't get tripped up by what the URI specified is; instead, focus on the namespace being declared and how that namespace is used in the document.

A short note is in order before continuing. This may seem a tough section to read through; if so, don't feel as if you aren't up to the task. The concepts involved in XML Schema are not trivial, and the specification is continuing to evolve. Although many content authors will *use* XML Schema, you are now learning to *understand* it; this subtle but important difference will result in more intelligent design choices and better applications. Of particular complexity is how DTDs and namespaces are used within schemas; happily, many of the constructs for constraining XML are more straightforward. So take heart, read slowly and with caffeine nearby, and continue on! It will be worth the time and effort in the long run.

Specifying Elements

We have come a long way since you first saw this heading in the section on DTDs. In a schema, specifying an element will feel quite a bit more logical. It also closely mirrors the structure, if not the syntax, of a Java declaration, with some additional options that can be specified. The `element` element is used for these specifications:

```
<element name="[Name of Element]"
         type="[Type of Element]"
         [Options...]
>
```

Here, `[Name of Element]` is the name of the element in the XML document being constrained. However, unlike DTDs, the namespace of the element should *not* prefix the element. Remember our discussion of the target namespace? Because we have said that our target namespace is `JavaXML`, all element specifications, as well as any user-defined types we create, are applied and assigned to that target namespace. This also aids in creating a cleaner schema, as the elements are defined and then the namespace applied. `[Type of Element]` is either a predefined XML Schema data type or a user-defined data type. Table 4-4 lists the data types supported by the current version of XML Schema.

Table 4-4. XML Schema Data Types

Type	Subtypes	Purpose
`string`	`NMTOKEN, language`	Character strings
`boolean`	N/A	Binary valued logic (true or false)
`float`	N/A	32-bit floating point type
`double`	N/A	64-bit floating point type
`decimal`	`integer`	Standard decimal notation, positive and negative
`timeInstant`	N/A	A combination of date and time representing one single instant of time
`timeDuration`	N/A	A duration of time
`recurringInstant`	`date, time`	A specific time that recurs over a `timeDuration`
`binary`	N/A	Binary data
`uri`	`enumeration`	A Uniform Resource Indicator (URI)

Although we will only use a few of these in our examples, you can see that XML Schema provides a much more comprehensive set of data types than DTDs.

Start at the bottom

Complex data types, defined by the user, are also possible within schemas. These types consist of combinations of elements. For example, we can define a `Book` type as being made up of a `Title` element, a `Contents` element, and a `Copyright` element (realize that we have stopped using the namespace when referring to elements, as XML Schema sees only the element name, and later applies the namespace). These elements can in turn be user-defined types, made up of more elements. What results is a sort of hierarchical pyramid; at the base of this pyramid are elements with basic XML Schema data types. Built on this base are layers of user-defined types, until the root element is finally defined at the top of the pyramid.

Because of this structure, it is generally wise to start with the elements that comprise the base of the hierarchy; in other words, those elements that can be defined as standard XML Schema data types. This is a bit different than in DTDs, where the order of the elements within the XML document is typically followed, but it does result in an easier schema creation process. Looking at our XML document, we can determine which elements are "primitive" data types, shown in Table 4-5.

Table 4-5. "Primitive" Elements

Element Name	Type
`Title`	`string`
`Heading`	`string`
`Topic`	`string`

With these elements determined, we can add each to our schema (see Example 4-12). For clarity, the example schema we build will omit the XML declaration and `DOCTYPE` declaration; although these will be a part of the final schema, they are left out to avoid clutter until the end of our schema creation.

Example 4-12. XML Schema with "Primitive" Elements

```
<schema targetNamespace="http://www.oreilly.com/catalog/javaxml"
        xmlns="http://www.w3.org/1999/XMLSchema"
        xmlns:JavaXML="http://www.oreilly.com/catalog/javaxml"
>

  <element name="Title" type="string" />
  <element name="Heading" type="string" />
  <element name="Topic" type="string" />

</schema>
```

If adding those elements seemed a little too easy to believe, great! It *is* that easy. By defining these "base" or "primitive" elements, we can now go on to construct our more complex elements.

User-defined data types

Similar to the way we started with our most atomic elements, we want to begin constructing our more complex elements at the bottom of the hierarchical pyramid of our document. This almost always means starting with the most nested level of elements and working outwards until the root element is reached. The most deeply nested elements in our example are `Heading` and `Topic`. Since we have already specified these elements as primitives, we can move outward a level, reaching the `Chapter` element. This element will be our first user-defined element, and it should be specified as being made up of one `Heading` element and one or more `Topic` elements. The `complexType` element within XML Schema allows us to define complex data types:

```
<complexType name="[Name of Type">
  <[Element Specification]>
  <[Element Specification]>
  ...
</complexType>
```

By defining this name type, we can then assign the new type to our element. For our `Chapter` element, we can now create a `ChapterType` data type:

```
<complexType name="ChapterType">
  ...
</complexType>
```

This creates the type, and of course makes that type a part of our target namespace, `JavaXML`. So to assign the type to our `Chapter` element, we can use the following element specification:

```
<element name="Chapter" type="JavaXML:ChapterType" />
```

Now whatever element structure we specify within the `ChapterType` element type will determine the constraints on the `Chapter` element. Also notice that the type of element referred to is `JavaXML:ChapterType`, not simply `ChapterType`. When the type was created, it was created within the target namespace, `JavaXML`. But the elements we have been using within the schema (`element`, `complexType`, etc.) are not prefixed with a namespace, as they belong to the default namespace, which is the XML Schema namespace. So if we tried to specify the type as simply `ChapterType`, the parser would search the default namespace (that of XML Schema) for the type, not find the type, and raise an exception. To tell our parser where to find the type definition, we must give it the correct namespace, which in this case is `JavaXML`.

With the type body complete, we now need to fill in the details. For this element, we need to define within the schema the two elements that should be nested within this type. Because we have already specified the two elements that are nested (the `Heading` and `Topic` element primitives), we must refer to those element specifications from within our new type:

```
<complexType name="ChapterType">
  <element ref="JavaXML:Heading" />
  <element ref="JavaXML:Topic" />
</complexType>
```

The `ref` attribute tells the XML parser that the definition for the element named is in another part of the schema. As in the case of specifying a type, we must tell the parser which namespace the elements are specified within, which is usually the target namespace. However, this is a bit redundant and verbose. We define the two elements as primitives, and then refer to them, resulting in four lines within our schema. But these elements are not used anywhere else within our document, so wouldn't it be clearer if we could define the element within the type? This would avoid having to refer to the element, causing readers of your schema to have to scan through the rest of the schema to find an element that is only used here. In fact, this is exactly what you should do here. Element specifications can be nested within user-defined types, so we can refine our schema to be more self-documenting:

```
<element name="Title" type="string" />
<element name="Chapter" type="JavaXML:ChapterType" />

<complexType name="ChapterType">
  <element name="Heading" type="string" />
  <element name="Topic" type="string" />
</complexType>
```

In addition to removing needless lines of XML, we have removed extra references to the `JavaXML` namespace, which may help reduce confusion for newer XML authors when reading through your schema. With our new knowledge of user-defined types, we can define the rest of our XML documents' elements, as in Example 4-13.

Example 4-13. XML Schema with All Elements Defined

```
<schema targetNamespace="http://www.oreilly.com/catalog/javaxml"
        xmlns="http://www.w3.org/1999/XMLSchema"
        xmlns:JavaXML="http://www.oreilly.com/catalog/javaxml"
>

  <element name="Book" type="JavaXML:BookType" />

  <complexType name="BookType">
    <element name="Title" type="string" />
```

Example 4-13. XML Schema with All Elements Defined (continued)

```
    <element name="Contents" type="JavaXML:ContentsType" />
    <element name="Copyright" type="string" />
  </complexType>

  <complexType name="ContentsType">
    <element name="Chapter" type="JavaXML:ChapterType" />
    <element name="SectionBreak" type="string" />
  </complexType>

  <complexType name="ChapterType">
    <element name="Heading" type="string" />
    <element name="Topic" type="string" />
  </complexType>

</schema>
```

This neatly and cleanly results in every XML element used being defined, as well as having a very readable schema. However, there are still a few problems.

Implicit types and empty content

So far we have used only named types, often called explicit types. An *explicit type* is one in which a name is given to the type, and the element that uses the type is generally in a different section of the file. This is very object-oriented, as the same explicit type could be used as the type for several different elements. However, there may be times when this level of structure is not needed; in other words, a type is so specific to the element it is assigned to that naming the type is not at all useful. In our example, we could consolidate the definition of the `Chapter` element by defining its type within its element definition. This is done using an *implicit type*, sometimes called a *nameless type*:

```
<complexType name="ContentsType">
  <element name="Chapter">
    <complexType>
      <element name="Heading" type="string" />
      <element name="Topic" type="string" />
    </complexType>
  </element>
  <element name="SectionBreak" type="string" />
</complexType>
```

This implicit type allows even more "streamlining" of a schema. However, no other element can be of the same type as defined within an implicit type, unless another implicit type is defined. In other words, only use implicit types when you are positive that the type will never be needed by multiple elements.

In addition to using implicit types for user-defined data types, they can also be used to specify information about the elements they are defining. For example, we currently have defined the type of `SectionBreak` as a `string`. This isn't really accurate, as we want to make the element an empty element. We can define the content of the element as empty by using an implicit type:

```
<element name="SectionBreak">
  <complexType content="empty" />
</element>
```

This may seem a little strange; why can't we simply assign an "empty" data type to the element? Did the XML Schema authors leave this out? Actually, just the reverse; earlier versions of the XML Schema specification defined an `empty` data type, but it has since been removed. This is to require the definition of an element type. To see why, consider that most elements that are empty may have attributes that are used to specify data:

```
<img src="images/myGif.gif" />
<comment text="Here is a comment" />
```

In these cases, specifying the type as `empty` would not allow an intuitive way to define what attributes are allowed for the empty element. However, by using a type for the element, this can be defined:

```
<element name="img">
  <complexType content="empty">
    <attribute name="src" type="string" />
  </complexType>
</element>
```

We will talk more about how these attributes are defined in the next section. For now, though, you should see that using implicit types can help us design our schema more intuitively, as well as allow the definition of more element properties, such as an element being empty.

How many?

The last item left to specify in our elements is their recurrence (or lack thereof!). A schema behaves similarly to a DTD in that for an element specification with no modifiers, the element must appear exactly one time. This is not always the desired case, as we found out in DTDs. Our book may have many chapters, may have no section break, and might have some chapters with headings and some without. We need to be able to specify these details in our schema. Like DTDs, there is a mechanism to do this, but unlike DTDs, an intuitive set of attributes is provided to specify these details, instead of the more cryptic recurrence operators in DTDs (?, +, *). In XML Schema, the attributes minOccurs and maxOccurs are used within an element specification:

```
<element name="[Element Name]"
         type="[Element Type]"
         minOccurs="[Minimum times allowed to occur]"
         maxOccurs="[Maximum times allowed to occur]"
>
```

Both these attributes, when unspecified, default to the value "1", resulting in the single required element per definition already discussed. If a maximum finite value is not determined, a wildcard character can be used to indicate an occurrence an unlimited number of times. These constructs allow easy additions to our schema setting the recurrence constraints on our defined elements, as shown in Example 4-14.

Example 4-14. XML Schema Complete with Element Specifications

```
<schema targetNamespace="http://www.oreilly.com/catalog/javaxml"
        xmlns="http://www.w3.org/1999/XMLSchema"
        xmlns:JavaXML="http://www.oreilly.com/catalog/javaxml">

  <element name="Book" type="JavaXML:BookType" />

  <complexType name="BookType">
    <element name="Title" type="string" />
    <element name="Contents" type="JavaXML:ContentsType" />
    <element name="Copyright" type="string" />
  </complexType>

  <complexType name="ContentsType">
    <element name="Chapter" maxOccurs="*">
      <complexType>
        <element name="Heading" type="string" minOccurs="0" />
        <element name="Topic" type="string" maxOccurs="*" />
      </complexType>
    </element>
    <element name="SectionBreak" minOccurs="0" maxOccurs="*">
      <complexType content="empty" />
    </element>
  </complexType>

</schema>
```

Looking at this, we have defined a single root element, Book, of type BookType. This element has three immediate child elements: Title, Contents, and Copyright. Of these, two are primitive XML strings, and the third (Contents) is another user-defined type, ContentsType. This element type, in turn, has a child element `Chapter`, which can appear one or more times, and a child element `SectionBreak`, which doesn't have to appear at all. The `Chapter` element has two nested elements, `Heading` and `Topic`. Each is a primitive XML string, and while `Heading` can appear zero or one times, `Topic` can appear one or more times. The `SectionBreak` element can appear zero or more times, and is an empty element. Our schema now has all the elements specified and detailed; all that is left is to add the attributes to the schema.

Defining Attributes

The process of defining attributes is much simpler than that of specifying elements, primarily because many of the considerations within elements are not present when determining what attributes can be used for an element. By default, an attribute does not have to appear, and nesting concerns are not relevant, as attributes are not nested within other attributes. Although there are many advanced constructs that can be used to handle attribute constraints, we only look at some of the basic ones we need to constrain our XML document. The XML Schema specification should be consulted for the more advanced features that XML Schema offers in regards to attribute definitions.

What's left out

There are some important omissions when constraining attributes for an XML document; all of these relate to the various namespace definitions in the referring document. An XML document, as discussed, must make several namespace definitions to refer to a schema, plus those definitions that apply to its own content. These are all accomplished through the `xmlns:[Namespace]` attribute in the root document element. None of these attributes should be defined in a schema. Trying to define every allowed namespace would result in a very confusing schema. Additionally, the location of the namespace declaration does not have to be fixed; as long as the namespace is available to all elements within it, the declaration can be relocated. For these reasons, the XML Schema group allows the omission of all namespace attribute definitions within a schema.

If you remember our section on DTDs, this is quite a change. For our DTD, we had to make an attribute definition as follows to allow the namespace declarations we made in our XML document:

```
<!ATTLIST JavaXML:Book
      xmlns:JavaXML CDATA #REQUIRED
>
```

To use a DTD, we didn't have to do anything but specify the namespace in our XML document, as DTDs don't have any "knowledge" of XML namespaces. This is a bit more complicated in XML Schema.

If you remember from our introductory discussion, there are actually three different attributes that are used to specify a schema for a document. These are repeated here to refresh your memory:

```
<addressBook xmlns:xsi="http://www.w3.org/1999/XMLSchema/instance"
             xmlns="http://www.oreilly.com/catalog/javaxml"
             xsi:schemaLocation="http://www.oreilly.com/catalog/javaxml/
                                 mySchema.xsd"
>
```

If you were going to write a schema based on your knowledge of DTDs, you would probably get ready to declare that the `xmlns:xsi`, `xmlns`, and `xsi:schemaLocation` attributes are all legal attributes for this root element. However, these declarations can be omitted, as XML Schema is namespace-aware, and is "smart" enough to not require that such declarations be defined in the XML document being constrained.

The definition

The attribute definition is accomplished through XML Schema's `attribute` element (confusing, isn't it?). In other words, similar to the `element` element, XML Schema defines an `attribute` element by which to specify which attributes are allowed for the enclosing element or type definition. The format of these is:

```
<attribute name="[Name of attribute]"
           type="[Type of Attribute]"
           [Attribute Options]
>
```

This should look very similar to how elements are defined, and in fact is almost identical. The same data types are available for attributes as are for elements. This means we can very easily add the attribute definitions to our schema. For any element with a type defined, we add the needed attributes within the type definition. For elements that do not currently have a type defined, we must add one. This is to let our schema know that the attributes we are declaring "belong" to the enclosing element type. In these new element types, we can specify the content type with the `content` attribute of the `contentType` element, preserving the original constraints, and add the attribute definitions. These changes result in the schema shown in Example 4-15.

Example 4-15. XML Schema with Attribute Definitions

```
<schema targetNamespace="http://www.oreilly.com/catalog/javaxml"
        xmlns="http://www.w3.org/1999/XMLSchema"
        xmlns:JavaXML="http://www.oreilly.com/catalog/javaxml">

  <element name="Book" type="JavaXML:BookType" />
```

Example 4-15. XML Schema with Attribute Definitions (continued)

```
  <complexType name="BookType">
    <element name="Title" type="string" />
    <element name="Contents" type="JavaXML:ContentsType" />
    <element name="Copyright" type="string" />
  </complexType>

  <complexType name="ContentsType">
    <element name="Chapter" maxOccurs="*">
      <complexType>
        <element name="Heading" type="string" minOccurs="0" />
        <element name="Topic" maxOccurs="*">
          <complexType content="string">
            <attribute name="subSections" type="integer" />
          </complexType>
        </element>
        <attribute name="focus" type="string" />
      </complexType>
    </element>
    <element name="SectionBreak" minOccurs="0" maxOccurs="*">
      <complexType content="empty" />
    </element>
  </complexType>

</schema>
```

You can see in the `Topic` element that we must create a type for the purpose of defining the `subSections` attribute. Within this type, we use the `content` attribute to require that the element's content be of type `integer`. This is the same functionality we used earlier to assign `SectionBreak` a type of `empty` to ensure it remained an empty element. The other attributes added required less modification, as types already existed for these more complex elements.

Required attributes, default values, and enumerations

All that is left to complete our schema is a set of odds and ends in our attribute definitions. Remember that we used the keywords `#IMPLIED`, `#FIXED`, and `#REQUIRED` to specify if attributes had to appear and whether they were assigned default values if not included in an XML document. As in the case of the recurrence operators on elements, XML Schema has refined how these constraints are notated, making them clearer. For requiring an attribute, the same `minOccurs` attribute used for element specifications can be used, and assigning a value of "1" effectively makes an attribute mandatory. In our example, if we wanted to ensure that an attribute called `section` is required for the `Chapter` element, we could add a line as follows:

```
<attribute name="section" type="string" minOccurs="1" />
```

Although we mentioned that the default for elements was for any defined element to occur a single time (minOccurs would default to 1), attributes are not required, and minOccurs defaults to 0 when defining an attribute.

The notion of a fixed value for attributes (#FIXED) is not employed in XML Schema; as we discussed earlier, it is not used commonly and is not an intuitive construct. However, specifying a default value for an attribute is a useful construct, and is handled quite simply by the default attribute of an attribute definition. For example, we determined that the default value for the focus attribute of the Chapter element should be "Java":

```
<attribute name="focus" type="string" default="Java" />
```

Hopefully, you are starting to love the simplicity and elegance of XML Schema! The intuitive choices of element and attribute names go a long way towards making XML significantly easier to constrain than with the mechanism that DTDs provided. To demonstrate this even further, let's look at the final option we want to use: enumerations.

For our focus attribute, we had used our DTD to specify that only the values Java and XML were allowed. Using parenthetical notation and the OR operator, we handled this like so:

```
<!ATTLIST JavaXML:Chapter
      focus (XML|Java) "Java"
>
```

While this isn't necessarily difficult, it is also not necessarily intuitive. The values allowed are not even in quotation marks, which is the *de facto* standard for representing data values. XML Schema, while requiring more lines of schema to achieve the same effect, makes this type of constraint much easier to follow. The attribute definition is opened up, and a simpleType element is used. This element allows an existing data type, such as string, to be narrowed in the values that it can take on. In this case, we want to include the two allowed enumerative values that the attribute can take on. Each of these values is specified with the enumeration element. We specify the base type of this element with the base keyword. Using all this information in concert, we can change our attribute definition for the focus attribute:

```
<attribute name="focus" default="Java">
  <simpleType base="string">
    <enumeration value="XML" />
    <enumeration value="Java" />
  </simpleType>
</attribute>
```

Again, this is quite a bit more verbose than our DTD for the same resulting constraint, but significantly easier to understand and grasp, particularly for newer users of XML. With this change, we have now completed our schema, and set forth all the constraints of our earlier DTD, all in much more readable form (see Example 4-16).

Example 4-16. Completed XML Schema

```
<?xml version="1.0"?>

<schema targetNamespace="http://www.oreilly.com/catalog/javaxml"
        xmlns="http://www.w3.org/1999/XMLSchema"
        xmlns:JavaXML="http://www.oreilly.com/catalog/javaxml">

  <element name="Book" type="JavaXML:BookType" />

  <complexType name="BookType">
    <element name="Title" type="string" />
    <element name="Contents" type="JavaXML:ContentsType" />
    <element name="Copyright" type="string" />
  </complexType>

  <complexType name="ContentsType">
    <element name="Chapter" maxOccurs="*">
      <complexType>
        <element name="Heading" type="string" minOccurs="0" />
        <element name="Topic" maxOccurs="*">
          <complexType content="string">
            <attribute name="subSections" type="integer" />
          </complexType>
        </element>
        <attribute name="focus" default="Java">
          <simpleType base="string">
            <enumeration value="XML" />
            <enumeration value="Java" />
          </simpleType>
        </attribute>
      </complexType>
    </element>
    <element name="SectionBreak" minOccurs="0" maxOccurs="*">
      <complexType content="empty" />
    </element>
  </complexType>

</schema>
```

What's Next?

We have now looked at two ways to constrain our XML documents: the "old" way, by using DTDs, and the "new" way, using XML Schema. Hopefully, you also are beginning to see the importance of document constraints, particularly with regard to applications. If an application does not understand the type of information that an XML document should contain, manipulating and understanding the document's data becomes a much more difficult task. In the next chapter, we extend our knowledge of the SAX Java classes by looking at the facilities for accessing DTDs and schemas within our Java program. We will add to the parser the example program we built in Chapter 3, allowing the program to read through document constraints and report errors if the XML documents read are not valid, as well as examining the callbacks available within the validation process.

In this chapter:

- *Configuring the Parser*
- *Output of XML Validation*
- *The DTDHandler Interface*
- *"Gotcha!"*
- *What's Next?*

5

Validating XML

Your knowledge base and accompanying bag of XML tricks should be starting to feel a little more solid by now. You can create XML, use the Java SAX classes to parse through that XML, and now constrain that XML. This leads us to the next logical step: validating XML with Java. Without the ability to validate XML, business-to-business and inter-application communication becomes significantly more difficult; while constraints enable portability of our data, validity ensures its consistency. In other words, being able to constrain a document doesn't help much if we can't ensure that those constraints are enforced within our XML applications.

In this chapter, we will look at using additional SAX classes and interfaces to enforce validity constraints in our XML documents. We will examine how to set features and properties of a SAX-compliant parser, allowing easy configuration of validation, namespace handling, and other parser functionality. In addition, the errors and warnings that can occur with validating parsers will be detailed, filling in the blanks from earlier discussions on the SAX error handlers.

Configuring the Parser

With the wealth of XML-related specifications and technologies emerging from the World Wide Web Consortium (W3C), adding support for any new feature or property of an XML parser has become difficult. Many parser implementations have added proprietary extensions or methods at the cost of the portability of the code. While these software packages may implement the SAX `XMLReader` interface, the methods for setting document and schema validation, namespace support, and other core features are not standard across parser implementations. To address this, SAX 2.0 defines a standard mechanism for setting important properties and features of a parser that allows the addition of new properties and features as they are accepted by the W3C without the use of proprietary extensions or methods.

Setting Properties and Features

Lucky for us, SAX 2.0 includes the methods needed for setting properties and features in the `XMLReader` interface. This means we have to change little of our existing code to request validation, set the namespace separator, and handle other feature and property requests. The methods used for these purposes are outlined in Table 5-1.

Table 5-1. Property and Feature Methods

Method	Returns	Parameters	Syntax
`setProperty()`	`void`	`String propertyID, Object value`	`parser.setProperty( "[Property URI]", "[Object parameter]");`
`setFeature()`	`void`	`String featureID, boolean state`	`parser.setFeature( "[Feature URI]", true);`
`getProperty()`	`Object`	`String propertyID`	`String separator = (String)parser.getProperty( "[Property URI]");`
`getFeature()`	`boolean`	`String featureID`	`if (parser.getFeature( "[Feature URI]")) { doSomething(); }`

For each of these, the ID of a specific property or feature is a URI. The core set of features and properties is listed in Appendix B, *SAX 2.0 Features and Properties*. Additional documentation on features and properties supported by your vendor's XML parser should also be available. Keep in mind, though, that these URIs are similar to namespace URIs; they are only used as associations for particular features. Good parsers ensure that you do not need network access to resolve these features; in this sense, you can think of them as simple constants that happen to be in URI form. These methods are simply invoked and the URI is de-referenced locally, often to a constant representing what action in the parser needs to be taken.

In the parser configuration context, a *property* requires some arbitrary object to be usable. For example, for lexical handling, a `LexicalHandler` implementation class might be supplied as the value for the property. In contrast, a *feature* is a flag used by the parser to indicate whether a certain type of processing should occur. Common features are validation, namespace support, and including external parameter entities.

The most convenient aspect of these methods is that they allow simple addition and modification of features. Although new or updated features will require a parser implementation to add supporting code, the method by which features and properties are accessed remains standard, as well as simple; only a new URI need be defined. Regardless of the complexity (or obscurity) of new XML-related ideas, this robust set of four methods should be sufficient to allow parsers to implement the new ideas.

Turning on Validation

So far, we have talked about how to set features and properties, but not about those functionalities themselves. In this chapter, we are most concerned with ensuring document validation during parsing. To illustrate the importance of these methods, a little history lesson is in order. In SAX 1.0, parser implementations had to provide their own (proprietary) solutions to handle parsing with validation and parsing without. Without the ability to turn validation on or off through a standard mechanism, it was easier to provide two independent parsing classes in order to remain standard in their use. For example, to use the early versions of Sun's Project X parser without validation, the code fragment in Example 5-1 would be employed.

Example 5-1. Using a Non-Validating Parser with SAX 1.0

```
try {
    // Register a parser with SAX
    Parser parser =
        ParserFactory.makeParser(
            "com.sun.xml.parser.Parser");

    // Parse the document
    parser.parse(uri);

} catch (Exception e) {
    e.printStackTrace();
}
```

Because no standard mechanism existed for requesting validation, a different class had to be loaded; this new class is an almost identical implementation of the SAX 1.0 `Parser` interface that performs validation. The code employed to use this parser is almost identical (see Example 5-2), with the exception of the class loaded for parsing.

Example 5-2. Using a Validating Parser with SAX 1.0

```
try {
    // Register a parser with SAX - use the validating parser
            Parser parser =
                ParserFactory.makeParser(
                    "com.sun.xml.parser.ValidatingParser");
```

Example 5-2. Using a Validating Parser with SAX 1.0 (continued)

```
    // Parse the document
    parser.parse(uri);

} catch (Exception e) {
    e.printStackTrace();
}
```

In addition to having to change and recompile source code when validation is turned on or off, this presents a little-realized problem in rolling out production-ready code that parses XML. A standard development environment will use code that validates all application-produced XML. This validation, although costly for performance, can ensure that the application is always producing correct XML documents, or that correct XML documents are always being received as input for the application's components. Often, these validation constraints, once thoroughly tested, can be removed, resulting in a significant performance yield in production. It is possible in this situation to remove validation from the parser's behavior because thorough testing has confirmed correct XML in development, but this change forces a source code modification and recompilation. Although this may sound fairly trivial, many companies do not allow code to go into production that has not run *unchanged* for a set length of time, often days if not weeks. This minor change to turn off validation can result in additional testing cycles, which are often redundant, and a lengthier time to market for applications.

A common argument here is that the name of the parser class to be used can be loaded from a properties file (we talked about this in Chapter 2, *Creating XML*, regarding XML application portability). However, consider the significance of changing a complete parser implementation class just before going into production. This is not a minor change, and should be tested thoroughly. When compared to changing the value of a feature set (supposing that the value to set the SAX validation feature is kept in a similar properties file), it is easy to determine which solution is preferred.

For all these reasons, SAX 2.0 added the methods we have been discussing to the `XMLReader` interface. With these methods, we can enable validation by using the URI specific to setting validation: *http://xml.org/sax/features/validation.* We could also request parsing of external entities and namespace processing, but for now we will simply add the validation feature to our parser shown in Example 5-3.

Example 5-3. Turning On Validation

```
// Get instances of our handlers
ContentHandler contentHandler = new MyContentHandler();
ErrorHandler errHandler = new ErrHandler();
```

Example 5-3. Turning On Validation (continued)

```
try {
    // Instantiate a parser
    XMLReader parser =
        XMLReaderFactory.createXMLReader(
            "org.apache.xerces.parsers.SAXParser");

    // Register the content handler
    parser.setContentHandler(contentHandler);

    // Register the error handler
    parser.setErrorHandler(errHandler);

    parser.setFeature("http://xml.org/sax/features/validation", true);

    // Parse the document
    parser.parse(uri);

} catch (IOException e) {
    System.out.println("Error reading URI: " + e.getMessage());
} catch (SAXException e) {
    System.out.println("Error in parsing: " + e.getMessage());
}
```

With these straightforward changes, we are now ready to modify our sample XML file to again include the DTD reference and entity reference (which we commented out in an earlier chapter):

```
<?xml version="1.0"?>

<!-- We don't need these yet
  <?xml-stylesheet href="XSL\JavaXML.html.xsl" type="text/xsl"?>
  <?xml-stylesheet href="XSL\JavaXML.wml.xsl" type="text/xsl"
                   media="wap"?>
  <?cocoon-process type="xslt"?>
-->

<!DOCTYPE JavaXML:Book SYSTEM "DTD\JavaXML.dtd">

<!-- Java and XML -->
<JavaXML:Book xmlns:JavaXML="http://www.oreilly.com/catalog/javaxml/">
 <JavaXML:Title>Java and XML</JavaXML:Title>
 <JavaXML:Contents>
...
<!-- Uncomment the entity reference as well -->
<JavaXML:Copyright>&OReillyCopyright;</JavaXML:Copyright>
```

Make sure you have the DTD we created in the last chapter in the directory specified here. Before running the example, you need to make sure you are connected to the Internet; remember that in validation, any entity references you make are attempted to be resolved. In our example file, we have such an entity reference: `OReillyCopyright`. In our DTD, we referenced the URI *http://www.oreilly.com/catalog/javaxml/docs/copyright.xml.* When validation takes place, if this URI is not available, validation errors will occur. If you do not have Internet access, or do not want to use that access, you can replace the reference with a local file reference. For example, you may create a one-line text file like Example 5-4.

Example 5-4. Local Copyright File

```
This is a sample shared copyright file.
```

Save this file in a directory that is accessible by the parser program, and replace the DTD entity declaration with the path to this new file:

```
<!ENTITY OReillyCopyright SYSTEM
         "entities/copyright.txt">
```

In this example, the text file should be saved as *copyright.txt* in a subdirectory named *entities/*. With this change, you are ready to run the sample program on the example XML file.

Output of XML Validation

Make sure your XML document, DTD, copyright file (if you created one), and compiled classes are assembled. You may then run the example program, and you might be surprised at the output (shown in Example 5-5).

Example 5-5. SAXParserDemo Output

```
D:\prod\JavaXML> java SAXParserDemo D:\prod\JavaXML\contents\contents.xml
Parsing XML File: D:\prod\JavaXML\contents\contents.xml


    * setDocumentLocator() called
Parsing begins...
**Parsing Error**
  Line:     13
  URI:      file:/D:/prod/JavaXML/contents/contents.xml
  Message: Document root element "JavaXML:Book", must match DOCTYPE root
           "JavaXML:Book".
```

This rather cryptic error is a significant problem when using DTDs and namespaces together. The error seems to be stating that the root specified in the `DOCTYPE` declaration (`JavaXML:Book`) does not match the root element of the document itself. But the root element is `JavaXML:Book`, right? Actually, it's not! By default, SAX 2.0 specifies that parsers must enable their namespace feature, making all SAX 2.0 parsers namespace-aware unless this feature is explicitly set to false.* We did not change this default, so our `XMLReader` implementation is namespace aware. The unexpected result of this is that our root element is seen (by the parser) as `Book`, with the namespace prefix of `JavaXML`. But remember that XML 1.0 and DTDs cannot distinguish between a prefix and element name, so the root element the DTD expects to find is `JavaXML:Book`. When it finds `Book`, it reports the error above.

The only way to get around this rather annoying "feature" of SAX is to turn off namespace awareness on documents that are being validated by DTDs. Add in the following code to your `SAXParserDemo` source file:

```
try {
    // Instantiate a parser
    XMLReader parser =
        XMLReaderFactory.createXMLReader(
            "org.apache.xerces.parsers.SAXParser");

    // Register the content handler
    parser.setContentHandler(contentHandler);

    // Register the error handler
    parser.setErrorHandler(errorHandler);

    // Turn on validation
    parser.setFeature("http://xml.org/sax/features/validation",
                      true);

    // Turn off namespace awareness
    parser.setFeature("http://xml.org/sax/features/namespaces",
                      false);

    // Parse the document
    parser.parse(uri);

} catch (IOException e) {
    System.out.println("Error reading URI: " + e.getMessage());
} catch (SAXException e) {
    System.out.println("Error in parsing: " + e.getMessage());
}
```

With this change, all elements names are treated as containing both the namespace prefix and the local name of the element. We will get back to dealing

* Namespace support being on by default was the SAX requirement as of the time of this writing; however, several groups within the XML community, such as the Apache Xerces development team, are campaigning to have this feature off by default. If you do not receive the results shown here, it is possible that the default for this feature has been changed in a revision of SAX.

with allowing namespaces to be used later in the chapter. For now, re-run the program with the changes compiled in, and you should get the output shown in Example 5-6.

Example 5-6. SAXParserDemo Output with Namespaces Disabled

```
D:\prod\JavaXML> java SAXParserDemo D:\prod\JavaXML\contents\contents.xml
Parsing XML File: D:\prod\JavaXML\contents\contents.xml


    * setDocumentLocator() called
Parsing begins...
startElement:  has no associated namespace
  Attribute: xmlns:JavaXML=http://www.oreilly.com/catalog/javaxml/
ignorableWhitespace: [
 ]
startElement:  has no associated namespace
characters: Java and XML
endElement: JavaXML:Title
...
```

You may find this almost disappointing. It doesn't look any different than our output from the non-validating parser in Chapter 3, *Parsing XML*! This is because our XML document is both well-formed and valid; there is nothing for the validating parser to report. This is important to realize: behavior of a validating parser on a valid document is almost identical to behavior of a non-validating parser on the same document. If this seems strange, remember that all validation seeks to achieve is to ensure that a document doesn't break any of a set of predefined rules. If all those rules are followed, the application should use the XML data as intended. It is only when rules are broken that a validating parser must perform extra behavior; these cases, which do produce different output than the non-validating parser, will be examined next.

Before looking at these errors, though, there is one difference in our output. Remember that previously, all of the whitespace between elements in our XML document was reported through the `characters()` callback method in our `ContentHandler` implementation. In a non-validated XML document, the XML parser has the option to report this whitespace through either that callback or the `ignorableWhitespace()` callback. We discussed that this is because the parser cannot safely make assumptions about the purpose of the whitespace between elements without a DTD to constrain the XML document. When running our parser example with validation, we instead see that all of the whitespace is reported through the `ignorableWhitespace()` method. With validation occurring, any whitespace is ignored and treated as if it were not present unless explicitly outlined in the DTD for the document. This allows the parser to determine if the content of XML elements conforms to the DTD without having to worry about whitespace surrounding the element contents. In other words, the parser is free to treat the following XML fragment:

```
<document>
  <element1>
    <element2>Hello!</element2>
  </element1>
</document>
```

identically to this fragment:

```
<document><element1><element2>Hello!</element2></element1></document>
```

While this second fragment is certainly less pleasing to the human eye, it follows the same constraints as the first document, and should be treated identically when validation is occurring. The lack of indentation should not affect the application using this XML data. If the whitespace used for indenting in the first document were reported through the `characters()` callback, it could seem to an application monitoring that callback method that the documents were *not* the same.

Warnings

There are almost no warnings that can arise as a result of validation being requested. All XML being validated that does not conform to the referenced DTD is considered to be in error. Invalidity in XML documents was considered by the W3C to be important enough to always warrant the generation of an error. For this reason it is difficult, particularly using a SAX 2.0 parser, to generate a warning. However, there are SAX 1.0 parsers that will generate a warning. For example, Sun's Project X parser package currently includes a class for validating XML documents while parsing, as well as a non-validating parser implementation. This should sound familiar, as we discussed this scenario earlier, in "Setting Properties and Features." If the validating parser is used on an XML document that does not explicitly declare a DTD, a warning will be generated. Because this is a specific issue with some SAX 1.0 parser implementations, we will not detail the code needed to generate such a warning. However, the output would look similar to the warnings we looked at in Chapter 3, and is shown here in Example 5-7.

Example 5-7. SAXParserDemo Output Issuing a Warning

```
D:\prod\JavaXML> java SAXParserDemo D:\prod\JavaXML\contents\contents.xml
Parsing XML File: D:\prod\JavaXML\contents\contents.xml


    * setDocumentLocator() called
Parsing begins...
**Parsing Warning**
  Line:    6
```

Example 5-7. SAXParserDemo Output Issuing a Warning (continued)

```
  URI:      file:/D:/prod/JavaXML/contents/contents.xml
  Message: Valid documents must have a <!DOCTYPE declaration.
```

This would occur if the <!DOCTYPE> construct was commented out or omitted in an XML document being parsed. As almost all XML parsers, including Sun's Project X parser, are moving to a SAX 2.0–compliant implementation, this is most likely a warning you will never encounter.

Non-Fatal Errors

The most common SAX problem you will receive when validating XML is a non-fatal error. This is generated any time that XML constraints are violated. To demonstrate this type of error, make the following change in your sample XML document, making it invalid:

```
<?xml version="1.0"?>

<!-- We don't need these yet
  <?xml-stylesheet href="XSL\JavaXML.html.xsl" type="text/xsl"?>
  <?xml-stylesheet href="XSL\JavaXML.wml.xsl" type="text/xsl"
                   media="wap"?>
  <?cocoon-process type="xslt"?>
-->

<!DOCTYPE JavaXML:Book SYSTEM "DTD\JavaXML.dtd">

<!-- Java and XML -->
<JavaXML:Book xmlns:JavaXML="http://www.oreilly.com/catalog/javaxml/"
              publicationDate="June 2000">
 <JavaXML:Title>Java and XML</JavaXML:Title>
 <JavaXML:Contents>
```

This change, while certainly legal and keeping the XML document well-formed, is not valid. Because no `publicationDate` attribute was declared in our DTD, an error will be generated on the parsing of this XML, shown in Example 5-8.

Example 5-8. SAXParserDemo Output Issuing an Error

```
D:\prod\JavaXML> java SAXParserDemo D:\prod\JavaXML\contents\contents.xml
Parsing XML File: D:\prod\JavaXML\contents\contents.xml


    * setDocumentLocator() called
Parsing begins...
**Parsing Error**
  Line:     10
  URI:      file:/D:/prod/JavaXML/contents/contents.xml
```

Example 5-8. SAXParserDemo Output Issuing an Error (continued)

```
Message: Attribute "publicationDate" must be declared for element type
        "JavaXML:Book".
```

Our parser sends the error to our `ErrorHandler` implementation, which reports the error, in this case an attribute that is not declared for the enclosing element being used. Certainly there are a variety of ways to manage to make our XML document invalid, and this is just one; however, all generate the same error, so experimentation with these errors will be left to you. Simply be aware that any violation of a DTD's constraints generates a non-fatal error, regardless of the type of violation. This includes element content being incorrect, illegal element nestings, attributes being misplaced or misused, and the variety of other well-formed but invalid conditions that can be created within an XML document.

Fatal Errors

What may come as a surprise is that a document that violates its DTD's constraints will never generate a fatal error. There are no conditions that arise in parsing invalid XML that would result in the parsing process stopping. While it may seem that continuing to parse an invalid document defeats the purpose of validation, realize that most of the time XML is application generated. In other words, the application receives XML input from another program or subprogram. If this input is invalid for some reason, the application attempting to use it should report an error to the application client rather than stop document processing. In fact, many times parsing must continue to allow a graceful exit of the process, in turn allowing the application to accurately report what errors occurred. While documents that are not well-formed will cause parsing to halt, invalid documents typically indicate either an error condition that can be corrected or one that the client should know about, such as invalid input. Consider the difficulty of writing an XML editor or IDE if every time you made a mistake in meeting your DTD's constraints, the editor crashed with a fatal error, or refused to parse your document long enough to let you know what mistake was made; in fact, some editors may attempt to correct validity errors for you! For these reasons, invalid documents cause warnings and errors, but never fatal errors.

The only fatal error you can encounter when using DTDs that you cannot receive in non-validated documents is a syntax error within the referenced DTD. This shouldn't surprise you, as syntax errors in an XML document also generate fatal errors. The same reasoning is used; it is impossible to continue parsing or validation if the constraints cannot be determined, which is the case when the syntax of the DTD is incorrect. You should be sure to realize this is not quite the same as the error generated when XML is not well-formed; the primary difference is that a DTD is never said to be well-formed because it is not true XML. However, the result of syntax errors in the DTD is the same as the result of parsing XML that is not well-formed.

The DTDHandler Interface

The last core document handler that SAX provides registers callback methods during the process of reading and parsing an XML document's DTD. This interface does *not* define events that take place during the process of validation, but only those that occur during the process of reading the DTD. In fact, in our section on "gotchas" we will look at some of the confusion this distinction often causes. This handler behaves in the same manner as the `ContentHandler` and `ErrorHandler` interfaces that we looked at in Chapter 3, defining two callback methods that occur during the parsing process.

As important as XML document validation is, the events involved with reading the DTD document are not very significant. With only two callback methods, and both of those not commonly used, you will probably not find many uses for the `DTDHandler` interface unless you are writing an XML editor or IDE and need to build or process DTD documents for correct syntax and notation. We will look at the two callback methods provided by SAX here, but will not spend much time on their use, as they are not significant in our use of XML for non-editor type applications. For information on an optional SAX handler that can help in reading further DTD information, refer to the `DeclHandler` interface in Appendix A, *API Reference*, under the `org.xml.sax.ext` package.

Unparsed Entity Declarations

The first callback method, `unparsedEntityDecl()`, is invoked when a DTD has an entity declaration signifying that the XML parser should not parse a particular entity. Though we have not looked at an example of this, unparsed entities are common in XML documents that reference images or other binary data, such as media files. This method takes in the name of the entity, the public and system IDs, and the *notation name* of the entity. Notation names are another XML term we have not yet looked at. Consider the example of an XML document fragment that refers to an image, possibly representing a logo, shown in Example 5-9.

Example 5-9. An XML Document with an Unparsed Entity

```
<document>
  <myLogo>&CompanyLogo;</myLogo>
</document>
```

When processing XML, the parser attempts to resolve all entity references and insert the parsed value of the reference into the document. However, an XML parser is not equipped to parse an image, and should leave the binary data unparsed. The parser can be instructed to do this in a document type definition:

```
<!ENTITY CompanyLogo SYSTEM "images/logo.gif" NDATA gif>
```

The NDATA keyword here instructs XML parsers not to parse the entity reference. Were this DTD to be processed with a registered DTDHandler implementation, the information in the entity declaration would be passed to the callback. Another key point here is that the callback occurs when the entity declaration is made in the DTD, not when it is parsed in the XML document. This means that even if the entity is not in the XML document, the callback would occur. This should make sense, as this callback is part of the DTDHandler interface, not the ContentHandler interface.

Notation Declarations

Notation declarations are always associated with one or more unparsed entity declarations, and are the subject of the second DTDHandler callback method. The final portion of the unparsed entity declaration seen above was the word "gif". This word specifies the type of the unparsed entity, and must refer to a type defined elsewhere in the DTD through the NOTATION construct. This specifies to the XML parser a URI reference for the type, often a public reference for common binary data types. This, in fact, is very similar to referencing a DTD in an XML document, as it associates a specific type of data (in this example, GIF images) with a public identifier or URI. The pairing of the NOTATION definition and unparsed entity declaration results in an XML parser leaving binary data untouched and unparsed, which is the desired behavior:

```
<!NOTATION gif SYSTEM "http://www.gif.com">
```

Occurrences of these declarations are reported to a registered handler through the notationDecl() callback method. This method, when invoked, receives the name of the notation declaration, the system identifier, and any public identifier that is present. As with unparsed entity declarations, this is a callback invoked upon reading the DTD, not the actual XML document.

Registering the Handler

Registering our DTDHandler implementation with our XML parser is no different than the procedure used for registering our error and document handlers. An instantiation of our implementation class can be passed to the setDTDHandler() method, and the parser will register SAX callback events with the class:

```
import java.io.IOException;


import org.xml.sax.Attributes;
```

```
import org.xml.sax.ContentHandler;
import org.xml.sax.DTDHandler;
import org.xml.sax.ErrorHandler;
import org.xml.sax.Locator;
import org.xml.sax.SAXException;
import org.xml.sax.SAXParseException;
import org.xml.sax.XMLReader;
import org.xml.sax.helpers.XMLReaderFactory;
...
        // Get instances of our handlers
        ContentHandler contentHandler = new MyContentHandler();
        ErrorHandler errHandler = new ErrHandler();
        DTDHandler dtdHandler = new MyDTDHandler();

        try {
            // Instantiate a parser
            XMLReader parser =
                XMLReaderFactory.createXMLReader(
                    "org.apache.xerces.parsers.SAXParser");

            // Register the content handler
            parser.setContentHandler(contentHandler);

            // Register the error handler
            parser.setErrorHandler(errorHandler);

            // Register the DTD handler
            parser.setDTDHandler(dtdHandler);

            // Turn on validation
            parser.setFeature("http://xml.org/sax/features/validation",
                              true);

            // Turn off namespace awareness
            parser.setFeature("http://xml.org/sax/features/namespaces",
                              false);

            // Parse the document
            parser.parse(uri);

        } catch (IOException e) {
            System.out.println("Error reading URI: " + e.getMessage());
        } catch (SAXException e) {
            System.out.println("Error in parsing: " + e.getMessage());
        }
```

The Rest of the Story . . .

It may seem we have skimmed over the handler interface for DTDs, particularly as compared to our treatment of our other handlers. However, applications that use XML rarely need to register this type of handler. While validation is often used in XML-aware systems, details of unparsed entity declarations rarely are relevant at higher levels of XML use. For this reason, we will move on to details that are more relevant to our goal of writing XML-aware applications.

You might expect to read a section on XML Schema validation next; however, schemas are increasingly being used not just for validation, but for pure data representation as well. For this reason we will save a complete discussion of handling schemas in Java for Chapter 14, *XML Schema*, and wait until we have seen both XSL and some more realistic uses of XML in applications before doing so. The SAX interfaces for handling a schema are much more robust than those for a `DTDHandler` and will require additional knowledge of XML to master. For now, we will complete our discussion of validating XML data with a look at the common problems you may encounter trying to use validation within your XML-aware applications.

"Gotcha!"

To continue with the theme of trying to provide some cautionary advice on your path to XML mastery, some additional pitfalls associated with XML validation are included here. These are often problems run into by newer XML developers, as the solutions are not immediately apparent. Take heed of them, as they have caused many a developer long hours of tedious debugging, or simple confusion at unexpected application output.

Handling Validation and Handling DTDs

One of the most common misunderstandings about using SAX for validation is thinking that validating an XML document is contingent upon registering a SAX `DTDHandler` implementation with the XML parser. Often, time and effort are spent to implement the `DTDHandler` interface and register it with the parser, and time is not spent setting the validation feature of the parser. This mistake arises from a mistaken association between handling a DTD and actually using the DTD for validation. In this case, the DTD would be parsed, and all DTD callback events would occur (if any were needed). However, the XML document itself would not be validated, but simply parsed. Keep in mind that the output from parsing a valid XML document looks almost identical to output from a non-validated XML document; always be aware when validation is occurring to avoid application bugs:

```
try {
    // Instantiate a parser
```

```
        XMLReader parser =
            XMLReaderFactory.createXMLReader(
                "org.apache.xerces.parsers.SAXParser");

        // Register the content handler
        parser.setContentHandler(contentHandler);

        // Register the error handler
        parser.setErrorHandler(errorHandler);

        // This has no effect on turning on validation!
        parser.setDTDHandler(dtdHandler);

        // Turn on validation
        parser.setFeature("http://xml.org/sax/features/validation", true);

        // Turn off namespace awareness
        parser.setFeature("http://xml.org/sax/features/namespaces", false);

        // Parse the document
        parser.parse(uri);

    } catch (IOException e) {
        System.out.println("Error reading URI: " + e.getMessage());
    } catch (SAXException e) {
        System.out.println("Error in parsing: " + e.getMessage());
    }
```

Be sure to realize that registering a DTD has nothing to do with the process of validation; a parser with a `DTDHandler` implementation registered does not always validate XML, and a parser without a registered handler may validate XML. It is the features (for SAX 2.0 implementations) or class (for pre–SAX 2.0 implementations) of the XML parser that determines if validation occurs, rather than the handler that is registered with it. Keep this in mind, as a `DTDHandler` implementation is not needed for validating XML, while setting a property or using a different parser class is.

Validate in Development, Cruise in Production

It is important to emphasize the value of knowing when to use validation and when not to. One of the biggest "gotchas" in using validation is to be surprised when your application seems sluggish in production, and you can't seem to determine why. The "gotcha" here is leaving validation on in a production environment. Typically, validation is part of testing; run an application numerous times through development and testing or quality assurance (QA) until you are confident of its results. If part of this application is the generation or modification of XML, validation of the resultant XML should be included as part of that testing.

However, this validation is costly, as the parser must process significantly more data and make many more decisions to validate a document.

Once you are assured of the output of your application, it is usually safe to turn off validation in the production environment. This results in a significant speed increase in most applications, and if testing was done properly, should not affect the application in any way. The only time disabling validation for production is not a good rule of thumb is when the application client is taking an active part in XML creation, as in an XML IDE or GUI tool, or when receiving XML from other applications, such as in e-business scenarios. Both of these are exceptions because the XML used as input, from a user or application, is outside of your control and may not be valid. In these cases, certainly validation is required, and even expected by the application client. In most situations, though, let your production application cruise without the heavyweight validation occurring.

What's Next?

By now you should feel very comfortable with XML documents and how to constrain those documents. We have also looked at all of the major aspects of using the SAX interfaces and classes, and you should have a solid understanding of the parsing and validating lifecycle, as well as what document callbacks are available. You should be able to easily configure and use an XML parser, as well as register the various types of SAX handlers with that parser. In the next chapter, we add to our specifications by taking a look at XSL, the Extensible Stylesheet Language. This will begin the transition from looking at XML data to looking at XML applications. Our discussions of XSL and XSL transformations will set the stage for a look at the Document Object Model and publishing engines, as well as more in-depth application programming throughout the rest of the book.

6

In this chapter:
- *The Purpose*
- *The Components*
- *The Syntax*
- *What's Next?*

Transforming XML

If you are a backend systems developer or a systems architect, you should be seeing the value of XML by now. A language that represents data in a vendor-neutral way, that is easy to parse, that is portable, and that you can use from Java? Could this be the data format that solves so many of your interoperability issues? It just might be. However, if you are a content developer, an application assembler, or are involved with application presentation, you may be a little confused. Certainly you have heard a lot about the promise of XML for generating content for various types of clients, and how it provides a separation of presentation and data. Yet we have been through five chapters without a word about how this is accomplished. You might be wondering if this technology is really right for you. In either case, read on, because XML's capabilities are just beginning to be showcased.

In this chapter, we begin the process of tackling XML transformations. This is a rather lengthy topic, and we begin in this chapter by discussing why XML transformations are important, the components involved, and the syntax used to accomplish transformations. The next chapter continues our discussion by looking at how Java XSLT processors can take an XML document and generate various types of content, often wildly different, from the same initial XML data, and how the Document Object Model (DOM) is used in this process. Throughout, we will continue to focus on the value of XML transformations to you, the application developer. Because XML transformations are such a large subject, we will not touch on every syntactical construct or possible use. For a short reference on transformations, you should pick up the *XML Pocket Reference*, by Robert Eckstein (O'Reilly & Associates). There is also an entire section of the World Wide Web Consortium's web site devoted to XML transformations, which can be accessed online at *http://www.w3.org/Style/XSL/*. These resources can fill in any blanks left by the next two chapters.

The Purpose

Before we dive into the components of XML transformations and the syntax involved, it is important to understand the purpose of XML transformations. Just as we spent time discussing the significance of constraining XML data and its effect on application interoperability, an understanding of the value of transforming XML data is critical to using these transformations appropriately. They are not the final solution in data presentation and should not be used in every situation; by the same token, there are times when transforming XML can save tens and even hundreds of hours of time that would be spent on discovering a comparable solution for a given problem.

We have spent a lot of time emphasizing the importance of XML as a pure data layer. In fact, there has been much more discussion of XML as pure data than as a new way of generating application content. This is in contrast to the hype that XML seems to be receiving as a content-driven language. In the next two chapters, we shift our focus to looking at how XML data can be presented to various clients. However, this does not necessarily mean that the focus is displaying a presentation layer to an end user. In fact, we will spend almost no time discussing the user point of view. If this confuses you a bit, that's okay. Let's reiterate what we mean by client.

The Client of the Client of the Client

The most common definition for a *client* or *application client* is an end user. The idea that some human using a web browser or a GUI interface is the client of an application is somewhat limiting, though. We've already discussed the variety of clients that might interact with your application; let's extend this definition even more. Consider a database engine; because the data within that database is rarely directly displayed to the end user without another program formatting that data, can we say that the database has no clients? In an application that parses the weather from another HTML page and displays it in a new format to a user, can we say that the weather data has two clients? How about the X Windows system, where the display is generated on the server, and the remote application is the client? Clearly, the commonly accepted definition of a client needs to be redefined.

For the duration of this book, we consider a *client* to be anything that uses data from an application, program, or engine. That would make the program using our database engine above a client, as well as the end user who views the formatted data. The program that formats the weather data is a client, as are the users who view that formatted data; and the program that reformats that data is a client, as well as its users. As you can see, the line between an end user and a program begins to get blurred. In a multi-tiered system where a database, Enterprise

JavaBeans container, servlet engine, and publishing framework may all exist, there are four, five, or more clients!

The point of this discussion is to make you understand that with XML, we do not distinguish between a human and a program using the data; they are both clients. This allows us to think about data transformations in a much more useful way; if application A needs data (in format A) from application B (which stores the data in format B), we will need to transform the data. The formats are simply details of the transformation, but do not affect the concepts involved. With our new definition of what a client is, we can also separate the details of the type of application needing the data. When application C then uses the formatted data in application B in format C, another transformation occurs. Whether these formats are HTML, SQL, XML conforming to different DTDs, or something entirely different, is not important. Whether the client is another program, an end user, or a legacy system, the details are still unimportant. The process is still simply a transformation from one format to another. Understanding this important point will help you see why we need to be able to transform XML data.

It's Greek to Me

As you may already be thinking, certainly the most common purpose for transforming XML is to put it into a format readable by a given client. Sometimes mutating an XML document that conforms to one DTD or schema into an XML document that conforms to another DTD or schema can do this. Other times, radically different documents may need to result from the same underlying XML data. In either case, our previous discussions about the importance of constraining and validating XML should be coming back to you. Even if an application knows the format it must read data in, it cannot correctly interpret another format with that information alone. It must use a DTD, schema, or another set of constraints for the originating document to understand what types of conversions can be accomplished and what data structures are present in the source data.

The problems arise when the permutations of application interoperability increase; in other words, the more application components, the more possibilities for data transformations. This can become unmanageable for the components, as each has to keep track of all other components' constraints and formats to allow them to exchange data. For this reason, a set of specifications and standards has been developed for XML transformations. These provide an intermediary layer that can act independently of application components to convert data from one format or style to another, leaving application components to perform business logic. We refer to this middle layer as a *processor*. It is the processor's task to take one or more documents, determine their formats and constraints, and apply a transformation, which results in data in another format, which might even result in multiple output files. This resulting document can then be used by the next component. Of course, this application may in turn hand its data to another processor, which hands off yet another transformed document to a third component, and so on down the line. In this way, applications that do not speak the same "language" can converse without having to implement complex rules for understanding each other's different data types. We look at the pieces of this process and how this nontrivial task is accomplished in the next section.

The Components

As useful as these XML transformations can be, they are not very simple to implement. In fact, rather than trying to specify the transformation of XML in the original XML 1.0 specification, three separate recommendations have come out to define how transformations should occur. Although one of these (XPath) is also used in the XPointer specification, by far the most common use of the components we outline here is to transform XML from one format into another.

Because these three specifications are tied together tightly, and are almost always used in concert, there is rarely a clear distinction between them. This can often make for a discussion that is easy to understand, but not necessarily technically correct. In other words, the term XSLT, which refers specifically to extensible stylesheet transformations, is often applied to both extensible stylesheets (XSL) and XPath. In the same fashion, XSL is often used as a grouping term for all three technologies. In this section, we will distinguish among the three recommendations, and remain true to the letter of the specifications outlining these technologies. However, in the interest of clarity, we will resume using XSL and XSLT interchangeably to refer to the complete transformation process throughout the rest of the book. Although this may not follow the letter of these specifications, it certainly follows their spirit, as well as helping to avoid unnecessary confusion.

The Extensible Stylesheet Language (XSL)

XSL is the extensible stylesheet language. It is defined as a language for expressing stylesheets. This broad definition is broken down into two parts:

- XSL is a language for transforming XML documents.
- XSL is an XML vocabulary for specifying the formatting of XML documents.

These definitions are similar, but one deals with moving from one XML document form to another, while the other is more focused on the actual presentation of content within each document. Perhaps a clearer definition would be to say that XSL handles the specification of how to transform a document from format A to format B. The components of the language handle the processing and identification of the constructs used to do this.

XSL and trees

The most important concept to begin to understand in XSL is that all data within XSL processing stages is in tree structures (see Figure 6-1). In fact, the rules you define using XSL are themselves held in a tree structure. This allows simple processing of the hierarchical structure of XML documents. Templates are used to match the root element of the XML document being processed. Then "leaf" rules are applied to "leaf" elements, filtering down to the most nested elements. At any point in this progression, elements can be processed, styled, ignored, copied, or have a variety of other things done to them.

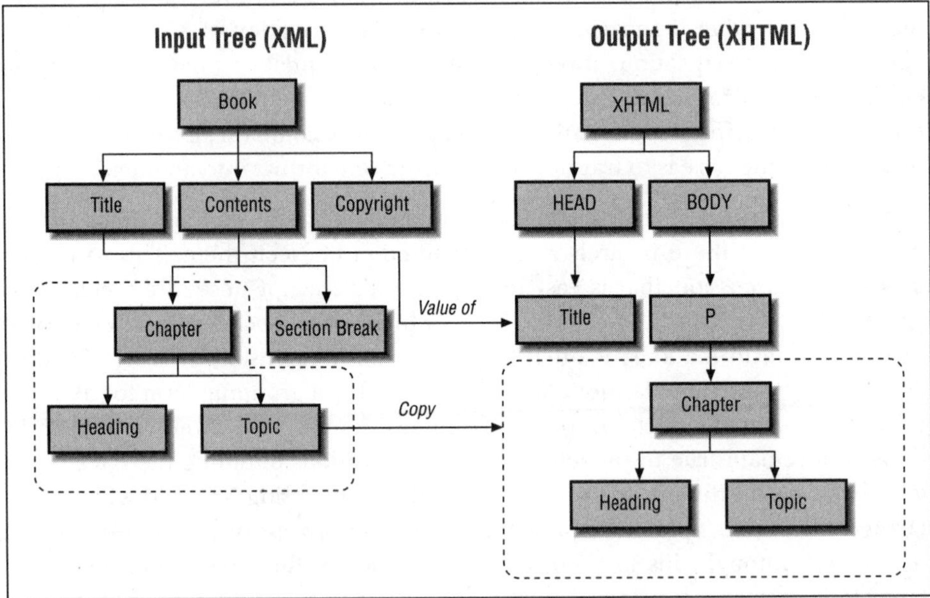

Figure 6-1. Tree operations within XSL

A nice advantage of this tree structure is that it allows the grouping of XML documents to be maintained. If element A contains elements B and C, and element A is moved or copied, the elements contained within it receive the same treatment.

This makes the handling of large data sections that need to receive the same treatment fast and easy to notate, as well as concise, in the XSL stylesheet. We will look more at how this tree is actually constructed when we talk specifically about XSLT in the next section.

Formatting objects

Almost the entirety of the XSL specification is concerned with defining *formatting objects*. A formatting object is based on a large model, not surprisingly called the formatting model. This model is all about a set of objects that are fed as input into a formatter. This formatter applies the objects to the document, either in whole or in part, and what results is a new document that consists of all or part of the data from the original XML document in a format specific to the objects the formatter used. Because this is such a vague, shadowy concept, the XSL specification attempts to define a concrete model these objects should conform to. In other words, a large set of properties and vocabulary make up the set of features that formatting objects can use. These include the types of areas that may be visualized by the objects, the properties of lines, fonts, graphics, and other visual objects, inline and block formatting objects, and a wealth of other syntactical constructs.

Formatting objects are used particularly heavily when converting textual XML data into binary formats, such as PDF files, images, or document formats such as Microsoft Word. For transforming XML data to another textual format, these objects are seldom used explicitly. Although an underlying part of the stylesheet logic, formatting objects are rarely directly invoked, since the resulting textual data often conforms to another predefined markup language such as HTML. Because most enterprise applications today are at least in some part based on web architecture, and use a browser as a client, we will spend most of our time looking at transformations to HTML and XHTML. While this causes us to cover formatting objects lightly, the topic is broad enough to merit its own coverage in a separate book or web site. For further information, you should consult the XSL specification at *http://www.w3.org/TR/WD-xsl*.

XSL Transformations (XSLT)

The second component of XML transformations is XSL Transformations. XSLT is the language that specifies the conversion of a document from one format to another. The syntax used within XSLT is generally concerned with the textual transformations we discussed earlier that do not result in binary data output. For example, XSLT is instrumental is generating HTML or WML (Wireless Markup Language) from an XML document. In fact, the XSLT specification outlines the syntax of an XSL stylesheet more explicitly than the XSL specification itself!

Just as in the case of XSL, XSLT is always well-formed, valid XML. A DTD is defined for XSL and XSLT that delineates the allowed constructs. For this reason, you should only have to learn new syntax to use XSLT as opposed to the entirely new structures that had to be digested to use DTDs themselves. Just as in XSL, XSLT is based on a hierarchical tree structure of data, where nested elements are leaves, or children, of their parents. XSLT provides a mechanism for matching patterns within the original XML document (using an XPath expression, which we look at next), and applying formatting to that data. This could result in simply outputting the data without the unwanted XML element names, or inserting the data into a complex HTML table and displaying it to the user with highlighting and coloring. XSLT also provides syntax for many common operators, such as conditionals, copying of document tree fragments, advanced pattern matching, and the ability to access elements within the input XML data in an absolute and relative path structure. All these constructs are designed to ease the process of transforming an XML document into a new format.

XML Path Language (XPath)

The final piece of the XML transformations puzzle, XPath provides a mechanism for referring to the wide variety of element and attribute names and values in an XML document. As we mentioned earlier, many XML specifications are now using XPath, but this discussion is only concerned with its use in XSLT. With the complex structure that an XML document can have, locating one specific element or set of elements can be difficult. This is made more difficult because access to a DTD or other set of constraints that outlines the document's structure cannot be assumed; documents that are not validated must be able to be transformed just as valid documents can. To accomplish this addressing of elements, XPath defines syntax in line with the tree structure of XML and the XSLT processes and constructs that use it.

Referencing any element or attribute within an XML document is most easily accomplished by specifying the path to the element relative to the current element being processed. In other words, if element B is the current element and element C and element D are nested within it, a relative path most easily locates them. This is similar to the relative paths used in operating system directory structures. At the same time, XPath also defines addressing for elements relative to the root of a document. This covers the common case of needing to reference an element not within the current element's scope; in other words, an element that is not nested within the element being processed. Finally, XPath defines syntax for actual pattern matching; find an element whose parent is element E and which has a sibling element F. This fills in the gaps left between the absolute and relative paths. In all these expressions, attributes can be used as well, with similar matching abilities. Several examples are shown in Example 6-1.

Example 6-1. XPath Expressions

```
<!-- Match the element named JavaXML:Book relative to
     the current element -->
<xsl:value-of select="JavaXML:Book" />
```

Example 6-1. XPath Expressions (continued)

```
<!-- Match the element named JavaXML:Contents nested within the
     JavaXML:Book element -->
<xsl:value-of select="JavaXML:Book/JavaXML:Contents" />

<!-- Match the JavaXML:Contents element using an absolute path -->
<xsl:value-of select="/JavaXML:Book/JavaXML:Contents" />

<!-- Match the focus attribute of the current element -->
<xsl:value-of select="@focus" />

<!-- Match the focus attribute of the JavaXML:Chapter element -->
<xsl:value-of select="JavaXML:Chapter/@focus" />
```

Because often the input document is not fixed, an XPath expression can result in the evaluation of no input data, one input element or attribute, or multiple input elements and attributes. This makes XPath very useful and handy; it also causes the introduction of some additional terms. The result of evaluating an XPath expression is generally referred to as a *node set*. This shouldn't be surprising, as we have already been loosely using the term "node" and will continue to do so; it is also in line with the idea of a hierarchical or tree structure, often dealt with in terms of its leaves, or nodes. The resultant node set can then be transformed, copied, or ignored, or have any other legal operation performed on it. In addition to expressions to select node sets, XPath also defines several node set functions, such as `not()` and `count()`. These functions take in a node set as input (typically in the form of an XPath expression) and then further pare the results. All of these expressions and functions are collectively part of the XPath specification and XPath implementations; however, XPath is also often used to signify any expression that conforms to the specification itself. This, like XSL and XSLT, while not always technically correct, makes it easier to talk about XSL and XPath.

To explain any of these three components' syntax by themselves would simply be a rehash of the specifications. Instead, we will again use our example XML document. As a demonstration of an XML transformation, we will look at how to create an HTML document fragment from our table of contents data. In this way we will look at XSL, XSLT, and XPath in the context of a practical use, continuing to try to make these discussions of syntax relevant to you as a developer.

The Syntax

Now that you have a conceptual understanding of the pieces of the XML transformation puzzle, let's begin to assemble these pieces into something meaningful. We will begin with our original XML file representing a portion of this book's table of contents. We would like to output this XML file in HTML, formatted to our liking. This is an extremely common task in Java applications today, and although we will only perform simple formatting on this file, the possibilities for the resultant HTML's complexity are only bounded by our knowledge and skill at XSLT. As we move step by step through the process of creating a stylesheet to apply to our XML, we will cover the most common constructs within XSLT and look at how they are often applied in XML applications.

Because this chapter is an introduction to XSLT, we will not look at the more complex transformations from one XML format to another. These transformations, while common in large business-to-business applications, are often more dependent upon application and business rules specific to a company. We will later touch on these types of XML transformations in our chapter on XML-RPC and XML for data storage, so if you are looking to use XML for data transport more than for presentation, we will not leave you out. The actual constructs used in transformation will be identical as well; only the resulting output will be different. With that understanding, let's generate some HTML!

XSL Is XML

The first task any XSL stylesheet must complete is to remain true to the XML specification. Remember that XSL has constructs of its own, but is really only one particular vocabulary of XML. That means that our XSL stylesheet must be well-formed, must contain an XML declaration, and must declare any namespaces that it uses. The XSL namespace, which uses the prefix `xsl`, defines the elements we need for performing transformations. This means that every element within our stylesheet that assists in the transformation process will be prefixed with that namespace. For example, the root element of all XSL stylesheets should be `xsl:stylesheet`. This namespace, in addition to identifying the XSL namespaces to the XML parser and processor, makes it easy to look at an XSL stylesheet and see what elements are parts of a transformation and what elements are not.

In addition to the XML declaration and the prescribed root element, we must reference the `xsl` namespace. By now this should not come as any great surprise; prefixing our elements with the XSL namespace requires that we let our parser know where to locate a URI to associate with that namespace. The namespace for XSL is located at the W3C, and the most recent version of the specification to refer to in this URI is *http://www.w3.org/1999/XSL/Transform*. You should consult the documentation available for your XSL processor to ensure you are using the latest supported version of XSL. In addition to the XSL namespace, we are going to be referring to elements in our XML table of contents that are within the `JavaXML` namespace. We must also include a namespace declaration for this namespace, identical to the one we used in our XML document. Remember that these namespaces are only used for association with the namespace each is assigned to, and do not represent a schema, DTD, or any other actual piece of data. With the initial declaration, the root element, and the namespace declarations, we can construct a very small skeleton of our XSL stylesheet, as shown in Example 6-2.

Example 6-2. The Skeleton XSL Stylesheet

```
<?xml version="1.0"?>

<xsl:stylesheet xmlns:xsl="http://www.w3.org/1999/XSL/Transform"
                xmlns:JavaXML="http://www.oreilly.com/catalog/javaxml/"
                version="1.0"
>

</xsl:stylesheet>
```

Note that we added a `version` attribute, now required for XSL stylesheets. While this is a legal stylesheet, it remains a useless one. We have not defined any rules within the stylesheet to match elements within our incoming XML data. We look at how to perform this matching now.

XSL Templates

Perhaps the most fundamental task within an XSL stylesheet is to locate a particular element or set of elements within the input XML document and apply a rule or set of rules to the resulting XML. In other words, in Java parlance, you want to call some accessor (`getMyNodes(criteria)`), and perform a computation (transformation) on the return value of your accessor. This is accomplished by using an XSL template. A template is defined as a set of rules that should be applied to XML that matches a specified XPath. So here we begin to use the various XSL components we have been talking about. We define the template using the XSL element `template`. This of course becomes `xsl:template` within our document to account for namespaces. This element should be defined with the attribute `match`. The value of this attribute must be the XPath expression that will match zero or more elements within the XML being processed. All of this results in the following:

```
<xsl:template match="[XPath expression]">
  <!-- Here are my rules and formatting -->
</xsl:template>
```

So the only real complexity in using these templates is creating an XPath expression that matches the XML element or elements you want to extract. The easiest of all XPath expressions are relative ones. In other words, similar to specifying the *lib/* directory when you are located at the root of a filesystem, we can specify elements by their name when we are at a level directly above them in the element hierarchy. Consider that the XSLT processor places us at the very top of the element hierarchy when processing begins, and it becomes simple to match the root element of a document; we simply use its name:

```
<xsl:stylesheet xmlns:xsl="http://www.w3.org/1999/XSL/Transform"
                xmlns:JavaXML="http://www.oreilly.com/catalog/javaxml/"
                version="1.0"
>

  <xsl:template match="JavaXML:Book">
    <!-- We can now perform formatting on the XML -->
  </xsl:template>

</xsl:stylesheet>
```

You should realize that although in this case we match exactly one element, an XPath expression might match many elements within the XML input, or none at all. We will look at examples of these scenarios as we continue.

Once you have matched an element, you of course want to do something with it. Within a template, you have access to all the elements within the matched element. Using the directory analogy, you have moved into the *lib/* directory. You can now relatively refer to any of the next-level elements (`JavaXML:Title` and `JavaXML:Contents`) by their name; referring to any other elements would require a more complex XPath expression. Before going on with that, though, let's actually produce some output. The typical "Hello World!" example could be accomplished by simply writing the text we want within our template:

```
<xsl:template match="JavaXML:Book">
  Hello World!
</xsl:template>
```

Of course, this isn't really that impressive; what we want is to get access to our XML data, not just push out textual content within the XSL itself. The easiest way to do this in XSL is to let the default behavior of XSL take over. If we match this root element, we have the entire XML element hierarchy loaded into the template. We can then specify that any other templates in the stylesheet should be applied. This may seem rather silly, as we have defined no other templates; however, since that is the case, the XSLT processor traverses the element hierarchy, and every time a leaf node with data is encountered, that data is added to the output of the transformation. The result is that all data within the XML document is printed out hierarchically without any formatting applied. The XSL construct we want to use here is `xsl:apply-templates`. Without any attributes specified for this element, this tells the processor to match any elements relative to the current one with any templates within the XSL stylesheet:

```
<xsl:template match="JavaXML:Book">
  <xsl:apply-templates />
</xsl:template>
```

Still, this manages to border on the useless and inane when it comes to handling transformations. All this data doesn't mean much without formatting applied. In our case, we should be able to apply some general HTML formatting tags to generate HTML output. As in the case of inserting the "Hello World" text, we can also insert standard HTML tags. We add an HTML `head` and `body` to the output, and then let the XML data output within that body using the `xsl:apply-templates` element we just discussed. Although this is a small improvement, it is our first step to creating HTML output. Make the additions noted in Example 6-3 to your stylesheet.

Example 6-3. Generating an HTML File As Output

```
<?xml version="1.0"?>

<xsl:stylesheet xmlns:xsl="http://www.w3.org/1999/XSL/Transform"
                xmlns:JavaXML="http://www.oreilly.com/catalog/javaxml/"
                version="1.0"
>

  <xsl:template match="JavaXML:Book">
    <html>
      <head>
        <title>Here is my HTML page!</title>
      </head>
      <body>
        <xsl:apply-templates />
      </body>
    </html>
  </xsl:template>

</xsl:stylesheet>
```

The result of transforming this data would be the HTML output shown in Example 6-4.

Example 6-4. HTML Output from Example 6-3 and XML Contents File

```
<html xmlns:JavaXML="http://www.oreilly.com/catalog/javaxml/">
<head>
<title>Here is my HTML page!</title>
</head>
<body>
 Java and XML



  Introduction
  What Is It?
```

Example 6-4. HTML Output from Example 6-3 and XML Contents File (continued)

```
    How Do I Use It?
    Why Should I Use It?
    What's Next?



    Creating XML
    An XML Document
    The Header
    The Content
    What's Next?

<!-- Additional chapters left out for brevity -->

  This is a sample shared copyright file.

</body>
</html>
```

We're definitely starting to get somewhere. Although we haven't had to use very complex XSL functionality yet, we are already seeing HTML-formatted results with very little effort. In the process of creating some HTML output, you may notice that in our stylesheet, items that had to be escaped, such as angle brackets, are passed through without problem to the output tree. This is because in the XSL stylesheet itself, elements (such as the HTML head and body elements) that are not part of the XSL specification are inserted into the output tree directly. This allows easy addition of markup language constructs without having to go to great lengths to escape your output.

The last item we want to discuss before moving on is matching a specific element within a template. In other words, suppose that we want the title of our HTML document to be the value of the `JavaXML:Title` element within our XML document. This would be a good time to extract that value without creating a template for that element; there is no formatting to apply, so building a template to match the element would seem to be overkill. Instead, we want to obtain the value and insert that value into our output "inline" within our HTML formatting. It shouldn't come as a surprise to you that this is a simple operation. Here we introduce another XSL construct, the `xsl:value-of` element. This construct, instead of matching an XPath expression for further processing, matches an XPath expression and obtains the value of the matched input. The XPath expression is supplied as a value for the `select` attribute on the element. As we go on, you will find that the `select` attribute is common to many XSL elements, and is always used to supply an XPath expression in this fashion. In our example stylesheet, we want to match the `JavaXML:Title` element, which is relative to the root element we are within in our template. In other words, we again have to do nothing special to construct the appropriate XPath expression. We simply name the element to match:

```
<xsl:template match="JavaXML:Book">
  <html>
    <head>
      <title><xsl:value-of select="JavaXML:Title" /></title>
    </head>
    <body>
      <xsl:apply-templates />
    </body>
  </html>
</xsl:template>
```

After processing, you get the following HTML fragment for your title:

```
<head>
  <title>Java and XML</title>
</head>
```

Before we move on to some more complicated structures and expressions, a final word to the wise is in order. Although in this last example we matched the `JavaXML:Title` element, selecting its value does not remove it from the element hierarchy used as an input to the XSLT processor. The somewhat surprising result is that not only will the value of the data within the element appear within the title, but also it will be duplicated within the body of the HTML due to the `xsl:apply-templates` construct. If this seems incorrect, consider that the input to the processor is immutable; you cannot change this input, only specify how it is traversed and add information. To avoid processing an element, you have to construct an XPath for matching templates that excludes the element, or have a template match the element and produce no output within that template. In other words, we could construct a template to explicitly match the `JavaXML:Title` element, and have it generate no output:

```
<xsl:template match="JavaXML:Title" />
```

When all templates are applied within the root element template, this is matched and the effect is that the element's content is ignored. Hopefully you see this as a clumsy sort of solution, and already are eager to see how to construct an XPath expression that ignores this particular element. Read on, and all shall be revealed!

Control Structures

XSL, like any good processing language, provides several useful control structures. Although these do not closely resemble the constructs you may be used to in languages like Java and C, they are helpful in controlling the traversal of the input tree given to the XSLT processor. We will look at the most common of these and see how they help us control not only what content we are able to access, but the order and fashion in which that content is accessed.

Using XPath for filtering

To begin our look at XSL control structures, we start with controlling the traversal of the document tree we have been discussing. While this does not require a special construct, it is easily accomplished with intelligent usage of XPath expressions. For example, specifying an XPath expression that avoids duplication of the title element from our last example is as much of a control structure as the constructs we will look at that direct program flow later in this section. In the example we have been looking at concerning the `JavaXML:Title` element, we can devise a simple solution. Remember that the set of nodes returned from an XPath expression is parsed hierarchically; in other words, our XSLT processor does not see all the elements in an XML document at one time. It sees all the elements at a specific level of nesting, and then begins to traverse down each element's tree structure. In our document, this means that the elements seen by the XSLT processor within the root element are the elements nested exactly one layer deep; in other words, only `JavaXML:Title`, `JavaXML:Contents`, and `JavaXML:Copyright`. We want to exclude the `JavaXML:Title` element, while processing the rest of the elements. This is best accomplished through our first XPath node set function, `not()`. This function can be used to generate a set of nodes that don't match a given XPath expression. First, we need to add the attribute allowing an XPath expression to our applying of templates. For now, we can use an asterisk as the value of the `select` attribute to signify we want all child nodes of the current node to be processed. This is called *selecting an axis* upon which to operate; here we select the child axis. This obviously doesn't completely accomplish the desired task, but it is a start:

```
<xsl:template match="JavaXML:Book">
 <html>
   <head>
     <title><xsl:value-of select="JavaXML:Title" /></title>
   </head>
   <body>
     <xsl:apply-templates select="*" />
   </body>
 </html>
</xsl:template>
```

Next we need to refine the result set. We add a set of brackets to the end of our selection criteria, within which we can add criteria. It is within this set of brackets that our node set expression should go, returning the nodes to process. In our example, we nest the `not()` function, and then specify the nodes we do *not* want to be processed along the child axis. This would look like the following:

```
<xsl:template match="JavaXML:Book">
  <html>
    <head>
      <title><xsl:value-of select="JavaXML:Title" /></title>
    </head>
    <body>
      <xsl:apply-templates select="*[not(myExpression)]" />
    </body>
  </html>
</xsl:template>
```

The expression we want should signify the name (including namespace prefix) of the element to ignore, in our case `JavaXML:Title`. However, we still have some extra work to do. Because we are selecting nodes along a specified axis, we must let the XSLT processor know where the node we are referring to comes from. If this seems silly (why should I have to specify myself as the origin?), consider that often the axis being selected is not the child axis, and so a frame of reference must be given for those cases. This, of course, means that in even our simple case, we still must specify that frame of reference. For this, we use the keyword `self`. This lets the processor know that the nodes referred to after `self` are children of the current node being processed (`JavaXML:Book`). To separate the keyword from the elements (actually a single element in our case), we use a double colon. This allows us to reserve the single colon for namespace separators, and results in the final expression:

```
<xsl:template match="JavaXML:Book">
  <html>
    <head>
      <title><xsl:value-of select="JavaXML:Title" /></title>
    </head>
    <body>
      <xsl:apply-templates select="*[not(self::JavaXML:Title)]" />
    </body>
  </html>
</xsl:template>
```

If you are scratching your head a bit by now, don't feel like you are the only one. Node sets, axes, and transformations are not a small or trivial part of the world of XML; an entire book could easily be written on the subject. For now, try to absorb what you can and make notes about what confuses you. After completing this and the next chapter, you may want to research online at the W3C (*http://www.w3.org*) anything you are still unclear about. You can also view and join the XSL mailing list and archives by visiting *http://www.mulberrytech.com* on the Web.

Looping and iteration

In addition to using XPath and functions to generate a specific traversal of the input tree, XSL also provides constructs to control processor flow that are analogous to standard programming language control structures. The first of these we look at is a looping construct, `xsl:for-each`. This is a perfect choice for iterating through data within the same element type. For example, our XML table of contents has several chapters defined within it, and we can loop through each chapter, printing out the title. To accomplish this task, we first want to add a new template to our XSL file to match the `JavaXML:Contents` element. This gives us a framework within which to build our looping structure. Without this outer template, we would have no templates that we could insert our looping into. While we could continue to add onto our original `JavaXML:Book` template, our stylesheet could easily become riddled with complex XPath expressions that reference nodes several layers deep. By creating another template for `JavaXML:Contents`, we are now able to write XPath expressions that begin with `JavaXML:Contents` as the current "base" element, rather than the `JavaXML:Book` element. This keeps our XPath expressions simple and our stylesheet readable.

Once within this new template, we can print out a heading specifying that we are about to display the table of contents. This is easily done with some HTML directly inserted into our stylesheet. We then add a horizontal rule (`<hr>`) to separate our title from the contents:

```
<xsl:template match="JavaXML:Contents">
  <center>
   <h2>Table of Contents</h2>
  </center>
  <hr>
</xsl:template>
```

Before we construct our loop, you should notice that something in our XSL is wrong. If you don't see it, remember that XSL must always remain well-formed XML. Even when we are adding static HTML, the HTML must conform to this rule (in essence, making it XHTML)! So when processing this stylesheet, we would receive an error, because our `<hr>` tag has no closing tag. From an XML point of view, this is certainly nothing surprising, but it may catch you off guard if you are used to coding HTML. The simple solution to this is to use the empty notation for this tag, which browsers ignore when parsing the generated HTML:

```
<xsl:template match="JavaXML:Contents">
  <center>
   <h2>Table of Contents</h2>
  </center>
  <hr />
</xsl:template>
```

This will take a little getting used to if you do lots of content development, but in time, it will feel as natural as coding the less-formal HTML standard did. With this detail worked out, we can add in our looping. The `xsl:for-each` construct takes in an XPath expression that should result in a node set to iterate over, specified via the `select` attribute; in our case, we want all of the `JavaXML:Chapter` elements to be the result of this expression. By now it should be easy for you to create this expression:

```
<xsl:template match="JavaXML:Contents">
  <center>
   <h2>Table of Contents</h2>
  </center>
  <hr />
  <xsl:for-each select="JavaXML:Chapter">
  </xsl:for-each>
</xsl:template>
```

With this in place, we merely have to add content. Within each iteration of this loop, the node being traversed becomes the current node in our hierarchy. This means that to refer to elements and attributes that are nested within the `JavaXML:Chapter` element, we refer to them relative to that element, rather than the element being traversed within the outer template, `JavaXML:Contents`. In our example, we can now print out the heading of each chapter. To make the result look nicer, we add each heading as an unnumbered list to our HTML output:

```
<xsl:template match="JavaXML:Contents">
  <center>
   <h2>Table of Contents</h2>
  </center>
  <hr />
  <ul>
   <xsl:for-each select="JavaXML:Chapter">
    <li><xsl:value-of select="JavaXML:Heading" /></li>
   </xsl:for-each>
  </ul>
</xsl:template>
```

The resulting HTML from this stylesheet is actually beginning to look like useful content! We'll look at how you can produce this content in your servlet engine in Chapter 9, *Web Publishing Frameworks*; the generated HTML would look like Example 6-5.

Example 6-5. HTML Output from Modified XSL Stylesheet

```
<html xmlns:JavaXML="http://www.oreilly.com/catalog/javaxml/">
<head>
<title>Java and XML</title>
</head>
```

Example 6-5. HTML Output from Modified XSL Stylesheet (continued)

```
<body>
<center>
<h2>Table of Contents</h2>
</center>
<hr>
<ul>
<li>Introduction</li>
<li>Creating XML</li>
<li>Parsing XML</li>
<li>Web Publishing Frameworks</li>
</ul>This is a sample shared copyright file.</body>
</html>
```

By now you're probably jumping at the chance to see how this transformation occurs; hold on until the next chapter, as a firm understanding of the constructs within XSL will be necessary before performing the transformations. The value of knowing XSL syntax before using an XSLT processor will pay off in our later discussions.

You may be asking yourself why we use a looping construct in XSL. Wouldn't it be simpler to create a new template for the element we want to format, such as `JavaXML:Chapter`, and handle the formatting within that template? It might be simpler (we did the same thing for our `JavaXML:Contents` element earlier); however, one consideration is readability. It is very clear in our stylesheet what the purpose of our looping is; certainly much clearer than if we applied templates to each `JavaXML:Heading` element individually. It is also very easy to display only the data we want made visible, in our case the heading, within this construct. While we are not forced to show other nested elements like the `JavaXML:Section` element in our template, the XML chapters are being used for formatting within a list structure (`<ul></ul>`) that is created in the `JavaXML:Contents` template. If we did construct a template for the chapters, you would have to remember (as would those who had to maintain your stylesheet when you moved on to your next XML project) that content within that template had to be a list item (`<li></li>`). This is clearly not very good style; as with many concepts in XML, the possibility of doing something doesn't always suggest the correctness of that thing. So yes, it might be simpler in the short term to create a template, but almost certainly a poorer decision in the long run.

Choosing elements to process

Next to looping through a set of nodes, one of the most common tasks you will encounter is processing only nodes that meet a certain criteria. This should remind wizened developers of the simple `if-then` construct in most languages. We can simulate this behavior with the `xsl:if` construct, which allows us to return nodes that conform to both an XPath expression *and* some user-defined criteria. This is helpful when all data of a certain type needs to be evaluated, and only a subset of that data should be displayed or formatted in a particular way. In our example, suppose that we want to separate the chapters focusing on Java from those that concentrate on XML. We have this data in our XML document as the value of the `focus` attribute ready for just such a use. The attribute that we use to complement the `xsl:if` element is the `test` attribute. The result of evaluating the expression within `test` should be either true or false; if true, the contents of the `xsl:if` element will be evaluated, and if false, ignored. Easy enough, right? Let's take a look at our example using this construct to only display chapters whose `focus` attribute is equal to the value 'Java':

```
<xsl:template match="JavaXML:Contents">
  <center>
   <h2>Table of Contents</h2>
  </center>
  <hr />
  <ul>
   <xsl:for-each select="JavaXML:Chapter">
    <xsl:if test="@focus='Java'">
     <li><xsl:value-of select="JavaXML:Heading" /></li>
    </xsl:if>
   </xsl:for-each>
  </ul>
</xsl:template>
```

There are few surprises here. You may be unfamiliar with the way we reference an XML attribute. Instead of using the name, as with elements, we prefix the attribute name with the `@` sign. This lets our XSLT processor know that an attribute is being referred to, not an element. We then compare it to the literal value 'Java', signified by the surrounding quotation marks as static text. For the two chapters where this is not true (Chapter 1, *Introduction*, and Chapter 2, *Creating XML*), the heading is not printed; the other two chapters, because they do meet the criteria specified, are processed and displayed to the screen.

Although this is a common and useful way to make decisions occur within your transformations, it is not the best solution for our document. Rather than only showing XML-based chapters or Java-based chapters, we would prefer to display the name of the chapter, and then the focus of the chapter in parentheses after the name. While we could use `xsl:if` to accomplish this, we would need two loops; the first to iterate through the chapters and test for the focus being XML, and the second to loop again and test for the focus being Java. Not only is this costly for performance, but it can result in the chapters being displayed out of order; all of the XML chapters would always appear first, and all Java chapters last. We want to make a choice based on a similar test, but perform an action in either case. The `xsl:choose` element makes this possible. With this construct, we can specify a test, perform one action if the test evaluates to true, and another if it evaluates to false. This element surrounds the block of actions to perform for either case. Inside this block, the element `xsl:when` is used, and a test is specified to its `test` attribute. This test and its format should be the same as that specified to the `xsl:if` element's `test` attribute. Within this element, processing that should occur if the test evaluates to true is included. The difference is that we also include an `xsl:otherwise` element, which contains the processing we wish to occur if the test evaluates to false. This behaves much like the `default` keyword in a Java `switch` statement. In our example, we can make some minor modifications to use this construct. In either case, we write the name of the element out, and then, based on our test, determine what focus to display:

```
<xsl:template match="JavaXML:Contents">
  <center>
   <h2>Table of Contents</h2>
  </center>
  <hr />
  <ul>
   <xsl:for-each select="JavaXML:Chapter">
    <xsl:choose>
     <xsl:when test="@focus='Java'">
      <li><xsl:value-of select="JavaXML:Heading" /> (Java Focus)</li>
     </xsl:when>
     <xsl:otherwise>
      <li><xsl:value-of select="JavaXML:Heading" /> (XML Focus)</li>
     </xsl:otherwise>
    </xsl:choose>
   </xsl:for-each>
  </ul>
</xsl:template>
```

As you're absorbing this example, realize that it only works because there are only two possible choices for a chapter's focus. Also realize that we could have just as easily used XSL to output the value of the `focus` attribute directly to the screen. Of course, that wouldn't have taught you as much about XSL, or been as fun! Seriously, the `xsl:choose` is very helpful for controlling the traversal and processing of a node set returned from an XPath expression, particularly when a certain subset of those nodes needs to be singled out and handled differently. In our case, this manages to further clean up our HTML output, as well as move it closer to looking like a real table of contents, shown in Example 6-6.

Example 6-6. HTML Output with XSL Control Structures

```
<html xmlns:JavaXML="http://www.oreilly.com/catalog/javaxml/">
<head>
<title>Java and XML</title>
</head>
```

Example 6-6. HTML Output with XSL Control Structures (continued)

```
<body>
<center>
<h2>Table of Contents</h2>
</center>
<hr>
<ul>
<li>Introduction (XML Focus)</li>
<li>Creating XML (XML Focus)</li>
<li>Parsing XML (Java Focus)</li>
<li>Web Publishing Frameworks (Java Focus)</li>
</ul>This is a sample shared copyright file.</body>
</html>
```

With these control structures, you should be able to handle a variety of tasks, as well as learn to use more complex XPath expressions and tests to further help you process only the specific data you need. Next we look at how to manipulate and create new elements and attributes within XSL to complement the ones available in your processor's input.

Elements and Attributes

You should be starting to see how much control a textual XSL stylesheet gives you. With as much control as you have over the processing of XML elements and attributes, it shouldn't come as a great shock to learn that you can also define attributes and elements within your XSL stylesheet. These can be used in computations, or simply created and added to the output of your transformation. They are most commonly used in some more advanced templates and in parameter parsing, which we won't spend much time on here. If you have a lot of interest in these more advanced uses of XSL, you may want to subscribe to the XSL list, which discusses these topics all day every day. You may get more information on the XSL list at *http://www.mulberrytech.com/xsl/xsl-list.*

One common reason to create elements and attributes within a stylesheet is to generate dynamic HTML references from XML data. To demonstrate, let's add a section of useful references within our XML file (no, this isn't really appropriate in a table of contents, but it's a great example!), nested within our `JavaXML:Book` element (we need to be sure to turn off validation, as we are now breaking rules in our DTD!):

```
<JavaXML:Book xmlns:JavaXML="http://www.oreilly.com/catalog/javaxml/"
              publicationDate="June 2000">
 <JavaXML:Title>Java and XML</JavaXML:Title>

 <!-- Our Chapters Content -->
```

```
</JavaXML:Contents>

<JavaXML:References>
 <JavaXML:Reference>
  <JavaXML:Name>The W3C</JavaXML:Name>
  <JavaXML:Url>http://www.w3.org/Style/XSL</JavaXML:Url>
 </JavaXML:Reference>
 <JavaXML:Reference>
  <JavaXML:Name>XSL List</JavaXML:Name>
  <JavaXML:Url>http://www.mulberrytech.com/xsl/xsl-list</JavaXML:Url>
 </JavaXML:Reference>
</JavaXML:References>

<!-- Copyright -->

</JavaXML:Book>
```

To set this up, we need to add a new template for this element in our stylesheet. We can also add in some HTML formatting, as well as an iteration through the references in the document, all using the techniques we have been discussing:

```
<xsl:template match="JavaXML:References">
 <p>
  <center><h3>Useful References</h3></center>
  <ol>
   <xsl:for-each select="JavaXML:Reference">
    <li><!-- The URL should go here --></li>
   </xsl:for-each>
  </ol>
 </p>
</xsl:template>
```

All that is left is to create our link in HTML. It should use the `JavaXML:name` element's value as the label, and the `JavaXML:url` element's value as the URL to link to. However, how do we add this into a tag we define? In other words, we want to do something like this in our XSL:

```
<a href="[value of the url element]">[value of the name element]</a>
```

The trick is that the attribute we are outputting needs to be constructed from an element inputted to the processor. A good way to accomplish this feat is to use the `xsl:element` and `xsl:attribute` constructs to set data values for these elements and attributes. The element construct takes a `name` attribute that gives the element its name, and its value is any data within the element. In other words, `<xsl:element name="myElement">Hello!</xsl:element>` would be outputted simply as `<myElement>Hello!</myElement>`. We can also add `<xsl:attribute>` tags to this definition, which function the same way. So in a more complete example, the following XSL:

```
<xsl:element name="myElement">
  <xsl:attribute name="myAttribute">
    Java
  </xsl:attribute>
  is Great!
</xsl:element>
```

would be evaluated, and the resulting output would be:

```
<myElement myAttribute="Java">is Great!</myElement>
```

Complex expressions can appear within the `xsl:element` and `xsl:attribute` elements, allowing virtually any values to be created inline. This gives us the tools we need to tackle our URL building problem. Let's take a look at a solution to our problem:

```
<xsl:template match="JavaXML:References">
 <p>
  <center><h3>Useful References</h3></center>
  <ol>
   <xsl:for-each select="JavaXML:Reference">
    <li>
     <xsl:element name="a">
      <xsl:attribute name="href">
       <xsl:value-of select="JavaXML:Url" />
      </xsl:attribute>
      <xsl:value-of select="JavaXML:Name" />
     </xsl:element>
    </li>
   </xsl:for-each>
  </ol>
 </p>
</xsl:template>
```

We are able to insert the values of elements, as well as generate an attribute, using an XSL element, which in turn becomes an HTML element and is interpreted as a hyperlink. The output of this transformation, shown in Example 6-7, is exactly what we want.

Example 6-7. HTML Output with XSL Styles for References

```
<html xmlns:JavaXML="http://www.oreilly.com/catalog/javaxml/">
<head>
<title>Java and XML</title>
</head>
<body>
<center>
<h2>Table of Contents</h2>
</center>
<hr>
```

Example 6-7. HTML Output with XSL Styles for References (continued)

```
<ul>
<li>Introduction (XML Focus)</li>
<li>Creating XML (XML Focus)</li>
<li>Parsing XML (Java Focus)</li>
<li>Web Publishing Frameworks (Java Focus)</li>
</ul>
<p>
<center>
<h3>Useful References</h3>
</center>
<ol>
<li>
<a href="http://www.w3.org/Style/XSL">The W3C</a>
</li>
<li>
<a href="http://www.mulberrytech.com/xsl/xsl-list">XSL List</a>
</li>
</ol>
</p>This is a sample shared copyright file.</body>
</html>
```

Data . . . Just the Data

It could be argued that in a perfect world, only one transformation would need to occur for any XML document. It also might be argued that the XML document would be pure data, without a single formatting tag or element that should remain unprocessed. However, we don't live in a perfect world, and the result is that sometimes elements in an XML document are intended to be used as data. If that just confused you, don't worry, as you are certainly not alone. However, there are probably some developers who are already nodding their heads out there. They are the developers who have had to produce HTML within XML, and try to figure out how to tell the XSLT processor to "leave my HTML alone!" They are the developers who have to chain stylesheets together, or generate elements that must go through unprocessed to be used in another XML-aware application. They are the developers who sometimes just want to see their output on the screen without it being processed. In short, if they aren't you yet, someday they will be!

The final construct we look at in XSLT processing is the construct that requests that no processing occur! Let's make this a little more applicable with an example. Instead of using the entity reference for the XML table of contents' copyright, let's insert some HTML data into that element. This could be data from another file, or some sort of generated data that is beyond your control. In other words, it is HTML that you are stuck with, something that happens quite a bit in applications today. So we can add some HTML into our XML document:

```
<JavaXML:Copyright>
  <center>
   <table cellpadding="0" cellspacing="1" border="1" bgcolor="Black">
    <tr>
     <td align="center">
      <table bgcolor="White" border="2">
       <tr>
        <td>
         <font size="-1">
          Copyright O'Reilly and Associates, 2000
         </font>
        </td>
       </tr>
      </table>
     </td>
    </tr>
   </table>
  </center>
</JavaXML:Copyright>
```

This is the type of HTML formatting that you may have to handle in your XML transformations. If you are thinking that this isn't such a big deal, you might be surprised by the results of running this change in your document through the XSLT processor; what you get is the text "Copyright O'Reilly and Associates, 2000," without any formatting included. This is only surprising until you remember our initial discussion on template matching. Remember that if a template is not specified for an element, nothing is outputted, and the input tree is continually traversed until data is encountered and printed out. What came into our processor as HTML tags was interpreted as XML, and all of our `center`, `table`, `tr`, `td`, and `font` tags were happily processed and ignored in our XML transformation, leaving us only the textual data, unformatted and unchanged. Fortunately, there is a simple solution to the problem of specifying some elements as data: the `xsl:copy-of` construct. This functions identically in form to the `xsl:value-of` construct, taking in an XPath expression through the value of the `select` attribute. However, instead of outputting the value of the node set returned, it passes the complete node set through the processor from the input directly to the output. All content within the node set is *not* transformed.

```
<xsl:template match="JavaXML:Copyright">
  <xsl:copy-of select="*" />
</xsl:template>
```

This passes through the `JavaXML:Copyright` element's contents (including the HTML) untouched. However, do not think this gives you freedom to break any XML rules! The content of this node set is parsed the same as any other XML before it ever hits the processing stage, and must be well-formed XML. In other words, using ampersands (&) or elements without closing tags (<br>) is just as illegal in a node set being copied as it is in one being transformed. Still, the advantages of being able to copy data from your input directly to your output, possibly for later processing, should become clear in situations where your data is not all XML, or when multiple stylesheets may need to be applied and all elements shouldn't be processed in the same stylesheet. Let's take a look at our completed XSL stylesheet, shown in Example 6-8, with this new template added in.

Example 6-8. Completed XSL Stylesheet

```
<?xml version="1.0"?>

<xsl:stylesheet xmlns:xsl="http://www.w3.org/1999/XSL/Transform"
                xmlns:JavaXML="http://www.oreilly.com/catalog/javaxml/"
                version="1.0"
>

  <xsl:template match="JavaXML:Book">
    <html>
      <head>
        <title><xsl:value-of select="JavaXML:Title" /></title>
      </head>
      <body>
        <xsl:apply-templates select="*[not(self::JavaXML:Title)]" />
      </body>
    </html>
  </xsl:template>

  <xsl:template match="JavaXML:Contents">
    <center>
     <h2>Table of Contents</h2>
    </center>
    <hr />
    <ul>
     <xsl:for-each select="JavaXML:Chapter">
      <xsl:choose>
       <xsl:when test="@focus='Java'">
        <li><xsl:value-of select="JavaXML:Heading" /> (Java Focus)</li>
       </xsl:when>
       <xsl:otherwise>
        <li><xsl:value-of select="JavaXML:Heading" /> (XML Focus)</li>
       </xsl:otherwise>
      </xsl:choose>
     </xsl:for-each>
    </ul>
  </xsl:template>

  <xsl:template match="JavaXML:References">
   <p>
    <center><h3>Useful References</h3></center>
```

Example 6-8. Completed XSL Stylesheet (continued)

```
    <ol>
     <xsl:for-each select="JavaXML:Reference">
      <li>
       <xsl:element name="a">
        <xsl:attribute name="href">
         <xsl:value-of select="JavaXML:Url" />
        </xsl:attribute>
        <xsl:value-of select="JavaXML:Name" />
       </xsl:element>
      </li>
     </xsl:for-each>
    </ol>
   </p>
  </xsl:template>

  <xsl:template match="JavaXML:Copyright">
    <xsl:copy-of select="*" />
  </xsl:template>

</xsl:stylesheet>
```

We can see how this copying allowed our HTML tables to pass through unmodified; Example 6-9 shows the output from the transformation.

Example 6-9. HTML Output with XHTML Content Copied Through

```
<html xmlns:JavaXML="http://www.oreilly.com/catalog/javaxml/">
<head>
<title>Java and XML</title>
</head>
<body>
<center>
<h2>Table of Contents</h2>
</center>
<hr>
<ul>
<li>Introduction (XML Focus)</li>
<li>Creating XML (XML Focus)</li>
<li>Parsing XML (Java Focus)</li>
<li>Web Publishing Frameworks (Java Focus)</li>
</ul>
<p>
<center>
<h3>Useful References</h3>
</center>
<ol>
<li>
```

Example 6-9. HTML Output with XHTML Content Copied Through (continued)

```
<a href="http://www.w3.org/Style/XSL">The W3C</a>
</li>
<li>
<a href="http://www.mulberrytech.com/xsl/xsl-list">XSL List</a>
</li>
</ol>
</p>This is a sample shared copyright file.</body>
</html>
```

Finally, as a preview of the next chapter on using an XSLT processor, Figure 6-2 shows the HTML as seen in a web browser.

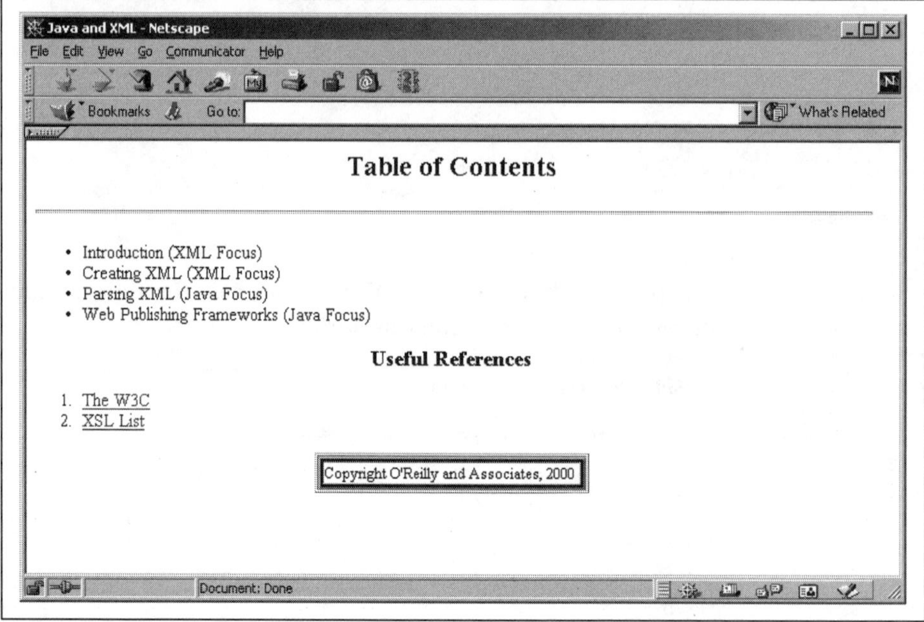

Figure 6-2. HTML output seen in a web browser

When Text Just Isn't Good Enough

As useful and common as transforming XML into another textual format is, sometimes it doesn't cover all the bases. We have stressed that XML data can be transformed into nearly *any* format, not just textual ones like HTML or WML. For example, XML can be processed and transformed into a PDF (Portable Document Format) to be viewed through Adobe Acrobat. To accomplish these binary transformations, formatting objects are used. We briefly discussed formatting objects earlier when talking about the XSL specification. Because XSL must output well-formed XML, it is impossible for an XSLT processor to directly output binary data. However, formatting objects define a set of XML elements and attributes that can be used to represent *areas* in an output format. An area is then used by a formatting objects processor to turn the specified XML area into a binary format. For example, consider the following XSL fragment, which transforms XML using formatting objects:

```
<xsl:template match="JavaXML:Title">
  <fo:block font-size="24pt" text-align-last="centered"
           space-before.optimum="24pt">
    <xsl:apply-templates/>
  </fo:block>
</xsl:template>
```

The output of the transformation for a `JavaXML:Title` element whose value was "Java and XML" would be this XML document fragment:

```
<fo:block font-size="24pt" text-align="centered"
         space-before.optimum="24pt">
  Java and XML
</fo:block>
```

On its own, this is fairly cryptic, and certainly not a PDF document fragment. However, a formatting objects processor, such as FOP from the Apache XML Group (*http://xml.apache.org*) can then take the area represented by this XML fragment and convert it into PDF-specific binary data. The result would be the title, "Java and XML," centered on the page with the correct font size. This same XML fragment could be turned into a Word document if a formatting processor was developed for Microsoft Word, or a Star Office spreadsheet if a Star Office processor was available.

In this way, XSL can generate XML "areas" using formatting objects; these representations of data can then be manipulated in ways that are specific to the binary data that should result. At the same time, the XML format is preserved in both the original and transformed documents, continuing to keep the data portable. In fact, the answer to when text isn't enough isn't to change the way things are done; the same XSL techniques are used, with a different set of transformation objects. The result is one source document with a variety of output formats.

What's Next?

We have now created a complete, functional, XSL stylesheet. You should have a pretty good idea of how to manipulate XML data and transform that data, as well as how to create new data within an XSL stylesheet. In order to use the pairing of XML and XSL, though, we need an XSLT processor. The XSLT processor, in our case written in Java, will handle the actual transformation and generate the output of our stylesheet being applied to our XML document. In the next chapter, we look at using XSLT processors, both from a command line in a standalone fashion and from within Java programs. We will also delve into the Document Object Model (DOM) to see how it is used to generate XML data in a format suitable for input into an XSLT processor. We will then end the book's section on basic XML syntax and use by seeing how all the parts of XML we have looked at so far can be assembled and used within larger XML applications.

In this chapter:
- *Getting the Output*
- *Getting the Input*
- *The Document Object Model (DOM)*
- *"Gotcha!"*
- *What's Next?*

7

Traversing XML

In the last chapter, we learned how to create stylesheets for our XML documents, beginning our section on XSL. In this chapter, we complete that discussion by taking a detailed look at how our document and stylesheet are processed and transformed into output. As in our previous pairs of chapters, this chapter gives you the Java application of the XML language structures we just learned about. We will look at Java XSLT processors, Java APIs for handling XML input in tree formats, and how these APIs differ from the SAX APIs we have already examined.

To begin this chapter, we take a look at how to make the transformations dangled in front of you throughout the last chapter actually occur on your own local machine. This should give you a "virtual playground" where you can experiment with all the various XSL and XSLT constructs on your own, as well as adding more complex formatting to the stylesheet we created last chapter. It will also begin our closer look into how an XSLT processor works. We then complement our view of a processor's output with a detailed look at the type of input it expects, and the format of this input. This leads us into a first look at the Document Object Model (DOM), an alternative to using SAX for getting to XML data. Finally, we will begin to move back a step from parsers, processors, and APIs, and look at how to put an XML application together. This will set the tone for the rest of the book, as we take a more topical approach on various types of XML applications and how to take advantage of proven design patterns and XML frameworks.

Before going on, you should understand not only the focus of the chapter, but also what it does *not* focus on. This chapter will not teach you how to write an XSLT processor, any more than previous chapters taught you to write an XML parser. Certainly the concepts here are very important, in fact critical, to using an XSLT processor, and are a great starting point for getting involved with existing efforts to enhance XSLT processors, such as the Apache Group's Xalan processor. However, parsers and processors are extremely complex programs, and to try to explain the inner workings of them within these pages would consume the rest of this book and possibly another! Instead, we continue to take the approach of an application developer or Java architect; we use the excellent tools that are available, and enhance them when needed. In other words, you have to start somewhere, and for a Java developer, using a processor should precede trying to code one.

Getting the Output

If you followed along with our examples in the last chapter, you should be ready to put your stylesheet and XML document through a processor and see the output for yourself. This is a fairly straightforward process with most XSLT processors. Continuing in our vein of using open source, best-of-breed products, we will use the Apache Xalan XSLT processor, which you can find information and downloads for at *http://xml.apache.org*. In addition to being contributed to by Lotus, IBM, Sun, Oracle, and some of the best open source minds in the business, Xalan fits in very well with Apache Xerces, the parser we looked at in earlier chapters. If you already have another processor, you should easily be able to find the programs and instructions needed to run the examples in this chapter; your output should also be identical or very close to the example output we look at here.

The first use of an XSLT processor we will investigate is invoking it from a command line. This is often done for debugging, testing, and offline development of content. Consider that many high-performance web sites generate their content offline, often nightly or weekly, to reduce the load and performance constraints of dynamically transforming XML into HTML or other markup languages when a user requests a page. We can also use this as a starting point for peeling back the layers of an XML transformation. Consult your processor's documentation for how to use XSLT from the command line. For Apache Xalan, the command used to perform this task is:

```
D:\prod\JavaXML> java org.apache.xalan.xslt.Process
                        -IN [XML Document]
                        -XSL [XSL Stylesheet]
                        -OUT [Output Filename]
```

Xalan, like any processor you choose, can take in many other command-line options, but these three are the primary ones we want to use. Xalan also uses the Xerces parser by default, so you will need to have both the parser and processor classes in your class path to run Xalan from the command line. You can specify a different XML parser implementation through the command line if you wish, although the support for Xerces is more advanced than for other parsers. You also do not need to reference a stylesheet in your XML document if generating a transformation this way; the XSLT processor will apply the stylesheet you specify on the command line to the XML document. We will use our XML document's internal stylesheet declarations in Chapter 9, *Web Publishing Frameworks*. So taking the names of our XML document and XSL stylesheet (in this case in a subdirectory), we can determine the syntax needed to run the processor. Since we are transforming our XML into HTML, we specify *contents.html* as the output for the transformation:

```
D:\prod\JavaXML> java org.apache.xalan.xslt.Process
                      -IN contents.xml
                      -XSL XSL/JavaXML.html.xsl
                      -OUT contents.html
```

Running this command from the appropriate directory should cause Xalan to begin the transformation process, giving you output similar to that shown in Example 7-1.

Example 7-1. Transforming XML with Apache Xalan

```
D:\prod\JavaXML>java org.apache.xalan.xslt.Process
                     -IN contents.xml
                     -XSL XSL/JavaXML.html.xsl
                     -OUT contents.html
========= Parsing file:D:/prod/JavaXML/XSL/JavaXML.html.xsl ==========

Parse of file:D:/prod/JavaXML/XSL/JavaXML.html.xsl took 1161 milliseconds
========= Parsing contents.xml ==========
Parse of contents.xml took 311 milliseconds
==============================
Transforming...
transform took 300 milliseconds
XSLProcessor: done
```

Once this is complete, you should be able to open the generated file, *contents.html*, in an editor or web browser. If you followed along with all the examples in the last chapter, your HTML document should look similar to Figure 7-1 (remember our preview of this HTML from the last chapter?).

As simple as that, you have a means to make changes and test the resultant output from XML and XSL stylesheets! The Xalan processor, when run from the command line, also has the helpful feature of identifying errors that may occur in your XML or XSL and the line numbers on which those errors are encountered in the source documents, aiding even further in testing and debugging.

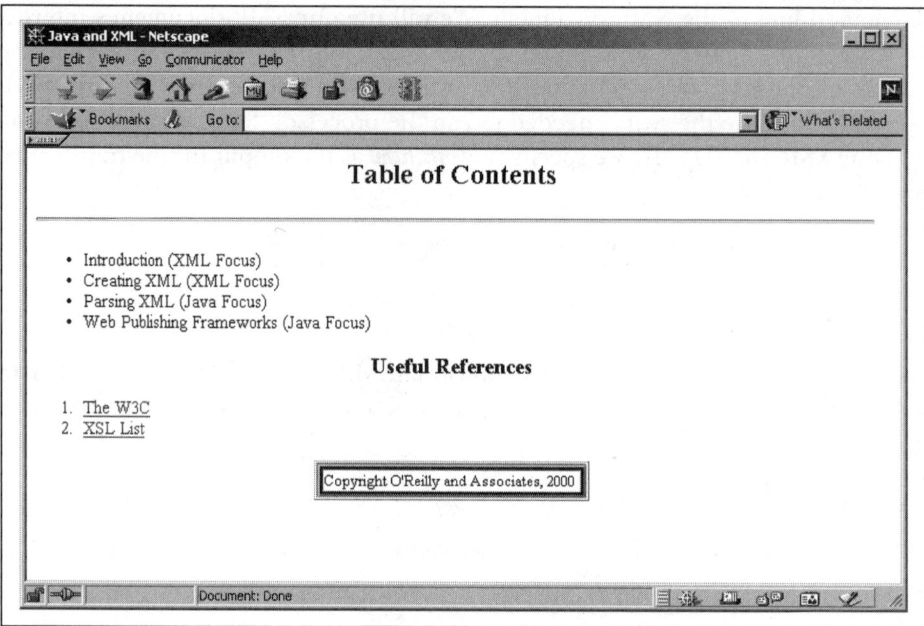

Figure 7-1. HTML from XML transformation

Getting the Input

Besides the reasons already mentioned for not going into how a processor works, there is an even better reason not to spend time on the issue: the inputs and outputs of the processor are far more interesting! You have seen how to parse a document incrementally with the SAX interfaces and classes. You can easily make decisions within the process about what to do with the elements encountered, how to handle particular attributes, and what actions error conditions should result in. However, there are some problems with using that model in various situations, and providing input to an XSLT processor is one of them.

SAX Is Sequential

The sequential model that SAX provides does not allow for random access to an XML document. In other words, in SAX you get information about the XML document as the parser does, and lose that information when the parser does. When element 2 comes along, it cannot access information in element 4, because element 4 hasn't been parsed yet. When element 4 comes along, it can't "look back" on element 2. Certainly, you have every right to save the information encountered as the process moves along; coding all these special cases can be very tricky, though. The other more extreme option is to build an in-memory representation of the XML document. We will see in a moment that a Document Object Model parser does exactly that for us, so performing the same task in SAX would be pointless, and probably slower and more difficult.

SAX Siblings

Another difficult task to achieve with the SAX model is moving laterally between elements. The access provided in SAX is largely hierarchical, as well as sequential. You are going to reach leaf nodes of the first element, then move back up the tree, then down again to leaf nodes of the second element, and so on. At no point is there any clear relation of what "level" of the hierarchy you are at. Although this can be implemented with some clever counters, it is not what SAX is designed for. There is no concept of a sibling element; no concept of the next element at the same level, or of which elements are nested within which other elements.

The problem with this lack of information is that an XSLT processor must be able to determine the siblings of an element, and more importantly, the children of an element. Consider the following code snippet in an XSL template:

```
<xsl:template match="myParentElement">
  <!-- Add content to the output tree -->
    <xsl:apply-templates select="myChildElement1|myChildElement2" />
  <!-- Add more content to the output tree -->
</xsl:template>
```

Here, templates are being applied via the `xsl:apply-templates` construct, but they are being applied to a specific node set that matches the given XPath expression. In this example, the template should be applied only to the elements `myChildElement1` or `myChildElement2` (separated by the XPath OR operator, the pipe). In addition, because a relative path is used, these must be direct children of the element `myParentElement`. Determining and locating these nodes with a SAX representation of an XML document would be extremely difficult. With an in-memory, hierarchical representation of the XML document, locating these nodes is trivial, another reason why the DOM approach is heavily used for input into XSLT processors.

Why Use SAX At All?

All these discussions about the "shortcomings" of SAX may have you wondering why one would ever choose to use SAX at all. If you are thinking along these lines, remind yourself that these shortcomings are all in regard to a specific application of XML data, in this case processing it through XSL. In fact, all of these "problems" with using SAX are the exact reason you would choose to use SAX. Confusing? Maybe not as much as you think.

Imagine parsing a table of contents represented in XML for an issue of *National Geographic.* This document could easily be 500 lines in length, more if there is a lot of content within the issue. Imagine an XML index for an O'Reilly book. Hundreds of words, with page numbers, cross-references, and more. And these are all fairly small, concise applications of XML. As an XML document grows in size, so does the in-memory representation when represented by a DOM tree. Imagine an XML document so large and with so many nestings that the representation of it using the DOM begins to affect the performance of your application. And now imagine that the same results could be obtained by parsing the same input document sequentially using SAX, and only need one-tenth, or one-hundredth, of your system's resources to accomplish the task.

The point of this example is that just as in Java there are many ways to do the same job, there are many ways to obtain the data in an XML document. In various scenarios, SAX is easily the better choice for quick, less-intensive parsing and processing. In other cases, the DOM provides an easy-to-use, clean interface to data in a desirable format. You, the developer, must always analyze your application and its purpose to make the correct decision as to which method to use, or how to use both in concert. As always, the power to make good or bad decisions lies in your knowledge of the alternatives. Keeping that in mind, let's look at this new alternative in more detail.

The Document Object Model (DOM)

The Document Object Model, unlike SAX, has its origins in the World Wide Web Consortium (W3C). Whereas SAX is public-domain software, developed through long discussions on the *XML-dev* mailing list, DOM is a standard just as the actual XML specification itself is. The DOM is also not designed specifically for Java, but to represent the content and model of documents across all programming languages and tools. Bindings exist for JavaScript, Java, CORBA, and other languages, allowing the DOM to be a cross-platform and cross-language specification.

In addition to being different from SAX in regard to standardization and language bindings, the DOM is organized into "levels" instead of versions. DOM Level One is an accepted Recommendation, and you can view the completed specification at *http://www.w3.org/TR/REC-DOM-Level-1/.* Level One details the functionality and navigation of content within a document. A document in the DOM is not just limited to XML, but can be HTML or other content models as well! Level Two, which should finalize in mid-2000, adds upon Level One by supplying modules and options aimed at specific content models, such as XML, HTML, and Cascading Style Sheets (CSS). These less-generic modules begin to "fill in the blanks" left by the more general tools provided in DOM Level One. You can view the current Level Two Candidate Recommendation at *http://www.w3.org/TR/DOM-Level-2/.*

Level Three is already being worked on, and should add even more facilities for specific types of documents, such as validation handlers for XML.

The DOM and Java

Using the DOM for a specific programming language requires a set of interfaces and classes that define and implement the DOM itself. Because the methods involved are not outlined specifically in the DOM specification, and instead the model of a document is focused upon, language bindings must be developed to represent the conceptual structure of the DOM for its use in Java or any other language. These language bindings then serve as APIs for us to manipulate documents in the fashion outlined in the DOM specification.

We are obviously concerned with the Java language binding. The latest Java bindings, the DOM Level Two Java bindings, can be downloaded from *http://www.w3.org/TR/DOM-Level-2/java-binding.html*. The classes you should be able to add to your IDE or class path are all in the `org.w3c.dom` package (and its subpackages). However, before downloading these yourself, you should check the XML parser and XSLT processor you purchased or downloaded; like the SAX package, the DOM package is often included with these products. This also ensures a correct match between your parser, processor, and the version of DOM that is supported.

Most processors do not handle the task of generating a DOM input themselves, but instead rely on an XML parser that is capable of generating a DOM tree. For this reason, it is often the XML parser that will have the needed DOM binding classes and not the XSLT processor. In addition, this maintains the loose coupling between parser and processor, letting one or the other be substituted with comparable products. As Apache Xalan, by default, uses Apache Xerces for XML parsing and DOM generation, it is the level of support for DOM that Xerces provides that is of interest to us.

Getting a DOM Parser

To give you an idea of how DOM works, we are going to look at how the Apache Xalan processor and other programs that need DOM input receive an XML document in the DOM tree structure. This will give us our first look at the DOM Java language binding, and start us towards understanding the concepts behind handling XML documents using the DOM.

One thing that the DOM does not specify is how a DOM tree is created. The specification instead focuses on the structure and APIs for manipulating this tree, which leaves a lot of latitude in how DOM parsers are implemented. Unlike the SAX `XMLReader` class, which dynamically loads a SAX `XMLReader` implementation, you will need to import and instantiate your vendor's DOM parser class explicitly. To begin, create a new Java file and call it *DOMParserDemo.java.* We will look at how to build a simple DOM parsing program to read in an XML document and print out its contents. Create the structure and skeleton of your example class first, as shown in Example 7-2.

Example 7-2. DOMParserDemo Class

```
// Import your vendor's DOM parser
import org.apache.xerces.parsers.DOMParser;

/**
 * <b><code>DOMParserDemo</code></b> will take an XML file and display
 *   the document using DOM.
 *
 * @version 1.0
 */
public class DOMParserDemo {

    /**
     * <p>
     * This parses the file, and then prints the document out
     *   using DOM.
     * </p>
     *
     * @param uri <code>String</code> URI of file to parse.
     */
    public void performDemo(String uri) {
        System.out.println("Parsing XML File: " + uri + "\n\n");

        // Instantiate your vendor's DOM parser implementation
        DOMParser parser = new DOMParser();
        try {
            // parser.parse(uri);

        } catch (Exception e) {
            System.out.println("Error in parsing: " + e.getMessage());
        }
    }

    /**
     * <p>
     * This provides a command-line entry point for this demo.
     * </p>
     */
    public static void main(String[] args) {
        if (args.length != 1) {
            System.out.println("Usage: java DOMParserDemo [XML URI]");
            System.exit(0);
        }
```

Example 7-2. DOMParserDemo Class (continued)

```
        String uri = args[0];

        DOMParserDemo parserDemo = new DOMParserDemo();
        parserDemo.performDemo(uri);
    }

}
```

This is set up in a fashion similar to our earlier `SAXParserDemo` class, but imports the Apache Xerces `DOMParser` class directly and instantiates it. We have commented out our actual invocation of the `parse()` method for the moment; before looking at what is involved in parsing a document into a DOM structure, we need to address issues of vendor neutrality in our choice of parsers.

Keep in mind that this is simple and works great for many applications, but is not portable across parser implementations as our SAX example was. The initial impulse would be to use Java constructs like `Class.forName(parserClass).newInstance()` to get an instance of the correct vendor parser class. However, different DOM implementations behave in a variety of fashions: sometimes the `parse()` method returns an `org.w3c.dom.Document` object (which we look at next); sometimes the parser class provides a `getDocument()` method; and sometimes different parameter types are required for the `parse()` method (`InputSource`, `InputStream`, `String`, `URI`, etc.) to be supplied with the URI. In other words, while the DOM tree created is portable, the method of obtaining that tree is not without fairly complex reflection and dynamic class and method loading.

DOM Parser Output

Remember that in SAX, the focus of interest in the parser was the lifecycle of the process, as all the callback methods provided us "hooks" into the data as it was being parsed. In the DOM, the focus of interest lies in the output from the parsing process. Until the entire document has been parsed and added into the output tree structure, the data is not in a usable state. The output of a parse intended for use with the DOM interfaces is an `org.w3c.dom.Document` object. This object acts as a "handle" to the tree your XML data is in, and in terms of the element hierarchy we have continually discussed, it is equivalent to one level above the root element in your XML document. In other words, it owns each and every element in the XML document input.

Unfortunately, the standardization with regard to DOM is focused on manipulating this data instead of obtaining it. This has resulted in some variety in the mechanism used to obtain the `Document` object after a parse. In many implementations, such as older versions of the IBM XML4J parser, the `parse()` method returned the Document object. The code to use such an implementation of a DOM parser would look like this:

```
public void performDemo(String uri) {
    System.out.println("Parsing XML File: " + uri + "\n\n");

    // Instantiate your vendor's DOM parser implementation
    DOMParser parser = new DOMParser();
    try {
        Document doc = parser.parse(uri);

    } catch (Exception e) {
        System.out.println("Error in parsing: " + e.getMessage());
    }
}
```

Most newer parsers, such as Apache Xerces, do not follow this methodology. In order to maintain a standard interface across both SAX and DOM parsers, the `parse()` method in these parsers returns void, as our SAX example of using the `parse()` method did. This change allows an application to use a DOM parser class and a SAX parser class interchangeably; however, it requires an additional method to obtain the Document object result from the XML parsing. In Apache Xerces, this method is named `getDocument()`. Using this type of parser, we can add the following example to our code to obtain the resulting DOM tree from parsing our input file:

```
public void performDemo(String uri) {
    System.out.println("Parsing XML File: " + uri + "\n\n");

    // Instantiate your vendor's DOM parser implementation
    DOMParser parser = new DOMParser();
    try {
        parser.parse(uri);
        Document doc = parser.getDocument();

    } catch (Exception e) {
        System.out.println("Error in parsing: " + e.getMessage());
    }
}
```

Also be sure to import the necessary DOM class:

```
import org.w3c.dom.Document;

// Import your vendor's DOM parser
import org.apache.xerces.parsers.DOMParser;
```

You should consult your vendor documentation to determine which of these mechanisms you need to employ to get the DOM result of your parse. In the next chapter, we look at Sun's JAXP API and other ways to have a more standardized means of accessing a DOM tree from any parser implementation. Although there is some variance in getting this result, all of the uses of this result we will look at are standard across the DOM specification, so you should not have to worry about any other implementation curveballs as we continue in the chapter.

Using a DOM Tree

Now that we have this "tree" object, let's look at doing something useful with it. For our example, we want to move through the tree structure we have access to and print out the tree of our XML data. The easiest way to do this is to take our initial `Document` object and at each node in the tree, process the current node and then recursively process the children of that node. This should sound familiar to you if you have ever done any work with tree structures. To understand how this works, we need to see the basic objects that our XML data will be accessible through; we have already seen the `Document` object, and this and the other core DOM object interfaces are listed here. These interfaces, shown in Figure 7-2 (which includes the less frequently used DOM interfaces as well), will be the means by which we manipulate all data within our DOM tree.

In addition to absorbing these interfaces, pay special attention to the `Node` interface, and notice that it is the base interface for the other interfaces. Anytime you see a design pattern like this, you should immediately think of runtime object-type discovery. In other words, we can write a method that takes in a node, discovers what type of DOM structure that node is, and prints it in the correct fashion. This allows us to easily print our entire DOM tree with one method! Once we print the node, we can use the common methods that are available to move on to the next sibling element in the tree, get the attributes if it is an element, and handle any other special cases that arise. Then, iterating through the child nodes, we can recursively invoke the same method on each, until our entire DOM tree is printed. This is a simple, clean way of handling DOM trees. We take a detailed look at how to accomplish this now.

Getting the ball rolling

Because our `Document` object itself is a DOM `Node`, we can pass it unchanged as the initial argument to our printing method. We can create the skeleton of this method, but first we need to add the appropriate import statements to our Java file:

```
import org.w3c.dom.Document;
import org.w3c.dom.Node;

// Import your vendor's DOM parser
import org.apache.xerces.parsers.DOMParser;
```

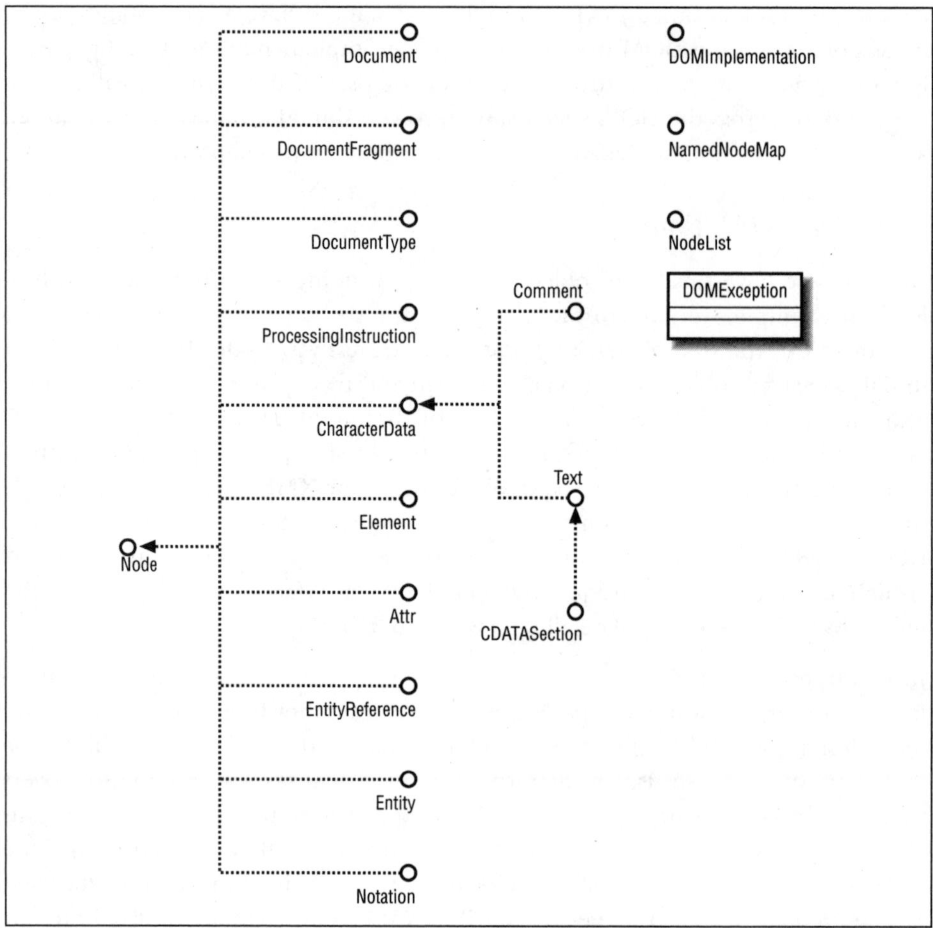

Figure 7-2. UML class model of DOM Level 2 core interfaces and classes

We then can add our method signature, which takes in a DOM `Node` and will print it out:

```
/**
 * <p>
 * This will print a DOM <code>Node</code> and then recurse
 *   on its children.
 * </p>
 *
 * @param node <code>Node</code> object to print.
 */
public void printNode(Node node)  {
    // Determine the type of node
    // Print the node
    // Recurse on children
}
```

Finally, with our skeleton method in place, we can invoke the method on our initial Document object, letting recursion continue the printing until the tree is completely output. This works because the Document interface extends from the common DOM Node interface:

```
public void performDemo(String uri) {
    System.out.println("Parsing XML File: " + uri + "\n\n");

    // Instantiate your vendor's DOM parser implementation
    DOMParser parser = new DOMParser();
    try {
        parser.parse(uri);
        Document doc = parser.getDocument();

        // Print the document from the DOM tree
        printNode(doc);

    } catch (Exception e) {
        System.out.println("Error in parsing: " + e.getMessage());
    }

}
```

At this point, you can compile your Java source file. Although there is no output, you can see that getting an application that uses a DOM output from an XML parser up and running is fairly simple. We next look at making this a usable demonstration.

Determining a node's type

Once within our printing method, our first task is to determine what type of node we have. Although we could approach this with a Java methodology, using instanceof and Java reflection, the DOM bindings for Java make our task much simpler. The Node interface defines a helper method, getNodeType(), which returns an integer value. This value can be compared against a set of constants defined within the Node interface, and the type of Node being examined can be quickly and easily determined. This also fits very naturally into the Java switch construct, which we can use within our method to break up printing into logical sections. We compare the type of our node with the most common node types; although there are some additional node types defined (see Figure 7-2), these are the most common and the concepts here can be applied to the less frequent node types as well:

```
private static void printNode(Node node) {

        // Determine action based on node type
        switch (node.getNodeType()) {
```

```
            case Node.DOCUMENT_NODE:
                // Print the contents of the Document object
                break;

            case Node.ELEMENT_NODE:
                // Print the element and its attributes
                break;

            case Node.TEXT_NODE:
            case Node.CDATA_SECTION_NODE:
                // Print the textual data
                break;

            case Node.PROCESSING_INSTRUCTION_NODE:
                // Print the processing instruction
                break;

            case Node.ENTITY_REFERENCE_NODE:
                // Print the entity reference
                break;

            case Node.DOCUMENT_TYPE_NODE:
                // Print the DTD declaration
                break;
        }
    }
```

Notice that for `CDATASection` and `Text` nodes, we handle output in a single `case` statement. In this example, we are not concerned with whether the text was in a CDATA section or not in the original document; we just want to print the text within the element. We now can add printing and recursion to the appropriate blocks of code, and have our application printing our DOM tree quickly and easily. We look at how to do this for the various DOM node types next.

The DOM Node Types

Now that you have seen how the concepts and structure of DOM work, you should only have to learn the syntax for the different node types to have a solid understanding of the DOM. In other words, you can now treat the DOM Java bindings as just another API, like the JNDI packages or the servlet extensions. Learning the concepts is typically the most difficult part of mastery, while using correct syntax only requires a reference and some example code. In this section, we give you that example code, demonstrating how to print out the most common node types as well as looking at traversing the DOM tree. You can then use the online documentation for the DOM at *http://www.w3.org/DOM* as your reference, as well as Appendix A, *API Reference*, which has an API reference for SAX, DOM, and JDOM (which we look at in the next chapter).

The Document node

Because the Document is an extension of the Node interface itself, we can use it interchangeably with our other node types. However, it is a bit of a special case, as it contains the root element as well as the XML document's DTD and some other special information not within the XML element hierarchy. Thus we need to extract the root element and pass that to our printing function when we run across this node. We also print out a simple version declaration to make our output conform to the XML specification:

```
case Node.DOCUMENT_NODE:
    System.out.println("<xml version=\"1.0\">\n");
    Document doc = (Document)node;
    printNode(doc.getDocumentElement());
    break;
```

WARNING Unfortunately, DOM Level 2 (as well as SAX 2.0) does not expose the XML declaration. This may not seem to be a big problem, until you consider that the encoding of the document is included in this declaration. DOM Level 3 is expected to address this deficiency, and should be available in a draft form in mid- to late 2000. Be careful not to write DOM applications that depend on this information until this problem is corrected.

Since we need to access a Document-specific method, we must first cast the Node implementation passed to the printing method to the Document interface; we can then invoke its getDocumentElement() method to obtain the root element of the XML input document, and then in turn pass that on to the printing method, starting the recursion and traversal of the DOM tree.

DOM elements

Of course, our most common task will be to take a DOM Element and print out its name, attributes, and value, and then print its children. As you would suspect, all of these are easily accomplishable with DOM method calls. First we need to get the name of the XML element, which is available through the getNodeName() method within the Node interface, and print it out. For now, we can leave space to add in the attributes, and then print out the closing angle bracket on our element. We then need to get the children of the current element and print these as well. A Node's children can be accessed through the getChildNodes() method, which returns an instance of a DOM NodeList.

WARNING While most Java APIs use a `Vector`, `Hashtable`, or other Java collections class to support traversing a list, the DOM API returns a DOM-specific interface, the `NodeList` interface. Don't expect to be handling attributes through the Java methods you are used to; instead, you will have to familiarize yourself with these structures when using DOM.

It is trivial to obtain the length of this list, and then iterate through the children calling the printing method on each, continuing our recursion. Finally, we can output the closing of our element.

First let's add in the new DOM interface we need:

```
import org.w3c.dom.Document;
import org.w3c.dom.Node;
import org.w3c.dom.NodeList;

// Import your vendor's DOM parser
import org.apache.xerces.parsers.DOMParser;
```

Now that we have the needed classes and interfaces accessible by their class name, we can add in the code we have been discussing. We obtain the name of the `Node` implementation, print it in XML format, print each of its children (checking for `null` to ensure that children exist), and then close our element. Although this code doesn't yet handle attributes, it should take care of printing out our XML elements for us throughout the entire DOM tree:

```
case Node.ELEMENT_NODE:
    String name = node.getNodeName();
    System.out.print("<" + name);
    // Print out attributes
    System.out.println(">");

    // recurse on each child
    NodeList children = node.getChildNodes();
    if (children != null) {
        for (int i=0; i<children.getLength(); i++) {
            printNode(children.item(i));
        }
    }

    System.out.println("</" + name + ">");
    break;
```

This seems fairly easy, right? It is just as simple to iterate through the attributes of our DOM `Element`. We use the `getAttributes()` method, again defined in the `Node` interface, to get a list of XML attributes, returned in a `NamedNodeMap`. This DOM interface is used for a collection of nodes that are unique with regard to their name, so is ideal for storing a list of our XML element's attributes. We then iterate through this list, printing out the name and value of each attribute. This is similar to the way we handled iteration through our element's child nodes, and we use the getNodeName() and getNodeValue() methods to obtain the values needed for printing. Let's take a look at how to do this here; add the import statement needed for NamedNodeMap and make the following changes to our code:

```
import org.w3c.dom.Document;
import org.w3c.dom.NamedNodeMap;
import org.w3c.dom.Node;
import org.w3c.dom.NodeList;

// Import your vendor's DOM parser
import org.apache.xerces.parsers.DOMParser;
...
            case Node.ELEMENT_NODE:
                String name = node.getNodeName();
                System.out.print("<" + name);
                NamedNodeMap attributes = node.getAttributes();
                for (int i=0; i<attributes.getLength(); i++) {
                    Node current = attributes.item(i);
                    System.out.print(" " + current.getNodeName() +
                                     "=\"" + current.getNodeValue() +
                                     "\"");
                }
                System.out.println(">");

                // recurse on each child
                NodeList children = node.getChildNodes();
                if (children != null) {
                    for (int i=0; i<children.getLength(); i++) {
                        printNode(children.item(i));
                    }
                }

                System.out.println("</" + name + ">");
                break;
...
```

At this point we have done quite a bit of work! With only a couple of hundred lines of code complete, we can iterate through a DOM tree and print out elements and attributes. In fact, it is this ease of use, particularly as compared to SAX, that has made DOM such a prevalent and popular way to handle XML data. Certainly it is not always the best choice, as we have already discussed and will again, but it provides a simple representation of XML that is easy to move through.

Applying formatting

If you haven't already, compile your Java source file and run it on the XML table of contents file we have been using. You should get output similar to the fragment shown in Example 7-3.

Example 7-3. DOMParserDemo Output

```
D:\prod\JavaXML>java DOMParserDemo D:\prod\JavaXML\contents.xml
Parsing XML File: D:\prod\JavaXML\ contents.xml


<xml version="1.0">

<JavaXML:Book xmlns:JavaXML="http://www.oreilly.com/catalog/javaxml/">
<JavaXML:Title>
</JavaXML:Title>
<JavaXML:Contents>
<JavaXML:Chapter focus="XML">
<JavaXML:Heading>
</JavaXML:Heading>
<JavaXML:Topic subSections="4">
</JavaXML:Topic>
<JavaXML:Topic subSections="5">
</JavaXML:Topic>
<JavaXML:Topic subSections="4">
</JavaXML:Topic>
<JavaXML:Topic subSections="1">
</JavaXML:Topic>
</JavaXML:Chapter>
...
```

This does exactly what we expected, but perhaps not in a very clear or usable way. It is very difficult to see where elements begin and end without the indenting we used in our original document. As you remember, whitespace between elements is stripped and typically ignored by parsers, so we need to add some whitespace back in to help in our output formatting. We can pass a simple indentation string into our printing method to handle this. Indentation can be added to as we recurse and traverse through the DOM tree:

```
/**
 * <p>
 * This will print a DOM <code>Node</code> and then recurse
 *   on its children.
 * </p>
 *
 * @param node <code>Node</code> object to print.
 * @param indent <code>String</code> spacing to insert
 *               before this <code>Node</code>
```

```
 */
public void printNode(Node node, String indent)  {
    switch (node.getNodeType()) {
      case Node.DOCUMENT_NODE:
            System.out.println("<xml version=\"1.0\">\n");
            Document doc = (Document)node;
            printNode(doc.getDocumentElement(), "");
            break;

      case Node.ELEMENT_NODE:
            String name = node.getNodeName();
            System.out.print(indent + "<" + name);
            NamedNodeMap attributes = node.getAttributes();
            for (int i=0; i<attributes.getLength(); i++) {
                Node current = attributes.item(i);
                System.out.print(" " + current.getNodeName() +
                                 "=\"" + current.getNodeValue() +
                                 "\"");
            }
            System.out.println(">");

            // recurse on each child
            NodeList children = node.getChildNodes();
            if (children != null) {
               for (int i=0; i<children.getLength(); i++) {
                   printNode(children.item(i), indent + "  ");
               }
           }

           System.out.println(indent + "</" + name + ">");
           break;

      case Node.TEXT_NODE:
      case Node.CDATA_SECTION_NODE:
           // Print the textual data
           break;

      case Node.PROCESSING_INSTRUCTION_NODE:
            // Print the processing instruction
            break;

      case Node.ENTITY_REFERENCE_NODE:
           // Print the entity reference
           break;

      case Node.DOCUMENT_TYPE_NODE:
            // Print the DTD declaration
            break;
    }
}
```

Then make a small change to feed our method an initial indent of an empty string:

```
public void performDemo(String uri) {
    System.out.println("Parsing XML File: " + uri + "\n\n");

    // Instantiate your vendor's DOM parser implementation
    DOMParser parser = new DOMParser();
    try {
    parser.parse(uri);
        Document doc = parser.getDocument();

        // Print the document from the DOM tree and
        //   feed it an initial indentation of nothing
        printNode(doc, "");

    } catch (Exception e) {
        System.out.println("Error in parsing: " + e.getMessage());
    }

}
```

With this minor change, you can see in Example 7-4 that our output is much more readable.

Example 7-4. DOMParserDemo Output with Indentation

```
D:\prod\JavaXML>java DOMParserDemo D:\prod\JavaXML\contents.xml
Parsing XML File: D:\prod\JavaXML\ contents.xml


<xml version="1.0">

<JavaXML:Book xmlns:JavaXML="http://www.oreilly.com/catalog/javaxml/">
  <JavaXML:Title>
  </JavaXML:Title>
  <JavaXML:Contents>
    <JavaXML:Chapter focus="XML">
      <JavaXML:Heading>
      </JavaXML:Heading>
      <JavaXML:Topic subSections="4">
      </JavaXML:Topic>
      <JavaXML:Topic subSections="5">
      </JavaXML:Topic>
      <JavaXML:Topic subSections="4">
      </JavaXML:Topic>
      <JavaXML:Topic subSections="1">
      </JavaXML:Topic>
    </JavaXML:Chapter>
...
```

With this formatting in place, we are ready to add in the textual data values of our elements.

Textual nodes

If you are wondering when we are going to handle integer nodes, numeric nodes, or Boolean nodes, we are not. As you should recall, all XML data within an element was reported through the SAX `characters()` callback. This should have given you your first clue that an XML parser handles all data as text, and an application must make data type conversions if needed. Thus, the DOM `Text` and `CDATASection` interfaces are all we need to worry about to print our elements' values. Printing is quite simple, as we only need to use the now familiar `getNodeValue()` method of the DOM `Node` interface to get the textual data and print it out:

```
case Node.TEXT_NODE:
case Node.CDATA_SECTION_NODE:
    System.out.print(node.getNodeValue());
    break;
```

With that in place, we are very close to having a complete DOM traversal. However, before moving on, let's take a look at a few less common but useful DOM interfaces (and their corresponding `Node` types): `ProcessingInstruction`, `DocumentType`, and `EntityReference`, all of which we have in our document.

Processing instructions

The DOM bindings for Java define an interface to handle processing instructions that are within the input XML document. This is useful, as these instructions do not follow the same markup model that XML elements and attributes do, but are still important for applications to know about. In our example document, we give instructions to the XSLT processor informing it about a stylesheet, as well as an instruction to a publishing framework, Apache Cocoon, letting it know what processing needs to occur. If you still have these PIs commented out in your XML table of contents, you should uncomment these now:

```
<?xml version="1.0"?>

<?xml-stylesheet href="XSL\JavaXML.html.xsl" type="text/xsl"?>
<?xml-stylesheet href="XSL\JavaXML.wml.xsl" type="text/xsl"
                 media="wap"?>
<?cocoon-process type="xslt"?>

<!DOCTYPE JavaXML:Book SYSTEM "DTD\JavaXML.dtd">

<!-- Java and XML -->
<JavaXML:Book xmlns:JavaXML="http://www.oreilly.com/catalog/javaxml/">
```

The PI node in the DOM is a little bit of a break from what we have seen so far: to fit the syntax into the Node interface model, the getNodeValue() method returns all data instructions within a PI in one String. This allows us to quickly output the PI to the screen; however, we still use getNodeName() to get the name of the PI. If you were writing an application that could receive PIs from an XML document, you might prefer to use the ProcessingInstruction interface; although it exposes the same data, the method names (getTarget() and getData()) are more in line with a PI's format. With this understanding, we can add in the code to print out our PIs:

```
case Node.PROCESSING_INSTRUCTION_NODE:
    System.out.println("<?" + node.getNodeName() +
                       " " + node.getNodeValue() +
                       "?>");
    break;
```

If you compile and run the sample program with this change, you may be in for a surprise: none of our XML document's PIs are outputted! Is something going on? Well, in a sense, no. Our code currently obtains the Document object from the XML parser, and only processes the root element of our XML input. Because our processing instructions are at the same level of the tree as that root element, they are ignored. To correct this, we need to change the section of code that handles a Node that is of type Document. We can make a modification similar to how we handled an element's children to process all of our "top-level" XML structures instead of just the root element:

```
case Node.DOCUMENT_NODE:
    System.out.println("<xml version=\"1.0\">\n");
    // recurse on each child
    NodeList nodes = node.getChildNodes();
    if (nodes != null) {
        for (int i=0; i<nodes.getLength(); i++) {
            printNode(nodes.item(i), "");
        }
    }
    /*
    Document doc = (Document)node;
    printNode(doc.getDocumentElement(), "");
    */
    break;
```

Compile this change in, and you should see the PIs at the top of your output, as expected. This is another subtle point of using DOM that you should remember: always be aware of what nodes you are processing, as well as what nodes you are *not* processing!

Document types

Like PIs, a DTD declaration can be helpful in exposing what set of constraints an XML document references. However, since there can be a public and system ID as well as other DTD-specific data, we need to cast our `Node` instance to the `DocumentType` interface to access this additional data. We can then use the helper methods to get the name of the `Node`, which returns the root element of the document it constrains, the public ID (if it exists), and the system ID of the DTD referenced. Using this information, we can reconstruct the DTD reference in the XML document:

```
import org.w3c.dom.Document;
import org.w3c.dom.DocumentType;
import org.w3c.dom.NamedNodeMap;
import org.w3c.dom.Node;
import org.w3c.dom.NodeList;

// Import your vendor's DOM parser
import org.apache.xerces.parsers.DOMParser;
...
case Node.DOCUMENT_TYPE_NODE:
    DocumentType docType = (DocumentType)node;
    System.out.print("<!DOCTYPE " + docType.getName());
    if (docType.getPublicId() != null)  {
        System.out.print(" PUBLIC \"" +
            docType.getPublicId() + "\" ");
    } else {
        System.out.print(" SYSTEM ");
    }
    System.out.println("\"" + docType.getSystemId() + "\">");
    break;
```

Entity references

The final node type we look at is the `EntityReference` interface. This handles the various entity references that can appear within an XML document, such as our copyright reference in our example XML document. There are no surprises in how we print this type of node:

```
case Node.ENTITY_REFERENCE_NODE:
    System.out.println("&" + node.getNodeName() + ";");
    break;
```

There are a few surprises that may trip you up when it comes to the output from a node such as this. The definition of how entity references should be processed within DOM allows a lot of latitude, and also relies heavily on the underlying parser's behavior. In fact, most XML parsers have expanded and processed entity references before the XML document's data ever makes its way into the DOM tree. So often, when expecting to see an entity reference within your DOM structure, you will find the text or values outputted rather than the entity itself. To test this for your parser, comment out or remove our HTML version of the `JavaXML:Copyright` element (we changed this last chapter, remember?) and replace it with the `OReillyCopyright` entity reference:

```
<!--
<JavaXML:Copyright>
  <center>
   <table cellpadding="0" cellspacing="1" border="1" bgcolor="Black">
    <tr>
     <td align="center">
      <table bgcolor="White" border="2">
       <tr>
        <td>
         <font size="-1">
          Copyright O'Reilly and Associates, 2000
         </font>
        </td>
       </tr>
      </table>
     </td>
    </tr>
   </table>
  </center>
 </JavaXML:Copyright>
-->

<JavaXML:Copyright>&OReillyCopyright;</JavaXML:Copyright>

</JavaXML:Book>
```

This can cause a nasty bug, and leave you staring at your XML wondering what is wrong. So what good is an entity reference node type if it is pre-processed by the parser? Well, it's actually intended more for use in creating XML than in parsing existing XML. We look at this next.

Mutability of a DOM Tree

The one glaring omission you will notice if you are familiar with the DOM is that we have not talked about the mutability of the DOM tree we have been using. It is possible to add nodes into the DOM tree very easily. In fact, next to the simplicity of use, this ability to modify and add to the tree is one of DOM's most used and heralded features.

This brings us back full circle to our original discussion on XML transformations. Why is the DOM so important for an XSLT processor? Not only is the input in an easily accessible data form, but an XSLT processor can create a new DOM tree for the output document, and easily copy, modify, add, and remove nodes from the input tree, creating an output tree as processing occurs. This is the "apples to apples" processing that is preferred in complex operations, as often input can be passed through to the output tree with little class casting or new object instantiation, greatly reducing complexity and increasing performance of the XSLT processor. For this reason, we have spent this chapter looking closely at the DOM.

However, you are probably still wondering when we talk about using this mutability; unfortunately, you will have to wait a little longer. To delve into that process now would take us quite a bit off track in our discussions on XSL; however, rest assured that the next chapters will spend time on how to create and modify XML. Before we dive into these more advanced topical chapters, let's take a look at some additional stumbling blocks that DOM can give you as a Java developer learning how to use these powerful APIs.

"Gotcha!"

As in previous chapters, we again revisit some of the common pitfalls for new XML Java developers. In this chapter, we have focused on the Document Object Model, and this section continues that emphasis. Although some of the points made here are more informational than directly affective on your programming, they can be helpful in making design decisions about when to use DOM, as well as instrumental in understanding what is going on "under the hood" of your XML applications.

Memory and Performance with DOM

We spent a lot of time earlier looking at the reasons to use DOM and the reasons to use SAX. Although it was emphasized that using the DOM requires that the entire XML document be read into memory and stored in a tree structure, enough cannot be said on the subject. All too common is the scenario where a developer loads up his extensive collection of complex XML documents into an XSLT processor and begins a series of offline transformations, leaving the process to grab a bite to eat. Upon returning, he finds that his Windows machine is showing the dreaded "blue screen of death" and his Linux box is screaming about memory problems. For this developer and the hundreds like him, beware the DOM for large data!

Using the DOM requires an amount of memory proportional to the size and complexity of an XML document. There is no way to avoid this relationship, and no way to lower the memory requirements. In addition, transformations themselves are often expensive operations; combined with the memory requirements of using the DOM, the two can easily chew into system resources very quickly. Is the motto never to use DOM? Certainly not! However, the motto is to be very careful and aware of the types of documents you are feeding into this model; if you have small, fractional-megabyte documents, you could probably use the DOM and never have a single problem. As you begin to transform larger documents, possibly lengthy technical manuals or textbook-length documents, beware that you don't eat into your system's resources and affect application performance.

DOM Parsers Throwing SAX Exceptions

In our examples of using DOM, we did not explicitly list the exceptions that could result from a document parse as we did in our SAX section. This was because we mentioned that the process of generating a DOM tree is left up to the parser implementation, and is not always the same. However, it is typically good practice to catch the specific exceptions that can occur and react to them differently, as the type of exception gives information about the problem that occurred. Rewriting our main parser loop this way might make a surprise facet of this process surface. For Apache Xerces this would be:

```
/**
 * <p>
 * This parses the file, and then prints the document out
 *   using DOM.
 * </p>
 *
 * @param uri <code>String</code> URI of file to parse.
 */
public void performDemo(String uri) {
    System.out.println("Parsing XML File: " + uri + "\n\n");

    // Instantiate your vendor's DOM parser implementation
    DOMParser parser = new DOMParser();
    try {
        parser.parse(uri);
        Document doc = parser.getDocument();

        // Print the document from the DOM tree and
        //   feed it an initial indentation of nothing
        printNode(doc, "");

    } catch (IOException e) {
        System.out.println("Error reading URI: " + e.getMessage());
    } catch (SAXException e) {
        System.out.println("Error in parsing: " + e.getMessage());
    }

}
```

The `IOException` seen here should not come as a surprise, as it signifies an error in locating the specified URI as it did in our SAX example. Something else in our

SAX section that might make you think something was amiss is the `SAXException` that can be thrown. Our DOM parser throws a SAX exception? Surely we have imported the wrong set of classes! In fact, you have the right classes. Remember that we said earlier that it would be possible to build a tree structure of the data in an XML document ourselves, using SAX, but that the DOM provided an alternative. This was true, but saying this does not preclude SAX from being used. In fact, SAX provides a lightweight, fast way to parse a document; in this case, it just happens that as it is parsed it is inserted into a DOM structure. Because no standard for the DOM creation exists, this is acceptable and not even uncommon. So don't be surprised or taken aback when you find yourself importing and catching `org.xml.sax.SAXException` in your DOM applications.

What's Next?

We have reached a significant milestone in our travels through XML land. You should now have working knowledge of XML, DTDs, XML Schema, and XSLT. These are the core and foundational technologies in the world of XML programming. Certainly there are more specifications and acronyms that you will come across in your development, but these fundamentals are key in using XML from the world of Java. In addition to the specifications, we have looked at both SAX and DOM, easily representing the majority of all XML use within Java. This officially makes you an XML Java developer!

In the next chapter, we wrap up our look at SAX and DOM by discussing where they shine, but more importantly, where they do not. Before diving into application code, which the rest of this book focuses on, JDOM is introduced to you. JDOM seeks to correct many of the problems and annoyances that developers continually face when using SAX and DOM. This API will also give you a good look at how XML can be used in new and creative ways with a little code and elbow grease.

8

In this chapter:

- *Parsers and the Java API for XML Parsing*
- *JDOM: Another API?*
- *Getting a Document*
- *Using a Document*
- *Outputting a Document*
- *What's Next?*

JDOM

We are at the midpoint of our travels through XML-land, and you should be starting to form some opinions about how useful the tools we have examined are, where some are handy and some are cumbersome, how to use these APIs and concepts in your applications, and most of all, what you want XML to do for you. In this chapter, however, we stop briefly to examine additional Java and XML APIs before diving into specific XML topics. First, we take a look at a helper API, the Java API for XML Parsing (JAXP). This API, developed by Sun, is intended to provide an abstraction layer over obtaining a SAX or DOM parser instance; as we saw in previous chapters, this is not always a standardized task (particularly when using DOM), and constitutes a serious gap in the process of using XML in a vendor-independent way.

After this look at JAXP, we introduce a new API, JDOM. Although not related to DOM in any structural or implementation manner, JDOM does provide a complete view of an XML document (as DOM does); however, it has been created for the specific purpose of solving the variety of problems that we have already discussed related to using SAX and DOM (remember all of those "Gotcha!" sections?), as well as for enhancing usability and performance of the current Java API offerings. We will discuss this API, its purpose, functionality, and future, and examine it as an alternative to using SAX, DOM, and JAXP. First, though, we need to look at what JAXP is and add it to our toolbox of XML APIs.

Parsers and the Java API for XML Parsing

If you have been doing much research or exploration into XML and Java, you have probably heard a little bit about Sun's Java API for XML Parsing, usually referred to as JAXP. We also briefly mentioned JAXP in Chapter 1, *Introduction*. Given that JAXP is often mentioned in the same breath as SAX and DOM, you may be surprised that we have waited until now to look at the API. However, the entire JAXP package, contained within `javax.xml.parsers`, is comprised of only six classes, four of which are abstract. The other two are exceptions that are thrown by the first four, making a concise look at JAXP possible.

You should have noticed that when using DOM (and SAX when not using the `XMLReaderFactory` helper class), we have had to explicitly import and reference a parser class from our vendor's Java code. In Apache Xerces these classes were `org.apache.xerces.parsers.SAXParser` and `org.apache.xerces.parsers.DOMParser`. The problem with this approach is that changing which parser class is used requires a change to the application code and a subsequent recompilation. While changes as large as whether to use one vendor's parser or another's are significant ones, it would be nice if the XML parser were completely pluggable. This "pluggability" layer is what JAXP seeks to provide.

With JAXP, instead of having to import a vendor's parser class directly, a system property can be used to specify the parser to use. JAXP then reads that property and handles the loading of the requested parser. In this way, changing the parser implementation to be used requires only a change to the system property specifying the parser class to JAXP, as the application code then uses the Sun-provided wrappers as an abstraction layer.

Using JAXP with SAX

When using SAX, the JAXP `SAXParser` and `SAXParserFactory` classes should be used. The former class wraps a SAX parser implementation and the latter handles the dynamic loading of the implementation. Before discussing these classes, let's look at an example of abstracting the specific XML parser implementation used with these classes, shown in Example 8-1.

Example 8-1. Using JAXP to Get a SAX Parser Implementation

```
import javax.xml.parsers.SAXParser;
import javax.xml.parsers.SAXParserFactory;
import javax.xml.parsers.ParserConfigurationException;

import org.xml.sax.SAXException;
import org.xml.sax.HandlerBase;

public class JAXPSAXText {

    public void doSomeParsing() {
        SAXParser parser;
        SAXParserFactory factory = SAXParserFactory.newInstance();
```

Example 8-1. Using JAXP to Get a SAX Parser Implementation (continued)

```
        HandlerBase myHandler = new MyHandlerBase();
        factory.setValidating(true);
        factory.setNamespaceAware(true);

        try {
            parser = factory.newSAXParser();
            parser.parse(myURI, myHandler);
        } catch (SAXException e) {
            // Handle SAX errors
        } catch (IOException e) {
            // Handle errors from reading the URI
        } catch (ParserConfigurationException e) {
            // Handle errors from the factory being unable to
            //   load the specified parser implementation
        }
    }

}
```

This shouldn't look too different from anything we have seen, but it does remove details of Apache Xerces or any other vendor from our parsing code. The `SAXParser` class wraps the instance of the implementation of parser used, and retrieves that instance from an instance of the `SAXParserFactory` class. One detail that is different from what we have seen in handling parsers is that validation and namespace awareness are set on the parser factory rather than the parser instance itself. The difference here is that any instances created from the factory are given these features; be careful you do not set a feature early in your code and forget that it is still set when retrieving a parser implementation from the same factory in later code.

Another deviation from using a SAX parser implementation directly is that an instance of the helper class `HandlerBase` from SAX is required for passing into the `parser()` method of `SAXParser`. This means that all content handlers, error handlers, and other SAX document handlers must be consolidated into a single subclass of `HandlerBase`. Be careful not to implement the SAX interfaces directly and expect to be able to use them individually (through the `setXXXHandler()` methods available in the SAX `Parser` interface). If the `HandlerBase` class does not ring any bells, you are most likely not familiar with SAX 1.0. Unfortunately, JAXP only supports SAX 1.0; the `DefaultHandler` class in SAX 2.0 replaces the `HandlerBase` class. That class implements the core SAX 1.0 interfaces, providing an empty implementation of each method defined in `ErrorHandler`, `DTDHandler`, `EntityResolver`, and `DocumentHandler` (which is deprecated in SAX 2.0 in favor of `ContentHandler`). In your `HandlerBase` subclass, you would override any callbacks you wish to have action occur within. Once this handler is created, the `parse()` method can be called on the instance of `SAXParser` with the URI to parse, as well as the `DefaultHandler` instance supplied as parameters.

Using JAXP with DOM

The principles of using JAXP to obtain a DOM parser implementation are identical to those used in obtaining a SAX implementation. There are analogs to the `SAXParser` and `SAXParserFactory` classes used to create a DOM tree: `DocumentBuilder` and `DocumentBuilderFactory`, which are also in the `javax.xml.parsers` package. In fact, these two classes use SAX APIs to communicate with the rest of the application, throwing the same exceptions as the SAX classes (including `SAXException`). Although the JAXP specification does not require that `DOMBuilder` implementations use SAX to construct the DOM tree, it does mandate that the SAX APIs be used to communicate with the application.

Code to use the JAXP DOM classes is almost identical to the SAX code we looked at earlier, and is shown in Example 8-2.

Example 8-2. Using JAXP to Get a DOM Parser Implementation

```
import javax.xml.parsers.DocumentBuilder;
import javax.xml.parsers.DocumentBuilderFactory;
import javax.xml.parsers.ParserConfigurationException;

import org.xml.sax.SAXException;
import org.w3c.dom.Document;

public class JAXPDOMTest {

    public void doSomeParsing() {
        DocumentBuilder parser;
        DocumentBuilderFactory factory =
            DocumentBuilderFactory.newInstance();
        factory.setValidating(true);
        factory.setNamespaceAware(true);

        try {
            parser = factory.newDocumentBuilder();
            Document doc = parser.parse(myURI);
        } catch (SAXException e) {
            // Handle SAX errors
        } catch (IOException e) {
            // Handle errors from reading the URI
        } catch (ParserConfigurationException e) {
            // Handle errors from the factory being unable to
            //   load the specified parser implementation
        }
    }
}
```

The DocumentBuilderFactory allows validation and namespace awareness to be set, and will maintain these settings for any DocumentBuilder instances obtained through its newDocumentBuilder() method. Once the location of the document to parse is determined, the parse() method can be called; this returns the DOM Document object resulting from the parsing. After the parsing, the standard DOM objects and methods can be used, abstracting the application from any vendor-specific parser details.

Selecting the Parser to Use

The one detail we have not yet covered in using JAXP is that of setting which parser is used. As mentioned, the purpose of JAXP is to allow easy change of parser implementations. However, this is not quite as simple as it might sound.

Because JAXP includes four abstract classes, each parser that supports JAXP must provide an implementation of the JAXP classes. For example, the Apache Xerces parser has the required implementation classes under org.apache.xerces.jaxp. The JAXP specification says that each implementation can provide any given parser as the default; in other words, the Apache Xerces implementation provides Apache Xerces as the default parser, while an Oracle implementation would most likely provide an Oracle parser as the default. To change this default parser class to another implementation, you can set the Java system property javax.xml.parsers.SAXParserFactory to point at a new SAX factory, or set the system property javax.xml.parsers.DocumentBuilderFactory to point at a new DOM factory. System properties can be set using the -D argument for command-line programs, or through System.setProperty() in Java code. This would allow the JAXP classes to read the system property and respond to calls to newSAXParser() and newDocumentBuilder() by providing instances using the factory specified. However, most applications using XML today are not command-line–based, but web-based, or part of a larger package that is not directly invoked through a command line. Additionally, using System.setProperty() in a generic way would probably mean having that code fragment read the information passed to setProperty() (such as the property name and SAX driver class) from a textual properties file. Of course, this cannot be an XML configuration file (which we discuss in more detail in Chapter 11, *XML for Configurations*), as no parser is available yet. The Java™ Development Kit (JDK) 1.3 does include the ability to specify properties within a *jar* file that is deployed; however, support for JDK 1.3 at the time of this writing was not available on major platforms such as Linux. In other words, the configurability of JAXP is still maturing.

Despite these shortcomings, the concepts and ideas outlined in JAXP are very important ones; additionally, Sun has recently donated JAXP and the Project X parser code to the Apache Xerces project (the code is code-named "Crimson"), which indicates Sun intends to allow faster growth of their API, as well as support open standards. Expect to see a JAXP 1.1 release in late 2000 that supports DOM Level 2, SAX 2.0, and a more generic means of configuration for selecting the parser class to use.

JDOM: Another API?

We have now covered the current API offerings for XML use within Java, and addressed their major strengths and weaknesses. However, the general level of acceptance and excitement over SAX, DOM, and JAXP has been average, at best. The XML community seems to feel that the necessary tools have been provided, while the Java community has been left a bit puzzled at the non-standard ways in which SAX and DOM behave, and the general difficulty in manipulating an XML document, as well as simply obtaining a parser! Therefore, in the tradition of open source software, Java development, and O'Reilly & Associates publishing, we decided to fix this problem, and let you in on the solution: a new API, JDOM.

What's in a Name?

Many of the early reviewers of JDOM were a little put off by its name, particularly as it is so close to DOM, an API that is more broad-sweeping in nature. However, since JDOM simply represents a document in Java, it was felt that the name was appropriate. In other words, the name was chosen for its accuracy despite its similarity to another API's name. Additionally, JDOM is only loosely coupled to XML. JDOM can support any hierarchical data format, and it can be serialized just as easily as it can be output to XML, by using an `OutputStream` or `File` and the JDOM output classes. In the same way, a JDOM `org.jdom.input.Builder` implementation provides a robust means by which to create a JDOM `Document`, and could construct that `Document` from a properties file in a non-standard format just as easily as it could from an XML format. JDOM seeks to provide these additional features, and truly represents any grouping of data within Java.

The JDOM API is comprised of a specification, written by Brett McLaughlin and Jason Hunter (K&A Software), with feedback and support from James Duncan Davidson (author of the JAXP specification). It defines behavior for a very lightweight view of an XML document. It includes standard input and output behavior suitable for creating a JDOM `Document` object from existing XML data and writing a `Document`'s data to any specified destination. The reference implementation, contained within the `org.jdom` package, is a complete 1.0 working product, and is currently available for download with the specification at *http://www.jdom.org.*

JDOM attempts to solve the deficiencies widely recognized in SAX, DOM, and JAXP. With this lightning-fast overview, let's see why another API was even needed—don't we have enough APIs and abbreviations already?

JDOM seeks to provide a Java-centric, high-performance alternative to SAX and DOM in most cases.* It is not based on DOM or SAX, but rather allows a user to deal with an XML document in tree form without the idiosyncrasies of DOM. At the same time, it provides the high performance of SAX, allowing very quick parsing and output. Additionally, it is namespace-aware, supports validation through DTDs (and will include XML Schema validation when the XML Schema specification finalizes), and never returns objects in the form of a `NodeList` or `Attributes`; instead, Java 2 collection classes, such as `List` and `Map`, are returned. Complete support for additional implementations is included, yet JDOM is comprised of concrete (non-abstract) classes, so no factory is needed for creation of elements, attributes, comments, and other JDOM constructs.

Specification Slowdown

While it is useful that standard APIs like DOM and SAX undergo so much review by the World Wide Web Consortium (W3C) and David Megginson and the XML community, respectively, often there is an enormous amount of time between revisions of the APIs. Additionally, the movement of software towards open source and public access (and modification, in many cases) demands a faster revision process, and a more up-to-date view of Java and XML specifications. JDOM, being completely open source software, is an attempt to provide this quicker time-to-market with regard to support for standards and emerging specifications. For example, JDOM already supports XML namespaces in all `Document` objects (even if the `Document` was built with a parser that is not namespace-aware!).

JDOM also eventually will be moved into a CVS tree with public access.† This allows suggestions and code contributions to be added to the code base, resulting in greater understanding of the code as well as a community vision of support and upgrades to functionality. The intent is that JDOM be constantly evolving, becoming a solution for the majority of Java developers' needs for using XML within their code.

* It is certainly true that in some cases, JDOM is not a good replacement for the larger DOM API; JDOM is not supported across multiple programming languages, and does not provide the strict tree representation that DOM does. However, JDOM does strive to provide at least the 80/20 rule of usability: 80% of the time, JDOM will solve your XML manipulation problems.

† At the time of this writing, putting JDOM into a public CVS tree was a task in process. The intent is that at this book's publication time, JDOM will already be available through CVS at *http://www.jdom.org*.

Java-Optimized

We have already mentioned that JDOM is a complete Java 2–based API, leveraging the power of the Java collection classes. There are no current plans to port the API to any other language; while this may decrease the standardization of the API across languages, it greatly increases its usability within Java, which is the goal of the project. The core JDOM classes are based on Java 2, allowing the use of `Collection` classes and weak references; however, a JDK 1.1 version is also available.

As JDOM is designed with you, the Java developer, in mind, it is easy to learn and use, and it follows proven Java design patterns. JDOM constructs (elements, comments, attributes, etc.) are created through direct object instantiation. An XML document (as well as any other document type) can be seen as a whole, and any member of that document is available at any time. Straightforward methods are provided for handling construction, removal, and modification of XML constructs, and Java classes are used for input and output (`URL`s, `InputStream`s, `OutputStream`s, `File`s, etc.).

Hopefully you see that trying to campaign for "reform" in SAX or DOM was certainly a slower (and arguably futile) process compared to developing and supplying JDOM as an alternative. The rest of this chapter, then, introduces this new API and demonstrates how it can be used for XML manipulation within Java.

Getting a Document

The first task in any process involving JDOM is to obtain a JDOM `Document` object. The `Document` object in JDOM is the core class that represents an XML document.

NOTE Like all other objects within the JDOM model, the `org.jdom.Document` class is detailed in Appendix A, *API Reference,* and all its method signatures are listed. Additionally, complete Javadoc on JDOM is available at *http://www.jdom.org.*

There are two ways to obtain a JDOM `Document` object: create one from scratch, when no existing XML data must be read, and build one from existing XML data.

Starting from Scratch

When no existing XML data is needed as a starting point, creating a JDOM `Document` is simply a matter of invoking a constructor:

```
Document doc = new Document(new Element("root"));
```

As we mentioned earlier, JDOM is a set of concrete classes, not a set of interfaces. This means that the more complicated code using factories to create objects as needed to create an `org.w3c.dom.Element` in DOM is unnecessary in JDOM. We simply perform the `new` operation on the `Document` object, and we have a viable JDOM `Document` that can be used.

This `Document` is not tied to any particular parser, either. XML often needs to be created from a blank template, rather than an existing XML data source, so there is a JDOM constructor for `org.jdom.Document` that requires only a root `Element` as a parameter. Example 8-3 builds an XML document from scratch using JDOM.

Example 8-3. Building a Document

```
import org.jdom.Document;
import org.jdom.Element;

/**
 * <p>
 * Demonstrate building a JDOM Document from scratch.
 * </p>
 *
 * @version 1.0
 */
public class FromScratch {

    /**
     * <p>
     * Build a simple XML document in memory.
     * </p>
     */
    public static void main(String[] args) {
        Document doc = new Document(new Element("root"));
        System.out.println("Document successfully built");
    }

}
```

This creates a new JDOM `Document` object with a new `Element` as its root (using the name "root" for the `Element`). This `Document` can be used for any purpose, manipulated in memory, and later output to a stream.

Building a Document from XML

As simple as creating a JDOM `Document` from no previous data is, it is more common to have existing data that needs to be read. Because JDOM documents may be created from many sources, a separate package is provided with classes for generating a JDOM `Document` object from these various forms of input. This package, org.jdom.input, defines the Builder interface, whose methods are shown in Example 8-4.

Example 8-4. The org.jdom.input.Builder Interface

```
public interface Builder {

    // Create a JDOM Document from an InputStream
    public Document build(InputStream in) throws JDOMException;

    // Create a JDOM Document from a File
    public Document build(File file) throws JDOMException;

    // Create a JDOM Document from a URL
    public Document build(URL url) throws JDOMException;
}
```

This provides a mechanism for a JDOM Document to be created from various input sources, and for different implementations to be built for various input formats. Currently, JDOM provides two builder implementations, SAXBuilder and DOMBuilder.* These allow current standards-based parsers to be used for creating JDOM Document objects, without those parsers having to provide additional support to their current DOM and SAX offerings.

SAXBuilder

Using the org.jdom.input.SAXBuilder class to create a JDOM document from an existing XML input source is fairly simple. The SAXBuilder constructor can take in two optional parameters: the name of the SAX parser class to use (which should implement org.xml.sax.XMLReader), and a flag indicating whether validation should occur. If neither is supplied, the default parser is used (currently Apache Xerces), and validation does not occur. We can create a simple SAXTest class to allow entry of a file on the command line, and then create a JDOM Document object using the SAXBuilder class and the supplied filename:

```
import java.io.File;

import org.jdom.Document;
import org.jdom.Element;
import org.jdom.JDOMException;
import org.jdom.input.SAXBuilder;

public class SAXTest {
```

* By the time you are reading this, it is possible that JDOM 1.0 will have additional Builder implementations available. While the 1.0 core API was frozen at the time of this writing, the helper packages (org.jdom.input, org.jdom.output, and org.jdom.adapters) were not. This allows for enhancements that do not affect the core API to be added during the book's publication cycle. Check *http://www.jdom.org* for updates.

```
    public static void main(String[] args) {
        if (args.length != 1) {
            System.out.println("Usage: SAXTest [filename to parse]");
            return;
        }

        try {
            // Request document building without validation
            SAXBuilder builder = new SAXBuilder(false);
            Document doc = builder.build(new File(args[0]));
            System.out.println("Document successfully read");
        } catch (JDOMException e) {
            e.printStackTrace();
        }
    }
}
```

Seems simple, doesn't it? This is because the `SAXBuilder` handles the chores of creating the various SAX handler classes, registering those with the `XMLReader` implementation, and building the JDOM `Document`. This is similar to how many DOM parsers might build a DOM `Document` object using SAX; however, to keep things simple, JDOM's `SAXBuilder` handles all `SAXExceptions` and converts them to `JDOMExceptions`. This isolates the SAX code from your `Document` building, and JDOM ensures the converted exceptions contain information about the specific problems that occurred in parsing and the line on which they occurred.

DOMBuilder

The `org.jdom.input.DOMBuilder` class is almost identical in function to the `SAXBuilder` class. Like `SAXBuilder`, it provides a means of producing a JDOM `Document`, but uses DOM and DOM parsers to accomplish the task. Because DOM does not define a standard parser interface, the `org.jdom.adapters` package supplies an abstraction level over vendor-specific parsers, providing a standard means of obtaining a DOM `Document` object. The constructor of a `DOMBuilder` takes in a flag indicating whether validation should occur, as well as the name of the adapter class to use. This can be any class (including user-defined ones), as long as it implements the `DOMAdapter` interface defined in `org.jdom.adapters`.

NOTE While the `org.jdom.adapters` package was created for use with JDOM, it can also be used in pure DOM applications as a flexible JAXP alternative. It provides a complete abstraction over the DOM parsing process, allowing the input of an `InputStream` or filename, as well as a validation flag, and will return a constructed DOM `Document` object. In other words, you could use these adapter classes in your applications to prevent having to import DOM-specific parser implementations. Additionally, the adapter classes are all built on reflection, so they do not require any parser implementations to be in your classpath at compile-time. This allows complete configurability and portability of an application with regard to the DOM parser implementation used.

Once the `DOMBuilder` has been created, it functions exactly the same as the `SAXBuilder`. The following example shows how to build a `Document` using DOM:

```
import java.io.File;

import org.jdom.Document;
import org.jdom.Element;
import org.jdom.JDOMException;
import org.jdom.input.DOMBuilder;

public class DOMTest {

    public static void main(String[] args) {
        if (args.length != 1) {
            System.out.println("Usage: DOMTest [filename to parse]");
            return;
        }

        try {
            // Request document building without validation, using Oracle parser
            DOMBuilder builder =
                new DOMBuilder("org.jdom.adapters.OracleV2DOMAdapter");
            Document doc = builder.build(new File(args[0]));
            System.out.println("Document successfully read");
        } catch (JDOMException e) {
            e.printStackTrace();
        }
    }
}
```

This uses the Oracle V2 XML parser to create a DOM tree, and then build a JDOM `Document` object from that DOM tree. To use the default parser, simply call `DOMBuilder builder = new DOMBuilder()`.

NOTE All current DOM parser implementations actually use SAX to create a DOM tree. For this reason, using `DOMBuilder` to create a JDOM `Document` object does not make much sense; it will always be slower than `SAXBuilder` (as SAX is used in both cases), and will always consume more memory, as the complete DOM tree exists for the duration of the conversion process into JDOM. `DOMBuilder`, then, should rarely be used. Its main value is the method it provides to create a JDOM `Document` object from an existing DOM tree (such as one received as input to your application from a non-JDOM application). This method, `build(org.w3c.dom.Document)`, is detailed in Appendix A.

Once the JDOM `Document` object has been created, there is no difference in the `Document` operation and functionality between varying builders.

Using a Document

Once we have our initial `Document` object (either from instantiating one directly or building one using the JDOM input classes), we can act on the `Document` independently of any particular format or API. There are no ties to SAX, DOM, or the original format of the data. There is also no coupling to the output format, as we will see in the next section. Any JDOM `Document` object can be output to any format desired!

The `Document` object itself has methods that deal with the four components it can have: a `DocType` (referencing an external DTD, or providing internal definitions), `ProcessingInstructions`, a root `Element`, and `Comments`. Each of these objects maps to an XML equivalent, and provides a Java representation of those constructs in XML.

The Document DocType

The JDOM `DocType` object is a simple representation of a `DOCTYPE` declaration in an XML document. Assume we have the following XHTML file:

```
<!DOCTYPE html
      PUBLIC "-//W3C//DTD XHTML 1.0 Transitional//EN"
            "http://www.w3.org/TR/xhtml1/DTD/xhtml1-transitional.dtd"
>

<html xmlns="http://www.w3.org/1999/xhtml" lang="en" xml:lang="en">
  <!-- etc -->
</html>
```

This code will print out the element, public ID, and system ID from the JDOM `DocType` object that maps to the declaration:

```
DocType docType = doc.getDocType();
System.out.println("Element: " + docType.getElementName());
System.out.println("Public ID: " + docType.getPublicID());
System.out.println("System ID: " + docType.getSystemID());
```

Its output is:

```
Element: html
Public ID: -//W3C//DTD XHTML 1.0 Transitional//EN
System ID: http://www.w3.org/TR/xhtml1/DTD/xhtml1-transitional.dtd
```

JDOM 1.0 supports referencing external DTDs, but does not yet allow inline definition of constraints.* A DocType object can be created with the name of the element being constrained (typically the root element of the document), and a system and public ID may be supplied to specify the location of an external DTD to reference. We can add a reference to the Document object with the following code:

```
Document doc = new Document(new Element("foo:bar"));
doc.setDocType(new DocType(
    "html",
    "-//W3C//DTD XHTML 1.0 Transitional//EN",
    "http://www.w3.org/TR/xhtml1/DTD/xhtml1-transitional.dtd"));
```

The DocType object is automatically created by the selected Builder implementation if the JDOM Document is constructed from existing XML data.

Processing Instructions

The ProcessingInstruction class provides a Java representation of an XML PI, with simple accessor and mutator methods. You can get a list of all PIs† from a Document using the following code:

```
// Get all PIs
List pis = doc.getProcessingInstructions();

// Iterate through them, printing out target and data
for (int i=0, size=pis.size(); i<size; i++) {
    ProcessingInstruction pi = (ProcessingInstruction)pis.get(i);
    String target = pi.getTarget();
    String data = pi.getData();
}
```

* Support for inline constraints is likely be added to a minor revision of JDOM, which may be available at the time of this book's publication.

† JDOM does support ProcessingInstruction objects nested within Elements in a Document. These nested PIs are not returned through the Document-level PI methods; because nested PIs are relatively uncommon, they are not specifically addressed here.

You can also retrieve a list of all PIs with a specific target name using getProcessingInstructions(String target).

A PI can be constructed by providing the target and data to the ProcessingInstruction constructor:

```
ProcessingInstruction pi =
  new ProcessingInstruction("cocoon-process", "type=\"xslt\"");
```

This would result in the following PI representation:

```
<?cocoon-process type="xslt"?>
```

There are several additional helper methods added to the class. It is common to supply the data for a PI in name/value pairs, as in the following example:

```
<?xml-stylesheet href="XSL\JavaXML.wml.xsl" type="text/xsl" media="wap"?>
```

To accommodate this, the ProcessingInstruction class provides a constructor that accepts a Map of values:

```
Map map = new HashMap();
map.put("href", "XSL\\JavaXML.wml.xsl");  // escape the '\'
map.put("type", "text/xsl");
map.put("media", "wap");
ProcessingInstruction pi =
  new ProcessingInstruction("xml-stylesheet", map);
```

The ProcessingInstruction class also has convenience methods to retrieve the data of the PI in name/value pair format. The most basic of these is the getValue() method. This method takes the name of the name/value pair being searched for in the PI's data, and returns its value if located, or an empty String is returned if the name/value pair cannot be found. For example, the following code would determine the media type for the xml-stylesheet PI shown earlier:

```
String mediaType = pi.getValue("media");
```

The resulting value would be the String "wap", which can then be used throughout the application. Since the data of a PI is not required to be in name/value pair form, getData() is also provided, which returns the raw String data for the ProcessingInstruction object. Adding ProcessingInstructions to a JDOM Document object can be done in any of the following ways:

```
Document doc = new Document(new Element("root"))
    .addProcessingInstruction(
        new ProcessingInstruction("instruction-1", "one way"))
    .addProcessingInstruction("instruction-2", "convenient way");
```

Here, a PI is added through:

```
addProcessingInstruction(ProcessingInstruction pi)
```

by supplying a created ProcessingInstruction object, and through the convenience method:

```
addProcessingInstruction(String target, String data)
```

which performs the same task using the supplied data.

Elements

The core of any Document is the data within it, which is enclosed within that Document's elements. The JDOM Element class is the Java representation of one of those elements, and provides access to all the data for the element it represents. A JDOM Element instance is namespace-aware, and all methods that operate upon the Element class and its Attributes can be invoked with a single String name, or the String local name of the Element and a Namespace reference (which we look at next). In other words, the following methods are all available to an Element instance:

```
// Create Element
Element element = new Element("elementName");

// Create Element with namespace
Element element = new Element ("elementName", Namespace.getNamespace(
                  "JavaXML", "http://oreilly.com/catalog/javaxml/"));

// Add an attribute
element.addAttribute("attributeName");
element.addAttribute("attributeName", Namespace.getNamespace(
                     "JavaXML", "http://www.oreilly.com/catalog/javaxml/"));

// Search for attributes with a specific name
List attributes = element.getAttributes("searchName");
```

The root element for a document is retrieved from the JDOM Document using doc.getRootElement(). Each Element then has methods provided to retrieve its children, through the getChildren() method. For convenience, the Element class provides several variations on getChildren(), providing a means to retrieve a specific Element through its namespace and local name, to retrieve all Elements with a specific name in the default namespace, or to retrieve all nested Elements regardless of name:

```
public class Element {

    // Retrieve all nested Elements for this Element
    public List getChildren();

    // Retrieve all nested Elements with the specified name
    //  (in the default namespace)
```

```
    public List getChildren(String name);

    // Retrieve all nested Elements with the specified name
    //   and namespace
    public List getChildren(String name, Namespace ns);

    // Retrieve the Element with the specified name - if multiple
    //   Elements exists with this name, return the first
    public Element getChild(String name) throws NoSuchElementException;

    // Retrieve the Element with the specified name - if multiple
    //   Elements exists with this name, return the first
    public Element getChild(String name, Namespace ns)
        throws NoSuchElementException;

    // Other methods

}
```

The versions that retrieve a specific `Element` can throw a `NoSuchElementException`, or in the case of the version that returns a `List`, an empty `List`. Children can be retrieved by name (with or without namespace), or all children can be retrieved regardless of name. To retrieve a child by name, use `getChild()`, and to retrieve all children, use `getChildren()`. Consider the following XML document:

```
<?xml version="1.0"?>

<linux-config>
  <gui>
    <window-manager>
      <name>Enlightenment</name>
      <version>0.16.2</version>
    </window-manager>

    <window-manager>
      <name>KWM for KDE</name>
      <version>1.1.2</version>
    </window-manager>
  </gui>
  <sound>
    <card>
      <name>Sound Blaster Platinum</name>
      <irq>7</irq>
      <dma>0</dma>
      <io start="D800" stop="D81F" />
    </card>
  </sound>
</linux-config>
```

When the document structure is known ahead of time, as in this example, a specific Element and its value can be retrieved from the JDOM Document object easily:

```
Element root = doc.getRootElement();

String windowManager = root.getChild("gui")
                           .getChild("window-manager")
                           .getChild("name")
                           .getContent();

String soundCardIRQ = root.getChild("sound")
                          .getChild("card")
                          .getChild("irq")
                          .getContent();
```

Note that here, only the *first* element named window-manager will be returned, which is the defined behavior of getChild(String name). To get all elements with a name, getChildren(String name) should be used:

```
List windowManagers = root.getChild("gui")
                          .getChildren("window-managers");
```

When an Element has pure textual data, it can be retrieved through the getContent() method as demonstrated in the previous example. When an Element has only Element children, they can be retrieved using getChildren(). In the fairly rare case that an Element has a combination of text content, child elements, and comment elements, it's said to have *mixed content*. The mixed content of an Element can be obtained through the getMixedContent() method. This method returns a List of the content that contains String, Element, ProcessingInstruction, and Comment objects.

NOTE Technically, getContent() actually returns the String data held within an Element. This can be seen as different than the content of the Element itself. Additionally, getChildren() technically only returns the nested Elements, not all the child objects of an Element. The task of retrieving *all* content of an Element is left to the more complicated getMixedContent() method. This simplification eases the task of manipulating XML files for Java developers, removing the need to perform instanceof operations on all method call results. The method names then, while not technically accurate, are modeled after developer and user patterns.

Elements are commonly added to other Elements through the addChild(Element) method. You can add several elements to a JDOM Document at once:

```
element
    .addChild(new Element("son").setContent("snips and snails"))
```

```
        .addChild(new Element("daughter").setContent("sugar and spice")
            .addChild(new Element("grandchild"))
        );
```

This example chains together the adding of elements for convenience. This shorthand is possible because `addChild()` returns the `Element` to which it was added. You must be very careful when placing parentheses so this technique will work correctly. With one mismatched parenthesis, what were supposed to be siblings may become parent and child! Child elements can be removed using the methods `removeChild()` and `removeChildren()`. They take the same parameters as `getChild()` and `getChildren()`.

`Elements` are constructed with their names. To accommodate namespaces, there are four constructors:

```
// Get a namespace reference
Namespace ns = Namespace.getNamespace("JavaXML",
                                       "http://www.oreilly.com/catalog/javaxml/");

// Create an element: JavaXML:Book
Element element1 = new Element("Book", ns);

// Create an element: JavaXML:Book
Element element2 = new Element("Book", "JavaXML",
                                       "http://www.oreilly.com/catalog/javaxml/");

// Create an element: Book
Element element3 = new Element("Book", "http://www.oreilly.com/catalog/javaxml/");

// Create an element: Book
Element element4 = new Element("Book");
```

The first two `Element` instances, `element1` and `element2`, have equivalent names, as the `Element` class will handle storing the supplied name and namespace. The third instance, `element3`, is assigned to the default namespace, and that namespace is given a URI. The fourth instance creates an `Element` without a namespace.

Element content is set using `setContent(String content)`. This replaces any existing content within the `Element`, including any `Element` children. To add the `String` as an additional "piece" of the `Element`'s overall mixed content, use the `addChild(String content)` method.

One powerful feature of JDOM is that `Elements` can be added and removed by manipulating the `List` returned from an invocation of `getChildren()`. Here the last "naughty" child is removed from the root (to set an example for the others):

```
// Get the root Element
Element root = doc.getRootElement();
```

```
// Get all "naughty" children
List badChildren = root.getChildren("naughty");

// Get rid of the last naughty child
if (badChildren.size() > 0) {
    badChildren.remove(badChildren.size()-1);
}
```

The Java 2 collection classes support features like set arithmetic and high-speed sorting, so while the convenience methods on JDOM objects are, well, convenient, for the advanced tasks, it's useful to manipulate the `List` objects directly. We now can look at adding namespace mappings to our `Document` object, as well as adding and accessing JDOM `Attributes`.

Namespaces

The XML namespaces Recommendation defines the process by which namespace prefixes are mapped to URIs. For a namespace prefix to be used, the prefix should be mapped to a URI through the `xmlns:[namespace prefix]` attribute. In using JDOM, all namespace-prefixes-to-URI mappings are handled automatically by JDOM at output time.

You have seen that XML namespaces are handled through the `org.jdom.Namespace` class, which doubles as a factory for creating new namespaces:

```
Namespace ns = Namespace.getNamespace("prefix", "uri");
```

The `ns` object can then be used by `Element` and `Attribute` objects. Additionally, the `Namespace` class will only create new objects when needed; requests for existing namespaces receive a reference to the existing object.

Attributes

An attribute of an `Element` is retrieved using the `getAttribute(String name)` method. This method returns an `Attribute` object whose value is retrieved using `getValue()`. The following code gets the "size" attribute on the given element.

```
element.getAttribute("size").getValue();
```

A variety of convenient methods are provided for accessing the attribute's value as a specific data type. These include methods for the Java primitives, such as `getIntValue()`, `getFloatValue()`, `getBooleanValue()`, and `getByteValue()`. The methods throw a `DataConversionException` if the value does not exist or could not be converted to the requested type. There are matching companions for each of these methods that allow a default value to be passed in, which is returned instead of throwing an exception if the requested data conversion cannot be done. This code snippet retrieves the size as an int, or returns 0 if a conversion cannot occur:

```
element.getAttribute("size")
       .getIntValue(0);
```

Adding attributes to an element is equally simple. An attribute can be added using an Element's addAttribute(String name, String value) method, or you can use the more formal addAttribute(Attribute attribute) method. The Attribute constructor takes in the name of the Attribute to create (either as a single String parameter, or as a namespace prefix and local name) and the value to assign to the Attribute:

```
doc.getRootElement()
    .addAttribute("kernel", "2.2.14")                          // easy way
    .addAttribute(new Attribute("dist", "Red Hat 6.1"));      // formal way
```

Comments

The JDOM Comment object represents data that is not part of the functional data of the Document, but is used for human readability and convenience. In XML it's represented by <!-- this syntax -->. Comments in JDOM are represented by the Comment class with instances kept either at the document level, or as children of an Element; in other words, both the JDOM Document object and its Elements can have comments.

To obtain the comments for a Document, the getMixedContent() method is provided, which returns a List containing all the Comment objects of the document as well as the root Element. Comments placed before the root appear in the list before the root, and those placed after the root appear later in the output. To obtain the comments for an Element, getMixedContent() should be called, which returns all Comment, Element, and String (textual data) objects nested within the Element in the order in which they appear. As an example, assume we have the following XML file:

```
<?xml version="1.0"?>

<!-- A comment at the root level: Java and XML, by Brett McLaughlin -->
<JavaXML:Book xmlns:JavaXML="http://www.oreilly.com/catalog/javaxml/">
  <JavaXML:Title>Java and XML</JavaXML:Title>

  <!-- A comment nested within the JavaXML:Book element: Contents -->
  <JavaXML:Contents>
     You're reading the contents!
  </JavaXML:Contents>
</JavaXML:Book>
```

Normally, the comments are not needed by applications, but should they be, this code would retrieve them:

```
List docContent = doc.getContent();
List elemContent = root.getMixedContent();

for (int i=0, size=docContent.size(); i<size; i++) {
    Object o = docContent.get(i);
    if (o instanceof Comment) {
        Comment c = (Comment)o;
        String text = c.getText();
    }
}

for (int i=0, size=elemContent.size(); i<size; i++) {
    Object o = elemContent.get(i);
    if (o instanceof Comment) {
        Comment c = (Comment)o;
        String text = c.getText();
    }
}
```

The `Comment` constructor takes in the text of the comment as its sole argument. The `Document` object provides a means for comments to be added through the `addComment(Comment)` method, and the `Element` class provides `addChild(Comment)` for the same purpose:

```
// Create the Comment
Comment docComment = new Comment("A comment at the root level");

// Add the comment to the Document object
doc.addComment(docComment);

// Create another Comment
Comment elemComment = new Comment("A comment nested within an element");

// Add the comment to an Element
doc.getRootElement()
   .getChild("Contents")
   .addChild(elemComment);
```

Outputting a Document

The process of outputting a JDOM `Document` object is even simpler than the process of creating one. The `org.jdom.output` package provides helper and utility classes for outputting a `Document` to various sources. No interface is provided to define required behavior, as output of a `Document` can be used in a variety of ways, from something as simple as writing to a file to something as complex as triggering events for another application component to use.

Standard XML Output

The most common use for XML data within a JDOM `Document` is to output that data as XML to a file or another application component, using an `OutputStream`. Of course, this stream may wrap a console's output, a file, a URL, or any other construct that can receive data. This task is handled in JDOM by the `org.jdom.output.XMLOutputter` class. This class provides the following constructors and output method:

```
public class XMLOutputter {

    // Accept defaults: 2 space indent and new line feeds on
    public XMLOutputter();

    // Specify indent, accept default for new line feeds (on)
    public XMLOutputter(String indent);

    // Specify the indention to use and if new line feeds should be used
    public XMLOutputter(String indent, boolean newlines);

    // Output a JDOM Document to a stream
    public void output(Document doc, OutputStream out)throws IOException;

}
```

When instantiated with the default constructor, this results in a "pretty printing" of the JDOM `Document`; other options can be supplied for more compact output (such as turning off new lines and removing indentation, resulting in the smallest file possible). The following example shows the `SAXTest` class we looked at earlier, revised to print the document to the standard output:

```
import java.io.File;
import java.io.IOException;

import org.jdom.Document;
import org.jdom.Element;
import org.jdom.JDOMException;
import org.jdom.input.SAXBuilder;
import org.jdom.output.XMLOutputter;

public class SAXTest {

    public static void main(String[] args) {
        if (args.length != 1) {
            System.out.println("Usage: SAXTest [filename to parse]");
            return;
        }

        try {
```

```
            // Request document building without validation
            SAXBuilder builder = new SAXBuilder(false);
            Document doc = builder.build(new File(args[0]));
            printDocument(doc);
        } catch (JDOMException e) {
            if (e.getRootCause() != null) {
                e.getRootCause().printStackTrace();
            }
            e.printStackTrace();
        } catch (Exception e) {
            e.printStackTrace();
        }
    }

    public static void printDocument(Document doc) throws IOException {
        XMLOutputter fmt = new XMLOutputter();
        fmt.output(doc, System.out);
    }
}
```

Notice that in our methods that build JDOM `Document` objects with `SAXBuilder` and `DOMBuilder`, we didn't perform any data massaging or manipulation after building; a built `Document` is immediately ready for output, making reading and writing XML (possibly from one source to another source) extremely easy.

Firing Off SAX Events

We have already discussed applications of JDOM even when the original XML is available only as a pre-built DOM tree; the `DOMBuilder` can convert the DOM tree to the much lighter-weight JDOM `Document` object, and the JDOM API can be used to manipulate the XML data. In the same manner, JDOM can communicate with other applications that expect SAX events as input. The `org.jdom.SAXOutputter` class provides the ability to fire off SAX events from a supplied JDOM `Document` object. This provides a complete isolation level between application components, allowing you to use JDOM while still interacting with applications that don't use JDOM (or just haven't caught up yet!). Additionally, a `DOMOutputter` class is being developed to perform the same type of task, converting a JDOM `Document` object into a DOM tree to pass to other application components. Both of these classes should be complete by the publication of this book, so visit *http://www.jdom.org* to obtain these updates, as well as the latest version of the JDOM implementation classes.

More important than these two specific classes is the flexibility they indicate: rather than being tied to a specific format, JDOM seeks to allow input and output from any type of input source and to any type of output source. An `ApacheOutputter` class, for example, could be created to output a JDOM

Document created with ApacheBuilder back into an Apache HTTP configuration file format. The output formats can be as varied as the input formats, as JDOM provides only an object model, rather than a specific XML model.

Putting JDOM to Work

As a more complete example of using JDOM, Example 8-5 is a JDOM "test suite" that builds a JDOM Document object from scratch, using both SAXBuilder and DOMBuilder.

Example 8-5. JDOM Test Suite

```
import java.io.File;
import java.io.IOException;
import java.io.OutputStream;

import org.jdom.Attribute;
import org.jdom.Comment;
import org.jdom.DocType;
import org.jdom.Document;
import org.jdom.Element;
import org.jdom.JDOMException;
import org.jdom.Namespace;
import org.jdom.ProcessingInstruction;
import org.jdom.input.DOMBuilder;
import org.jdom.input.SAXBuilder;
import org.jdom.output.XMLOutputter;

/**
 * <p>
 * Demonstrate building JDOM Documents from scratch and existing XML
 *   data sources.
 * </p>
 *
 * @version 1.0
 */
public class JDOMTest {

    public JDOMTest() {
    }

    /**
     * <p>
     * Build a JDOM <code>Document</code> from scratch
     * </p>
     *
     * @param out <code>OutputStream</code> to write created XML to
     * @throws <code>IOException</code> when output errors occur.
```

Example 8-5. JDOM Test Suite (continued)

```
     */
    public void newDocument(OutputStream out)
        throws IOException, JDOMException {

       Namespace ns = Namespace.getNamespace("linux", "http://www.linux.org");
       Document doc =
         new Document(new Element("config", ns))
           .setDocType(new DocType("linux:config",
                                   "DTD/linux.dtd"))
           .addProcessingInstruction("cocoon-process",
                                     "type=\"xsp\"")
           .addProcessingInstruction(
               new ProcessingInstruction("cocoon-process",
                                         "type=\"xslt\""));

         doc.getRootElement()
              .addAttribute("kernel", "2.2.14")          // easy way
              .addAttribute(
                  new Attribute("dist", "RedHat 6.1"))  // hard way
              .addChild(new Element("gui", ns)
                 .setContent("No Window Manager Installed"))
              .addChild(new Comment("Sound Card Configuration"))
              .addChild(new Element("sound")
                .addChild(new Comment("Sound Blaster Card"))
                .addChild(new Element("card")
                    .addChild(new Element("name")
                        .setContent("Sound Blaster Platinum")))
                );

       XMLOutputter fmt = new XMLOutputter();
       fmt.output(doc, out);
    }

    public void domDocument(File file, OutputStream out)
        throws IOException, JDOMException {

        DOMBuilder builder = new DOMBuilder(true);
        Document doc = builder.build(file);

        XMLOutputter fmt = new XMLOutputter();
        fmt.output(doc, out);
    }

    public void saxDocument(File file, OutputStream out)
        throws IOException, JDOMException {

        SAXBuilder builder = new SAXBuilder(true);
        Document doc = builder.build(file);
```

Example 8-5. JDOM Test Suite (continued)

```
        XMLOutputter fmt = new XMLOutputter();
        fmt.output(doc, out);
    }

    /**
     * <p>
     * Static entry point for JDOM testing.
     * </p>
     */
    public static void main(String[] args) {
        if (args.length != 1) {
            System.out.println("Usage: JDOMTest [filename to parse]");
            System.exit(-1);
        }

        try {
            JDOMTest test = new JDOMTest();

            System.out.println(
                "\n\n---------------------------------------");
            System.out.println(
                "Testing creating Document from scratch ...");
            System.out.println(
                "---------------------------------------\n\n");
            test.newDocument(System.out);

            System.out.println(
                "\n\n---------------------------------------");
            System.out.println(
                "Testing reading Document using DOM ...");
            System.out.println(
                "---------------------------------------\n\n");
            test.domDocument(new File(args[0]), System.out);

            System.out.println(
                "\n\n---------------------------------------");
            System.out.println(
                "Testing reading Document using SAX ...");
            System.out.println(
                "---------------------------------------\n\n");
            test.saxDocument(new File(args[0]), System.out);

            System.out.println(
                "\n\n---------------------------------------");
            System.out.println(
                "Tests complete. Successful build in place.");

        } catch (Exception e) {
```

Example 8-5. JDOM Test Suite (continued)

```
            e.printStackTrace();
            if (e instanceof JDOMException) {
                System.out.println(((JDOMException)e).getRootCause()
                                                     .getMessage());
            } else {
                System.out.println(e.getMessage());
            }
        }
    }

}
```

Compile the JDOMTest class, and let's take a look at its output. Supplying an XML file to the class, we can see the file output twice, once built with SAX and once built with DOM, which follows the new XML data created from scratch. Example 8-6 shows parts of this output.

Example 8-6. Output from JDOMTest Class

```
$ java JDOMText contents.xml

----------------------------------------
Testing creating tree from scratch ...
----------------------------------------

<?xml version="1.0" encoding="UTF-8"?>
<!DOCTYPE linux:config SYSTEM "DTD/linux.dtd">

<?cocoon-process type="xsp"?>
<?cocoon-process type="xslt"?>


<linux:config xmlns:linux="http://www.linux.org" kernel="2.2.14"
              dist="RedHat 6.1">
  <linux:gui>No Window Manager Installed</linux:gui>
  <!--Sound Card Configuration-->
  <sound>
    <!--Sound Blaster Card-->
    <card>
      <name>Sound Blaster Platinum</name>
    </card>
  </sound>
</linux:config>

----------------------------------------
Testing reading tree using DOM ...
----------------------------------------
```

Example 8-6. Output from JDOMTest Class (continued)

```
<?xml version="1.0" encoding="UTF-8"?>
<!DOCTYPE JavaXML:Book SYSTEM "DTD\JavaXML.dtd">

<?xml-stylesheet href="XSL\JavaXML.html.xsl" type="text/xsl"?>
<?xml-stylesheet href="XSL\JavaXML.wml.xsl" type="text/xsl"
                 media="wap"?>
<?cocoon-process type="xslt"?>
<!--  Java and XML  -->

<JavaXML:Book xmlns:JavaXML="http://www.oreilly.com/catalog/javaxml/">
  <JavaXML:Title>Java and XML</JavaXML:Title>
  <JavaXML:Contents>
    <JavaXML:Chapter focus="XML">
      <JavaXML:Heading>Introduction</JavaXML:Heading>
      <JavaXML:Topic subSections="7">What Is It?</JavaXML:Topic>

...

----------------------------------------
Testing reading tree using SAX ...
----------------------------------------


<?xml version="1.0" encoding="UTF-8"?>
<!DOCTYPE JavaXML:Book SYSTEM "DTD\JavaXML.dtd">

<?xml-stylesheet href="XSL\JavaXML.html.xsl" type="text/xsl"?>
<?xml-stylesheet href="XSL\JavaXML.wml.xsl" type="text/xsl"
                 media="wap"?>
<?cocoon-process type="xslt"?>
<!--  Java and XML  -->

<JavaXML:Book xmlns:JavaXML="http://www.oreilly.com/catalog/javaxml/">
  <JavaXML:Title>Java and XML</JavaXML:Title>
  <JavaXML:Contents>
    <JavaXML:Chapter focus="XML">
      <JavaXML:Heading>Introduction</JavaXML:Heading>
...
```

This output was the result of running `JDOMTest` with the `contents.xml` document we have been working with through the various chapters. The `JavaXML:References` element (and its children) is commented out, as our DTD does not allow those elements in the document. Leaving those elements in results in the following error message (when validation is requested in creating a `SAXBuilder` or `DOMBuilder` instance):

```
org.jdom.JDOMException: Error on line 59 of XML document: Element type
    "JavaXML:References" must be declared.
        at org.jdom.input.DOMBuilder.build(DOMBuilder.java:121)
        at org.jdom.input.AbstractBuilder.build(AbstractBuilder.java:58)
        at JDOMTest.domDocument(JDOMTest.java:46)
        at JDOMTest.main(JDOMTest.java:79)
Error on line 59 of XML document: Element type "JavaXML:References"
    must be declared.
```

One of the key features of JDOM is this error testing; this provides detailed information about the location within the XML input where errors occurred, making validation and well-formedness checking simple. Because input and output of an XML source takes only four lines of code (as shown in the `domDocument()` and `saxDocument()` methods), JDOM can be used to provide a means to ensure your XML documents are well-formed and valid.

NOTE For those of you paying close attention, you may have noticed something we did *not* have to worry about in the code above: validation and namespaces cooperating! Because JDOM handles namespaces internally (rather than depending on DOM Level 2 or SAX 2.0 to supply namespace information), it can perform validation while still providing namespace support. In fact, JDOM actually turns namespace-awareness off in `SAXBuilder` and `DOMBuilder`! Not only does this allow validation to occur, but it actually speeds up processing of XML documents.

As a final look at JDOM, we revisit the `SAXParserDemo` and `DOMParserDemo` from Chapters 3 and 7 briefly. Both of these programs printed out XML documents from an input file; while the `SAXParserDemo` provided more of a lifecycle view of the SAX parsing process, `DOMParserDemo` was essentially a "pretty-printer" class, outputting the DOM tree in human-readable format. Both classes allowed a look at an XML document; Example 8-7 shows the source for `com.oreilly.xml.PrettyPrinter`, a utility class that performs this same task using JDOM.

Example 8-7. The com.oreilly.xml.PrettyPrinter Utility Class

```
package com.oreilly.xml;

import java.io.File;

import org.jdom.Document;
import org.jdom.input.SAXBuilder;
import org.jdom.output.XMLOutputter;

/**
 * <b><code>PrettyPrinter</code></b> will output the XML document at a
 *   given URI
```

Example 8-7. The com.oreilly.xml.PrettyPrinter Utility Class (continued)

```
 *
 * @author
 *    <a href="mailto:brettmclaughlin@earthlink.net">Brett McLaughlin</a>
 * @author <a href="mailto:jhunter@servlets.com">Jason Hunter</a>
 * @version 1.0
 */
public class PrettyPrinter {

    /**
     * <p>
     * Pretty prints a given XML URI
     * </p>
     */
    public static void main(String[] args) {
        if (args.length != 1) {
            System.out.println("Usage: " +
                "java com.oreilly.xml.PrettyPrinter [XML_URI]");
            return;
        }

        String filename = args[0];

        try {
            // Build the Document with SAX and Xerces, no validation
            SAXBuilder builder = new SAXBuilder();

            // Create the document (without validation)
            Document doc = builder.build(new File(filename));

            // Output the document, use standard formatter
            XMLOutputter fmt = new XMLOutputter();
            fmt.output(doc, System.out);
        } catch (Exception e) {
            e.printStackTrace();
        }
    }
}
```

At this point, we have taken a bit of a whirlwind tour through JDOM, and only seen a glimpse of its full functionality. The complete API is documented in Appendix A, and includes all JDOM classes and interfaces, as well as the methods available for each. The support packages for JDOM, `org.jdom.adapters`, `org.jdom.input`, and `org.jdom.output`, are also documented in Appendix A. To continue to illustrate how JDOM is used (as we do with SAX and DOM), we will use JDOM in the examples throughout the rest of the book. Additionally, we compare JDOM to SAX and DOM in each example, ensuring that you can perform tasks using all three

APIs when needed. Ultimately, you can decide when each API is useful, and code accordingly. Finally, the most current version of JDOM and the corresponding Javadoc are available online at *http://www.jdom.org* and *http://www.newInstance.com.*

What's Next?

With JDOM added to our arsenal, and with our look at JAXP, we are ready to begin looking at specific applications of XML. Using SAX, DOM, and JDOM, we will discuss web publishing frameworks, business-to-business applications, XML-RPC, Rich Site Summary (RSS), XML configurations, and a variety of related topics in the latter half of the book. All topics focus on leveraging existing tools and adding code to enhance functionality rather than trying to recreate solutions that are already in place.

9

Web Publishing Frameworks

In this chapter:
- *Selecting a Framework*
- *Installation*
- *Using a Publishing Framework*
- *XSP*
- *Cocoon 2.0 and Beyond*
- *What's Next?*

This chapter begins our look at specific Java and XML topics. So far, we have covered the basics of using XML from Java, looking at the SAX and DOM APIs to manipulate XML and the fundamentals of using and creating XML itself. We've also looked at how JDOM can provide a more Java-centric means of using our XML data and documents within Java programs. Now that you have a grasp on using XML from your code, we will spend time on specific applications. The next six chapters represent the most significant applications of XML, and, in particular, how those applications are implemented in the Java space. While there are literally hundreds and soon to be thousands of important applications of XML, the topics in these chapters are those that continually seem to be in the spotlight, and that have a significant potential to change the way traditional development processes occur.

We begin our look at these hot topics with the one XML application that seems to have generated the largest amount of excitement in the XML and Java communities: the web publishing framework. Although we have continually emphasized that generating presentation from content is perhaps over-hyped when compared to the value of the portable data that XML provides, using XML for presentation styling is still very important. This importance increases when looking at web-based applications.

Over the next five years, virtually every major application will either be completely web-based, or at a minimum have a web frontend. At the same time, users are demanding more functionality, and marketing departments are demanding more flexibility in look and feel. The result has been the rise of the web artist; this new role is different from the webmaster in that little to no Perl, ASP, JavaScript, or other scripting language coding is part of the job description. The web artist's entire day is comprised of HTML creation, modification, and development. The rapid changes in business and market strategy can require a complete application or site overhaul as often as once a week, often forcing the web artist to spend days changing hundreds of HTML pages. While Cascading Style Sheets (CSS) have helped, the difficulty of maintaining consistency across these pages has required a huge amount of time. Even if this less than ideal situation were acceptable, no computer developer wants to spend his or her life making HTML changes to web pages.

With the advent of server-side Java, this problem has only grown. Servlet developers find themselves spending long hours modifying their `out.println()` statements to output HTML, and often glance hatefully at the marketing department when changes to a site's look require modifications to their code. The entire Java Server Pages (JSP) specification arguably stemmed from this situation; however, JSP is not a solution, as it only shifts the frustration to the HTML developer, who constantly has to avoid making incidental changes to embedded Java code. In addition, JSP does not provide the clean separation between content and presentation it promises. What was called for was a means to generate pure data content, and have that content uniformly styled either at predetermined times (static content generation), or dynamically at runtime (dynamic content generation).

Of course, you should be nodding your head at this familiar problem if you have ever done any web development, and hopefully your mind is wandering into the XSL and XSLT technology space. The problem is that an engine must exist to handle content generation, particularly in the dynamic sense. Having hundreds of XML documents on a site does no good if there is no mechanism to apply transformations on them when requested. Add to this the need for servlets and other server-side components to output XML that should be consistently styled, and you have defined a small set of requirements for the web publishing framework. In this chapter, we take a look at this framework, how it can allow you to toss out those long hours of HTML coding, and how it can help you convert all of those "web artists" into XML and XSL gurus, making you happy, them happy, and allowing your applications to change look and feel as often as you want.

A web publishing framework attempts to address these complicated issues. Just as a web server is responsible for responding to a URL request for a file, a web publishing framework is responsible for responding to a similar request; however, instead of responding with a file, it often will respond with a *published* version of a file. In this case, a published file refers to a file that may have been transformed with XSLT, or massaged at an application level, or converted into another format such as a PDF. The requestor does not see the raw data that may underlie the published result, but also does not have to explicitly request that publication occur. Often, a URI base (such as *http://yourHost.com/publish*) signifies that a publishing engine that sits on top of the web server should handle requests. As you may suspect, the concept is much simpler than the actual implementation of a framework like this, and finding the correct framework for your needs is not a trivial task.

Selecting a Framework

If you're getting an idea of the importance of the web publishing framework, you might expect to find a list of hundreds of possible solutions. This is because the Java language offers an easy interface into the various XML tools used by web publishing frameworks. Additionally, Java servlets offer a simple means of handling web requests and responses. However, the list of frameworks is small, and the list of good and stable ones is even smaller. One of the best resources for seeing what products are currently available is XML Software's list at *http://xmlsoftware.com/publishing/*. This list changes frequently enough that it is not worth repeating here. Still, some important criteria for determining what framework is right for you are worth mentioning.

Stability

Don't be surprised if you have a hard time finding a product whose version tag is greater than 2.x. In fact, you may have to search diligently to even find a second-generation framework. While a higher version number is not a guarantee of stability, it often reflects the amount of time, effort, and review that a framework has undergone. The XML publishing system is such a new beast that the market is being flooded with 1.0 and 1.1 products that simply are not stable enough for practical use.

You can also often ascertain stability of a product by the stability of other products from the same vendor. Often, an entire suite of tools is released by a vendor; if their other tools do not offer SAX 2.0 and DOM Level 2 support, or are all also 1.0 and 1.1 products, you might be wise to pass on the framework until it has matured a little more, and has conformed to newer XML standards. You should also try to steer away from platform-specific technologies—if the framework is tied to a platform (such as Windows), you aren't dealing with a pure Java solution. Remember that a publishing framework must serve clients on any platform; why be happy with a product that can't also run on any platform?

Integration with Other XML Tools and APIs

Once you have ensured that your framework is stable enough for your needs, you should make sure that it has support for a variety of XML parsers and processors. If a framework is tied to a specific parser or processor, you are really just buying an XML version of Microsoft—you have tied yourself to one specific implementation of a technology. Although frameworks often integrate well with a particular parser vendor, determine if parsers can be interchanged. If you have a favorite processor (or one left to you from previous projects), make sure that processor can still be used.

Support for SAX and DOM is a must. Also, try to find a framework whose developers are monitoring the specifications of XML Schema, XLink, XPointer, and other emerging XML technologies. This will indicate if you can expect to see revisions of the framework add support for these XML specifications, an important indication of the framework's longevity. Don't be afraid to ask questions about how quickly new specifications can be expected to be integrated into the product, and insist on a firm answer.

Production Presence

The last, and perhaps most important, question to answer when looking for a web publishing framework is determining if it is used in production applications. If you cannot be supplied with at least a few reference applications or sites that are using the framework, don't be surprised if there aren't any. Vendors (and developers, in the open source realm) should be happy and proud to let you know where you can check out their frameworks in action. Hesitance in this area is a sign that you may be more of a pioneer with a product than you wish to be.

Making the Decision

Once you have evaluated these criteria, you will probably have a clear answer. Very few frameworks can positively answer all the questions raised here, not to mention your application specific concerns. In fact, at the time of this writing, less than five publishing frameworks exist that support the latest versions of SAX, DOM, and JAXP, are in production at even one application site, and have at least three significant revisions of code under their belt. These are not listed here because, honestly, in six months they may not exist, or may be radically changed. The world of web publishing frameworks is in such flux that trying to recommend you to four or five options and be assured they will be in existence months from now has a greater chance of misleading you than helping you.

However, one publishing framework has consistently succeeded and received notice within the Java and XML community; when considering the open source community in particular, this framework is often the choice of Java developers. The Apache Cocoon project, founded by Stefano Mazzocchi, has been a solid framework since its inception. Developed while most of us were still trying to figure out what XML was, Cocoon is now entering its second generation as an XML publishing framework based completely in Java. It also is part of the Apache XML project, and has default support for Apache Xerces and Apache Xalan. It allows any conformant XML parser to be used, and is based on the immensely popular Java servlet architecture. In addition, there are several production sites using Apache Cocoon (in its 1.x form) that push the boundaries of traditional web application development yet still perform extremely well. For this reason, and again in keeping with the spirit of open source software, we use Apache Cocoon as the framework of choice in this chapter.

In previous chapters, our choice of XML parser and processor was fairly open; in other words, examples would work with only small modifications to code when using different vendor implementations. However, the web publishing framework is not standardized, and each framework implements wildly different features and conventions. For this reason, the examples in this chapter using Apache Cocoon are not portable; however, the popularity of the concepts and design patterns used within Cocoon merit an entire chapter on using the framework. If you do not choose Cocoon, you should at least look over the examples, as the concepts in web publishing are usable across any vendor implementation, even though the specifics of the code are not.

Installation

In other chapters, installation instructions generally involved pointing you at a web site where you could obtain a distribution of the software and letting you add the included *jar* file to your class path. Installing a framework such as Cocoon is not such a trivial task, and we document the procedures to make this happen here. If you want the very latest versions of the framework, you should download a copy of CVS, the Concurrent Versioning System. This allows you to obtain the code from the actual source code repository rather than the less frequent code releases, which usually occur at version releases. You can get CVS from *http://www.cyclic.com/cyclic-pages/howget.html*.

With Cocoon, we look at the 1.x version of the framework. Although by the time you are reading this, the public 2.0 release will probably be available in a beta form, at this time, Cocoon 2.0 is in an alpha state, and is only available through CVS access. Because of the high amount of change still anticipated in the Cocoon 2.0 framework, we will focus on the 1.x version tree, as that is being used most often today. At the end of this chapter, we do take a brief look at the upcoming features of Cocoon 2, which is scheduled for a full release late in 2000. If you are looking at using Cocoon in a production environment today, you will definitely want to stay with the 1.x branch until Cocoon 2 has been released and stabilized.

If going through the procedures you find yourself encountering problems, you should take advantage of the online resources available for Cocoon. The Apache XML project, located at *http://xml.apache.org*, hosts the Cocoon project. There are mailing lists available at *http://xml.apache.org/mail.html*, as well as a very informative FAQ at *http://xml.apache.org/cocoon/faqs.html*. Don't be afraid to ask questions and get involved; installation of complex application frameworks is rarely simple, and chances are that others may share your problems and frustrations. With that in mind, let's get down to business.

Getting Ant

Unix and Linux veterans are probably already gearing up to type those familiar commands when compiling source code:

```
/home/bmclaugh (mejis)> ./configure
/home/bmclaugh (mejis)> make
/home/bmclaugh (mejis)> make install
```

The association between source code, `make`, and `autoconf` is old and long-standing. However, `make` does not translate well with Java code—Windows users have to have additional tools for compiling on a Windows platform, lengthy configuration has to be performed to allow Javadoc and other extra commands to be run, RMI compiles (`rmic`) are complex, and the list goes on. The solution designed to work so well with Perl, shell scripts, and C code is not robust enough for the Java paradigm.

Luckily, James Duncan Davidson (of Jakarta, JAXP, and the servlet specification fame) spent some long nights doing more than just complaining. He began what is now called Ant, which is part of the Apache Jakarta project. Ant is a Java-based build tool; its configuration is XML based, it is cross-platform, and can handle any task needed. RMI compiles, Javadoc, external commands, and more can all be run within this environment. It is Ant that is used for building the Cocoon sources.

The current version of Ant is included when you obtain Cocoon, and is located in the Cocoon *lib/* directory. You can also get the latest version of Ant from the Jakarta web site, located at *http://jakarta.apache.org*. Instructions for using Ant with Cocoon are included with the Cocoon distribution, while more general documentation on Ant is available at the Jakarta web site.

Getting Cocoon

With Ant in place, you are ready to obtain the source for Cocoon 1.x. In addition to being able to download Cocoon from the Apache XML project (*http://xml.apache.org*), the latest version with new features is available via CVS. If you are just starting out with Cocoon, you may want to download a packaged distribution; however, by this time you should be pretty comfortable with Java and XML code. You may want to obtain the very newest version of Cocoon, the 1.x.dev version, from the Apache XML CVS repository. You can get the code from CVS with:

```
cvs -d :pserver:anoncvs@xml.apache.org:/home/cvspublic login
Password: ******* (Password is 'anoncvs')
```

```
cvs -d :pserver:anoncvs@xml.apache.org:/home/cvspublic checkout xml-cocoon
...
```

You will then get the Cocoon source distribution in the *xml-cocoon* directory. This contains the build file used by Ant, all the required libraries to build Cocoon, and the source itself. Change into the created directory and you are ready to build Cocoon.

Building Cocoon

At this point, you need to be sure you are back into the main directory of the Cocoon project. To perform the build, enter the following command on Windows systems:

```
D:\dev\xml-cocoon> build.bat
```

A shell script is provided for use on Unix and Linux systems:

```
$ sh build.sh
```

The *lib/* subdirectory contains all the libraries needed for building Cocoon. These supplied build scripts will add each *jar* file in this directory to your class path, which includes the latest versions of Apache Xerces, Apache Xalan, and other dependencies that work with Cocoon 1.x. Even if you already have some of these libraries (such as Xerces or Xalan), it is recommended that you use the supplied libraries (which the scripts take care of), as they are certified to work with the version of Cocoon retrieved from CVS. When finished, your class path will include the following libraries:

- JDK Tools: *tools.jar*
- Jakarta Ant: *ant.jar*
- Servlet API 2.2: *servlet_2_2.jar*
- Apache Xerces: *xerces_x_y_z.jar*
- Apache Xalan: *xalan_x_y_z.jar*
- Apache FOP*: *fop_x_y_z.jar*
- Apache Stylebook†: *stylebook-x.y-z.jar*

The build script then tells Ant to use the *build.xml* in the current directory to build the project. Once executed, your output should look like this:

* This is the same FOP (Formatting Objects Processor) we looked at in Chapter 6, *Transforming XML*, when discussing converting XML to non-textual formats.

† Stylebook is a project that handles generation of very complex documents, including HTML, and is used to generate the Cocoon documentation and web site. The Stylebook project is set to integrate with Cocoon in Cocoon 2.0.

```
Cocoon Build System
-------------------
Building with classpath /usr/java/lib/tools.jar;./lib/xerces_1_0_3.jar;
./lib/xalan_1_0_0.jar;./lib/fop_0_12_1.jar;./lib/servlet_2_2.jar;
./lib/ant.jar
Starting Ant...
Buildfile: build.xml
Project base dir set to: /home/bmclaugh/projects/cocoon
Executing Target: init
------------------- Cocoon 1.7.3-dev [1999-2000] ----------------
Executing Target: prepare
Created dir: /home/bmclaugh/projects/cocoon/build
Executing Target: prepare-projectx
Copying 1 files to /home/bmclaugh/projects/cocoon/src
Executing Target: prepare-xt
Executing Target: prepare-ecma
Executing Target: prepare-ldap
Copying 5 files to /home/bmclaugh/projects/cocoon/build/src
Executing Target: prepare-src
Created dir: /home/bmclaugh/projects/cocoon/build/classes
Copying 109 files to D:\dev\xml-cocoon\build\src
Executing Target: compile
Compiling 98 source files to /home/bmclaugh/projects/cocoon/build/classes
Copying 12 support files to /home/bmclaugh/projects/cocoon /build/classes
Executing Target: package
Building jar: /home/bmclaugh/projects/cocoon/build/cocoon.jar
Completed in 24 seconds
```

You may see slight differences in the version or exact number of files, but no errors should occur; if they do, make the corrections to your class path indicated by the build program and re-run the build command. At the end of this process, you should have the complete Cocoon distribution in a single *jar* file, *cocoon.jar*, located in the *build/* subdirectory. You should also verify that you have the sample properties file that Cocoon comes with, *cocoon.properties*, in the *bin/* directory of the project. If you cannot locate this file, it is also located in the *build/classes/org/apache/cocoon/* subdirectory.

You can also use Ant to generate documentation, Javadoc, and perform other tasks related to the project. These tasks are accomplished by specifying *targets* to the build command. Targets are keywords supplied as arguments to Ant; the complete list of supported targets for Cocoon is listed in the build file, *build.xml*. The target for documentation is `docs`, and for Javadoc it is `javadocs`. For example, to generate the Cocoon project documentation, perform:

```
$ sh build.sh docs
Building with classpath /usr/java/lib/tools.jar;./lib/xerces_1_0_3.jar;
./lib/xalan_1_0_0.jar;./lib/fop_0_12_1.jar;./lib/servlet_2_2.jar;
./lib/ant.jar
```

```
Starting Ant...
Buildfile: build.xml
Project base dir set to: /home/bmclaugh/projects/cocoon
Executing Target: init
------------------ Cocoon 1.7.3-dev [1999-2000] ---------------
Executing Target: prepare-docs
Replacing ./docs/dtd/ --> dtd/
Replacing ./docs/dtd/ --> dtd/
Executing Target: docs
...
```

This generates complete project documentation in the *build/docs/* subdirectory. Once you have built Cocoon and any desired optional targets, you should be ready to set up your servlet engine to use Cocoon.

Configuring the Servlet Engine

Once you have built Cocoon, you need to configure your servlet engine to use Cocoon and tell it which requests Cocoon should handle. We look at setting up Cocoon to work with the Jakarta Tomcat servlet engine here;* as this is the reference implementation for the Java Servlet API 2.2, you should be able to mimic these steps for your own servlet engine if you are not using the Tomcat implementation.

The Cocoon framework is built to operate at an engine level rather than as another servlet in your engine. Therefore, we need to add Cocoon and its dependencies to the core servlet engine class path rather than in a particular servlet zone or context. Copy the Cocoon *jar* file and the Xerces, Xalan, and FOP *jar* files into the Tomcat *lib/* subdirectory, off of the main Tomcat installation directory. You then need to add these libraries to the engine class path; in Tomcat, this is accomplished through editing the Tomcat initialization script. For Windows platforms, this is *<TOMCAT_HOME>/bin/tomcat.bat*; for Unix platforms, *<TOMCAT_HOME>/bin/tomcat.sh.* In these files, you will see the lines that set the class path used by Tomcat when starting up. You should add the Cocoon distribution and its dependencies *before* these other entries in the configuration file. On Windows, this will look like:

```
set CLASSPATH=.
set CLASSPATH=%TOMCAT_HOME%\classes

rem Cocoon classes and libraries
set CLASSPATH=%CLASSPATH%;%TOMCAT_HOME%\lib\xerces_1_0_3.jar
set CLASSPATH=%CLASSPATH%;%TOMCAT_HOME%\lib\xalan_1_0_0.jar
```

* Although the 3.1 build is used in these examples, Cocoon only requires a 2.x version of the servlet API. In addition, configuration options in Tomcat should not be subject to change with revisions of the engine; in other words, the instructions within this chapter should apply to any 3.x version of Tomcat.

```
set CLASSPATH=%CLASSPATH%;%TOMCAT_HOME%\lib\fop_0_12_1.jar
set CLASSPATH=%CLASSPATH%;%TOMCAT_HOME%\lib\cocoon.jar

set CLASSPATH=%CLASSPATH%;%TOMCAT_HOME%\lib\webserver.jar
set CLASSPATH=%CLASSPATH%;%TOMCAT_HOME%\lib\jasper.jar
set CLASSPATH=%CLASSPATH%;%TOMCAT_HOME%\lib\xml.jar
set CLASSPATH=%CLASSPATH%;%TOMCAT_HOME%\lib\servlet.jar
set CLASSPATH=%CLASSPATH%;%JAVA_HOME%\lib\tools.jar
```

On Unix platforms, the modified file should look like this:

```
CLASSPATH=.

# Cocoon classes and libraries
CLASSPATH=${CLASSPATH}:${TOMCAT_HOME}/lib/xerces_1_0_3.jar
CLASSPATH=${CLASSPATH}:${TOMCAT_HOME}/lib/xalan_0_20_0.jar
CLASSPATH=${CLASSPATH}:${TOMCAT_HOME}/lib/fop_0_12_1.jar
CLASSPATH=${CLASSPATH}:${TOMCAT_HOME}/lib/cocoon.jar

for i in ${TOMCAT_HOME}/lib/* ; do
  CLASSPATH=${CLASSPATH}:$i
done

CLASSPATH=${CLASSPATH}:${JAVA_HOME}/lib/tools.jar
```

It is important to ensure that the Cocoon classes precede the rest of the Tomcat classes, particularly *xml.jar*. While Xerces, Xalan, and Cocoon all use SAX 2 and DOM Level 2 classes and interfaces, the Sun Project X parser contained in *xml.jar* does not yet have SAX 2 and DOM Level 2 support; if this class and its SAX and DOM versions are found first, the Cocoon framework will error out.

With these libraries added, all that is left is to specify to Cocoon the location of its properties file (we will look at what this file does a little later). Copy the *cocoon.properties* file from the Cocoon root directory into *<TOMCAT_HOME>/conf/*. In this same directory, you will see *web.xml*, which configures the properties for engine-wide servlets. In this file are properties and mappings for various engine-level servlets; we need to add configuration for Cocoon here. Insert the following entries into the engine configuration file:

```
<servlet>
    <servlet-name>
        org.apache.cocoon.Cocoon
    </servlet-name>
    <servlet-class>
        org.apache.cocoon.Cocoon
    </servlet-class>
    <init-param>
        <param-name>
            properties
```

```
            </param-name>
            <param-value>
                cocoon.properties
            </param-value>
        </init-param>
    </servlet>
    <servlet-mapping>
        <servlet-name>
            org.apache.cocoon.Cocoon
        </servlet-name>
        <url-pattern>
            *.xml
        </url-pattern>
    </servlet-mapping>
```

The location within the file does not matter, as long as you ensure that element nestings are not disrupted; in other words, the resulting file must remain well-formed XML. You will also need to insert the correct path to the *cocoon.properties* file for the value of the `properties` parameter. This tells the engine to pass this parameter to the main Cocoon servlet, enabling it to configure itself and the rest of the Cocoon framework. The `servlet-mapping` then instructs the engine to direct all URI requests that end in *.xml* to the Cocoon framework. With these changes made, you can start (or restart) Tomcat; ensure that no errors occur and the Cocoon install can be tested.

If everything has been configured correctly, you should be able to access *http://<hostname>:<port>/Cocoon.xml* in your web browser. If no errors occur, the HTML output should look like that shown in Figure 9-1.

If there are errors, you should see a stack trace indicating what problems were encountered. These typically relate to classes not being in the engine class path that Cocoon needs, the properties file not being specified in an initial argument to the servlet, or the file specified being unreadable by the servlet. Correct any errors that result, and restart the engine. Once you receive the output above, you are ready to see Cocoon in action and configure Cocoon to handle a variety of requests.

Using a Publishing Framework

Using a good publishing framework like Cocoon doesn't require any special instruction; it is not a complex application that users must learn to adapt to. In fact, all the uses of Cocoon are based on simple URLs entered into a standard web browser. Generating dynamic HTML from XML, viewing XML transformed into PDF files, and even seeing VRML applications generated from XML is simply a matter of typing the URL to the desired XML file into your browser and watching Cocoon and the power of XML take action.

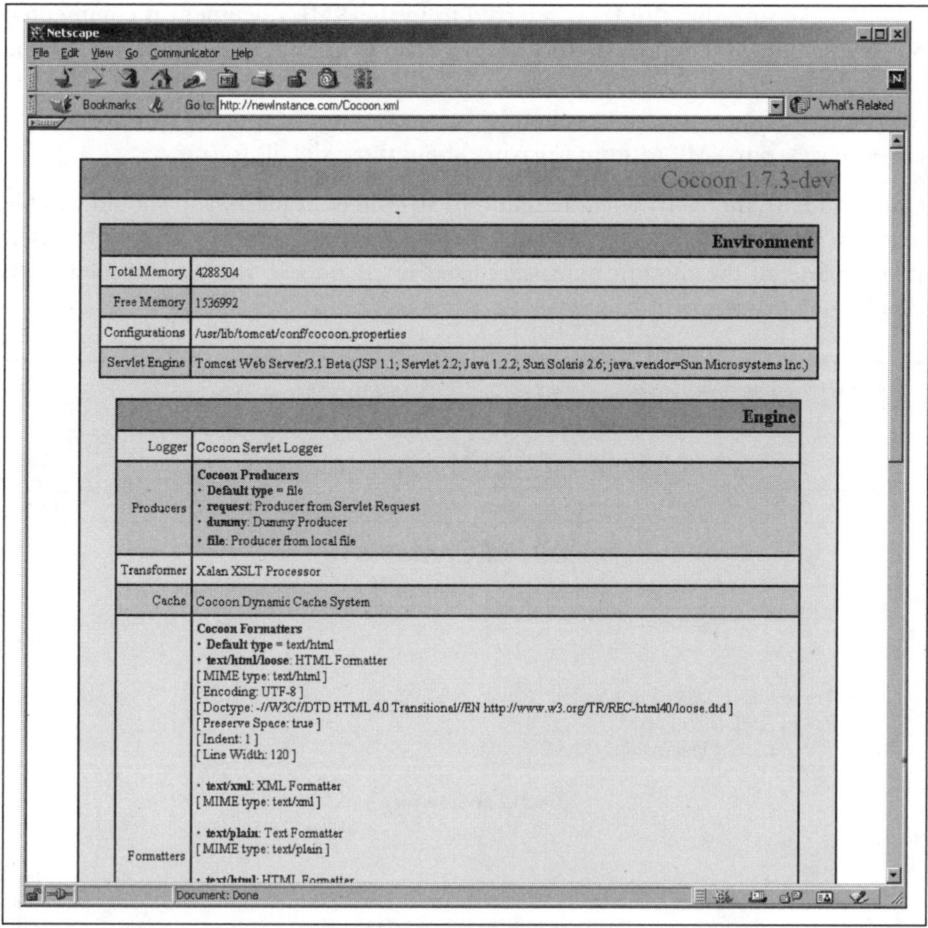

Figure 9-1. The output of the Cocoon configuration URI when properly configured

Viewing XML Converted to HTML

Now that our framework is in place and correctly handling requests that end in *.xml*, we can begin to see it publish our XML files. Cocoon comes with several sample XML files and associated XSL stylesheets in the project's *samples/* subdirectory. However, we have our own XML and XSL from earlier chapters, so let's transform the partial XML table of contents for our book with the XSL stylesheet we built in Chapter 6, *Transforming XML*. The XML file should be named *contents.xml* (and is also available from the book's web site). Locate where you saved this file, and copy it into the servlet engine's document root. On a default installation of Tomcat, this is under *<TOMCAT_ROOT>/webapps/ROOT/*. The document refers to the stylesheet *XSL/JavaXML.html.xsl*. Create the XSL directory in your web document root, and copy the stylesheet we built in Chapter 6 into that directory. You should make sure that the DTD referred to in the XML document is commented out (remember, validation should rarely occur in production); also convert the `OReillyCopyright` entity reference to HTML as discussed in Chapter 6. Although validation and external entity references are supported by Cocoon, it is easier to view our XML without worrying about those details for now.

Once you have the XML document and its stylesheet in place, you should be able to access it with the URL *http://<hostname>:<port>/contents.xml* in your web browser. If you made all the modifications discussed in Chapter 6, the transformed XML should look like Figure 9-2.

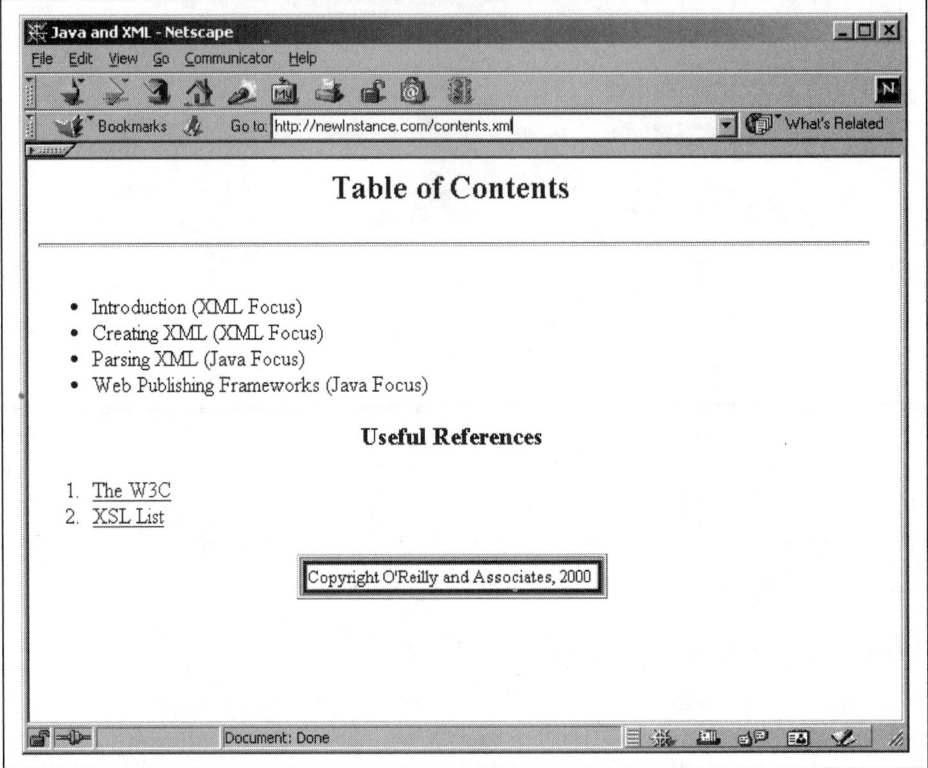

Figure 9-2. Transformed XML from Chapter 6

This should have seemed almost trivial to you; once Cocoon is set up and configured, serving up dynamic content is a piece of cake! The mapping from XML extensions to Cocoon should work across your entire servlet engine.

Viewing PDFs from XML

So far, we have talked almost exclusively about converting XML documents to HTML; when not looking at this, we have assumed our data was being used in an application-to-application manner. The format was entirely arbitrary, as both the sending and receiving applications parsed the XML using the specified DTD or schema. However, a publishing framework offers many more possibilities. Not only are a variety of markup languages supported as final document formats, but in addition, Java provides libraries for converting XML to some non-markup-based formats. The most popular and stable library in this category is the Apache XML group's Formatting Objects Processor, FOP, which we discussed briefly in Chapter 6. This gives Cocoon or any other publishing framework the ability to turn XML documents into Portable Document Format (PDF) documents, which are generally viewed with Adobe Acrobat (*http://www.adobe.com*).

The importance of being able to convert a document from XML into a PDF cannot be overstated; particularly for document-driven web sites, such as print media or publishing companies, this could revolutionize web delivery of data. Consider the following XML document, an XML-formatted excerpt from Chapter 1, *Introduction*, shown in Example 9-1.

Example 9-1. XML Version of Chapter 1

```
<?xml version="1.0"?>

<?cocoon-process type="xslt"?>
<?xml-stylesheet href="XSL/JavaXML.fo.xsl" type="text/xsl"?>

<book>
 <cover>
  <title>Java and XML</title>
   <author>Brett McLaughlin</author>
 </cover>

 <contents>
  <chapter id="chapterOne">
   <title>Chapter 1: Introduction</title>

   <paragraph>XML.  These three letters have brought shivers to
   almost every developer in the world today at some point in the
   last two years.  While those shivers were often fear at another
   acronym to memorize, excitement at the promise of a new technology,
   or annoyance at another source of confusion for today's
   developer, they were shivers all the same.  Surprisingly, almost every
   type of response was well merited with regard to XML.  It is another
   acronym to memorize, and in fact brings with it a dizzying array of
   companions: XSL, XSLT, PI, DTD, XHTML, and more.  It also brings with
```

Example 9-1. XML Version of Chapter 1 (continued)

```
    it a huge promise—what Java did for portability of code, XML claims
    to do for portability of data.  Sun has even been touting the
    rather ambitious slogan "Java + XML = Portable Code + Portable
    Data" in recent months.  And yes, XML does bring with it a
    significant amount of confusion.  We will seek to unravel and
    demystify XML, without being so abstract and general as to be
    useless, and without diving in so deeply that this becomes just
    another droll specification to wade through.  This
    is a book for you, the Java developer, who wants to understand the
    hype and use the tools that XML brings to the table.</paragraph>

    <paragraph>Today's web application now faces a wealth of problems
    that were not even considered ten years ago.  Systems that are
    distributed across thousands of miles must perform quickly and
    flawlessly.  Data from heterogeneous systems, databases, directory
    services, and applications must be transferred without a single
    decimal place being lost.  Applications must be able to communicate
    not only with other business components, but other business systems
    altogether, often across companies as well as technologies.  Clients
    are no longer limited to thick clients, but can be web browsers that
    support HTML, mobile phones that support Wireless Application
    Protocol (WAP), or handheld organizers with entirely different markup
    languages altogether. Data, and the transformation of that data, has
    become the crucial centerpiece of every application being developed
    today.</paragraph>
   </chapter>

  </contents>
</book>
```

We have already seen how XSL stylesheets allow us to transform this document into HTML. But converting an entire chapter of a book into HTML could result in a gigantic HTML document, and certainly an unreadable format; potential readers wanting online delivery of a book generally would prefer a PDF document. On the other hand, generating PDF statically from the chapter means changes to the chapter must be matched with subsequent PDF file generation. Keeping a single XML document format means the chapter can be easily updated (with any XML editor), formatted into SGML for printing hard copy, transferred to other companies and applications, and included in other books or compendiums. Now add to this robust set of features the ability for web users to type in a URL and access the book in PDF format, and you have a complete publishing system.

Although we don't have the time to cover formatting objects and the FOP for Java libraries in detail, you can review the entire formatting objects definition within the XSL specification at the W3C at *http://www.w3.org/TR/xsl/*. Example 9-2 is an

XSL stylesheet that uses formatting objects to specify a transformation from XML to a PDF document, appropriate for our XML version of Chapter 1.

Example 9-2. XSL Stylesheet to Transform Example 9-1 into a PDF Document

```
<xsl:stylesheet version="1.0"
  xmlns:xsl="http://www.w3.org/1999/XSL/Transform"
  xmlns:fo="http://www.w3.org/1999/XSL/Format">

  <xsl:template match="book">
    <xsl:processing-instruction name="cocoon-format">
      type="text/xslfo"
    </xsl:processing-instruction>
    <fo:root xmlns:fo="http://www.w3.org/1999/XSL/Format">
      <fo:layout-master-set>
      <fo:simple-page-master
        page-master-name="right"
        margin-top="75pt"
        margin-bottom="25pt"
        margin-left="100pt"
        margin-right="50pt">
        <fo:region-body margin-bottom="50pt"/>
        <fo:region-after extent="25pt"/>
      </fo:simple-page-master>
      <fo:simple-page-master
        page-master-name="left"
        margin-top="75pt"
        margin-bottom="25pt"
        margin-left="50pt"
        margin-right="100pt">
        <fo:region-body margin-bottom="50pt"/>
        <fo:region-after extent="25pt"/>
      </fo:simple-page-master>
      </fo:layout-master-set>

      <fo:page-sequence>

        <fo:sequence-specification>
          <fo:sequence-specifier-alternating
            page-master-first="right"
            page-master-odd="right"
            page-master-even="left"/>
        </fo:sequence-specification>

        <fo:static-content flow-name="xsl-after">
          <fo:block text-align-last="centered" font-size="10pt">
            <fo:page-number/>
          </fo:block>
        </fo:static-content>
```

Example 9-2. XSL Stylesheet to Transform Example 9-1 into a PDF Document (continued)

```
        <fo:flow>
          <xsl:apply-templates/>
        </fo:flow>
      </fo:page-sequence>

    </fo:root>
  </xsl:template>

  <xsl:template match="cover/title">
    <fo:block font-size="36pt" text-align-last="centered"
              space-before.optimum="24pt">
      <xsl:apply-templates/>
    </fo:block>
  </xsl:template>

  <xsl:template match="author">
    <fo:block font-size="24pt" text-align-last="centered"
              space-before.optimum="24pt">
      <xsl:apply-templates/>
    </fo:block>
  </xsl:template>

  <xsl:template match="chapter">
    <xsl:apply-templates/>
  </xsl:template>

  <xsl:template match="chapter/title">
    <fo:block font-size="24pt" text-align-last="centered"
              space-before.optimum="24pt">
      <xsl:apply-templates/>
    </fo:block>
  </xsl:template>

  <xsl:template match="paragraph">
    <fo:block font-size="12pt" space-before.optimum="12pt"
              text-align="justified">
      <xsl:apply-templates/>
    </fo:block>
  </xsl:template>
</xsl:stylesheet>
```

If you create both of these files, saving the chapter as *chapterOne.xml*, and the XSL stylesheet as *JavaXML.fo.xsl* within a subdirectory called *XSL/*, you can see the result of the transformation in a web browser. Make sure you have the Adobe Acrobat Reader and plug-in for your web browser, and then access the XML document just created. Figure 9-3 shows the results.

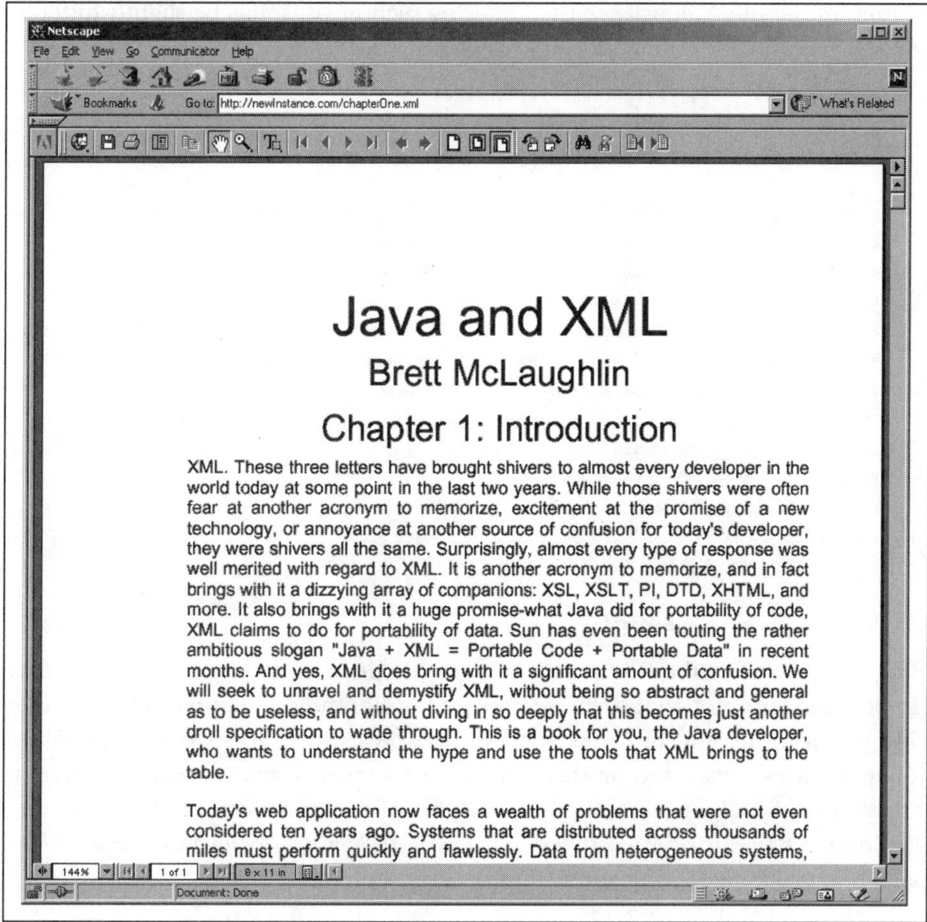

Java and XML

Brett McLaughlin

Chapter 1: Introduction

XML. These three letters have brought shivers to almost every developer in the world today at some point in the last two years. While those shivers were often fear at another acronym to memorize, excitement at the promise of a new technology, or annoyance at another source of confusion for today's developer, they were shivers all the same. Surprisingly, almost every type of response was well merited with regard to XML. It is another acronym to memorize, and in fact brings with it a dizzying array of companions: XSL, XSLT, PI, DTD, XHTML, and more. It also brings with it a huge promise-what Java did for portability of code, XML claims to do for portability of data. Sun has even been touting the rather ambitious slogan "Java + XML = Portable Code + Portable Data" in recent months. And yes, XML does bring with it a significant amount of confusion. We will seek to unravel and demystify XML, without being so abstract and general as to be useless, and without diving in so deeply that this becomes just another droll specification to wade through. This is a book for you, the Java developer, who wants to understand the hype and use the tools that XML brings to the table.

Today's web application now faces a wealth of problems that were not even considered ten years ago. Systems that are distributed across thousands of miles must perform quickly and flawlessly. Data from heterogeneous systems,

Figure 9-3. PDF document from Example 9-1 and Example 9-2.

Browser-Dependent Styling

In addition to specifically requesting certain types of transformations, such as a conversion to a PDF, Cocoon allows for dynamic processing to occur based on the request. A common example of this is applying different formatting based on the media of the client. In a traditional web environment, this would allow an XML document to be transformed differently based on the browser being used. A client using Internet Explorer could be served a different presentation than a client using Netscape; with the recent wars between versions of HTML, DHTML, and JavaScript brewing between Netscape and Microsoft, this is a powerful feature to have available. Cocoon provides built-in support for many common browser types. Locate the *cocoon.properties* file you referenced earlier, open it, and scroll to the bottom of the file. You will see the following section (this may be slightly different for newer versions):

```
##########################################
# User Agents (Browsers)                 #
##########################################

# NOTE: numbers indicate the search order. This is very important since
# some words may be found in more than one browser description. (MSIE is
# presented as "Mozilla/4.0 (Compatible; MSIE 4.01; ...")
#
# for example, the "explorer=MSIE" tag indicates that the XSL stylesheet
# associated to the media type "explorer" should be mapped to those
# browsers that have the string "MSIE" in their "user-Agent" HTTP header.

browser.0 = explorer=MSIE
browser.1 = opera=Opera
browser.2 = lynx=Lynx
browser.3 = java=Java
browser.4 = wap=Nokia
browser.5 = wap=UP
browser.6 = netscape=Mozilla
```

The keywords after the first equals sign are the items to take note of: `explorer`, `lynx`, `java`, and `netscape`, for example, all differentiate between different user-agents, the codes the browsers send with requests for URLs. As an example of applying stylesheets based on this property, let's create a sample XSL stylesheet to apply when the client accesses our XML table of contents document with Internet Explorer. Copy our original stylesheet, *JavaXML.html.xsl*, to *JavaXML.explorer-html.xsl*. Then make the modifications shown in Example 9-3.

Example 9-3. Internet Explorer XSL Stylesheet

```
<?xml version="1.0"?>

<xsl:stylesheet xmlns:xsl="http://www.w3.org/1999/XSL/Transform"
                xmlns:JavaXML="http://www.oreilly.com/catalog/javaxml/"
>

  <xsl:template match="JavaXML:Book">
    <html>
      <head>
        <title>
          <xsl:value-of select="JavaXML:Title" /> (Explorer Version)
        </title>
      </head>
      <body>
        <xsl:apply-templates select="*[not(self::JavaXML:Title)]" />
      </body>
```

Example 9-3. Internet Explorer XSL Stylesheet (continued)

```
    </html>
  </xsl:template>

  <xsl:template match="JavaXML:Contents">
    <center>
      <h2>Table of Contents (Explorer Version)</h2>
      <small>
        Try <a href="http://www.netscape.com">Netscape</a> today!
      </small>
    </center>
...
```

While this is a trivial example, dynamic HTML could be inserted for Internet Explorer 5.0, and standard HTML could be used for Netscape Navigator, which has less DHTML support. With this in place, we need to let our XML document know that if the media type (or user-agent) matches up with the `explorer` type defined in the properties file, a different XSL stylesheet should be used. The additional processing instruction shown in Example 9-4 handles this, and can be added to the *contents.xml* file.

Example 9-4. XML Document with Multiple Stylesheets Based on Media Type

```
<?xml version="1.0"?>
<?xml-stylesheet href="XSL\JavaXML.html.xsl" type="text/xsl"?>
<?xml-stylesheet href="XSL\JavaXML.explorer-html.xsl" type="text/xsl"
                 media="explorer"?>
<?xml-stylesheet href="XSL\JavaXML.wml.xsl" type="text/xsl"
                 media="wap"?>
<?cocoon-process type="xslt"?>
...
```

Accessing the XML in your Netscape browser yields the same results as before; however, if you access the page in Internet Explorer, you will see that the document has been transformed with the alternate stylesheet, and looks like Figure 9-4.

WAP and WML

One of the real powers in this dynamic application of stylesheets lies in the use of wireless devices. Remember our properties file?

```
browser.0 = explorer=MSIE
browser.1 = opera=Opera
browser.2 = lynx=Lynx
browser.3 = java=Java
browser.4 = wap=Nokia
browser.5 = wap=UP
browser.6 = netscape=Mozilla
```

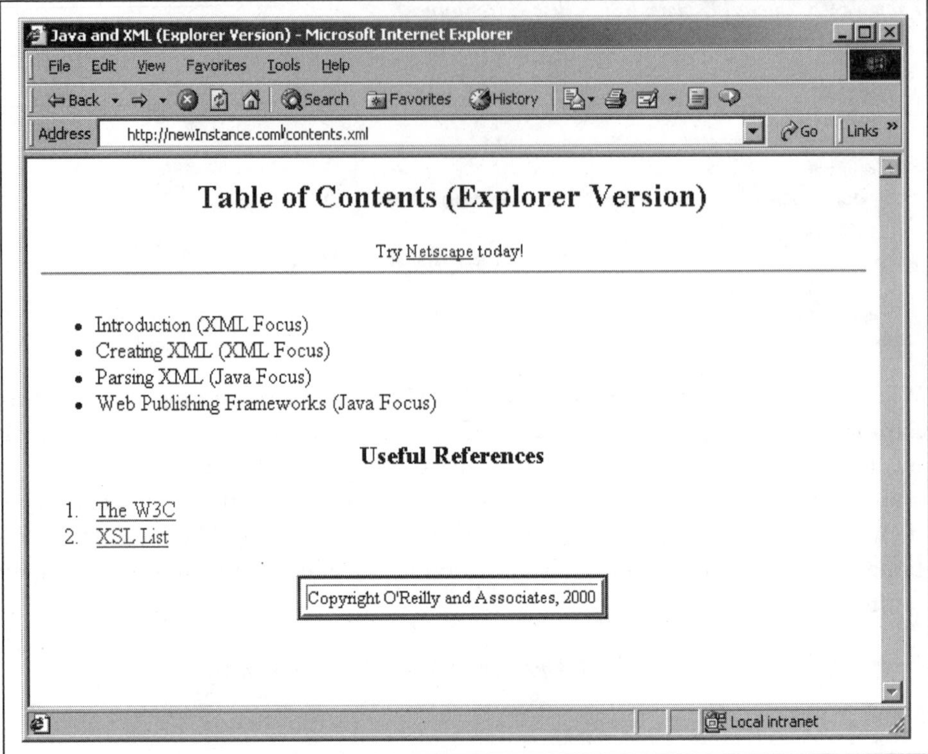

Figure 9-4. Internet Explorer version of generated HTML

The two highlighted entries detect that a wireless agent, such as an Internet-capable phone, is being used to access content. Just as Cocoon detected whether the incoming web browser was Internet Explorer or Netscape, responding with the correct stylesheet, a WAP device can be handled by yet another stylesheet. So far we have looked at the line that specifies a stylesheet to use for WAP media in our *contents.xml* file without paying it much attention:

```
<?xml-stylesheet href="XSL\JavaXML.html.xsl" type="text/xsl"?>
<?xml-stylesheet href="XSL\JavaXML.explorer-html.xsl" type="text/xsl"
                 media="explorer"?>
<?xml-stylesheet href="XSL\JavaXML.wml.xsl" type="text/xsl"
                 media="wap"?>
<?cocoon-process type="xslt"?>
```

Now we take a look at this in more detail. When building a stylesheet for a WAP device, the Wireless Markup Language (WML) is typically used. This is a variant on HTML, but has a slightly different method of representing different pages. When a wireless device requests a URL, the returned response must be within a `wml` element. Within that root element, several *cards* can be defined, each through the WML `card` element. The device downloads multiple cards at one time (often referred to as a *deck*) so that it does not have to go back to the server for the additional screens. Example 9-5 shows a simple XML page using these constructs.

Example 9-5. A Simple WML Page

```
<wml>
 <card id="index" title="Home Page">
  <p align="left">
   <i>Main Menu</i><br />
   <a href="#title">Title Page</a><br />
   <a href="#myPage">My Page</a><br />
  <p>
 </card>

 <card id="title" title="My Title Page">
  Welcome to my Title Page!<br />
  So happy to see you.
 </card>

 <card id="myPage" title="Hello World">
  <p align="center">
   Hello World!
  </p>
 </card>
</wml>
```

This simple example would serve requests with a menu, and two screens that could be accessed from links within that menu. The complete WML 1.1 specification is available online at *http://updev.phone.com/dev/ts/* by signing up for a free membership to phone.com's developer website, located at *http://updev.phone.com*. Additionally, the UP.SDK can be downloaded; this is a software emulation of a wireless device that allows testing of your WML pages. With this software, we can develop an XSL stylesheet to output WML for WAP devices, and test the results by pointing our UP.SDK browser to *http://<hostname>:<port>/contents.xml*.

Because phone displays are much smaller, we only want to show a subset of the information in our XML table of contents. Example 9-6 is an XSL stylesheet that outputs three cards in WML. The first is a menu with links to the other two cards. The second card generates a table of contents listing from our *contents.xml* document. The third card is a simple copyright screen. This stylesheet can be saved as *JavaXML.wml.xsl* in the *XSL/* subdirectory of your web server's document root.

Example 9-6. XSL Stylesheet to Output WML from XML Table of Contents

```
<?xml version="1.0"?>

<xsl:stylesheet version="1.0"
                xmlns:xsl="http://www.w3.org/1999/XSL/Transform"
```

Example 9-6. XSL Stylesheet to Output WML from XML Table of Contents (continued)

```
                xmlns:JavaXML="http://www.oreilly.com/catalog/javaxml/"
                exclude-result-prefixes="JavaXML"
>

 <xsl:template match="JavaXML:Book">
  <xsl:processing-instruction name="cocoon-format">
   type="text/wml"
  </xsl:processing-instruction>

  <wml>
   <card id="index" title="{JavaXML:Title}">
    <p align="center">
     <i><xsl:value-of select="JavaXML:Title" /></i><br />
     <a href="#contents">Contents</a><br/>
     <a href="#copyright">Copyright</a><br/>
    </p>
   </card>

   <xsl:apply-templates select="JavaXML:Contents" />

   <card id="copyright" title="Copyright">
    <p align="center">
     Copyright 2000, O&apos;Reilly &amp; Associates
    </p>
   </card>
  </wml>
 </xsl:template>

 <xsl:template match="JavaXML:Contents">
  <card id="contents" title="Contents">
   <p align="center">
    <i>Contents</i><br />
    <xsl:for-each select="JavaXML:Chapter">
     <xsl:number value="position()" format="1: " />
     <xsl:value-of select="JavaXML:Heading" /><br />
    </xsl:for-each>
   </p>
  </card>
 </xsl:template>

</xsl:stylesheet>
```

Other than the WML tags, most of this example should look familiar. A new XSL function is introduced, `position()`, and a new XSL element, `xsl:number`, displays it. This adds output that indicates the position in the `xsl:for-each` loop each element is at; the `format` attribute allows the specification of the output format. In our case, we want output similar to this:

```
1: Introduction
2: Creating XML
...
```

We also added a processing instruction for Cocoon, with the target specified as `cocoon-format`. The data sent, `type="text/wml"`, instructs Cocoon to output this stylesheet with a content header specifying the output is `text/wml` (instead of the normal `text/html` or `text/plain`). The last new construct is an important one, and is seen as an attribute added to the root element of the stylesheet:

```
<xsl:stylesheet version="1.0"
                xmlns:xsl="http://www.w3.org/1999/XSL/Transform"
                xmlns:JavaXML="http://www.oreilly.com/catalog/javaxml/"
                exclude-result-prefixes="JavaXML"
>
```

By default, any XML namespace declarations other than the XSL namespace are added to the root element of the transformation output. In our example, the root element of our transformed output, `wml`, would have the `JavaXML` namespace declaration added to it:

```
<wml xmlns:JavaXML="http://www.oreilly.com/catalog/javaxml/">
...
</wml>
```

This would cause a WAP browser to report an error, as `xmlns:JavaXML` is not an allowed attribute for the `wml` element. The browser is not as forgiving as an HTML browser, and the rest of our content would not be shown. However, we must declare the namespace so our XSL stylesheet can handle template matching for the input document, which does use the `JavaXML` namespace. To handle this problem, XSL allows the attribute `exclude-result-prefixes` to be added to the `xsl:stylesheet` element. The namespace prefix specified to this attribute will not be added to the transformed output, which is exactly what we want. Our output would now look like this:

```
<wml>
...
</wml>
```

This is understood perfectly by a WAP browser. If you've downloaded the UP.SDK browser, you can point it to our XML table of contents, and see the results. Figure 9-5 shows the main menu that results from the transformation using our WML stylesheet when a WAP device requests our *contents.xml* file through Cocoon.

Figure 9-6 shows the generated table of contents, accessed by clicking the "Link" button when the "Contents" link is indicated in the display.

Figure 9-5. WML main menu

For more information on WML and WAP, visit *http://www.phone.com* and *http://www.wapforum.org*; both sites have extensive online resources for wireless device development.

By now, you should have a pretty good idea of the variety of output that can be created with Cocoon. With a minimal amount of effort and an extra stylesheet, the same XML document can be served in multiple formats to multiple types of clients; this is one of the reasons the web publishing framework is such a powerful tool. Without XML and a framework like this, separate sites would have to be created for each type of client. Now that you have seen how flexible the generation of output is when using Cocoon, we move on to looking at how Cocoon provides technology that allows for dynamic creation and customization of the input to these transformations.

Figure 9-6. WML table of contents

XSP

XSP stands for *Extensible Server Pages*, and is perhaps the most important development coming out of the Cocoon project. Certainly you, Constant Reader, are familiar with Java Server Pages (JSP). JSP (in a nutshell) allow tags and inline Java code to be inserted into an otherwise normal HTML page, and then when the JSP page is requested, the resulting code is executed and the results are inserted right into the output HTML.* This has taken the Java and ASP worlds by storm, ostensibly

* This is a drastic oversimplification; the JSP is actually precompiled into a servlet, and a `PrintWriteractually` handles output. For more information on JSP, refer to *Java Servlet Programming*, by Jason Hunter (O'Reilly & Associates).

simplifying server-side Java programming and allowing a separation of output and logic. However, there are still some significant problems. First, JSP does not really provide a separation of content and presentation. This is the same problem we have been talking about time and time again; changes to a banner, the color of a font, and text sizes require the JSP (with the inline Java and JavaBean references) to be modified. It also mingles content (pure data) with presentation in the same way static HTML does. Second, there is no ability to transform the JSP into any other format, or use it across applications, because the JSP specification is designed primarily for delivery of output.

XSP remedies both these problems. First, XSP is, at its heart, simply XML. Take a look at the sample XSP page in Example 9-7.

Example 9-7. Sample XSP Page

```
<?xml version="1.0"?>
<?cocoon-process type="xsp"?>
<?cocoon-process type="xslt"?>
<?xml-stylesheet href="myStylesheet.xsl" type="text/xsl"?>

<xsp:page language="java"
          xmlns:xsp="http://www.apache.org/1999/XSP/Core"
>

 <xsp:logic>
  private static int numHits = 0;

  private synchronized int getNumHits() {
   return ++numHits;
  }
 </xsp:logic>

 <page>
  <title>Hit Counter</title>

  <p>I've been requested <xsp:expr>getNumHits()</xsp:expr> times.</p>
 </page>
</xsp:page>
```

All XML conventions are followed; for now, think of the `xsp:logic` element contents as "off-limits" to the XML parser; we'll discuss that later. Other than that, the entire document is XML with some new elements. In fact, it references an XSL stylesheet that has nothing remarkable about it at all, as seen in Example 9-8.

Example 9-8. XSL Stylesheet for Example 9-7

```
<?xml version="1.0"?>

<xsl:stylesheet version="1.0"
```

Example 9-8. XSL Stylesheet for Example 9-7 (continued)

```
                xmlns:xsl="http://www.w3.org/1999/XSL/Transform"
>

  <xsl:template match="page">
    <xsl:processing-instruction name="cocoon-format">
      type="text/html"
    </xsl:processing-instruction>
    <html>
      <head>
        <title><xsl:value-of select="title"/></title>
      </head>
      <body>
        <xsl:apply-templates select="*[not(self::title)]" />
      </body>
    </html>
  </xsl:template>

  <xsl:template match="p">
    <p align="center">
      <xsl:apply-templates />
    </p>
  </xsl:template>

</xsl:stylesheet>
```

Thus, XSP easily handles the first major problem of JSP: it allows the separation of content from presentation. This separation allows developers to handle content generation (as the XSP page can be generated from a servlet or other Java code as well as being static), while XML and XSL authors can handle presentation and styling through modification of the XSL stylesheet applied to the XSP page. Just as easily, XSP solves the other significant deficiency of JSP: because XSP processing occurs before any stylesheets are applied, the resultant XML document can be transformed into any other format. This maintains all the advantages of XML, as the XSP page can be transferred between applications as well as being used just for presentation.

Creating an XSP Page

Now that you have had a taste of XSP, let's build our own XSP page. For this example, let's continue looking at the XML documents we have already created. We revisit the XML document we constructed earlier. This document represents a portion of the first chapter of this book, and was transformed into a PDF document. Instead of simply using this document for display, let's assume that the author (me!) wants to let his editor view the document as it is being written. However, in addition to the text of the book, the editor should be able to see comments from the author that the public should not see: for example, questions about style and formatting. First, let's add the comment to the *chapterOne.xml* file we built earlier:

```
...
 <contents>
  <chapter id="chapterOne">
   <title>Chapter 1: Introduction</title>

   <paragraph>XML.  These three letters have brought shivers to
   almost every developer in the world today at some point in the
   last two years.  While those shivers were often fear at another
   acronym to memorize, excitement at the promise of a new technology,
   or annoyance at another source of confusion for today's
   developer, they were shivers all the same.  Surprisingly, almost every
   type of response was well merited with regard to XML.  It is another
   acronym to memorize, and in fact brings with it a dizzying array of
   companions: XSL, XSLT, PI, DTD, XHTML, and more.  It also brings with
   it a huge promise-what Java did for portability of code, XML claims
   to do for portability of data.  Sun has even been touting the
   rather ambitious slogan "Java + XML = Portable Code + Portable
   Data" in recent months.  And yes, XML does bring with it a
   significant amount of confusion.  We will seek to unravel and
   demystify XML, without being so abstract and general as to be
   useless, and without diving in so deeply that this becomes just
   another droll specification to wade through.  This
   is a book for you, the Java developer, who wants to understand the
   hype and use the tools that XML brings to the table.</paragraph>

   <authorComment>Is the formatting of this first paragraph OK?  I
   wonder if we should break this into two separate paragraphs.  Let
   me know what you think, Mike.</authorComment>

   <paragraph>Today's web application now faces a wealth of problems
   that were not even considered ten years ago.  Systems that are
   distributed across thousands of miles must perform quickly and
   flawlessly.  Data from heterogeneous systems, databases, directory
   services, and applications must be transferred without a single
   decimal place being lost.  Applications must be able to communicate
   not only with other business components, but other business systems
   altogether, often across companies as well as technologies.  Clients
   are no longer limited to thick clients, but can be web browsers that
   support HTML, mobile phones that support Wireless Application
   Protocol (WAP), or handheld organizers with entirely different markup
   languages altogether. Data, and the transformation of that data, has
   become the crucial centerpiece of every application being developed
   today.</paragraph>
  </chapter>

 </contents>
</book>
```

With this comment now in our XML document, let's add a corresponding entry into our XSL stylesheet, *JavaXML.fo.xsl*:

```
<xsl:template match="paragraph">
  <fo:block font-size="12pt" space-before.optimum="12pt"
            text-align="justified">
    <xsl:apply-templates/>
  </fo:block>
</xsl:template>

<xsl:template match="authorComment">
  <fo:block font-size="10pt" font-style="italic" color="blue"
            space-before.optimum="12pt"
            text-align="justified">
    <xsl:apply-templates/>
  </fo:block>
</xsl:template>
```

With this new entry, the comments will appear slightly smaller than the rest of the text, italicized, and in blue. Now let's turn our XML document into an XSP page (as in Example 9-9) by adding the needed processing instructions for Cocoon, and surrounding the elements within a new root element, `xsp:page`.

Example 9-9. XSP Version of Example 9-1

```
<?xml version="1.0"?>

<?cocoon-process type="xsp"?>
<?cocoon-process type="xslt"?>
<?xml-stylesheet href="XSL/JavaXML.fo.xsl" type="text/xsl"?>

<xsp:page
  language="java"
  xmlns:xsp="http://www.apache.org/1999/XSP/Core"
>
<book>
  <cover>
    <title>Java and XML</title>
    <author>Brett McLaughlin</author>
  </cover>

  <!-- Content of Chapter -->

</book>
</xsp:page>
```

Before adding XSP logic to determine whether or not to show the comment, let's build a simple HTML page letting the viewer select whether he or she is the book's editor. In a real application, this could be a page that handles authentication and determines a user's role; for our example, it lets the user select if they are the author, the editor, or just a curious reader, and enter a password for verification. An HTML page that does this is shown in Example 9-10. You can save this file as *entry.html* in your web server's document root.

Example 9-10. HTML Frontend for User to Select a "Role"

```
<html>
 <head>
  <title>Welcome to the Java and XML Book in Progress</title>
 </head>

 <body>
  <h1 align="center"><i>Java and XML</i> Book in Progress</h1>
  <center>
   <form action="/chapterOne.xml" method="POST">
    Select your role:
    <select name="userRole">
     <option value="author">I'm the Author</option>
     <option value="editor">I'm the Editor</option>
     <option value="reader">I'm a Reader</option>
    </select>
    <br />
    Enter your password:
    <input type="password" name="password" size="8" />
    <br /><br />
    <input type="submit" value="Take me to the Book!" />
   </form>
  </center>
 </body>
</html>
```

Also notice that we submit the HTML form directly to our XSP page. In this example, our XSP acts similarly to a servlet. We want it to read the request parameters, determine what user role was selected, authenticate that role using the password supplied, and finally determine whether we should show the comment. To begin, let's define a `boolean` variable; this variable will hold the result of comparing the request parameters to see if the user is an author or editor and supplied a correct password. We then check the value of that variable, and if it is `true`, display the `authorComment` element:

```
<xsp:page
  language="java"
  xmlns:xsp="http://www.apache.org/1999/XSP/Core"
>

<book>
  <cover>
    <title>Java and XML</title>
```

```
    <author>Brett McLaughlin</author>
  </cover>
...
   is a book for you, the Java developer, who wants to understand the
   hype and use the tools that XML brings to the table.</paragraph>

   <xsp:logic>
    boolean authorOrEditor = false;

    // Perform logic to see if user is an author or editor

    if (authorOrEditor) {
      <xsp:content>
       <authorComment>Is the formatting of this first paragraph OK?  I
       wonder if we should break this into two separate paragraphs.  Let
       me know what you think, Mike.</authorComment>
      </xsp:content>
    }
   </xsp:logic>

   <paragraph>Today&apos;s web application now faces a wealth of problems
   that were not even considered ten years ago.  Systems that are
...
```

This shouldn't look too odd to you; other than the XSP-specific tags, we're just defining a variable and checking its value. If the variable evaluates to `true`, the `authorComment` element is added to the XSP page's output; otherwise, the element is not included in the output. One interesting thing to note is that we surround the actual XML document output within the `xsp:logic` block with an `xsp:content` element (which in turn is within the outer `xsp:page` element). This ensures that the XSP processor does not try to interpret any elements or text within the block as XSP structures. This again is an improvement to JSP; the same code in JSP might look like this:

```
<%
 if (authorOrEditor) {
%>
  <authorComment> Is the formatting of this first paragraph OK?  I
  wonder if we should break this into two separate paragraphs.  Let
  me know what you think, Mike.</authorComment>
<%
 }
%>
```

This is not very structured, as the JSP block ends before the `authorComment` element begins; then a new block is appended after the element, which closes the brackets opened in the first JSP block. It is very easy to mismatch coding structures or forget to add matching JSP blocks; the XSP paradigm forces every open element to be closed (standard XML well-formedness) and one block of code is matched with one element.

With our logical structures in place, we just need to interpret the request parameters. We use the built-in XSP variable `request`, which mimics the Servlet `HttpServletRequest` object. The following code additions read the value of the `userRole` and `password` request parameters (if they exist); the value is then compared with the roles that can see the comments (author and editor). If a match occurs, the password is checked as well. If the password matches the key for the supplied role, the `boolean` variable is set to `true`, and the `authorComments` element is part of the XML output:

```
<xsp:logic>
 boolean authorOrEditor = false;

 // Perform logic to see if user is an author or editor
 <![CDATA[
 String[] roleValues = request.getParameterValues("userRole");
 String[] passwordValues = request.getParameterValues("password");
 if ((roleValues != null) && (passwordValues != null)) {
   String userRole = roleValues[0];
   String password = passwordValues[0];
   if (userRole.equals("author") && password.equals("brett")) {
     authorOrEditor = true;
   } else
   if (userRole.equals("editor") && password.equals("mike")) {
     authorOrEditor = true;
   }
 ]]>
 }

 if (authorOrEditor) {
   <xsp:content>
    <authorComment>Is the formatting of this first paragraph OK?  I
    wonder if we should break this into two separate paragraphs. Let
    me know what you think, Mike.</authorComment>
   </xsp:content>
 }
</xsp:logic>
```

Notice that we enclose a good bit of this logic within a CDATA tag. Remember that XSP is still evaluated as XML, and must follow the rules of an XML document; but the double quotes and ampersands we use in the Java fragments are not allowed in XML documents; instead of escaping these characters, and getting a very strange XSP fragment, we use the CDATA tag so that we can write standard Java code. Without this, we would have to code as follows:

```
<xsp:logic>
 boolean authorOrEditor = false;
```

```
String[] roleValues =
  request.getParameterValues(&quot;userRole&quot;);
String[] passwordValues =
  request.getParameterValues(&quot;password&quot;);
if ((roleValues != null) &amp;&amp;
    (passwordValues != null)) {
  String userRole = roleValues[0];
  String password = passwordValues[0];
  if (userRole.equals("author") &amp;&amp;
      password.equals("brett")) {
    authorOrEditor = true;
  } else
  if (userRole.equals("editor") &amp;&amp;
      password.equals("mike")) {
    authorOrEditor = true;
  }
}
...
</xsp:logic>
```

You can now test out our entry page and the resultant PDF generated from the XML. You should get output similar to Figure 9-7 if you direct your web browser to *http://<hostname>:<port>/entry.html.*

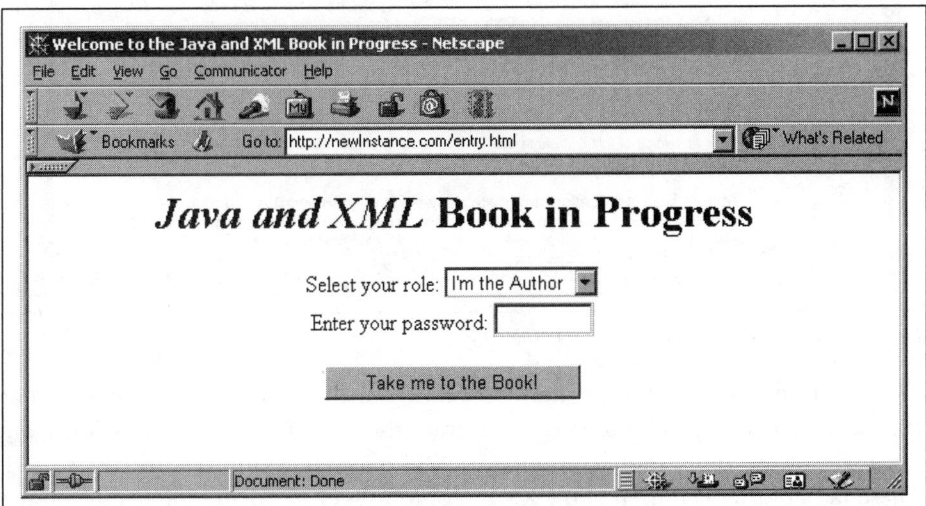

Figure 9-7. Entry HTML page

Select the role of author, and use the password "brett"; otherwise use the editor role with the password "mike." Either case gives you the PDF output shown in Figure 9-8.

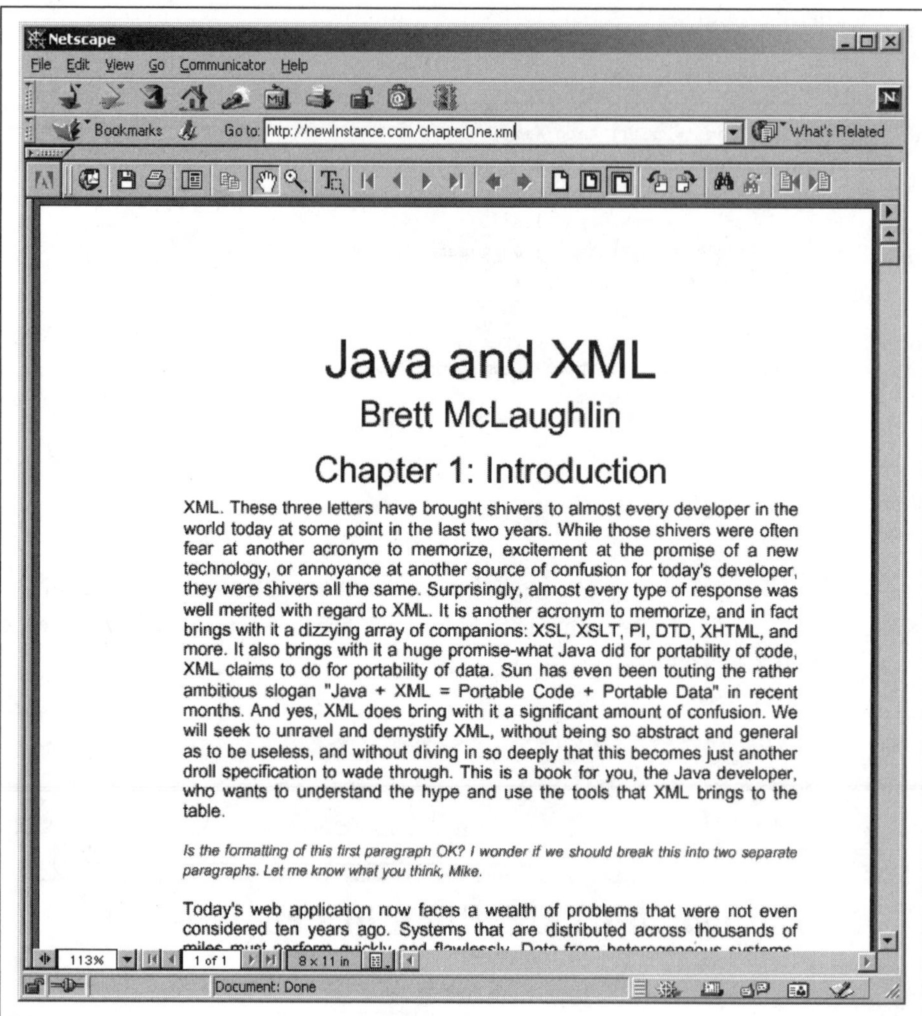

Figure 9-8. Generated PDF with comments showing

The one thing we have not yet done is isolate our logic from our content. Just as JSP allows inclusion of JavaBeans to abstract the content and presentation from the logic of an application component, XSP allows tag libraries to be created. These tag libraries can then allow XML tags to trigger the matching code within a tag library.

Using XSP Tag Libraries

In addition to showing comments based on the user, we should indicate that the chapter is in a draft state; additionally, the current date can be shown to indicate the date of the draft (the intention would be that the date be frozen when the chapter is considered complete). Instead of adding inline Java tags to load the current date, we can create a custom tag library for this purpose. While we are at it, let's look at creating an XSP element that takes in the chapter number and title and formats the complete title. This function will handle the insertion of the draft date we have been talking about. To do this, we first need to create a tag library that is available to our XSP page. Much of the tag library is based on an XSL stylesheet. We can start with the skeleton in Example 9-11, which passes anything it receives through as output. Save this skeleton as *JavaXML.xsp.xsl* in the *XSL/* subdirectory. Be sure to include the `JavaXML` namespace declaration, as we will use it to match elements within that namespace used in our XSP pages.

Example 9-11. XSP Logicsheet

```
<?xml version="1.0"?>

<xsl:stylesheet version="1.0"
  xmlns:xsl="http://www.w3.org/1999/XSL/Transform"
  xmlns:xsp="http://www.apache.org/1999/XSP/Core"
  xmlns:JavaXML="http://www.oreilly.com/catalog/javaxml/"
>
  <xsl:template match="xsp:page">
    <xsp:page>
      <xsl:copy>
        <xsl:apply-templates select="@*"/>
      </xsl:copy>

      <xsl:apply-templates/>
    </xsp:page>
  </xsl:template>

  <xsl:template match="@*|*|text()|processing-instruction()">
    <xsl:copy>
      <xsl:apply-templates
           select="@*|*|text()|processing-instruction()"/>
    </xsl:copy>
  </xsl:template>

</xsl:stylesheet>
```

By matching the `xsp:page` tag, we ensure that all elements are matched and handled within this stylesheet, or *logicsheet* in XSP parlance. We can now add Java methods for the templates within this logicsheet to call:

```
  <xsl:template match="xsp:page">
    <xsp:page>
      <xsl:copy>
        <xsl:apply-templates select="@*"/>
      </xsl:copy>
```

```
    <xsp:structure>
      <xsp:include>java.util.Date</xsp:include>
      <xsp:include>java.text.SimpleDateFormat</xsp:include>
    </xsp:structure>

    <xsp:logic>
      private String getDraftDate() {
        return (new SimpleDateFormat("MM/dd/yyyy"))
          .format(new Date());
      }

      private String getTitle(int chapterNum, String chapterTitle) {
        return "Chapter " + chapterNum + ": " + chapterTitle;
      }
    </xsp:logic>

    <xsl:apply-templates/>
  </xsp:page>
</xsl:template>
```

Several new XSP elements are introduced here. First, `xsp:structure` is used to surround several `xsp:include` statements. These work just like their Java counterpart, `import`, by making the specified Java classes available for use by their unqualified name (rather than the complete package name). Once these are available, we define and implement two methods: one that creates a chapter title from the chapter number and textual title, and one that returns the current date as a formatted `String`. These methods are available to any elements within this logicsheet.

We now need to define the element that specifies when an XSP result should replace an XML element. We have already defined the `JavaXML` namespace in the document root element, so we use that as the namespace for our tag library elements. Add the following template:

```
<!-- Create formatted title -->
<xsl:template match="JavaXML:draftTitle">
  <xsp:expr>getTitle(<xsl:value-of select="@chapterNum" />,
                     "<xsl:value-of select="@chapterTitle" />")
  </xsp:expr> - <xsp:expr>getDraftDate()</xsp:expr>
</xsl:template>

<xsl:template match="@*|*|text()|processing-instruction()">
  <xsl:copy>
    <xsl:apply-templates
         select="@*|*|text()|processing-instruction()"/>
  </xsl:copy>
</xsl:template>
```

When a document with this tag library uses the element `JavaXML:draftTitle`, the result of the method `getTitle()` will be prepended to a dash (`-`), and then the returned value of the `getDraftDate()` method will be appended to that result. The `JavaXML:draftTitle` element also expects two attributes to be declared: the chapter number and the textual title of the chapter. We signify to the XSP processor that we are calling a defined method by enclosing the method call within a set of `<xsp:expr>` tags. To indicate that the second argument (the chapter title) is a `String`, we enclose it within quotes. Since the chapter number should be treated as an `int`, it is left without quotation marks.

Once you have completed the XSP logicsheet (available online at the book's web site as well), you need to make it accessible to Cocoon. This can be done one of two ways: the first is to specify the location of the file as a URI, which allows the servlet engine (and therefore Cocoon) to locate the logicsheet. For example, to add our XSP logicsheet to Cocoon's set of resources through its URI, you could add the following line to your *cocoon.properties* file on a Unix-based system:

```
processor.xsp.library.context.java =
  resource://org/apache/cocoon/processor/xsp/library/java/context.xsl
processor.xsp.library.cookie.java =
  resource://org/apache/cocoon/processor/xsp/library/java/cookie.xsl
processor.xsp.library.global.java =
  resource://org/apache/cocoon/processor/xsp/library/java/global.xsl
processor.xsp.library.request.java =
  resource://org/apache/cocoon/processor/xsp/library/java/request.xsl
processor.xsp.library.response.java =
  resource://org/apache/cocoon/processor/xsp/library/java/response.xsl
processor.xsp.library.session.java =
  resource://org/apache/cocoon/processor/xsp/library/java/session.xsl
processor.xsp.library.util.java =
  resource://org/apache/cocoon/processor/xsp/library/java/util.xsl

processor.xsp.library.JavaXML.java =
  file:///usr/local/jakarta-tomcat/webapps/ROOT/XSL/JavaXML.xsp.xsl
```

For Windows systems, this would be:

```
processor.xsp.library.context.java =
  resource://org/apache/cocoon/processor/xsp/library/java/context.xsl
processor.xsp.library.cookie.java =
  resource://org/apache/cocoon/processor/xsp/library/java/cookie.xsl
processor.xsp.library.global.java =
  resource://org/apache/cocoon/processor/xsp/library/java/global.xsl
processor.xsp.library.request.java =
  resource://org/apache/cocoon/processor/xsp/library/java/request.xsl
processor.xsp.library.response.java =
  resource://org/apache/cocoon/processor/xsp/library/java/response.xsl
processor.xsp.library.session.java =
```

```
  resource://org/apache/cocoon/processor/xsp/library/java/session.xsl
processor.xsp.library.util.java =
  resource://org/apache/cocoon/processor/xsp/library/java/util.xsl

processor.xsp.library.JavaXML.java =
  file:///C:/java/jakarta-tomcat/webapps/ROOT/XSL/JavaXML.xsp.xsl
```

While this is handy for testing, it is not a very good solution for uncoupling your logicsheets from the servlet engine, and also adds quite a bit of maintenance overhead when adding new logicsheets: a new line would have to be added to the Cocoon properties file for new logicsheets to be available.* An alternative method for loading logicsheets is to allow specification of a resource in the servlet engine's classpath. This allows all of your custom logicsheets to be added to a *jar* file, and that *jar* file to be added to the servlet engine classpath. In addition, new logicsheets can be put within the *jar* file, providing a central location for storing your custom XSP logicsheets. From the *XSL/* subdirectory in your web server's document root, perform the following command to create a *jar* file that contains our logicsheet:

```
jar cvf logicsheets.jar JavaXML.xsp.xsl
```

Move the created *logicsheets.jar* archive into your *<TOMCAT_HOME>/lib/* directory with the other Cocoon libraries. Now we need to add this library to Tomcat's class path; edit the *tomcat.sh* or *tomcat.bat* file, located in the *<TOMCAT_HOME>/bin/* directory. In Unix, the edited file would look like this:

```
CLASSPATH=.

# Cocoon classes and libraries
CLASSPATH=${CLASSPATH}:${TOMCAT_HOME}/lib/xerces_1_0_3.jar
CLASSPATH=${CLASSPATH}:${TOMCAT_HOME}/lib/xalan_0_20_0.jar
CLASSPATH=${CLASSPATH}:${TOMCAT_HOME}/lib/fop_0_12_1.jar
CLASSPATH=${CLASSPATH}:${TOMCAT_HOME}/lib/cocoon.jar
CLASSPATH=${CLASSPATH}:${TOMCAT_HOME}/lib/logicsheets.jar

for i in ${TOMCAT_HOME}/lib/* ; do
  CLASSPATH=${CLASSPATH}:$i
done

CLASSPATH=${CLASSPATH}:${JAVA_HOME}/lib/tools.jar
```

And on Windows:

```
set CLASSPATH=.
set CLASSPATH=%TOMCAT_HOME%\classes
```

* Additionally, there are some rare occurrences where the 1.7.x version of the Cocoon engine has problems loading a logicsheet from a `file://` reference. Using the classpath and `resource://` alternative is a way to be sure you avoid these problems.

```
rem Cocoon classes and libraries
set CLASSPATH=%CLASSPATH%;%TOMCAT_HOME%\lib\xerces_1_0_3.jar
set CLASSPATH=%CLASSPATH%;%TOMCAT_HOME%\lib\xalan_1_0_0.jar
set CLASSPATH=%CLASSPATH%;%TOMCAT_HOME%\lib\fop_0_12_1.jar
set CLASSPATH=%CLASSPATH%;%TOMCAT_HOME%\lib\cocoon.jar
set CLASSPATH=%CLASSPATH%;%TOMCAT_HOME%\lib\logicsheets.jar

set CLASSPATH=%CLASSPATH%;%TOMCAT_HOME%\lib\webserver.jar
set CLASSPATH=%CLASSPATH%;%TOMCAT_HOME%\lib\jasper.jar
set CLASSPATH=%CLASSPATH%;%TOMCAT_HOME%\lib\xml.jar
set CLASSPATH=%CLASSPATH%;%TOMCAT_HOME%\lib\servlet.jar
set CLASSPATH=%CLASSPATH%;%JAVA_HOME%\lib\tools.jar
```

With our logicsheet available, we can now let Cocoon know where to look for `JavaXML` namespace references within XSP pages. Edit the *cocoon.properties* file you earlier put in the <TOMCAT_HOME>*/conf/* directory. Locate the section that lists the various Cocoon XSP resources, and add the new logicsheet reference:

```
processor.xsp.library.context.java =
  resource://org/apache/cocoon/processor/xsp/library/java/context.xsl
processor.xsp.library.cookie.java =
  resource://org/apache/cocoon/processor/xsp/library/java/cookie.xsl
processor.xsp.library.global.java =
  resource://org/apache/cocoon/processor/xsp/library/java/global.xsl
processor.xsp.library.request.java =
  resource://org/apache/cocoon/processor/xsp/library/java/request.xsl
processor.xsp.library.response.java =
  resource://org/apache/cocoon/processor/xsp/library/java/response.xsl
processor.xsp.library.session.java =
  resource://org/apache/cocoon/processor/xsp/library/java/session.xsl
processor.xsp.library.util.java =
  resource://org/apache/cocoon/processor/xsp/library/java/util.xsl

processor.xsp.logicsheet.JavaXML.java = resource://JavaXML.xsp.xsl
```

Because our logicsheet is not nested within any subdirectories in the *logicsheets.jar* file, we simply use the name of the logicsheet as its resource path. Finally, you will need to restart the servlet engine. This will reload the *cocoon.properties* file, and the logicsheet will be available for use. As the Cocoon engine is used to handle requests, any XSP page that declares that it uses the `JavaXML` will have available to it the logicsheet specified as the `JavaXML` library. So our XSP page needs to add a namespace declaration for the `JavaXML` namespace:

```
<?xml version="1.0"?>

<?cocoon-process type="xsp"?>
<?cocoon-process type="xslt"?>
<?xml-stylesheet href="XSL/JavaXML.fo.xsl" type="text/xsl"?>
```

```
<xsp:page
  language="java"
  xmlns:xsp="http://www.apache.org/1999/XSP/Core"
  xmlns:JavaXML="http://www.oreilly.com/catalog/javaxml/"
>
<book>
...
```

With the tag library now available for use, we can finally add in the `JavaXML:draftTitle` element to our XML document, *chapterOne.xml*:

```
<contents>
  <chapter id="chapterOne">
    <title>
      <JavaXML:draftTitle chapterNum="1"
                          chapterTitle="Introduction"
      />
    </title>
```

We replace the hardcoded chapter title with the element defined in our tag library. This should generate the title with the chapter number, chapter title, and the date of the draft. Accessing this new version of our XSP page results in the output shown in Figure 9-9.

Certainly these are simple examples, and we have only scratched the surface of what XSP allows. Even this simple example allows the title to be converted to a different form when the chapter is complete, without modifying the content or presentation of the page, but only the XSP logicsheet. In the same way, XSP allows the creation of very strict contracts separating presentation from content from application logic. Adding server-side Java components such as Enterprise JavaBeans can bring business logic into the equation. Rather than using a less flexible solution like JSP that is coupled to HTML and a presentation format, using XSP allows a looser coupling of components and thus a better solution for application development. XSP also promises to be key in the upcoming version of Cocoon, Cocoon 2.0, which we look at now.

Cocoon 2.0 and Beyond

The next generation of Cocoon, Cocoon 2.0, promises to take the web publishing framework a gigantic leap forward. Cocoon 1.x, which is primarily based on XML being transformed via XSL, still has some serious limitations. First, it does not reduce the management costs of large sites significantly. While one XML document can be transformed into different client views, a significant number of documents will still exist. Generally, either long URIs (such as */content/publishing/books/javaxml/contents.xml*), a large number of virtual path mappings (*/javaxml* mapped to */content/publishing/books/javaxml*), or a combination of the two, result. In

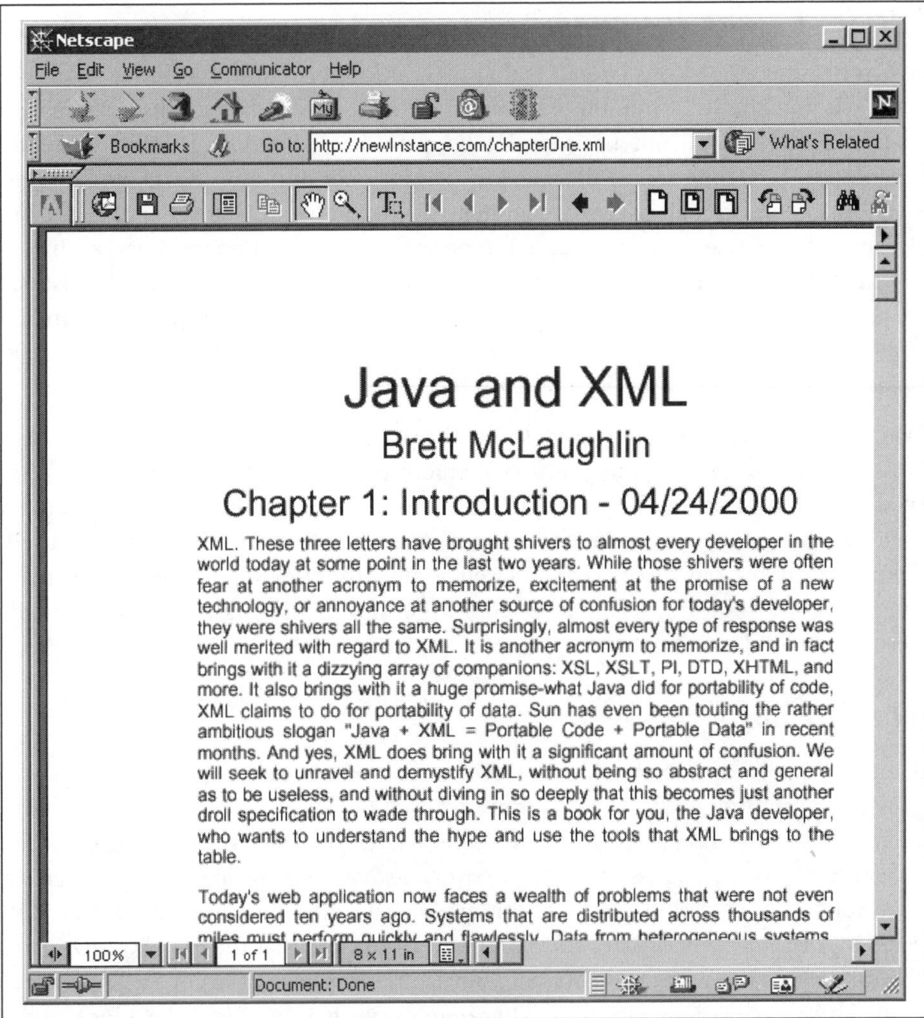

Figure 9-9. Output of XSP using a tag library

addition, a strict separation of presentation from content from logic is still difficult to accomplish, and even more difficult to manage.

Cocoon 2 focuses on enforcing the contracts between these different layers, therefore reducing management costs. XSP is a centerpiece in this design. In addition, the sitemap (which we look at in a moment) allows the distinction between XSP, XML, and static HTML pages to be hidden from the prying user. Advanced precompilation and memory considerations will also be introduced to make Cocoon 2 an even more significant advance over Cocoon 1.x than Cocoon 1.x was over a standard web server.

Servlet Engine Mappings

A significant change in Cocoon 2 is that it is no longer requires a simple mapping for XML documents. While this works well in the 1.x model, it still leaves management of non-XML documents completely up to the webmaster, possibly someone completely different from the person responsible for the XML documents. Cocoon 2 seeks to take over management of the entire web site. For this reason, the main Cocoon servlet (`org.apache.cocoon.servlet.CocoonServlet` in the 2.0 model) is generally mapped to a URI, such as */Cocoon*. This could also be mapped to the root of the web server itself (simply "/") to completely control a site. The URL requested then follows the servlet mapping: *http://myHost.com/Cocoon/myPage.xml* or *http://myHost.com/Cocoon/myDynamicPage.xsp*, for example.

With this mapping in place, even static HTML documents can be grouped with XML documents. This allows the management of all files on the server to be handled by a central person or group. If HTML and XML documents must be mixed in a directory, no confusion needs to occur, and uniform URIs can be used. Cocoon 2 will happily serve HTML as well as any other document type; with a mapping from the root of a server to Cocoon, the web publishing framework actually becomes invisible to the client.

The Sitemap

Another important introduction to Cocoon 2 is the *sitemap*. In Cocoon, a sitemap provides a central location for administration of a web site. Cocoon uses this sitemap to decide how to process the request URIs it receives. For example, when Cocoon receives a request like *http://myCocoonSite.com/Cocoon/javaxml/chapterOne.html*, the Cocoon servlet dissects the request and determines that the actual URI requested is */javaxml/chapterOne.html*. However, suppose that the file *chapterOne.html* should map not to a static HTML file, but to the transformation of an XML document (as in our earlier examples). The sitemap can handle this. Take a look at the sitemap shown in Example 9-12.

Example 9-12. Sample Cocoon 2.0 Sitemap

```
<sitemap>
 <process match="/javaxml/*.html">
  <generator type="file" src="/docs/javaxml/*.xml"
  <filter type="xslt">
   <parameter name="stylesheet" value="/styles/JavaXML.html.xsl"/>
  </filter>
  <serializer type="html"/>
 </process>

 <process match="/javaxml/*.pdf">
```

Example 9-12. Sample Cocoon 2.0 Sitemap (continued)

```
    <generator type="file" src="/docs/javaxml/*.xml"
    <filter type="xslt">
     <parameter name="stylesheet" value="/styles/JavaXML.pdf.xsl"/>
    </filter>
    <serializer type="fop"/>
   </process>
  </sitemap>
```

WARNING Although the sitemap DTD is being finalized as this book goes to production, changes could be introduced in beta-testing. Take the example sitemap as a flavor of what is to come in Cocoon 2 rather than a definitive sample.

Cocoon matches the URI */javaxml/chapterOne.html* to the sitemap directive `/javaxml/*.html`. It then determines that this is an actual file, and the source for that file should be determined by using the mapping `/docs/javaxml/*.xml`, which translates to */docs/javaxml/chapterOne.xml* (the filename we want to have transformed). The XSLT filter is then applied; the stylesheet to use, *JavaXML.html.xsl*, is also specified in the sitemap. The resulting transformation is then displayed to the user. In addition, the XML file could be an XSP file that is processed before being converted to XML and then styled.

This same process can render a PDF from the request *http://myCocoonSite.com/Cocoon/javaxml/chapterOne.pdf*, all with a few extra lines in the sitemap (shown above). This also means that the processing instructions in the individual XML documents can be completely removed, a significant change from Cocoon 1.x. First, uniform application of stylesheets and processing can occur based on a directory location. Simply creating XML and placing it in the */docs/javaxml/* directory in the example means the document can be accessed as HTML or PDF. It is also trivial to change the stylesheet used for all documents, something very difficult and tedious to do in Cocoon 1.x. Instead of making a change to each XML document, only the single line in the sitemap needs to be changed.

The Cocoon sitemap is still being developed, and there will probably be quite a few additional enhancements and changes to its format and structure by the time Cocoon 2.0 goes final. To get involved, join the mailing lists at *cocoon-users@xml.apache.org* and *cocoon-dev@xml.apache.org*. The Apache XML project at *http://xml.apache.org* has details about how to get involved with these lists and the Cocoon project.

Producers and Processors

One final improvement that Cocoon 2 will include is precompiled and event-based *producers* and *processors.* In Cocoon, a producer handles the transformation of a request URI into an XML document stream. A processor then takes an input stream (currently the XML document in a DOM tree) into output readable by the client. We have not covered producers and processors in the Cocoon 1.x model because they are going to drastically change in the Cocoon 2.0 model; any producers and processors currently being used will most likely be useless and have to be rewritten in Cocoon 2.0.

Cocoon 2 moves from using DOM for these structures to the more event-based SAX (or even JDOM!), wrapped within a DOM structure. As a producer had to generate an XML document in memory, the corresponding DOM structure could get extremely large. This eventually drained system resources, particularly when performing complex tasks such as large transformations or handling formatting objects (PDF generation). For these reasons, DOM will be a simple wrapper around SAX-based events in Cocoon 2, allowing producers and processors to be very slim and efficient.

In addition, producers and processors will be pre-complied versions of other formats. For example, XSL stylesheets can be precompiled into processors, and XSP pages can be precompiled into producers. This further increases performance while removing load from the client. These and other changes continue to use a component model, allowing Cocoon to be a very flexible, very pluggable framework. Keep up on the latest changes by monitoring the Cocoon web site, and look for Cocoon 2 in late 2000.

What's Next?

In the next chapter, we take a look at a technology that allows XML to be used as a data format in an important request and response model: XML-RPC. XML Remote Procedure Calls allow clients in a distributed system to request that tasks be executed on a server (or servers) on another portion of the network. Until recently, RPC has declined in popularity, mostly due to the surge of RMI-based technologies in the Java space (most notably, EJB). However, with XML as a data format, XML-RPC is a new solution for many problems that could not be solved cleanly or efficiently without RPC. We take a look at XML-RPC next, and in particular, at the Java libraries available.

In this chapter:

- *RPC Versus RMI*
- *Saying Hello*
- *Putting the Load on the Server*
- *The Real World*
- *What's Next?*

10

XML-RPC

We now take a look at yet another exciting development associated with XML: XML-RPC. XML-RPC is actually just a specific flavor of RPC, which stands for Remote Procedure Calls. If you are new to development, or have only worked with the Java language, remote procedure calls may be new ground for you; if you've been around the block in the development world, you may be a bit rusty, as RPC has fallen out of vogue in recent years. In this chapter we look at why those three little letters in front of RPC are revolutionizing what was becoming a computing dinosaur, and how to use XML-RPC from the world of Java. We also spend some time at the end of this chapter looking at real-world applications of XML-RPC, trying to shed some light not only on how to use this technology, but when to use it.

If you are part of the tidal wave of object-oriented development that has come along in the past three to five years, even hearing the word "procedure" may send shivers running down your back. Procedural languages such as PL/SQL and ANSI C are not popular, for a long list of very good reasons. You have probably been scolded for calling a Java method a function or procedure before, and almost certainly know better than to write "spaghetti code," code that has method after method chained together in a long line. RPC has fallen by the wayside much as these languages and techniques have, because of the new, object-oriented ways of achieving the same results, often with better design and performance. Surprisingly, though, the rise of XML has brought with it the rise and prominence of APIs specifically built for XML-RPC, and a gradual trend towards using XML-RPC in specific situations despite the connotations it carries.

Before trying to use these APIs, it is worth spending some time looking at what RPC is and how it compares to similar Java technologies, most notably Remote Method Invocation (RMI). If you do choose to use XML-RPC in your applications (and you almost surely will want to at some point), be assured that you will probably have to justify your choice to other developers, particularly those who may have just read books on EJB or RMI. Certainly there are places for all these technologies, but understanding the proper application of each is critical to your success not only as a developer, but as a team member and mentor. Keeping in mind these reasons for understanding the concepts behind these remote methodologies, let's take a look at the two most popular ways to operate with objects across a network: RPC and RMI.

RPC Versus RMI

If you haven't been under a rock for the last year, you should be aware that RMI is taking the Java world by storm. The entire EJB (Enterprise JavaBeans) specification is founded upon RMI principles, and you will be hard-pressed to write a three-tier application without using RMI, even if indirectly. In other words, if you don't know how to use RMI yet, you may want to pick up *Java Enterprise in a Nutshell*, by David Flanagan, Jim Farley, William Crawford, and Kris Magnusson, or *Java Distributed Computing*, by Jim Farley (both published by O'Reilly & Associates) and spend some time looking into this useful technology.

What Is RMI?

In short, RMI is *remote method invocation*. That seems fairly simple: RMI allows a program to invoke methods on an object when the object is not located on the same machine as the program. This is at the heart of distributed computing in the Java world, and is the backbone of EJB as well as many enterprise application implementations. Without getting into too much detail, RMI uses client stubs and skeletons to describe the methods a remote object has available for invocation. The client acts upon these stubs (typically Java interfaces), and RMI handles the "magic" of translating requests to a stub into network calls. This call invokes the method on the machine with the actual object, and then streams the result back across the network. Finally, the stub returns this result to the client that made the original method call, and the client moves on. The main idea you should get a hold on is that the client doesn't typically worry about the RMI and network details; it uses the stub as if it *were* the actual object with implemented methods. RMI (using JRMP™, Java's remote protocol) makes all this network communication happen behind the scenes, allowing the client to deal with a generic exception (`java.rmi.RemoteException`) and spend more time handling business rules and application logic. RMI also allows different protocols (such as Internet Inter-ORB Protocol [IIOP]) to be used, allowing communication between Java and CORBA objects, often in different languages such as C or C++.

RMI does carry with it a cost, though. First, using RMI is resource intensive. There are quite a few classes that must be used, and although these are part of the core

Java Development Kit (JDK), they still use memory and resources when instantiated. In addition, JRMP provides very poor performance, and writing a remote protocol to replace it is not a simple task. As clients issue RMI calls, sockets must be opened and maintained, and the number of sockets can affect system performance, particularly when the system is accessible via a network (which then requires more sockets to be opened for HTTP access). RMI also requires a server or provider to bind objects to. Until an object is bound to a name on one of these providers, the object is not accessible to other programs. This requires using an RMI registry, a Lightweight Directory Access Protocol (LDAP) directory server, or a variety of other Java Naming and Directory Interface (JNDI) services. Finally, RMI can involve a lot of coding, even with all the helpful RMI server classes you get with the JDK; a remote interface describing the methods available to be invoked must be coded (as well as quite a few other interfaces if you are using EJB). This also means that adding an additional method to the server class results in a change to the interface and recompilation of the client stubs, something that is often not desirable and sometimes not possible.

What Is RPC?

RPC is *remote procedure calls.* Where RMI lets you interoperate directly with a Java object, RPC is built in more of a dispatch fashion. Instead of dealing with objects, RPC lets you use standalone methods (yes, we can call them procedures here!) across a network. Although this limits interactivity, it does make for a slightly simpler interface to the client. You can think of RPC as being a way to use "services" on remote machines, while RMI allows you to use "servers" on remote machines; the subtle difference is that RMI typically is driven entirely by the client, with events occurring when methods are invoked remotely. RPC is often built more as a class or set of classes that work to perform tasks with or without client intervention; however, at times these classes service requests from clients, and execute "mini" tasks for the clients. We will look at some examples shortly to help clarify these definitions.

RPC, while not as interactive an environment as RMI, does offer some significant advantages. RPC allows disparate systems to work together. While RMI allows the use of IIOP for connecting Java to CORBA servers and clients, RPC allows literally any type of application intercommunication because the transport protocol can be HTTP. Since virtually every language in use today has some means of communicating via HTTP, RPC is very attractive for programs that must connect to legacy systems. RPC is also typically more lightweight than RMI (particularly when using XML as the encoding, which we look at next); while RMI often has to load entire Java classes over the network (such as code for applets and custom helper classes for EJB), RPC only has to pass across the request parameters and the resulting response, generally encoded as textual data. RPC also fits very nicely into the API model, allowing systems that are not part of your specific application to still access information from your application; this means that changes to your server do not have to result in changes to other clients' application code; with pure textual data transfer and requests, additional methods can be added without client recompilation, and minor changes are sufficient to use these new methods.

The problem with RPC has traditionally been the encoding of data in transfer; imagine trying to represent a Java `Hashtable` or `Vector` in a very lightweight way through text. When you consider that these structures can, in turn, hold other Java object types, the data representation quickly becomes tricky to write; it also has to remain a format that is usable by all the disparate programming languages, or the advantages of RPC are lessened. Until recently, an inverse relationship had been developing between the quality and usability of the encoding and its simplicity; in other words, the easier it became to represent complex objects, the more difficult it became to use the encoding in multiple programming languages without proprietary extensions and code. Elaborate textual representations of data were not standardized and required completely new implementations in every language to be usable. Certainly by now you should see where this discussion is leading.

XML-RPC

The greatest obstacle to using RPC has traditionally been its encoding. And then XML came along, and changed everything! Not only did XML provide a very simple, textual representation of data, it provided a standard for the structure of that data. Concerns about proprietary solutions became moot when the W3C released the XML 1.0 specification, assuring RPC coders that XML was not going anywhere anytime soon. In addition, SAX provided a lightweight, standard way to access XML, making it much easier to implement RPC libraries. This left only transmission over HTTP (something people have been doing for over a decade) and the specific encoding and decoding APIs for XML-RPC implementers to write. After a few beta implementations of XML-RPC libraries, it became clear that XML was also a very fast and lightweight encoding, resulting in better performance for XML-RPC libraries than expected; XML-RPC is now a viable and stable solution for remote procedure calls.

For you, the Java developer, XML-RPC provides a way to handle simple creation of "hooks" into your application and its services, for your own use as well as for other application clients in different divisions or even companies. It also uncouples these APIs from Java if clients are unable to use the Java language directly. Finally, XML-RPC removes RMI from the technologies that have to be learned to use distributed services (at least initially). We spend this chapter looking at how to implement an XML-RPC server and client, as well as an example of how a server can operate independently of clients, yet still provide XML-RPC accessible interfaces to interoperate with and query its data. Although we do not take a look at RMI in depth in this chapter, we will continually compare the XML-RPC solution to RMI, pointing out why XML-RPC is a better solution for some types of tasks.

Saying Hello

If you've made it through these several pages of discussion, you probably are at least partially convinced that XML-RPC has some usefulness and that it might be the right solution for some of your development problems. To try to elaborate on XML-RPC, we now look at building some actual working Java code using XML-RPC. In the great tradition of programming, we start with a simple "Hello World" type program. We want to have our XML-RPC server register a handler. This handler takes in a Java `String` parameter, the user's name, and returns "Hello" and the user's name; for example, the method might return "Hello Brett" when invoked. Then we need a server to make our handler available for XML-RPC clients. Finally, we build a simple client to connect to the server and request the method invocation.

In a practical case, the XML-RPC server and handler would be on one machine, usually a heavy-duty server, and the client on another machine, invoking the procedure calls remotely. However, if you don't have multiple machines available, you can still use the examples locally. Although this will be much faster than an actual client and server, you can still see how the pieces fit together and get a taste of XML-RPC.

Getting XML-RPC Libraries

As we said earlier, a lot of work has already gone into RPC, and more recently XML-RPC. Like using SAX, DOM, and JDOM for XML handling, there is no reason to reinvent the wheel when there are good, even exceptional, Java packages in existence for your desired purpose. The center for information about XML-RPC and links to libraries for Java as well as many other languages is *http://www.xml-rpc.com*. Sponsored by Userland (*http://www.userland.com*), this site has a public specification on XML-RPC, information on what data types are supported, and some tutorials on XML-RPC use. Most importantly, it directs you to the XML-RPC package for Java. Following the link on the main page, you are directed to Hannes Wallnofer's site at *http://helma.at/hannes/xmlrpc*.

On Hannes's site is a description of the classes in his XML-RPC package as well as instructions on use. Download the archive file and expand the files into your development area or IDE. You should then be able to compile these classes; there is one Java servlet example that requires the servlet classes (*servlet.jar* for Servlet API 2.2).

You can obtain these classes with the Tomcat servlet engine by pointing your web browser to *http://jakarta.apache.org*. If you do not wish to play with the servlet example, the servlet classes are not required for the programs in this chapter.

NOTE The XML-RPC classes are packages within a zip file, *xmlrpc-java.zip*. You will need to extract from this archive all the source code within the *xmlrpc-java/src/* directory. There is no included *jar* distribution, so manual compilation of these classes is required. Once compiled, you may want to *jar* the classes yourself for easy inclusion in your classpath.

The core distribution (which does not include the applet or regular expression examples in the downloaded archive) is made up of eight classes, all in the `helma.xmlrpc` package. They are `XmlRpc`, the core class; `XmlRpcClient`, which is used to connect to an XML-RPC server; `XmlRpcServer`, which is the server itself; `XmlRpcHandler`, which allows fine-grained control over XML encoding and processing; and several support and helper classes. `XmlRpcException` is the exception thrown by these classes; `XmlRpcServlet` demonstrates how to use a servlet as the HTTP response handler; `WebServer` is a lightweight HTTP server built specifically for handling XML-RPC requests; and `Benchmark` allows timing a roundtrip XML-RPC request using a specific SAX driver. Not included in the distribution, but required for operation, are the SAX classes (which you should have from earlier examples) and a SAX driver; in other words, you need a complete XML parser implementation that supports SAX. We continue to use Apache Xerces in our examples, although the libraries support any SAX 1.0–compatible driver.

Once you have all the source files compiled, ensure that the XML-RPC classes, SAX classes, and your XML parser classes are all in your environment's class path. This should have you ready to write your own custom code and start the process of "saying hello." Keep the XML-RPC source files handy, as looking at what is going on under the hood can aid in your understanding of our example.

Writing the Handler

The first thing we need to do is write the class and method we want to be invoked remotely. This is often called a *handler*. Beware, though, as the XML-RPC server mechanism that dispatches requests is also often called a handler; again, naming ambiguity rears its ugly head. A clearer distinction can be drawn as follows: an *XML-RPC handler* is a method or set of methods that takes an XML-RPC request, decodes its contents, and dispatches the request to a class and method. A *response handler*, or simply *handler*, is any method that can be invoked by an XML-RPC handler. With the XML-RPC libraries for Java, we do not need to write an XML-RPC handler, as one is included as part of the `helma.xmlrpc.XmlRpcServer` class. We only need to write a class with one or more methods that we register with the server.

It might surprise you to learn that creating a response handler requires no subclassing or other special treatment in our code. Any method can be invoked via XML-RPC as long as its parameter and return types are supported (able to be encoded) by XML-RPC. Table 10-1 lists all currently supported Java types that can be used in XML-RPC method signatures.

Table 10-1. XML-RPC Supported Java Types

XML-RPC Data Type	Java Data Type
`int`	`int`
`boolean`	`boolean`
`string`	`java.lang.String`
`double`	`double`
`dateTime.iso8601`	`java.util.Date`
`struct`	`java.util.Hashtable`[a]
`array`	`java.util.Vector`[a]
`base64`	`byte[]`

[a] Of course, the `struct` and `array` types must only contain other legal XML-RPC types.

Although this list includes only a small number of types, you will find that they handle most of the XML-RPC requests that can be made over a network. Because we only want to take in one `String` parameter, and return a `String`, our method fits these requirements. We can write our simple handler class now (shown in Example 10-1).

Example 10-1. Handler Class with Method to Be Invoked Remotely

```
/**
 * <b><code>HelloHandler</code></b> is a simple handler that can
 *   be registered with an XML-RPC server.
 *
 * @version 1.0
 */
public class HelloHandler {

    /**
     * <p>
     * This will take in a <code>String</code> and return
     *   a hello message to the user indicated.
     * </p>
     *
     * @param name <code>String</code> name of person to say Hello to.
     * @return <code>String</code> - hello message.
```

Example 10-1. Handler Class with Method to Be Invoked Remotely (continued)

```
     */
    public String sayHello(String name) {
        return "Hello " + name;
    }

}
```

This really is as simple as it seems. The method signature takes in and returns legal XML-RPC parameters, so we can safely register it with our XML-RPC server and know it will be callable via XML-RPC.

Writing the Server

With our handler ready, we need to write a program to start up the XML-RPC server, listen for requests, and dispatch these requests to the handler. For our example, we will use the `helma.xmlrpc.WebServer` class as the request handler. Although we could use a Java servlet, using this lightweight web server implementation allows us to avoid running a servlet engine on our XML-RPC server. We spend more time at the end of this chapter discussing servlets in the context of an XML-RPC server. For our server, we want to allow the specification of a port to start the server on, and then have the server listen for XML-RPC requests until shut down. We then need to register the class we created with the server, and specify any other application-specific parameters to the server.

We can create the skeleton for this class (shown in Example 10-2) now; we need to import the `WebServer` class and also ensure that a port number is given to the program on the command line when the server is started.

Example 10-2. Skeleton for Hello XML-RPC Server

```
import helma.xmlrpc.WebServer;

/**
 * <b><code>HelloServer</code></b> is a simple XML-RPC server
 *   that will make the <code>HelloHandler</code> class available
 *   for XML-RPC calls.
 *
 * @version 1.0
 */
public class HelloServer {

    /**
     * <p>
     * Start up the XML-RPC server and register a handler.
     * </p>
     */
```

Example 10-2. Skeleton for Hello XML-RPC Server (continued)

```
    public static void main(String[] args) {
        if (args.length < 1) {
            System.out.println(
                "Usage: java HelloServer [port]");
            System.exit(-1);
        }

        // Start the server on specified port
    }

}
```

Before actually starting the server, we need to specify the SAX driver for use in parsing and encoding XML. The default SAX driver for these libraries is James Clark's XP parser, available at *http://www.jclark.com*. We instead request the Apache Xerces parser by specifying the SAX `Parser` implementation class to the XML-RPC engine.* This is done through the `setDriver()` method, a static method belonging to the `XmlRpc` class. This class underpins the `WebServer` class, but we must import it and use it directly to make this change in SAX drivers. The `ClassNotFoundException` is thrown by this method, so must be caught in case the driver class cannot be located in your class path at runtime. Add the necessary `import` statement and methods to your `HelloServer` class now:

```
import helma.xmlrpc.WebServer;
import helma.xmlrpc.XmlRpc;
...
    /**
     * <p>
     * Start up the XML-RPC server and register a handler.
     * </p>
     */
    public static void main(String[] args) {
        if (args.length < 1) {
            System.out.println(
                "Usage: java HelloServer [port]");
            System.exit(-1);
        }

        try {
            // Use the Apache Xerces SAX Driver
```

* Currently there are no XML-RPC libraries that support SAX 2.0 and implement the `XMLReader` interface. It is expected that by late 2000, these updates will occur; as the Apache Xerces `SAXParser` class implements both the SAX 1.0 `Parser` interface and SAX 2.0 `XMLReader` interface, no code needs to be changed in the examples if SAX 2.0 updates are made to the libraries. However, if you are using a different vendor's parser, you may need to specify a SAX 2.0 class if the XML-RPC libraries are modified to use SAX 2.0.

```
                XmlRpc.setDriver("org.apache.xerces.parsers.SAXParser");

                // Start the server

            } catch (ClassNotFoundException e) {
                System.out.println("Could not locate SAX Driver");
            }
        }
    ...
```

At this point, we are ready to add the main portion of our code, which creates the HTTP listener that services XML-RPC requests, and then registers some handler classes that are available for remote procedure calls. Creating the listener is very simple; the `WebServer` helper class we have been discussing can be instantiated by supplying it the port to listen to, and just that easily, our server is servicing XML-RPC requests. Although as of yet we have no classes available to be called, we do have a working XML-RPC server. Let's add in the line to create and start the server, as well as a status line for display purposes. We also need to add another `import` statement and exception handler, this one for `java.io.IOException`. Because the server must start up on a port, it can throw an `IOException` if the port is inaccessible or if other problems occur in server startup. The modified code fragment is:

```
import java.io.IOException;

import helma.xmlrpc.WebServer;
import helma.xmlrpc.XmlRpc;
...
    /**
     * <p>
     * Start up the XML-RPC server and register a handler.
     * </p>
     */
    public static void main(String[] args) {
        if (args.length < 1) {
            System.out.println(
                "Usage: java HelloServer [port]");
            System.exit(-1);
        }

        try {
            // Use the Apache Xerces SAX Driver
            XmlRpc.setDriver("org.apache.xerces.parsers.SAXParser");

            // Start the server
            System.out.println("Starting XML-RPC Server...");
            WebServer server = new WebServer(Integer.parseInt(args[0]));

        } catch (ClassNotFoundException e) {
```

```
            System.out.println("Could not locate SAX Driver");
        } catch (IOException e) {
            System.out.println("Could not start server: " +
                e.getMessage());
        }
    }
...
```

Compile this class and give it a try; it is completely functional, and should print out the status line and then pause, waiting for requests. We now need to add our handler class to the server so that it can receive requests.

One of the most significant differences between RMI and RPC is how methods are made available. In RMI, a remote interface has the method signature for each remote method. If a method is implemented on the server class, but no matching signature is added to the remote interface, the new method cannot be invoked by an RMI client. This makes for quite a bit of code modification and recompilation in the development of RMI classes. This process is quite a bit different, and is generally considered easier and more flexible, in RPC. When a request comes in to an RPC server, the request contains a set of parameters and a textual value, usually in the form "classname.methodname." This signifies to the RPC server that the requested method is in the class "classname" and is named "methodname." The RPC server then tries to find a matching class and method that takes as input to that method parameter types that match the types within the RPC request. Once a match is made, the method is called, and the result is encoded and sent back to the client.

What this fairly long and somewhat complex discussion means is that the method requested is never explicitly defined in the XML-RPC server, but rather in the request from the client. Only a class instance is registered with the XML-RPC server. You can add methods to that class, restart the XML-RPC server with no code changes (allowing it to register an updated class instance), and then immediately request the new methods within your client code. As long as you can determine and send the correct parameters to the server, the new methods are instantly accessible. This is one of the advantages of XML-RPC over RMI, in that it more closely can represent an API; there are no client stubs, skeletons, or interfaces that must be updated. If a method is added, the method signature can be published to the client community and used immediately.

Now that you've read how easily an RPC handler can be used, let's register one in our example. The `WebServer` class allows the addition of a handler through the `addHandler()` method. This method takes as input a name to register the handler class to, and an instance of the handler class itself. This is typically accessed by instantiating a new class with its constructor (using the new keyword), although in the next section we look at using other methods, in the event that an instance should be shared instead of created by each client. In our current example, instantiating a new class is an acceptable solution. Let's register our `HelloHandler` class to the name "hello." We also add some additional status lines to let us see what is occurring in the server as it adds the handler:

```
/**
 * <p>
 * Start up the XML-RPC server and register a handler.
 * </p>
 */
public static void main(String[] args) {
    if (args.length < 1) {
        System.out.println(
            "Usage: java HelloServer [port]");
        System.exit(-1);
    }

    try {
        // Use the Apache Xerces SAX Driver
        XmlRpc.setDriver("org.apache.xerces.parsers.SAXParser");

        // Start the server
        System.out.println("Starting XML-RPC Server...");
        WebServer server = new WebServer(Integer.parseInt(args[0]));

        // Register our handler class
        server.addHandler("hello", new HelloHandler());
        System.out.println(
            "Registered HelloHandler class to \"hello\"");

        System.out.println("Now accepting requests...");

    } catch (ClassNotFoundException e) {
        System.out.println("Could not locate SAX Driver");
    } catch (IOException e) {
        System.out.println("Could not start server: " +
            e.getMessage());
    }
}
```

You can now recompile this source file and start up the server. Your output should look similar to Example 10-3.*

* If you are on a Unix machine, you must be logged in as the root user to start a service up on a port lower than 1024. To avoid these problems, consider using a higher numbered port, as shown in Example 10-3.

Example 10-3. Starting the HelloServer XML-RPC Server Class

```
$ java HelloServer 8585
Starting XML-RPC Server...
Registered HelloHandler class to "hello"
Now accepting requests...
```

Believe it or not, it is really that simple! We can write a client for our server, and then test communications across a network using XML-RPC. This is another advantage of XML-RPC; the barrier for entry into coding servers and clients is extremely low, particularly compared to the complexity of using RMI. Read on, and see that creating a client is just as straightforward.

Writing the Client

With our server running and accepting requests, we have taken care of the hardest part of coding our XML-RPC application (believe it or not, that was the hard part!). Now we need to construct a simple client to call our `sayHello()` method remotely. This is made simple by using the `helma.xmlrpc.XmlRpcClient`. This class takes care of many of the details on the client side that its analogs, `XmlRpcServer` and `WebServer`, do on the server. To write our client, we need this class as well as the `XmlRpc` class; our client must handle encoding of the request, so we must again set the SAX driver class to use with the `setDriver()` method. Let's begin our client code with these required import statements, checking for an argument to pass as the parameter to our `sayHello()` method on the server, and some exception handling. Create the Java source file shown in Example 10-4 and save it as *HelloClient.java*.

Example 10-4. An XML-RPC Client

```
import helma.xmlrpc.XmlRpc;
import helma.xmlrpc.XmlRpcClient;

/**
 * <b><code>HelloClient</code></b> is a simple XML-RPC client
 *   that makes an XML-RPC request to <code>HelloServer</code>.
 *
 * @version 1.0
 */
public class HelloClient {

    /**
     * <p>
     * Connect to the XML-RPC server and make a request.
     * </p>
     */
    public static void main(String args[]) {
```

Example 10-4. An XML-RPC Client (continued)

```
        if (args.length < 1) {
            System.out.println(
                "Usage: java HelloClient [your name]");
            System.exit(-1);
        }

        try {
            // Use the Apache Xerces SAX Driver
            XmlRpc.setDriver("org.apache.xerces.parsers.SAXParser");

            // Specify the Server

            // Create request

            // Make a request and print the result

        } catch (ClassNotFoundException e) {
            System.out.println("Could not locate SAX Driver");
        }
    }

}
```

As with the rest of the code in this chapter, this should seem simple and straightforward. To create an XML-RPC client, we need to instantiate the `XmlRpcClient` class, which requires the hostname of the XML-RPC server to connect to. This should be a complete URL, including the `http://` protocol prefix. In creating the client, a `java.net.MalformedURLException` can be thrown when this URL is in an unacceptable format. We can add this class to our list of imported classes, instantiate our client, and add the required exception handler:

```
import java.net.MalformedURLException;

import helma.xmlrpc.XmlRpc;
import helma.xmlrpc.XmlRpcClient;
...
    /**
     * <p>
     * Connect to the XML-RPC server and make a request.
     * </p>
     */
    public static void main(String args[]) {
        if (args.length < 1) {
            System.out.println(
                "Usage: java HelloClient [your name]");
            System.exit(-1);
        }
```

```
        try {
            // Use the Apache Xerces SAX Driver
            XmlRpc.setDriver("org.apache.xerces.parsers.SAXParser");

            // Specify the server
            XmlRpcClient client =
                new XmlRpcClient("http://localhost:8585/");

            // Create request

            // Make a request and print the result

        } catch (ClassNotFoundException e) {
            System.out.println("Could not locate SAX Driver");
        } catch (MalformedURLException e) {
            System.out.println(
                "Incorrect URL for XML-RPC server format: " +
                e.getMessage());
        }
    }
...
```

Although no actual RPC calls are being made, we now have a fully functional client application. You can compile and run this application, although you won't see any activity, as no connection is made until a request is initiated.

WARNING Make sure you use the port number in your source code that you plan to specify to the server when you start it up. Obviously, this is a poor way to implement connectivity between our client and server; changing the port the server listens to requires changing the source code of our client! In the next chapter, we will look at how to address this issue.

Hopefully you are excited about the ease with which this client and our server are coming together, and how little work is required to make use of XML-RPC.

Still, our program is not of much use until it actually makes a request and receives a response. To encode the request, we must invoke the `execute()` method on our `XmlRpcClient` instance. This method takes in two parameters: the name of the class identifier and method to invoke, which is one single `String` parameter, and a `Vector` of the method parameters to pass in to the specified method. The *class identifier* is the name we registered to our `HelloHandler` class on the XML-RPC server; although this identifier can be the actual name of the class, it is often something more readable and meaningful to the client, and in our case it is "hello." The name of the method to invoke is appended to this, separated from the class identifier with a period, in the form `[class identifier].[method name]`. The parameters must be in the form of a Java Vector, and should include any parameter objects that are needed by the specified method. In our simple sayHello() method, this is a String with the name of the user, which should have been specified on the command line.

Once the XML-RPC client encodes this request, it sends the request to the XML-RPC server. The server then locates the class that matches the request's class identifier, and looks for a matching method name. If a matching method name is found, the parameter types for the method are compared with the parameters in the request. If a match occurs, the method is executed. If multiple methods are found with the same name, the parameters determine which method is invoked; this process allows normal Java overloading to occur in the handler classes. The result of the method invocation is encoded by the XML-RPC server, and sent back to the client as a Java Object (which in turn could be a Vector of Objects!). This result can then be cast to the appropriate Java type, and used in the client normally. If a matching class identifier/method/parameter signature is not found, an XmlRpcException is thrown back to the client. This ensures that the client is not trying to invoke a method or handler that does not exist, or sending in incorrect parameters.

All this happens with a few additional lines of Java code: we must import the XmlRpcException class, as well as java.io.IOException; this latter is thrown when communication between the client and server causes error conditions. We then add the Vector class and instantiate it, adding to it our single String parameter. This allows us to invoke the execute() method with the name of our handler, the method to call, and our parameters; the result of this call is cast to a String which is then printed out to the screen. In this example, the local machine is running the XML-RPC server on port 8585:

```
import java.io.IOException;
import java.net.MalformedURLException;
import java.util.Vector;

import helma.xmlrpc.XmlRpc;
import helma.xmlrpc.XmlRpcClient;
import helma.xmlrpc.XmlRpcException;
...
    /**
     * <p>
     * Connect to the XML-RPC server and make a request.
     * </p>
     */
    public static void main(String args[]) {
        if (args.length < 1) {
            System.out.println(
                "Usage: java HelloClient [your name]");
```

```
            System.exit(-1);
        }

        try {
            // Use the Apache Xerces SAX Driver
            XmlRpc.setDriver("org.apache.xerces.parsers.SAXParser");

            // Specify the server
            XmlRpcClient client =
                new XmlRpcClient("http://localhost:8585/");

            // Create request
            Vector params = new Vector();
            params.addElement(args[0]);

            // Make a request and print the result
            String result =
               (String)client.execute("hello.sayHello", params);

         System.out.println("Response from server: " + result);

        } catch (ClassNotFoundException e) {
            System.out.println("Could not locate SAX Driver");
        } catch (MalformedURLException e) {
            System.out.println(
                "Incorrect URL for XML-RPC server format: " +
                e.getMessage());
        } catch (XmlRpcException e) {
            System.out.println("XML-RPC Exception: " + e.getMessage());
        } catch (IOException e) {
            System.out.println("IO Exception: " + e.getMessage());
        }
    }
...
```

Surprisingly enough, that's all that is required to make this work! You can compile this code, and then open a command shell for running our example code.

Talk to Me

Make sure that you have the XML-RPC classes and our example classes in your environment's class path. You also need to confirm that Apache Xerces or your chosen SAX driver is in your class path and accessible, as the examples must load these classes for parsing. Once that is set up, start the `HelloServer` class by giving it a port number. On Windows, use the `start` command to start the server in a separate process:

```
D:\prod\Java and XML\WEB-INF\classes>start java HelloServer 8585
Starting XML-RPC Server...
```

```
Registered HelloHandler class to "hello"
Now accepting requests...
```

In Unix, use the background processing command (&) to make sure you can run your client as well (or open another terminal window and duplicate your environment settings):

```
$ java HelloServer &
Starting XML-RPC Server...
Registered HelloHandler class to "hello"
Now accepting requests...
```

You can then run your client by specifying your name to the program as a command-line argument. You should quickly see a response (similar to that shown in Example 10-5) as the `HelloServer` receives your request, handles it, and returns the result of the `sayHello()` method, which is then printed by our client.

Example 10-5. Running the HelloClient Class

```
$ java HelloClient Brett
Response from server: Hello Brett
```

You have just seen XML-RPC in action. Certainly this is not a particularly useful example, but it should have given you an idea of the basics and shown you the simplicity of coding an XML-RPC server and client in Java. With these fundamentals, we can move on to a more realistic example. In the next section, we build a more practical and useful server, and take a look at what XML-RPC handlers more often look like. We then create a client (similar to our `HelloClient`) to test our new code.

Putting the Load on the Server

As instructional as our `Hello` example has been in demonstrating how to use XML-RPC with Java, it isn't very realistic. In addition to being a trivial example, the server is not very flexible and the handler itself doesn't give any indication of how a practical XML-RPC handler might operate. Here we try to give examples of using XML-RPC in a production environment by increasing the usefulness of the handler and the usability of the server. These, while still not code you might want to immediately add to your current project, should at least begin to demonstrate to you how XML-RPC might be of use in your future projects, and how to build applications that can use XML-RPC but are not limited by it.

A Shared Handler

Our `HelloHandler` class was simple but useless in a practical application. Remember that we said most XML-RPC uses relate to letting events occur on a server that is more suited for complex tasks, while allowing a thin client to request procedures be executed and use the returned results. In addition, it is possible that part or even all of the computations needed to respond to a request can be done in advance; in other words, the handler class may be running tasks and ensuring that results are already available when a method call comes in. As a Java coder, threads and shared instance data should leap to your mind. Here we take a look at a very simple `Scheduler` class to illustrate these principles.

Our scheduler should allow clients to add and remove events. We also want to be able to query our scheduler for a list of all events in the queue. To make this a little more practical (and to have a task for our server to perform later), we want the result of an events query to return the events sorted by the time they occur. These events for our example will simply be a `String` event name and a time for the event (in a `java.util.Date` format). Though this is not a complete scheduler implementation, it can demonstrate how to let the server do some behind-the-scenes work for us.

First we will code our `addEvent()` and `removeEvent()` methods. Because these are both client-triggered events, there is nothing particularly remarkable about them; what is worth thinking about is how to store these events in our `Scheduler` class. Although our XML-RPC server will instantiate this class, and that instance will be used for all XML-RPC calls that come into that server, it is possible and even probable that other classes or even XML-RPC servers may interact with our scheduler as well. If we store a list of events as a member variable of our class, multiple instances will not be able to share data. To solve this problem in our example, we will make our storage static, causing it to be shared across all `Scheduler` class instances. To store both an event name and an event time, a `Hashtable` would seem appropriate, allowing the use of key-value pairs. In addition to this `Hashtable`, we store the names of the events in a `Vector`. Although this uses some extra storage space (and memory in the Java Virtual Machine), we can sort our `Vector` and not have to deal with sorting our `Hashtable`; the advantage here is that we can swap the event names in our `Vector` (a single swap) and not have to swap the event times in our `Hashtable` (two swaps for each exchange). Let's code the skeleton of this class, and add these first two methods to allow addition and removal of events. For now, we add our storage as well, but we leave the implementation of the retrieval and sorting of events for later. Example 10-6 is a code listing for this new handler.

Example 10-6. The Scheduler Class

```
import java.util.Date;
import java.util.Hashtable;
import java.util.Vector;
```

Example 10-6. The Scheduler Class (continued)

```
/**
 * <b><code>Scheduler</code></b> is a class that allows
 *   addition, removal, and retrieval of a list of events, sorted
 *   by their occurrence time.
 *
 * @version 1.0
 */
public class Scheduler {

    /** List of event names (for sorting) */
    private static Vector events = new Vector();

    /** Event details (name, time) */
    private static Hashtable eventDetails = new Hashtable();

    /**
     * <p>
     * This will initialize the storage.
     * </p>
     */
    public Scheduler() {
    }

    /**
     * <p>
     * This will add the requested event.
     * </p>
     *
     * @param eventName <code>String</code> name of event to add.
     * @param eventTime <code>Date</code> of event.
     * @return <code>boolean</code> - indication of if event was added.
     */
    public boolean addEvent(String eventName, Date eventTime) {
        // Add this event to the list of events
        if (!events.contains(eventName)) {
            events.addElement(eventName);
            eventDetails.put(eventName, eventTime);
        }

        return true;
    }

    /**
     * <p>
     * This will remove the requested event.
     * </p>
     *
     * @param eventName <code>String</code> name of event to remove.
```

Example 10-6. The Scheduler Class (continued)

```
     * @return <code>boolean</code> - indication of if event was removed.
     */
    public synchronized boolean removeEvent(String eventName) {
        events.remove(eventName);
        eventDetails.remove(eventName);

        return true;
    }

}
```

Our `addEvent()` method adds the name of the event to both storage objects, and the time to the `Hashtable`. Our `removeEvent()` method does the converse. Both methods return a `boolean` value. Although in the example this value is always `true`, in a more complex implementation, this value could be used to indicate problems in the addition or removal of events.

With the ability to add and remove events, we now need to add a method that returns a list of events. This method returns all events added to the event store, regardless of what client or application added those events; in other words, these could be events added by a different XML-RPC client, a different XML-RPC server, another application, or a standalone implementation of this same scheduler. Since we have to return a single `Object` result, we can return a `Vector` of formatted `String` values that contain the name of each event and its time. Certainly, in a more useful implementation this might return the `Vector` of events, or some other form of the events in a typed format (with the date as a `Date` object, etc.). This method acts more as a view of the data, though, and does not allow the client to further manipulate it. To return this list of events, we use the event store and the `java.text.SimpleDateFormat` class, which allows textual formatting of `Date` objects. Iterating through all events, a `String` is created with the event name and the time it is set for; each `String` is inserted into the `Vector` result list, and this list is then returned to the client. Let's add the required import statement and the code to return the events in the store to the scheduler code:

```
import java.text.SimpleDateFormat;
import java.util.Date;
import java.util.Hashtable;
import java.util.Vector;
...
    /**
     * <p>
     * This returns the current listing of events.
     * </p>
     *
     * @return <code>Vector</code> - list of events.
```

```
    */
    public Vector getListOfEvents() {
        Vector list = new Vector();

        // Create a Date Formatter
        SimpleDateFormat fmt =
            new SimpleDateFormat("hh:mm a MM/dd/yyyy");

        // Add each event to the list
        for (int i=0; i<events.size(); i++) {
            String eventName = (String)events.elementAt(i);
            list.addElement("Event \"" + eventName +
                            "\" scheduled for " +
                            fmt.format(
                                (Date)eventDetails.get(eventName)));
        }

        return list;
    }
...
```

At this point, we could use this class as an XML-RPC handler without any problems. However, the point of this exercise is to look at how work can be done by the server while the client is performing other tasks. The `getListOfEvents()` method assumes that the event list (the `Vector` variable `events`) is ordered in the correct way when this method is called; this means that sorting has already occurred. We haven't written code to sort our events yet, but more importantly, we haven't written code to trigger this sorting. Furthermore, as the event store gets large, sorting it can be very time-consuming, and this task should not cause the client to wait for it to complete. First we must add a method that our class can use to sort the events. For simplicity, a bubble sort is used; discussion of sorting algorithms is beyond the scope of this book, so this code is presented without any explanation of its workings. At the end of the method, though, the `Vector` variable `events` is sorted in order of the time the events within it occur. For information on this and other sorting algorithms, you should refer to *Algorithms in Java*, by Robert Sedgewick and Tim Lindholm (Addison-Wesley). The algorithm and method to handle sorting of the events is presented here, and should be added to your code:

```
import java.text.SimpleDateFormat;
import java.util.Date;
import java.util.Enumeration;
import java.util.Hashtable;
import java.util.Vector;

/**
 * <b><code>Scheduler</code></b> is a class that allows
```

```
 *   addition, removal, and retrieval of a list of events, sorted
 *   by their occurrence time.
 *
 * @author <a href="mailto:brettmclaughlin@earthlink.net">Brett McLaughlin</a>
 * @version 1.0
 */
public class Scheduler {

    /** List of event names (for sorting) */
    private static Vector events = new Vector();

    /** Event details (name, time) */
    private static Hashtable eventDetails = new Hashtable();

    /** Flag to indicate if events are sorted */
    private static boolean eventsSorted;

    // Other existing method implementations

    /**
     * <p>
     * Sort the events in the current list.
     * <p>
     */
    private synchronized void sortEvents() {
        if (eventsSorted) {
            return;
        }

        // Create array of events as they are (unsorted)
        String[] eventNames = new String[events.size()];
        events.copyInto(eventNames);

        // Bubble sort these
        String tmpName;
        Date date1, date2;
        for (int i=0; i<eventNames.length - 1; i++) {
            for (int j=0; j<eventNames.length - i - 1; j++) {
                // Compare the dates for these events
                date1 = (Date)eventDetails.get(eventNames[j]);
                date2 = (Date)eventDetails.get(eventNames[j+1]);
                if (date1.compareTo(date2) > 0) {

                    // Swap if needed
                    tmpName = eventNames[j];
                    eventNames[j] = eventNames[j+1];
                    eventNames[j+1] = tmpName;

                }
            }
```

```
        }

        // Put into new Vector (ordered)
        Vector sortedEvents = new Vector();
        for (int i=0; i<eventNames.length; i++) {
            sortedEvents.addElement(eventNames[i]);
        }

        // Update the global events
        events = sortedEvents;
        eventsSorted = true;

    }
  ...
  }
```

In addition to the core algorithm, we import the `java.util.Enumeration` class and add a `boolean` member variable, `eventsSorted`. This flag allows short-circuiting of the execution of the sorting when the events are already ordered. Although we have not yet added code to update this flag, we can easily do so. Our sorting method already indicates that events are sorted at its completion. Our constructor should initially set this value to `true`, indicating that all events are in order. It is only when events are added that the list may become unordered, so in our `addEvents()` method we need to set this flag to `false` if an event is added. This will let our `Scheduler` class know that something should occur that will trigger the sort. Then when the `getListOfEvents()` method is invoked, the events will be ordered and ready for retrieval. Let's add code to our constructor and the method for adding events that will update this flag:

```
    /**
     * <p>
     * This will initialize the storage.
     * </p>
     */
    public Scheduler() {
        eventsSorted = true;
    }

    /**
     * <p>
     * This will add the requested event.
     * </p>
     *
     * @param eventName <code>String</code> name of event to add.
     * @param eventTime <code>Date</code> of event.
     * @return <code>boolean</code> - indication of if event was added.
     */
    public boolean addEvent(String eventName, Date eventTime) {
```

```
        // Add this event to the list of events
        if (!events.contains(eventName)) {
            events.addElement(eventName);
            eventDetails.put(eventName, eventTime);
            eventsSorted = false;
        }

        return true;
    }
```

We do not need to make any changes to the `removeEvent()` method, as removing an entry does not affect the order of the events. The ideal mechanism to handle server-side processing while freeing the client for further action is a thread that sorts events. With this thread started in the JVM, client processing can continue without waiting for the thread to complete. This is particularly important in a multi-threaded environment where synchronization and threads waiting for object locks would be in use. In this example, we avoid those issues (this is a chapter about XML-RPC, not threading), but you can add the relevant code to handle these issues fairly easily. In our example, we want to create an inner class that extends `Thread`, and does nothing but invoke the `sortEvents()` method. We then add to our `addEvents()` method code that creates and starts this thread when events are added. This results in the addition of events triggering a re-sorting of the events, but allows the client to continue with its actions (which might include adding additional events, which in turn starts more threads to sort the data). When the client does request the list of events, the events should be sorted when returned, all without the client ever waiting on this action to occur, or having to spend processing power to make it happen. The addition of the inner class to sort, and code to run that class as a thread in our `addEvents()` method rounds out the `Scheduler` class:

```
public class Scheduler {
...
    public boolean addEvent(String eventName, Date eventTime) {
        // Add this event to the list of events
        if (!events.contains(eventName)) {
            events.addElement(eventName);
            eventDetails.put(eventName, eventTime);
            eventsSorted = false;

            // Start thread on server sorting
            SortEventsThread sorter = new SortEventsThread();
            sorter.start();
        }

        return true;
    }
...
    /**
```

```
         * <p>
         * This inner class handles starting the sorting as
         *   a <code>Thread</code>.
         */
        class SortEventsThread extends Thread {

            /**
             * <p>
             * Start the sorting.
             * </p>
             */
            public void run() {
                sortEvents();
            }
        }

    }
```

You can now compile the modified source code, and we have a threaded scheduler that performs the process-intensive task of sorting on the server, allowing any clients to work uninterrupted while that sorting occurs. This is still a simple example of using a handler class properly, but it does introduce the concepts of resource distribution and letting a server handle the workload when possible. To complement this more advanced handler class, we next look at building a more robust XML-RPC server implementation.

A Configurable Server

Our XML-RPC server class still needs some work. The current version requires us to specifically add our handler classes to the server in the code. This means that the addition of a new handler class requires coding and recompilation. Not only is this undesirable from a change control perspective, but it is annoying and time-consuming. Obtaining the newest code from a source control system, adding the change, and testing to add one or two handlers is not practical, and won't win you friends among your management. What is preferred is to have a robust server that can read this sort of information from a configuration file and load the needed classes at runtime. We can build a lightweight server to do this now.

To begin, we create a new server class. You can either start from scratch, or copy and paste from the `HelloServer` class given earlier in this chapter. We start by setting up our framework, adding the required import statements, and instantiating our server, similar to the earlier example; however, we do not add any code that registers handlers, as we will write a helper method to load the needed information from a file. The one change from our earlier version is that we require an additional command-line parameter; this parameter should be the name of a file.

We will read this file in our methods later to add handlers to the server. You can create the `LightweightXmlRPcServer` class (part of the `com.oreilly.xml` utility package), which continues to use the thin `WebServer` helper class, with the code shown in Example 10-7. The complete `com.oreilly.xml` package is also available for download at *http://www.oreilly.com/catalog/javaxml* or *http://www.newInstance.com.*

Example 10-7. The LightweightXmlRpcServer Class

```
package com.oreilly.xml;

import java.io.IOException;

import helma.xmlrpc.XmlRpc;
import helma.xmlrpc.WebServer;

/**
 * <b><code>LightweightXmlRpcServer</code></b> is a utility class
 *   that will start an XML-RPC server listening for HTTP requests
 *   and register a set of handlers, defined in a configuration file.
 *
 * @author
 *   <a href="mailto:brettmclaughlin@earthlink.net">Brett McLaughlin</a>
 * @version 1.0
 */
public class LightweightXmlRpcServer {

    /** The XML-RPC server utility class */
    private WebServer server;

    /** Port number to listen on */
    private int port;

    /** Configuration file to use */
    private String configFile;

    /**
     * <p>
     * This will store the requested port and configuration file
     *   for the server to use.
     * </p>
     *
     * @param port <code>int</code> number of port to listen to
     * @param configFile <code>String</code> filename to read for
     *                   configuration information.
     */
    public LightweightXmlRpcServer(int port, String configFile) {
        this.port = port;
        this.configFile = configFile;
```

Example 10-7. The LightweightXmlRpcServer Class (continued)

```
    }

    /**
     * <p>
     * This will start up the server.
     * </p>
     *
     * @throws <code>IOException</code> when problems occur.
     */
    public void start() throws IOException {
        try {
            // Use Apache Xerces SAX Parser
            XmlRpc.setDriver("org.apache.xerces.parsers.SAXParser");

            System.out.println("Starting up XML-RPC Server...");
            server = new WebServer(port);

            // Register handlers

        } catch (ClassNotFoundException e) {
            throw new IOException("Error loading SAX parser: " +
                e.getMessage());
        }
    }

    /**
     * <p>
     * Provide a static entry point.
     * </p>
     */
    public static void main(String[] args) {

        if (args.length < 2) {
            System.out.println(
                "Usage: " +
                "java com.oreilly.xml.LightweightXmlRpcServer " +
                "[port] [configFile]");
            System.exit(-1);
        }

        LightweightXmlRpcServer server =
            new LightweightXmlRpcServer(Integer.parseInt(args[0]),
                                        args[1]);

        try {
            // Start the server
            server.start();
        } catch (IOException e) {
```

Example 10-7. The LightweightXmlRpcServer Class (continued)

```
            System.out.println(e.getMessage());
        }
    }

}
```

There is really nothing remarkable here. We ensure that the required parameters are passed in and start the server on the requested port. We now need to add in methods to load our handlers from a file, and then add those handlers one by one to our server.

Because each handler needs a name and an associated class, we can create a configuration file that has these two pieces of information. With Java, it is easy to load and instantiate a class with its complete package and name. This means we can completely represent a new handler with a pair of textual values. Within this file, we can add both our original `HelloHandler` class as well as our new `Scheduler` class. Since we are writing the file parser as well, we can arbitrarily decide to use commas as delimiters and the pound sign (#) as a comment marker. In fact, you can use whatever format you wish as long as you write code that uses your conventions in parsing the file. Create the configuration file shown in Example 10-8 that will add the `HelloHandler` class under the class identifier "hello" and the `Scheduler` class under the class identifier "scheduler," and save it as *xmlrpc.conf*.

Example 10-8. XML-RPC Handler Configuration File

```
# Hello Handler: sayHello()
hello,HelloHandler

# Scheduler: addEvent(), removeEvent(), getEvents()
scheduler,Scheduler
```

For documentation purposes, we specify the methods available to each handler in our comments. This allows future maintainers of our code to know what methods are available for each handler.

Java's I/O classes make it easy to load this file and read its contents. We can create a helper method that reads the specified file and stores the pairs of values in a Java `Hashtable`. This object can then be passed on to another helper that loads and registers each handler. This example method does not do extensive error checking, which a production ready server might, and it simply ignores any line without a pair of comma-separated values; certainly it is easy enough to add in error handling if you want to use this code in your applications. Once we find a line with a pair of values, the line is broken up and the class identifier and class name are stored as an entry within the `Hashtable`. Add the `import` statements for the required classes and then the new `getHandlers()` method to the `LightweightServer` class now:

```
import java.io.BufferedReader;
import java.io.FileReader;
import java.io.IOException;
import java.util.Hashtable;

import helma.xmlrpc.XmlRpc;
import helma.xmlrpc.WebServer;
...
    /**
     * <p>
     * This is a method that parses the configuration file
     *   (in a very simplistic manner) and reads the handler
     *   definitions supplied.
     * </p>
     *
     * @return <code>Hashtable</code> - class id/class pairs.
     * @throws <code>IOException</code> - when errors occur in
     *                                    reading/parsing the file.
     */
    private Hashtable getHandlers() throws IOException {

        Hashtable handlers = new Hashtable();

        BufferedReader reader =
            new BufferedReader(new FileReader(configFile));
        String line = null;

        while ((line = reader.readLine()) != null) {
            // Syntax is "handlerName, handlerClass"
            int comma;

            // Skip comments
            if (line.startsWith("#")) {
                continue;
            }

            // Skip empty or useless lines
            if ((comma = line.indexOf(",")) < 2) {
                continue;
            }

            // Add the handler name and the handler class
            handlers.put(line.substring(0, comma),
                         line.substring(comma+1));
```

```
        }

        return handlers;
    }
...
```

Instead of adding code to save the result of this method, we can use that result as input to a method that iterates through the `Hashtable` and adds each handler to the server. The code needed to accomplish this task is not complicated; the only notable items are that the `addHandler()` method of `WebServer` requires an instantiated class as a parameter. This requires us to take the name of the class to register from the `Hashtable`, load that class into the JVM with `Class.forName()`, and then instantiate that class with `newInstance()`. This is the methodology used in class loaders and other dynamic applications in Java, but may be unfamiliar to you if you are new to Java or have not had to dynamically instantiate classes from a textual name before. Once the class is loaded in this way, it and the class identifier are passed to the `addHandler()` method, and the iteration continues. Once the contents of the `Hashtable` are loaded, the server is set up and ready to go. We use the `Enumeration` class to cycle through the keys in the `Hashtable`, so we must add this `import` statement to our file:

```
import java.io.BufferedReader;
import java.io.FileReader;
import java.io.IOException;
import java.util.Enumeration;
import java.util.Hashtable;

import helma.xmlrpc.XmlRpc;
import helma.xmlrpc.WebServer;
...
    /**
     * <p>
     * This will register the handlers supplied in the XML-RPC
     *   server (typically from <code>{@link #getHandlers()}</code>.
     * </p>
     *
     * @param handlers <code>Hashtable</code> of handlers to register.
     */
    private void registerHandlers(Hashtable handlers) {
        Enumeration handlerNames = handlers.keys();

        // Loop through the requested handlers
        while (handlerNames.hasMoreElements()) {
            String handlerName = (String)handlerNames.nextElement();
            String handlerClass = (String)handlers.get(handlerName);

            // Add this handler to the server
            try {
```

```
                server.addHandler(handlerName,
                    Class.forName(handlerClass).newInstance());

                System.out.println("Registered handler " + handlerName +
                                   " to class " + handlerClass);
            } catch (Exception e) {
                System.out.println("Could not register handler " +
                                   handlerName + " with class " +
                                   handlerClass);
            }
        }
    }
...
```

This is simply a complement to our `getHandlers()` method; in fact, it takes the result of that method as input. It uses the `String` values within the `Hashtable` and registers each, and just that simply, our server is running and will have any handlers in the configuration file loaded and available for remote calls. Be aware that we could have just as easily consolidated these methods into one larger method. However, the purpose of the two methods is significantly different; while one, `getHandlers()`, deals with parsing a file, the other, `registerHandlers()`, deals with registering handlers once information about the handlers is available. With this methodology, we can change the way we parse the configuration file (or even have it read from a database or other medium) without having to worry about the way the handlers are registered. In fact, in the next chapter we remove the `getHandlers()` method in lieu of a helper class that reads this information from an XML configuration file! In this case, a good design decision early in the process (here) avoids a lot of change to our working code later in the process (in the next chapter).

Once you have added these two helper methods, add their invocation to the `start()` method of our server class:

```
    /**
     * <p>
     * This will start up the server.
     * </p>
     *
     * @throws <code>IOException</code> when problems occur.
     */
    public void start() throws IOException {
        try {
            // Use Apache Xerces SAX Parser
            XmlRpc.setDriver("org.apache.xerces.parsers.SAXParser");

            System.out.println("Starting up XML-RPC Server...");
            server = new WebServer(port);
```

```
            // Register handlers
            registerHandlers(getHandlers());

        } catch (ClassNotFoundException e) {
            throw new IOException("Error loading SAX parser: " +
                e.getMessage());
        }
    }
```

We add a `try-catch` block around the method invocations we have added so that we can distinguish between exceptions that occur in the server itself (the outer block) as opposed to exceptions that occur specifically related to the loading of handlers. In this latter case, we report the error as being generated by our handler methods. Compile this code, ensure you have created the configuration file, and our server is ready for use.

A Useful Client

Our client has no new concepts or techniques in it; just as our `HelloClient` class was simple, so is the `SchedulerClient` class. It needs to start up an XML-RPC client, invoke handler methods, and print out the result of those handlers. The complete code for the client is here. Comments indicate what is occurring, and since this is all ground we have covered you can simply enter the code in Example 10-9 into your editor and compile it.

Example 10-9. The SchedulerClient Class

```
import java.io.IOException;
import java.net.MalformedURLException;
import java.util.Calendar;
import java.util.Date;
import java.util.Enumeration;
import java.util.Hashtable;
import java.util.Vector;

import helma.xmlrpc.XmlRpc;

import helma.xmlrpc.XmlRpcClient;
import helma.xmlrpc.XmlRpcException;

/**
 * <b><code>SchedulerClient</code></b> is an XML-RPC client
 *   that makes XML-RPC requests to <code>Scheduler</code>.
 *
 * @version 1.0
 */
public class SchedulerClient {
```

Example 10-9. The SchedulerClient Class (continued)

```
    /**
     * <p>
     * Add events to the Scheduler.
     * </p>
     *
     * @param client <code>XmlRpcClient</code> to connect to
     */
    public static void addEvents(XmlRpcClient client)
        throws XmlRpcException, IOException {

        System.out.println("\nAdding events...\n");

        // Parameters for events
        Vector params = new Vector();

        // Add an event for next month
        params.addElement("Proofread final draft");

        Calendar cal = Calendar.getInstance();
        cal.add(Calendar.MONTH, 1);
        params.addElement(cal.getTime());

        // Add the event
        if (((Boolean)client.execute("scheduler.addEvent", params))
                             .booleanValue()) {
            System.out.println("Event added.");
        } else {
            System.out.println("Could not add event.");
        }

        // Add an event for tomorrow
        params.clear();
        params.addElement("Submit final draft");

        cal = Calendar.getInstance();
        cal.add(Calendar.DAY_OF_MONTH, 1);
        params.addElement(cal.getTime());

        // Add the event
        if (((Boolean)client.execute("scheduler.addEvent", params))
                             .booleanValue()) {
            System.out.println("Event added.");
        } else {
            System.out.println("Could not add event.");
        }

    }
```

Example 10-9. The SchedulerClient Class (continued)

```
    /**
     * <p>
     * List the events currently in the Scheduler.
     * </p>
     *
     * @param client <code>XmlRpcClient</code> to connect to
     */
    public static void listEvents(XmlRpcClient client)
        throws XmlRpcException, IOException {

        System.out.println("\nListing events...\n");

        // Get the events in the scheduler
        Vector params = new Vector();
        Vector events =
            (Vector)client.execute("scheduler.getListOfEvents", params);
        for (int i=0; i<events.size(); i++) {
            System.out.println((String)events.elementAt(i));
        }
    }

    /**
     * <p>
     * Static entry point for the demo.
     * </p>
     */
    public static void main(String args[]) {

        try {
            // Use the Apache Xerces SAX Parser Implementation
            XmlRpc.setDriver("org.apache.xerces.parsers.SAXParser");

            // Connect to server
            XmlRpcClient client =
            new XmlRpcClient("http://localhost:8585/");

            // Add some events
            addEvents(client);

            // List events
            listEvents(client);

        } catch (Exception e) {
            System.out.println(e.getMessage());
        }

    }

}
```

As you are entering this code, notice that the events are added in reverse order of the event time. Our server should rearrange these events with the `sortEvents()` method to facilitate correctly ordered results when the `getListOfEvents()` method is called. We can see that our server takes care of this sorting next.

Talk to Me (Again)

Once you have entered in the code for the handler, server, and client, compile all of the source files. You also will need to create the configuration file that lists handlers to register with the XML-RPC server that we discussed in that section. First, start up the XML-RPC server as a separate process:

```
D:\prod>start java com.oreilly.xml.LightweightXmlRpcServer 8585
                   D:\prod\conf\xmlrpc.conf
```

In Unix, use:

```
$ java com.oreilly.xmlrpc.LightweightServer 8585 conf/xmlrpc.conf &
```

You should see the server indicate that the handlers in the supplied configuration file are registered to the names you provided:

```
Starting up XML-RPC Server...
Registered handler scheduler to class Scheduler
Registered handler hello to class HelloHandler
```

WARNING If you never stopped the previous XML-RPC server, `HelloServer`, you will get an error trying to start another server on the same port. Be sure to stop the `HelloServer` before trying to start the `LightweightXmlRpcServer`.

Finally, execute your client and see the results:

```
$ java SchedulerClient

Adding events...

Event added.
Event added.

Listing events...

Event "Submit final draft" scheduled for 10:13 AM 02/14/2000
Event "Proofread final draft" scheduled for 10:13 AM 03/13/2000
```

You should not notice a significant pause as your client adds and lists events, yet the server still sorts the events in a separate thread within the server JVM (and bubble sorting is not a quick algorithm!). You have written your first useful XML-RPC application!

The Real World

We conclude this chapter with a short look at some important details of using XML-RPC in the real world. This continues the focus on allowing you to use XML not because it is the newest and neatest technology, but because it is the best for solving certain situations. All of the knowledge within this book, all the XML specifications, and other XML books will not make your application operate as well as it could, if you do not know when and how to use XML and XML-RPC *correctly*! This section, then, highlights some of the common issues that arise in using XML-RPC.

Where's the XML in XML-RPC?

After working through this chapter, you may have been surprised that we didn't write any SAX, DOM, or JDOM code. In fact, we used very little XML directly at all. This is because the XML-RPC libraries were responsible for the encoding and decoding of the requests that our client sent to and from the server. While this may seem a little bit of a letdown, as you didn't write any code that directly manipulates XML, you are definitely using XML technology. The simple request to the `sayHello()` method was actually translated to an HTTP call that looks like Example 10-10.

Example 10-10. XML-RPC Request After Encoding

```
POST /RPC2 HTTP/1.1
User-Agent: Tomcat Web Server/3.1 Beta (Sun Solaris 2.6)
Host: newInstance.com
Content-Type: text/xml
Content-length: 234

<?xml version="1.0"?>
<methodCall>
  <methodName>hello.sayHello</methodName>
  <params>
    <param>
      <value><string>Brett</string></value>
    </param>
  </params>
</methodCall>
```

The XML-RPC libraries on the server receive this and decode it, matching it with a handler method (if one is available that matches). The requested Java method is then invoked, and the server encodes the result back into XML, as shown in Example 10-11.

Example 10-11. XML-RPC Response After Encoding

```
HTTP/1.1 200 OK
Connection: close
Content-Type: text/xml
Content-Length: 149
Date: Mon, 11 Apr 2000 03:32:19 CST
Server: Tomcat Web Server/3.1 Beta-Sun Solaris 2.6

<?xml version="1.0"?>
<methodResponse>
  <params>
    <param>
      <value><string>Hello Brett</string></value>
    </param>
  </params>
</methodResponse>
```

All this communication happens without you having to worry about the details.

Shared Instances

In our examples, we looked at using static data objects to share data across multiple instances of the same class. However, there are times when an instance itself is shared. This may not be because of an XML-RPC need, but because of a need to use the class differently on the server. For example, the singleton design pattern in Java mandates that only one instance of a class ever be created, and that instance is shared across all applications. This is usually accomplished by using a static method called `getInstance()` instead of constructing the object:

```
Scheduler scheduler;
// Get the single instance, which is managed in the Scheduler class
scheduler = Scheduler.getInstance();
// Add an event for right now
scheduler.addEvent("Picnic", new Date());
```

To ensure that no classes directly instantiate the `Scheduler` class, the constructor is usually made private or protected. While this works fine in that it forces clients to use the code shown above to get an instance, it can also cause confusion when trying to use the class as an XML-RPC handler. Remember that registering a handler has always been accomplished with the instantiation of the handler class. However, the `WebServer` class requires only a valid instance as a parameter, not necessarily a new instance. For example, the following code would be a perfectly acceptable way to add a handler:

```
WebServer server = new WebServer(8585);
// Create a handler class
HelloHandler hello = new HelloHandler();
server.addHandler("hello", hello);
```

The server class does not distinguish between these methodologies, as long as the handler class is instantiated when it gets passed into the addHandler() method. So we can make a small change to this code if we want to add an instance of the singleton Scheduler class described previously:

```
WebServer server = new WebServer(8585);
// Pass in the singleton instance
server.addHandler("scheduler", Scheduler.getInstance());
```

This passes in the shared instance just as if the class was being instantiated through a constructor with the new keyword, and preserves any information shared across the singleton class. You will find that many classes used in services such as XML-RPC are built as singletons to avoid the use of static data variables, as a shared instance allows the data to be stored in member variables; the single instance then operates upon those member variables for all client requests.

To Servlet or Not To Servlet

The use of a servlet as an XML-RPC server has become a popular option recently (for more details on servlets, see Jason Hunter's *Java Servlet Programming* [O'Reilly & Associates]). In fact, the XML-RPC Java classes that you downloaded include a servlet with the distribution. It is both legal and common to use a servlet in this way, having the servlet do nothing but field XML-RPC requests. However, this is not always the best idea.

If you have a machine that must serve other HTTP requests for Java tasks, then certainly a servlet engine is a good choice for handling the details of these requests. In this case, running a servlet as an XML-RPC server would be a good idea. However, one of the advantages of XML-RPC is it allows handler classes with complex, process-intensive tasks to be separated from other application code. Our Scheduler class could be placed on a server with classes that performed complex indexing, algorithmic modeling, and perhaps graphical transformations. All of these functions are very expensive for application clients to perform. However, to add a servlet engine and accept application requests for other tasks as well as the XML-RPC handling greatly reduces the processing power available to these handler classes. In this case, the only requests that should be coming to the server are for these handler classes.

In the case where only XML-RPC requests are accepted (as indicated above), it is rarely a good idea to use a servlet for the XML-RPC server. The provided WebServer class is very small, very light, and designed specifically for handling XML-RPC requests over HTTP. A servlet engine is designed for accepting any HTTP request, and is not tuned as well for XML-RPC requests in particular. Over time, you will begin to see performance degradation in the servlet engine as compared to the WebServer class. Unless you have a compelling reason to use a servlet for other non-XML-RPC tasks, it would be wise to stick with the lightweight XML-RPC server designed for the purpose you need.

What's Next?

By now you should start to feel you could use XML in a variety of ways, as our topical chapters give you some practical applications of XML. The next chapter continues the focus on XML in the real world by looking at XML for configurations. Enterprise JavaBeans are using XML for EJB deployment descriptors files, many server products are using XML for configuration files, and XML is coming into its own as a format for configuration data. We will look at why this trend has started, and examine how to use XML for storing data purely for application use and not for transferal between applications. We also spend time discussing why databases and directory servers are not going away anytime soon, and how to ensure you use XML wisely, but not in inappropriate situations.

In this chapter:
- *EJB Deployment Descriptors*
- *Creating an XML Configuration File*
- *Reading an XML Configuration File*
- *The Real World*
- *What's Next?*

11

XML for Configurations

In this chapter, we look at the use of XML for configuration data. This differs from our XML coverage in other chapters in that we are not using XML to transfer data between applications, or for generating a presentation layer; we are simply using XML to store data. To understand the motivation for using XML for configuration data, you need only write an application that uses extensive properties files, or code a server that is configured via files on a filesystem rather than command-line arguments. In both cases, the format of the files to supply information to the application becomes arbitrary and usually proprietary. The developer working on configuration often decides on a format, codes a file reader, and the application becomes locked into that format forever. Certainly this is not the most long-term view of application programming and development.

As developers and system engineers realized the maintenance problems that an approach like this can cause (forgetting where a comma belongs, being unsure what marks a comment, etc.), it became clear that a standard was needed to represent this type of data that would not immediately cause an application's configuration mechanism to become proprietary. One standard solution that is being used today, but is still lacking functionality, is Java properties files and the `java.util.Properties` class. Introduced in the Java Development Kit (JDK) 1.0, these constructs provide a more Java-centric means of storing data and configuration information. However, they do not provide for any sort of grouping or hierarchy. A client application had just as much access and visibility into a server's information as the server did into the client's data, and developers were unable to perform any sort of logical grouping within these files. In addition, having hierarchical configuration parameters had become popular; this nesting of information was difficult to accomplish in other solutions without creating even more complex (and still very proprietary) file formats. XML nicely solved all of these issues and offered a standard, simple way to represent application configuration information.

The format also lends itself to being a multi-purpose administration tool. Consider that XML allows a generic application to be coded that can load a DTD or schema and then a configuration file, and allows a user to add, update, delete, and modify information with such a tool. With one XML configuration file or hundreds, from one format to many, this same application could provide an interface for administration. Compared to the variety of password, shadow, user and group, initialization script, and other files on servers today, this is a significant improvement in simplicity and ease of use.

Because XML was being used in many applications already, it became a natural extension to add parsing and handling of configuration files that were converted to XML. Applications that do not utilize XML can easily begin to use XML by introducing XML configuration files; this is much easier to do than to add support for XML data transferal or XML transformations. All in all, it seemed an excellent fit for a variety of applications. When the Enterprise JavaBeans (EJB) 1.1 specification was released, dictating that all EJB deployment descriptors would be in XML format, the use of XML for configuration information exploded. Many who were concerned about introducing the overhead of an XML parser or worried about the longevity of XML suddenly found themselves having to use XML to deploy their business objects in EJB servers. This made a migration of all application configuration data to XML logical and even decreased the complexity of many applications. In this chapter we look at how you can use XML for configuration data within your applications.

First we spend some time looking at a current use of XML for configuration data. The EJB deployment descriptor is examined with an eye towards important design decisions made in the specification of that file. This will prepare us to write our own configuration files in XML. We then create a configuration file for our XML-RPC server and clients that we built in Chapter 10, *XML-RPC*. With this file built, we look at coding some utility classes to parse and load this information into our XML-RPC classes, adding flexibility to our server and clients. Using the JDOM interfaces for parsing, we can easily load the configuration information. Finally, we end with a look at XML in relation to other important data storage mechanisms, databases and directory servers. This will cast our use of XML for configuration data in the light of the "real world" and help you make wise decisions about when to use XML as a data source and when not to.

EJB Deployment Descriptors

Before we begin creating our own configuration files and programs to read and use those files, a look at existing formats and patterns in this area will help. Although this is not a book about EJB, spending some time investigating the EJB deployment descriptors can aid us in understanding how XML-based configuration files work, as well as suggest ideas on how to structure our file format and data. We discuss some of the most important design decisions here and relate them to the EJB deployment descriptor.

Before looking at the design of the deployment descriptor itself, though, we should look at why its overall EJB design lent itself to using XML at all. The EJB 1.0 specification required serialized deployment descriptors; unfortunately, that was the only guideline given. This resulted in each EJB vendor providing a proprietary format for their server's deployment descriptors, and then forcing the application developer to run a tool (or even write their own tool) to serialize the descriptor. EJB, and Java in general, had lost its claim to WORA, Write Once Run Anywhere. XML provided a standard means of handling the deployment descriptor, as well as removing the need for proprietary tools to serialize the descriptors. In addition, Sun provides an EJB DTD that ensures each vendor's deployment descriptors conform to the same specifications, allowing EJBs to be highly platform- and vendor-independent.

The Basics

As with any XML document, the EJB deployment descriptor has a DTD to which it conforms. A schema, as we have already discussed, will probably replace this in future revisions of the specification. In either case, the important concept here is that XML documents used for configuration, even more so than for other purposes, must have a set of constraints put upon them. Without constraints, the information could be incorrect or useless to a server, often causing an entire application to fail as a result. Once the constraints have been identified, the deployment descriptor begins with its root element, `ejb-jar`. Although this may seem a trivial item to note, the naming of a root element is an important part of authoring any XML document. This element faces the rather enormous task of having to represent all the information within the XML document it belongs to. Particularly when others may have to use or maintain your documents, proper naming here can avoid confusion, and poor naming can cause it. The relevant portions of an XML deployment descriptor that adheres to the EJB specification are shown here:

```
<?xml version="1.0"?>

<!DOCTYPE ejb-jar PUBLIC "-//Sun Microsystems, Inc.//DTD Enterprise
JavaBeans 1.1//EN" "http://java.sun.com/j2ee/dtds/ejb-jar_1_1.dtd">

<ejb-jar>
  <description>
    This ejb-jar file contains assembled enterprise beans that are
     Part of the employee self-service application.
  </description>
```

```
...
</ejb-jar>
```

Using namespaces (which were in their infancy when the EJB 1.1 specification was developed) can add clarity to the naming of your document's root and other elements. This aids in identification of the purpose of the document; consider the ambiguity removed by using a namespace such as `DeploymentDescriptor` or even simple `EJB-DD` in the EJB deployment descriptor. Any questions about the use of the document are removed when viewing these namespace prefixes on elements.

Organization

Just as naming is critical for document clarity, organization is crucial to the usability of your configuration files in XML. Not only do the organization and nesting of elements and attributes in your document help in understanding the purpose of a document, they can ensure that applications can share configurations and reuse similar information. It is equally important to know when *not* to try to store information across configurations. This is particularly relevant as we look at the EJB deployment descriptor; each EJB is intended to act independently of all others, knowing only the information supplied to it by its container. It is a problem if beans can operate with each other outside the strict confines designed by the bean developer, as performance and business logic can be subverted. For this reason, each EJB entry is completely independent of all others.

In the following example, a session bean is described in XML:

```
<enterprise-beans>
  <session>
    <description>
      The EmployeeServiceAdmin session bean implements the session
      used by the application's administrator.
    </description>

    <ejb-name>EmployeeServiceAdmin</ejb-name>
    <home>com.wombat.empl.EmployeeServiceAdminHome</home>
    <remote>com.wombat.empl.EmployeeServiceAdmin</remote>
    <ejb-class>com.wombat.empl.EmployeeServiceAdmin-Bean</ejb-class>
    <session-type>Stateful</session-type>
    <transaction-type>Bean</transaction-type>

    <resource-ref>
      <description>
        This is a reference to a JDBC database.
        EmployeeService keeps a log of all the transactions
        being performed through the EmployeeService bean
        for auditing purposes.
      </description>
```

```
      <res-ref-name>jdbc/EmployeeAppDB</res-ref-name>
      <res-type>javax.sql.DataSource</res-type>
      <res-auth>Container</res-auth>
    </resource-ref>

  </session>
</enterprise-beans>
```

In addition to the isolation of this session bean from any other beans, elements are used to logically group elements and data. The `resource-ref` element encloses information relevant to a particular environment entry. This makes it easy for the application parsing and using the data as well as developers and system administrators maintaining the application to locate and update information about the bean or EJB server.

A larger grouping not as immediately evident is the `enterprise-beans` element. This would allow information specific to the container that does not apply to beans to be included without being mixed in with information specific to EJBs. This is an important distinction, and we will use it to separate configuration information from our XML-RPC server and our XML-RPC clients later in this chapter. Finally, any number of beans can be added to this "parent" element; although we only looked at one session bean here, multiple elements can be added of type `session` and `entity`, representing multiple beans in the *jar* file that would be created.

Although we have only briefly looked at this XML file, you should be starting to think about what sort of naming and organization should be used in your own applications as well as our XML-RPC example. Hopefully, you have some ideas of your own about structuring configuration files; almost every application has different needs and will require a unique XML document structure and set of constraints. Now that you have seen an example use of configuring an application server in XML and have started thinking about creating a configuration file of your own, let's do just that for our XML-RPC classes.

Creating an XML Configuration File

To try to put some of this knowledge into use, we look at using an XML-based configuration file for the XML-RPC classes we wrote in the last chapter. Certainly this is an excellent example of using XML for configuration information; we already have an XML parser available (used in the XML-RPC server), and it is possible that we could use this same configuration file for both clients and servers. Additionally, this configuration could be edited by XML IDEs instead of our having to create a proprietary interface for editing the file in a proprietary format. This can reduce the code that needs to be written for complex applications.

Before we start writing our configuration file, we need to define the information that will be in this file. The pieces of information we want to include are:

- Port for the XML-RPC server to start on
- Parser class for the server to use as a SAX driver
- Handlers for the XML-RPC server
- Class identifier
- Class name
- Hostname for the XML-RPC clients to connect to
- Port for XML-RPC clients to connect to
- Parser class for the server to use as a SAX driver

This provides all the information needed for both our clients and server to start without needing any user input other than the location of the XML configuration file itself. With these requirements in mind, let's begin writing the XML configuration file.

Getting Started

Just as in the case of the EJB deployment descriptor, our file must include the standard XML prolog information. This is simple enough, and the only other details we need to decide on are a namespace and root element for our document. Although in a production situation we might use a namespace indicative of the purpose of the document, such as `XMLRPC` or `XmlRpcConfig`, here we continue to use `JavaXML` to identify the configuration file with the examples in the rest of the book. We use the same namespace declaration as in other chapters and examples as well. The root element then becomes an identifier of what the document actually is used for; simply using `xmlrpc-config` seems a good choice for this. It is often the case, particularly in more complex XML documents, that the simplest solutions are the best ones. Naming XML elements and attributes is no exception to this rule.

With these initial determinations and decisions made, let's start creating our XML configuration file for our XML-RPC classes. The initial XML declaration and root element with namespace declaration are given here:

```
<?xml version="1.0"?>

<JavaXML:xmlrpc-config
  xmlns:JavaXML="http://www.oreilly.com/catalog/javaxml/"
>

</JavaXML:xmlrpc-config>
```

Other options that can be added at this point include a reference to a DTD or schema to constrain the document as well as processing instructions to applications that might parse and use this configuration. For our example, we omit these, as our program will simply parse the document as is and return the needed configuration information to the XML-RPC server and clients.

Organization

With the skeleton of the configuration file set, organization of the file needs to be determined. This includes both grouping of elements and a determination of whether any configuration information will be shared across servers and clients. The best methodology for making organizational decisions is to group the file much as you would group the configuration information if writing it by hand. Our original information requirements are small, and this process is easy to perform.

The following pieces of information are simple, and we can consider them part of the information needed by our server:

- Port for XML-RPC server to start on
- Parser class for server to use as a SAX driver

The following pieces of information will be repeated numerous times, and can be grouped into a set of handlers, with each handler within that set having a class identifier and a class name:

- Handlers for XML-RPC server
- Class identifier
- Class name

The XML-RPC client uses the last three pieces of information; however, the port used by the client is the same for the XML-RPC server, and the SAX driver is most likely the same as well. It makes sense to share this information so that changes only need to be made in one XML element, rather in separate elements for the client and server. With the port and SAX driver class being shared, it makes sense to also group the hostname into this set of shared information. Even though only the client uses it, it fits in well with the port number to use for XML-RPC requests.

- Hostname for XML-RPC clients to connect to
- Port for XML-RPC clients to connect to
- Parser class for client to use as a SAX Driver

By simply "talking through" the information to be included, we have determined that we have two basic groups of configuration information: "shared information" used by both the server and client, and "handler information," which has "handler" entries for each XML-RPC handler. This will result in two basic groupings in our configuration file, with the latter of these two having elements nested within it describing each grouping. We look at each in turn next.

Shared information

There is very little to note in adding a hostname, port number, and SAX driver class for our server and clients to use at startup and connection time. Even the element names for these three pieces of information are simple to arrive at: `hostname`, `port`, and `parserClass`. Again, simple solutions are generally the most effective. As an example of using attributes as well as elements, we add in an attribute for the `port` element named `type`. The idea is that the value of this element is either "protected" or "unprotected." When the port is protected, some additional actions would need to take place to connect, such as encoding the request through SSL. In our example XML-RPC classes, the server listens on an unprotected port; however, using this attribute adds flexibility if we want to use secure ports at a later point in the application's evolution:

```
<JavaXML:xmlrpc-config
  xmlns:JavaXML="http://www.oreilly.com/catalog/javaxml/"
>

  <!-- Configuration Information for Server and Clients -->
  <JavaXML:hostname>newInstance</JavaXML:hostname>
  <JavaXML:port type="unprotected">8585</JavaXML:port>
  <JavaXML:parserClass>
    org.apache.xerces.parsers.SAXParser
  </JavaXML:parserClass>

</JavaXML:xmlrpc-config>
```

XML-RPC handlers

The first thing we want to do in defining our handlers is to ensure they are only used by our XML-RPC server. Although we have no other information besides the handler configuration applicable to only the server, it is possible and even probable that at some point, more server-specific information will be added to the configuration file. Rather than having our parser look for a specific set of elements (and adding to those elements when we add new configuration information), we can have it look for a server-specific element name, such as `xmlrpc-server`. Server applications can read this information, while clients can ignore it without having to know the specifics of the information contained within the grouping. It also makes the information's purpose easier to discern for human eyes. We use this element (`xmlrpc-server`) to enclose our handler information.

We also should group all of our handlers together, and use an element simply named `handlers` to do this. Again, this grouping makes it simple to determine the purpose and use of the configuration information within the file. Add the configuration information needed for specifying the `HelloHandler` and `Scheduler` classes as XML-RPC handlers to the XML-RPC server configuration section:

```
<JavaXML:xmlrpc-config
  xmlns:JavaXML="http://www.oreilly.com/catalog/javaxml/"
>

  <!-- Configuration Information for Server and Clients -->
  <JavaXML:hostname>newInstance.com</JavaXML:hostname>
  <JavaXML:port type="unprotected">8585</JavaXML:port>
  <JavaXML:parserClass>
    org.apache.xerces.parsers.SAXParser
  </JavaXML:parserClass>

  <!-- Server Specific Configuration Information -->
  <JavaXML:xmlrpc-server>

    <!-- List of XML-RPC handlers to register -->
    <JavaXML:handlers>
      <JavaXML:handler>
        <JavaXML:identifier>hello</JavaXML:identifier>
        <JavaXML:class>HelloHandler</JavaXML:class>
      </JavaXML:handler>

      <JavaXML:handler>
        <JavaXML:identifier>scheduler</JavaXML:identifier>
        <JavaXML:class>Scheduler</JavaXML:class>
      </JavaXML:handler>
    </JavaXML:handlers>

  </JavaXML:xmlrpc-server>

</JavaXML:xmlrpc-config>
```

Even in this small document, alternatives for data representation are available. It would also be possible to use the following structure for representing our handlers:

```
<handler id="hello" class="HelloHandler" />
```

In almost any document, you will have to make choices about not only what data is stored, but also *how* that data is stored. In our example, we choose to use a `handler` element; this is based on the possibility that we may later want to add additional information about that handler, such as a description or a network location to load the class from. By using an element with nested child elements, we can easily add this information as new child elements; adding attributes for each new piece of data could make our XML configuration class hard to read with long lines of text for a single element.

Document Constraints

We mentioned that in the EJB deployment descriptor file, a DTD was referenced to ensure that no illegal elements or attributes were used, and that any server could read the XML file. We need to do the same thing with our XML configuration file. Creating a DTD (simple with such a small file) can ensure that our applications have a set of constraints they can expect the configuration file to adhere to. Example 11-1 is a complete DTD for the configuration file we have created.

Example 11-1. DTD for XML-RPC Configuration File

```
<!ELEMENT JavaXML:xmlrpc-config (JavaXML:hostname,
                                 JavaXML:port,
                                 JavaXML:parserClass,
                                 JavaXML:xmlrpc-server)>
<!ATTLIST JavaXML:xmlrpc-config
     xmlns:JavaXML CDATA #REQUIRED
>
<!ELEMENT JavaXML:hostname (#PCDATA)>
<!ELEMENT JavaXML:port (#PCDATA)>
<!ATTLIST JavaXML:port
     type (protected|unprotected) "unprotected"
>
<!ELEMENT JavaXML:parserClass (#PCDATA)>
<!ELEMENT JavaXML:xmlrpc-server (JavaXML:handlers)>
<!ELEMENT JavaXML:handlers (JavaXML:handler)+>
<!ELEMENT JavaXML:handler (JavaXML:identifier,
                           JavaXML:class)>
<!ELEMENT JavaXML:identifier (#PCDATA)>
<!ELEMENT JavaXML:class (#PCDATA)>
```

With this file in place, we only need to reference it within our XML configuration file:

```
<?xml version="1.0"?>

<!DOCTYPE JavaXML:xmlrpc-config SYSTEM "DTD/XmlRpc.dtd">

<JavaXML:xmlrpc-config
  xmlns:JavaXML="http://www.oreilly.com/catalog/javaxml/"
>
...
</JavaXML:xmlrpc-config>
```

In this example, the DTD is saved as *XmlRpc.dtd* in a *DTD/* subdirectory.

Final Preparations

We have moved very swiftly through creating our configuration file and its constraints; once you understand the mechanics of XML, the only difficulty in creating a configuration format is making good design decisions. This means using simple and clear names, grouping elements in logical ways, and determining when information should be shared for multiple applications. Once these decisions are made, actually creating the XML file can take only a few minutes. With our example, the information we need to include in the configuration file is minimal, making our job even easier. The complete configuration file is shown in Example 11-2 so you can see how simple this file actually is.

Example 11-2. The Complete XML Configuration File for the XML-RPC Classes

```
<?xml version="1.0"?>

<!DOCTYPE JavaXML:xmlrpc-config SYSTEM "DTD/XmlRpc.dtd">

<JavaXML:xmlrpc-config
  xmlns:JavaXML="http://www.oreilly.com/catalog/javaxml/"
>

  <!-- Configuration Information for Server and Clients -->
  <JavaXML:hostname>newInstance.com</JavaXML:hostname>
  <JavaXML:port type="unprotected">8585</JavaXML:port>
  <JavaXML:parserClass>
    org.apache.xerces.parsers.SAXParser
  </JavaXML:parserClass>

  <!-- Server Specific Configuration Information -->
  <JavaXML:xmlrpc-server>

    <!-- List of XML-RPC handlers to register -->
    <JavaXML:handlers>
      <JavaXML:handler>
        <JavaXML:identifier>hello</JavaXML:identifier>
        <JavaXML:class>HelloHandler</JavaXML:class>
      </JavaXML:handler>

      <JavaXML:handler>
        <JavaXML:identifier>scheduler</JavaXML:identifier>
        <JavaXML:class>Scheduler</JavaXML:class>
      </JavaXML:handler>
    </JavaXML:handlers>

  </JavaXML:xmlrpc-server>

</JavaXML:xmlrpc-config>
```

Once you have created this file, save it as *xmlrpc.xml* and make sure it is accessible by your Java application code. Next we look at adding a SAX class that reads this information and makes it available to the XML-RPC server and clients for use.

Reading an XML Configuration File

To allow our XML-RPC classes to use our configuration file, we must create a helper class that parses the information and then makes it available to the server and clients. Although we could build this behavior into methods within the XML-RPC classes (similar to how the `getHandlers()` method was used in our `LightweightServer` class), using a separate class allows this class to be shared by both the clients and server, reducing duplication of code. We have already determined the information that needs to be obtained and can begin by writing a skeleton class with accessor methods for that data. The actual contents of the member variables we use will be populated by the parsing behavior we write in a moment.

Getting the Configuration Information

We could add code directly to the `com.oreilly.xml.LightweightXmlRpc-Server` class to parse a configuration file; we could then add similar code to our XML-RPC clients that performed the same task. However, this results in a lot of duplicate code. Instead, another `com.oreilly.xml` utility class is introduced here: `XmlRpcConfiguration`. The beginnings of this class are shown in Example 11-3; a constructor takes in either a filename or an `InputStream` to read XML configuration data from. Simple accessor methods are also provided to access the configuration data once it has been loaded. By isolating the input and output of the class from specific XML constructs, we can change the parsing mechanism (which we look at next) without changing our XML-RPC server and client code; this is a much more object-oriented approach than embedding XML parsing code within our server and client code.

Example 11-3. The XmlRpcConfiguration Class to Read XML Configuration Data

```
package com.oreilly.xml;

import java.io.FileInputStream;
import java.io.FileNotFoundException;
import java.io.InputStream;
import java.io.IOException;
import java.util.Hashtable;

/**
 * <b><code>XmlRpcConfiguration</code></b> is a utility class
 *   that will load configuration information for XML-RPC servers
 *   and clients to use.
```

Example 11-3. The XmlRpcConfiguration Class to Read XML Configuration Data (continued)

```
 *
 * @author
 *    <a href="mailto:brettmclaughlin@earthlink.net">Brett McLaughlin</a>
 * @version 1.0
 */
public class XmlRpcConfiguration {

    /** The stream to read the XML configuration from */
    private InputStream in;

    /** Port number server runs on */
    private int portNumber;

    /** Hostname server runs on */
    private String hostname;

    /** SAX Driver Class to load */
    private String driverClass;

    /** Handlers to register in XML-RPC server */
    private Hashtable handlers;

    /**
     * <p>
     * This will set a filename to read configuration
     *   information from.
     * </p>
     *
     * @param filename <code>String</code> name of
     *                 XML configuration file.
     */
    public XmlRpcConfiguration(String filename)
        throws IOException {

        this(new FileInputStream(filename));
    }

    /**
     * <p>
     * This will set a filename to read configuration
     *   information from.
     * </p>
     *
     * @param in <code>InputStream</code> to read
     *           configuration information from.
     */
    public XmlRpcConfiguration(InputStream in)
        throws IOException {
```

Example 11-3. The XmlRpcConfiguration Class to Read XML Configuration Data (continued)

```
        this.in = in;
        portNumber = 0;
        hostname = "";
        handlers = new Hashtable();

        // Parse the XML configuration information
    }

    /**
     * <p>
     * This returns the port number the server listens on.
     * </p>
     *
     * @return <code>int</code> number of server port.
     */
    public int getPortNumber() {
        return portNumber;
    }

    /**
     * <p>
     * This returns the hostname the server listens on.
     * </p>
     *
     * @return <code>String</code> hostname of server.
     */
    public String getHostname() {
        return hostname;
    }

    /**
     * <p>
     * This returns the SAX driver class to load.
     * </p>
     *
     * @return <code>String</code> - name of SAX driver class.
     */
    public String getDriverClass() {
        return driverClass;
    }

    /**
     * <p>
     * This returns the handlers the server should register.
     * </p>
     *
     * @return <code>Hashtable</code> of handlers.
     */
```

Example 11-3. The XmlRpcConfiguration Class to Read XML Configuration Data (continued)

```
    public Hashtable getHandlers() {
        return handlers;
    }

}
```

With this skeleton in place, we can add JDOM parsing behavior to load the member variables with configuration data. To ensure that this information is ready when needed, we call the parsing method in the class constructor. The intent of providing these basic accessor methods is to hide the details of how the configuration information is obtained from the classes and applications that use the information. Changes to JDOM version, or even to using an entirely different method of accessing the XML data, affect only this class; changes do not have to be made to the XML-RPC clients and server. This provides a highly maintainable method of getting configuration information.

Loading the Configuration Information

With our class skeleton created, we can begin outlining the details of the parsing behavior we need. In this situation, we have a simple task because we know the structure of the XML document coming in (thanks to our DTD and its constraints). Thus we can directly access the elements in the document for which we need to obtain values. The best way to think about this is as a hierarchical tree structure; we can then "walk" the tree and obtain values for the elements we need information from. Figure 11-1 shows our XML configuration file represented in this fashion.

With this model in mind, it is simple to use the `getChildren()` and `getChild()` methods that JDOM provides to navigate to each of the XML elements we want to obtain data from; we can then invoke `getContent()` on the resultant elements and use those values in our application. We need to import the needed JDOM classes (and the Java support classes), create a new method to parse our configuration, and then invoke that method from the `XmlRpcConfiguration` constructor. The code to load the configuration information from the XML document is shown here:

```
import java.io.FileInputStream;
import java.io.FileNotFoundException;
import java.io.InputStream;
import java.io.IOException;
import java.util.Hashtable;
import java.util.Iterator;
import java.util.List;
```

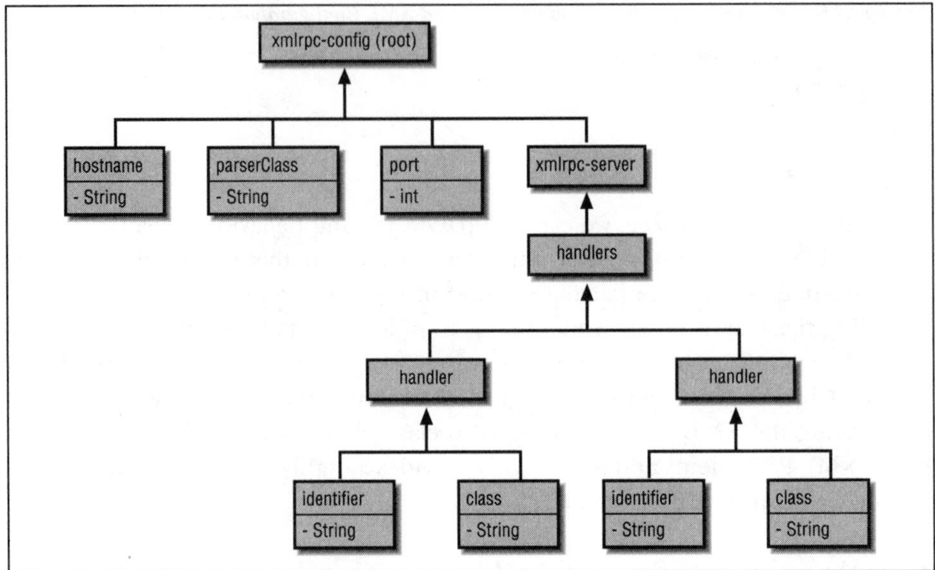

Figure 11-1. Tree view of XML configuration file

```
import org.jdom.Document;
import org.jdom.Element;
import org.jdom.JDOMException;
import org.jdom.Namespace;
import org.jdom.input.DOMBuilder;
...
    /**
     * <p>
     * This will set a filename to read configuration
     *   information from.
     * </p>
     *
     * @param in <code>InputStream</code> to read
     *           configuration information from.
     */
    public XmlRpcConfiguration(InputStream in)
        throws IOException {

        this.in = in;
        portNumber = 0;
        hostname = "";
        handlers = new Hashtable();

        // Parse the XML configuration information
        parseConfiguration();
    }
...
    /**
```

```
     * <p>
     * Parse the XML configuration information and
     *   make it available to clients.
     * </p>
     *
     * @throws <code>IOException</code> when errors occur.
     */
    private void parseConfiguration() throws IOException {
        try {
            // Request DOM Implementation and Xerces Parser
            DOMBuilder builder =
                new DOMBuilder("org.jdom.adapters.XercesDOMAdapter");

            // Get the Configuration Document, with validation
            Document doc = builder.build(in);

            // Get the root element
            Element root = doc.getRootElement();

            // Get the JavaXML namespace
            Namespace ns = Namespace.getNamespace("JavaXML",
                           "http://www.oreilly.com/catalog/javaxml/");

            // Load the hostname, port, and handler class
            hostname =
                root.getChild("hostname", ns).getContent();
            driverClass =
                root.getChild("parserClass", ns).getContent();
            portNumber =
                    root.getChild("port", ns).getIntContent(0);

            // Get the handlers
            List handlerElements =
                root.getChild("xmlrpc-server", ns)
                    .getChild("handlers", ns)
                    .getChildren("handler", ns);

            Iterator i = handlerElements.iterator();
            while (i.hasNext()) {
                Element current = (Element)i.next();
                handlers.put(current.getChild("identifier", ns)
                                    .getContent(),
                             current.getChild("class", ns)
                                    .getContent());
            }
        } catch (JDOMException e) {
            // Log an error
            throw new IOException(e.getMessage());
        }
    }
```

Once the class has been instantiated, the information needed to configure both XML-RPC servers and clients is parsed and loaded into member variables. The only feature not implemented here is error logging; this should be added in a production application, but is omitted here for the sake of space and clarity in the code. Once the root element has been obtained (`doc.getRootElement()`), JDOM is used to locate the elements based on the tree structure we looked at in Figure 11-1; once each element is located, its textual content is obtained and used to populate member data.

NOTE In this example, we used the `DOMBuilder` class to generate the JDOM `Document` object. This is a completely arbitrary decision, as once the `Document` object is built, there are no ties to either SAX or DOM. It would be just as easy (and actually much faster) to use SAX for creating the JDOM `Document` through the `SAXBuilder` class; throughout the book, both models are used to demonstrate the flexibility of JDOM. This also illustrates the possibility of completely new implementations being developed to create the tree, based neither on SAX nor DOM.

Since there are multiple handler elements, we use the `getChildren()` method to obtain a `List` of those elements, and then iterate through the list handling each element individually. With this addition, your compiled class is ready for use in our XML-RPC classes from last chapter.

Using the Configuration Information

Not surprisingly, we have taken care of the hard part of using XML for configuration data. With our `XmlRpcConfiguration` class, we have an easy means of getting at this configuration data. All our server and client now need as arguments is the XML configuration file to pass to the `XmlRpcConfiguration` helper class. In a production application, this could also be specified as a constant within a constants file or class, or specified as an initial argument if the application was a Java servlet.

Updating the server

First we can make the modifications to our `LightweightXmlRpcServer` class to use the XML configuration information instead of the textual properties file from last chapter. We also remove the command-line argument specifying a port, as that is now included within the configuration file. This involves modifying our constructor to only take in a configuration file, using the `XmlRpcConfiguration` class to access the port number and handlers to register, and removing the `getHandlers()` method from our server class. These changes are shown in Example 11-4.

Example 11-4. The LightweightXmlRpcServer Class Using an XML Configuration File

```
/**
 * <b><code>LightweightXmlRpcServer</code></b> is a utility class
 *   that will start an XML-RPC server listening for HTTP requests
 *   and register a set of handlers, defined in a configuration file.
 *
 * @author
 *   <a href="mailto:brettmclaughlin@earthlink.net">Brett McLaughlin</a>
 * @version 1.0
 */
public class LightweightXmlRpcServer {

    /** The XML-RPC server utility class */
    private WebServer server;

    /** Configuration file to use */
    private XmlRpcConfiguration config;

    // The port number and filename variables are removed

    /**
     * <p>
     * This will store the configuration file for the server to use.
     * </p>
     *
     * @param configFile <code>String</code> filename to read for
     *                   configuration information.
     * @throws <code>IOException</code> when the server cannot read
     *         its configuration information.
     */
    public LightweightXmlRpcServer(String configFile)
        throws IOException {

        config = new XmlRpcConfiguration(configFile);
    }

    /**
     * <p>
     * This will start up the server.
     * </p>
     *
     * @throws <code>IOException</code> when problems occur.
     */
    public void start() throws IOException {
        try {
            // Load the SAX Driver class
            XmlRpc.setDriver(config.getDriverClass());

            System.out.println("Starting up XML-RPC Server...");
```

Example 11-4. The LightweightXmlRpcServer Class Using an XML Configuration File (continued)

```
            server = new WebServer(config.getPortNumber());

            // Register handlers
            registerHandlers(config.getHandlers());

        } catch (ClassNotFoundException e) {
            throw new IOException("Error loading SAX parser: " +
                e.getMessage());
        }
    }

    // The getHandlers() method is removed from the source code

    /**
     * <p>
     * Provide a static entry point.
     * </p>
     */
    public static void main(String[] args) {

        if (args.length < 1) {
            System.out.println(
                "Usage: " +
                "java com.oreilly.xml.LightweightXmlRpcServer " +
                "[configFile]");
            System.exit(-1);
        }

        // Creation of server moved into try/catch block
        //   to let client know if errors occur in startup

        try {
            // Load configuration information
            LightweightXmlRpcServer server =
                new LightweightXmlRpcServer(args[0]);

            // Start the server
            server.start();
        } catch (IOException e) {
            System.out.println(e.getMessage());
        }
    }

}
```

These changes enable our server to use the new XML file for loading its configuration information, as well as to report errors when they occur in loading the configuration information. Our existing `registerHandlers()` method works well with the returned `Hashtable` from a call to the `getHandlers()` method from the `XmlRpcConfiguration` class, so no changes are necessary there. While the output from starting up the XML-RPC server with these changes does not seem very exciting (shown in Example 11-5), we have made a major improvement to our application.

Example 11-5. Output from the Modified LightweightXmlRpcServer Class

```
$ java com.oreilly.xml.LightweightXmlRpcServer conf/xmlrpc.xml
Starting up XML-RPC Server...
  Port: 8585
  Registered handler scheduler to class Scheduler
  Registered handler hello to class HelloHandler
```

Updating the client

Modifying our client to use the new configuration information is even easier than modifying our server was! With the `XmlRpcConfiguration` class imported, our `SchedulerClient` can retrieve the hostname and port number to connect to for making XML-RPC requests. Make the changes shown in Example 11-6.

Example 11-6. The SchedulerClient Class Using an XML Configuration File

```
import java.io.IOException;
import java.net.MalformedURLException;
import java.util.Calendar;
import java.util.Date;
import java.util.Enumeration;
import java.util.Hashtable;
import java.util.Vector;

import com.oreilly.xml.XmlRpcConfiguration;

import helma.xmlrpc.XmlRpc;

import helma.xmlrpc.XmlRpcClient;
import helma.xmlrpc.XmlRpcException;

public class SchedulerClient {

    // addEvents() and listEvents() method implementations

    public static void main(String args[]) {
        if (args.length < 1) {
            System.out.println(
                "Usage: java SchedulerClient [configFile]");
            System.exit(-1);
        }
```

Example 11-6. The SchedulerClient Class Using an XML Configuration File (continued)

```
        try {
            // Load Configuration File
            XmlRpcConfiguration config =
                new XmlRpcConfiguration(args[0]);

            // Load the SAX Driver class
            XmlRpc.setDriver(config.getDriverClass());

            // Connect to server
            XmlRpcClient client =
                new XmlRpcClient("http://" +
                                 config.getHostname() + ":" +
                                 config.getPortNumber());

            // Add some events
            addEvents(client);

            // List events
            listEvents(client);

        } catch (MalformedURLException e) {
            System.out.println(
                "Incorrect URL for XML-RPC server format: " +
                e.getMessage());
        } catch (XmlRpcException e) {
            System.out.println("XML-RPC Exception: " +
                e.getMessage());
        } catch (IOException e) {
            System.out.println("IO Exception: " + e.getMessage());
        } catch (ClassNotFoundException e) {
            System.out.println("Couldn't locate SAX parser: " +
                e.getMessage());
        }
    }

    ...
}
```

These same changes can be easily made to the `HelloClient` example as well. Both clients will (almost disappointingly) output exactly the same results as in the last chapter; however, as in the case of our server, a major improvement has been made. Changing the host and port number that accepts requests requires one XML (textual) change, and affects both the server and client classes as soon as they are restarted. This is a significant aid in configurability and application maintenance. Before moving on to the next chapter, we do want to look at some other alternatives for storing this type of configuration information, and see how they compare with XML.

The Real World

As we continue through our topical discussions, the line between a realistic use of XML and our examples is becoming thinner. Our XML-RPC server in this chapter is close to being ready for production use; it has a flexible configuration file format, it registers handlers dynamically, and maintains a lightweight structure for handling XML-RPC requests. However, the use of XML for pure data, as discussed in this chapter, is as new an idea as most of our other XML topics. As with RMI versus RPC, it is possible to overuse the technology. In this section, we compare XML as a data storage medium with other more traditional formats, discussing when one format is preferable over the other, as well as comparing JDOM with other solutions for accessing our underlying XML data.

XML Versus Databases

Depending on who you ask, databases (and, in particular, relational databases) are either here, never to be replaced, or are any minute going to literally disappear off the face of the planet in favor of object-oriented databases and XML data stores. As is usually the case, the reality of the situation is somewhere in the middle of these two extremes. Ten years ago, anyone questioning the longevity of a relational database management system (RDBMS) would have been laughed at. Five years ago, this possibility might have been acknowledged with the advent of the object-oriented database management system (OODBMS), but still received with skepticism and some chuckles. However, the last two years have made this a serious consideration; with the OODBMS, XML has rocketed to the forefront, and there are serious computer scientists and developers who claim that XML can completely replace traditional backend database systems for storage.

The truth of the matter? The RDBMS is not going anywhere anytime soon, if ever. Even ignoring serious issues such as relational data representation in XML, the DBMS technology is a core part of too many applications in use today. Although XML may be a realistic possibility for some smaller applications without legacy data or legacy application dependencies, most large-scale production applications must interface with existing data. This data is almost always maintained in a relational database (with Oracle being the most popular commercial product, and MySQL the most popular free product). Since almost all of the major players in the commercial world, as well as those influential in technology development, use these systems, it is not a wise bet to assume that XML is going to replace, or even crowd, the database management system space. The pure size of the data stored in many of these established systems (gigabytes and often terabytes) makes XML a poor choice for a data representation. Even in the ideal project for XML, which would be a new project without any ties to existing data or applications that depend on a DBMS, it is likely that at some point the application will have to interface with older systems. Certainly, selling management on an expensive migration of legacy data to an XML format is difficult when traditional development practices work equally well. So don't count on seeing Oracle's data storage format go XML, or on Sybase closing down their doors anytime soon; use XML for configuration and transport as much as possible, but leaving legacy data in large quantities alone for now is the wise choice.

Still, there is something of a happy medium for those of you anxious to use XML as a pure storage medium. Products are being released today that provide an XML layer over relational data, as well as other types of data (directory services, for example, which we look at next). As these mapping tools continue to mature, proponents of dealing with data in an XML format can choose to add a thin mapping layer over their existing legacy databases, effectively creating an XML data repository. In the same way, newer companies that do choose to use complete XML data store solutions can interact with older systems through these same mapping tools. The most promising product to date has been Castor, an open source project under the ExoLab* umbrella. For more information on Castor and ML data binding tools, visit *http://castor.exolab.org*.

XML Versus Directory Services and LDAP

Another fairly recent upstart in the technology and data space is the Lightweight Directory Access Protocol (LDAP) and directory services. From the first steps in research at Berkeley and Michigan to Netscape's now widespread Directory Server (*http://www.netscape.com*), LDAP has become a hot topic in its own right. With the rise of XML, there has been a fair bit of confusion as to when directory services are appropriate to use instead of XML. While directory services are well recognized as useful for company directories and integration of company-wide mail, addressing, and calendaring services, using the LDAP protocol has become popular for configuration information. Storing information about application configuration as well as about how to respond to key application events (such as authentication) is commonly handled with a directory server. This provides faster search and retrieval than a database, and the hierarchical format of most directory servers lends itself well to configuration information. With this chapter on XML for storing the same type of data, the question of when to use LDAP and when to use XML is particularly pertinent.

* Although we have not mentioned ExOffice and the ExoLab group before, they are strong proponents of open source technologies, particularly as those technologies relate to XML and Java. For more information, check out *http://www.exolab.org* online.

The surprising answer to this query is that the question itself is not valid! There is really not a comparison between LDAP and XML, as the two serve orthogonal purposes. Where LDAP and directory services are about making technology or components available by some specific name, XML is about the storage and transmission of the data involved with those components. In fact, a more appropriate question is "When will LDAP and XML integrate?" The answer lies in the same technologies for XML data binding that we mentioned in regards to databases; the Castor project actually has a complete XML-to-LDAP binding. Additionally, directory services are moving towards a uniform data storage medium; XML certainly could be this medium. As the hierarchical structures of LDAP and XML are close matches, don't be surprised to see a marriage between LDAP services and XML storage.

JDOM, SAX, or DOM

In looking at alternatives to XML, it is also important to address alternatives to how we access XML. Although you have seen how easily JDOM allowed us to access our XML configuration information, we take a brief look here at those alternatives. As you implement XML applications in the real world, understanding why a choice is made is often as important as making the choice itself. For that reason, let's look at our alternatives for accessing XML data from Java.

In accessing our XML configuration data, we used JDOM in our method to get the desired values:

```
private void parseConfiguration() {
    try {
        // Request DOM Implementation and Xerces Parser
        DOMBuilder builder =
            new DOMBuilder("org.jdom.adapters.XercesDOMAdapter");

        // Get the Configuration Document, with validation
        Document doc = builder.build(in);

        // Get the root element
        Element root = doc.getRootElement();

        // Get the JavaXML namespace
        Namespace ns = Namespace.getNamespace("JavaXML",
                       "http://www.oreilly.com/catalog/javaxml/");

        // Load the hostname, port, and handler class
        hostname =
            root.getChild("hostname", ns).getContent();
        driverClass =
            root.getChild("parserClass", ns).getContent();
        portNumber =
                root.getChild("port", ns).getIntContent(0);
```

```
            // Get the handlers
            List handlerElements =
                root.getChild("xmlrpc-server", ns)
                    .getChild("handlers", ns)
                    .getChildren("handler", ns);

            Iterator i = handlerElements.iterator();
            while (i.hasNext()) {
                Element current = (Element)i.next();
                handlers.put(current.getChild("identifier", ns)
                                    .getContent(),
                             current.getChild("class", ns)
                                    .getContent());
            }
        } catch (JDOMException e) {
            // Log an error
            throw new IOException(e.getMessage());
        }
    }
```

To give you an idea of how JDOM is different from SAX and DOM, the next two sections show how this information could be accessed using SAX or DOM.

SAX

The biggest challenge in writing SAX code is that it does not follow an object-oriented style as much as it does a hierarchical one. Because SAX events occur sequentially, it is not possible to deal with children of elements directly. Instead, storage has to be allocated to save the name of the element being processed, as the data for that element occurs in a subsequent callback. SAX parsing generally involves reading a document and storing the data passed to the `characters()` callback with the name of the element last processed (through the `startElement()` callback). Then at the end of processing the element (`endElement()`) or the document (`endDocument()`), this information is loaded from storage and used. While SAX and this sequential approach are sometimes faster than DOM (or JDOM with a DOM implementation), the resulting code is generally not as clear and easy to debug. The `parseConfiguration()` method, rewritten to use SAX, is shown here:

```
    private void parseConfiguration() {
        try {
            XMLReader parser =
                XMLReaderFactory.createXMLReader(
                    "org.apache.xerces.parsers.SAXParser");

            parser.setContentHandler(new ConfigurationHandler());
```

```
            parser.parse(new InputSource(in));

        } catch (Exception e) {
            // Log an error
        }
    }
```

A SAX XMLReader implementation is loaded and then a ContentHandler implementation is registered. As is typical with SAX, the bulk of application code is within the ContentHandler instance, shown here:

```
    /**
     * <p>
     * This inner class will handle callbacks indicating
     *   when configuration information is read.
     * </p>
     */
    class ConfigurationHandler extends DefaultHandler {

        /** Storage for element contents */
        private Hashtable storage;

        /** The name of the element last reported */
        private String currentElement;

        /** Element name constants */
        private static final String HOSTNAME_ELEMENT = "hostname";
        private static final String PORTNUMBER_ELEMENT = "port";
        private static final String DRIVER_CLASS_ELEMENT = "parserClass";
        private static final String HANDLER_ELEMENT = "handler";
        private static final String HANDLER_ID_ELEMENT = "identifier";
        private static final String HANDLER_CLASS_ELEMENT = "class";

        /**
        * <p>
        * This will initialize the storage.
         * </p>
         */
        public ConfigurationHandler() {
            storage = new Hashtable();
        }

        /**
         * <p>
         * Capture the name of the element being reported.
         * </p>
         */
        public void startElement(String namespaceURI, String localName,
                                 String rawName, Attributes atts)
            throws SAXException {
```

```
        currentElement = localName;
    }

    /**
     * <p>
     * Add whatever character data is being reported
     *   to the data for the current element already
     *   in storage.
     * </p>
     */
    public void characters(char[] ch, int start, int end)
        throws SAXException {

        String data = new String(ch, start, end).trim();

        if (storage.containsKey(currentElement)) {
            data =
                (String)storage.get(currentElement) +
                data.trim();
        }

        storage.put(currentElement, data);
    }

    /**
     * <p>
     * Since nested information is stored within a handler element,
     *   and that element can occur multiple times, handle
     *   storage of a handler's data every time the end
     *   of that element is reached.
     * </p>
     */
    public void endElement(String namespaceURI, String localName,
                           String rawName) throws SAXException {

        // Add handler if completed
        if (localName.equals(HANDLER_ELEMENT)) {
            String handlerName =
                (String)storage.get(HANDLER_ID_ELEMENT);
            String handlerClass =
                (String)storage.get(HANDLER_CLASS_ELEMENT);

            // Add this to the outer class's storage
            handlers.put(handlerName, handlerClass);

            storage.remove(HANDLER_ID_ELEMENT);
            storage.remove(HANDLER_CLASS_ELEMENT);
        }
    }
```

```
        /**
         * <p>
         * Save collected information at the end of a
         *   document, since we can be guaranteed all elements
         *   have been processed.
         * </p>
         */
        public void endDocument() throws SAXException {
            hostname = (String)storage.get(HOSTNAME_ELEMENT);
            driverClass = (String)storage.get(DRIVER_CLASS_ELEMENT);

            try {
                portNumber =
                    Integer.parseInt(
                        (String)storage.get(PORTNUMBER_ELEMENT));
            } catch (NumberFormatException e) {
                // Log error
            }
        }
    }
```

Javadoc is provided to describe what is occurring at each step. When the `startElement()` method is invoked, the name of the reported element is stored. This is then the key for the `Hashtable` of element/data values, which is populated through each call to `characters()`. After processing each `handler` element, the class identifier and class name must be saved, as subsequent reports of another `handler` element would overwrite the current data. Finally, in `endDocument()`, the hostname, port, and parser class are saved as well.

While this code is certainly functional, and even not too complex (with the help of good documentation), it is a lot more code that is a lot less readable than our method using JDOM. Additionally, as the number of elements in an XML document increases to fifty, one hundred, or more, the SAX code becomes increasingly complex, as more constants are defined and more logic is added to the callback methods. The JDOM fragment, however, does not increase nearly as quickly in complexity, because JDOM provides access to the complete XML document through its API.

DOM

Using DOM to access XML data is, in a sense, the opposite extreme of SAX. DOM does provide a complete view of an XML document, but in fact dictates that the document is completely read into memory before it is ever accessed programmatically. Although this is not a significant problem with smaller files, it can be cumbersome with large XML documents.

Additionally, DOM does not provide a standard interface for acquiring the DOM `Document` object. This results in explicit imports of vendor-specific classes or advanced reflection to avoid those imports. It also provides a very formal representation of a tree structure; the textual content of an element is only available as a child `Node` of that element, and must be accessed in that manner, rather than directly from the element itself. The `parseConfiguration()` method using DOM is shown here:

```
private void parseConfiguration() {
    org.apache.xerces.parsers.DOMParser parser =
        new org.apache.xerces.parsers.DOMParser();
    handlers = new Hashtable();
    parser.setFeature("http://xml.org/sax/features/namespaces", true);

    try {
        parser.parse(uri);
        doc = parser.getDocument();
        Element root = doc.getDocumentElement();

        // Get hostname
        NodeList nodes =
            root.getElementsByTagNameNS(NAMESPACE_URI, "hostname");

        if (nodes.getLength() > 0) {
            hostname = nodes.item(0).getFirstChild()
                                    .getNodeValue();
        } else {
            hostname = "";
        }

        // Get port number
        nodes =
            root.getElementsByTagNameNS(NAMESPACE_URI, "port");
        if (nodes.getLength() > 0) {
            portNumber =
                Integer.parseInt(
                    nodes.item(0).getFirstChild()
                                 .getNodeValue());
        } else {
            portNumber = 0;
        }

        // Get handlers
        nodes =
            root.getElementsByTagNameNS(NAMESPACE_URI, "handler");
        for (int i=0; i<nodes.getLength(); i++) {
            Element handlerNode = (Element)nodes.item(i);
            NodeList handlerNodes =
```

```
                handlerNode.getElementsByTagNameNS(
                    NAMESPACE_URI, "identifier");

            String handlerID =
                handlerNodes.item(0).getFirstChild()
                                    .getNodeValue();

            handlerNodes =
                handlerNode.getElementsByTagNameNS(
                    NAMESPACE_URI, "class");
            String handlerClass =
                handlerNodes.item(0).getFirstChild()
                                    .getNodeValue();

            handlers.put(handlerID, handlerClass);
        }

    } catch (Exception e) {

        // Set to default values
        portNumber = 0;
        hostname = "";
    }
}
```

While certainly a shorter code fragment than our SAX example, DOM is still very verbose. In addition to the direct interaction with the Apache Xerces parser (or whatever vendor you are using for DOM tree creation), there are several other non-intuitive structures to work with. Notice how the textual value of a node is obtained:

```
hostname = nodes.item(0).getFirstChild()
                        .getNodeValue();
```

Because the `hostname` element is considered to have child nodes, which include textual values for the element, the first child's value has to be obtained, rather than the value of the `Node` representing the `hostname` element itself. This is a prime cause of bugs when using DOM: a DOM Element has no textual value; instead, it may have children that are `Text Nodes`, and those actually have the value desired.

Finally, the structure returned from calls like `getElementsByTagName()` and `getChildNodes()` is a DOM `NodeList` instead of a Java `Vector` or `List`. This object has its own accessor methods (`getLength()` and `item()`), which differ from what Java collection classes have available. This design makes using DOM less Java-centric than dealing with JDOM, which uses standard Java objects for return types.

Certainly both SAX and DOM can accomplish the tasks that JDOM can; the question is if there is anything they offer that makes using them worth the penalties paid in readability of code. Additionally, with the JDOM `SAXBuilder` class, JDOM can perform at a level comparable to SAX, while still allowing a tree structure to be kept in memory (through the JDOM `Document` object), and while still remaining more lightweight than DOM. You can check for later versions and implementations of JDOM online at *http://www.jdom.org*. Finally, JDOM provides an abstraction layer over parsers and implementations that SAX emulates through `XMLReaderFactory` and that DOM ignores altogether. Sun's JAXP begins to help this situation, but is still slow to show support for newer versions of SAX and DOM. Ultimately, you will need to decide which API supports your projects best, as well as provides the simplest entry point for the new developers you will have to add to your teams.

What's Next?

At this point, we have read, parsed, transformed, and used XML in a variety of formats. We have used XML for content and presentation, for procedure calls across a network, and for telling an application how to behave on startup and execution. Next, we complement this store of reading and using XML with writing XML. In Chapter 12, *Creating XML with Java*, we look at the other half of XML handling, mutability. This will round out your XML toolbox to include the ability to have your applications generate XML documents at runtime, often changing the inputs of other application components.

In this chapter:

- *Loading the Data*
- *Modifying the Data*
- *XML from Scratch*
- *The Real World*
- *What's Next?*

12

Creating XML with Java

We now take a look at the one portion of manipulating XML that we have yet to address: creating and modifying XML. So far, all of our applications have used existing XML documents as constant data, never making changes to the original document. This is often the case in programming XML-based applications today; however, more and more leading edge technologies create XML documents in memory (such as XSP, which we looked at in Chapter 9, *Web Publishing Frameworks*). Other common applications that might need to modify XML data include XML editors and development environments as well as configuration managers, which we explore in this chapter.

In the last chapter, we created an XML configuration file for storing information related to configuring our XML-RPC classes. The assumption we made at that point was that changes to these configuration parameters would require a user (most likely a systems administrator) to edit the configuration file by hand and make modifications. Then (hopefully) the user would validate the modified XML document and restart the XML-RPC server and clients. However, this can be a very error-prone approach. First, it assumes that no mistakes are made when entering the new information. Second, it assumes that the user making the changes has the self-discipline to validate the modified XML document, ensuring correct and valid data has been entered. Even if both of these events occur every time modifications are made, which is unlikely in a real-world scenario, the configuration becomes more complicated if the client and server are on different machines. If the XML-RPC server is distributed as well, the configuration file then exists in another location; it is possible and even probable that four, five, or even more separate copies of the file exist, all on different servers. Any change to one of these files must result in the change being duplicated to all the other files. A Java application or servlet to modify the configuration file and then automatically update all the various locations is a good solution for this problem, and in this situation, the Java code must be able to modify XML.

We will explore modifying an XML document, and then saving the changed document, in this chapter. This final format could be another XML text file on a hard drive, a stream that is passed to another application component, or XML that is transformed and output as HTML. The Java APIs for programmatically working with XML make all of this possible.

Loading the Data

As in the previous chapters, the best way to learn to use these technologies and APIs is to actually code something useful with them. To demonstrate how to go about doing this, we take a look at further enhancing the functionality of our suite of XML-RPC classes and tools. In the last chapter, we migrated all of our configuration information to an XML configuration file. We have already created a class to read in this information and to use the loaded information for starting up our XML-RPC clients and server using the JDOM interfaces (as well as having looked at SAX and DOM alternatives). Now we will write a simple tool to update and modify this configuration information and then save the changes to the original configuration file.

In this section, we look at two components of this process: our utility class, `com.oreilly.xml.XmlRpcConfiguration`, that currently loads the configuration data, and a Java servlet to provide a user interface for editing the data. First we add mutator methods to our utility class that complement our accessor methods from Chapter 11, *XML for Configurations*. These will allow the servlet we build, as well as other applications, to modify the data within the utility class. Once we have created this entry point for applications to modify the configuration data, we will create a servlet to display the information, as well as to let users modify the data through an HTML form.

An Entry Point for Modification

Because our utility class, `XmlRpcConfiguration`, encapsulates the process of reading and writing to the underlying XML document on the filesystem, we can add mutator methods to the class now, and then later add behavior to write changes out to the actual file. This provides an abstraction layer that allows us to build applications in parallel: once the mutator methods are in place, one developer or group can work on the servlet interface, using the supplied accessor and mutator methods, while another developer or group can work on the method within the utility class that saves the updated configuration. Example 12-1 shows the `XmlRpcConfiguration` class with these mutator methods implemented, as well as a `saveConfiguration` method skeleton that will eventually use Java APIs to update the underlying configuration data, given either a filename or an `OutputStream` to write the updated configuration to.

Example 12-1. Utility Class with Mutator Methods

```
package com.oreilly.xml;

import java.io.FileInputStream;
import java.io.FileNotFoundException;
import java.io.FileOutputStream;
import java.io.InputStream;
import java.io.IOException;
import java.util.Hashtable;
import java.util.Iterator;
import java.util.List;

import org.jdom.Document;
import org.jdom.Element;
import org.jdom.JDOMException;
import org.jdom.Namespace;
import org.jdom.input.DOMBuilder;

/**
 * <b><code>XmlRpcConfiguration</code></b> is a utility class
 *   that will load configuration information for XML-RPC servers
 *   and clients to use.
 *
 * @author
 *   <a href="mailto:brettmclaughlin@earthlink.net">Brett McLaughlin</a>
 * @version 1.0
 */
public class XmlRpcConfiguration {

    /** The stream to read the XML configuration from */
    private InputStream in;

    /** Port number server runs on */
    private int portNumber;

    /** Hostname server runs on */
    private String hostname;

    /** SAX Driver Class to load */
    private String driverClass;

    /** Handlers to register in XML-RPC server */
    private Hashtable handlers;
```

Example 12-1. Utility Class with Mutator Methods (continued)

```
    /** JDOM Document tied to underlying XML */
    private Document doc;

    /**
     * <p>
     * This will set a filename to read configuration
     *   information from.
     * </p>
     *
     * @param filename <code>String</code> name of
     *                 XML configuration file.
     */
    public XmlRpcConfiguration(String filename)
        throws IOException {

        this(new FileInputStream(filename));
    }

    /**
     * <p>
     * This will set a filename to read configuration
     *   information from.
     * </p>
     *
     * @param in <code>InputStream</code> to read
     *           configuration information from.
     */
    public XmlRpcConfiguration(InputStream in)
        throws IOException {

        this.in = in;
        portNumber = 0;
        hostname = "";
        handlers = new Hashtable();

        // Parse the XML configuration information
        parseConfiguration();
    }

    /**
     * <p>
     * This returns the port number the server listens on.
     * </p>
     *
     * @return <code>int</code> - number of server port.
     */
    public int getPortNumber() {
```

Example 12-1. Utility Class with Mutator Methods (continued)

```
        return portNumber;
    }

    /**
     * <p>
     * This will set the port number to listen to.
     * </p>
     *
     * @param portNumber <code>int</code> port to listen to.
     */
    public void setPortNumber(int portNumber) {
        this.portNumber = portNumber;
    }

    /**
     * <p>
     * This returns the hostname the server listens on.
     * </p>
     *
     * @return <code>String</code> - hostname of server.
     */
    public String getHostname() {
        return hostname;
    }

    /**
     * <p>
     * This will set the hostname for the server to listen to.
     * </p>
     *
     * @param hostname <code>String</code> name of server's host.
     */
    public void setHostname(String hostname) {
        this.hostname = hostname;
    }

    /**
     * <p>
     * This returns the SAX driver class to load.
     * </p>
     *
     * @return <code>String</code> - name of SAX driver class.
     */
    public String getDriverClass() {
        return driverClass;
    }

    /**
```

Example 12-1. Utility Class with Mutator Methods (continued)

```
     * <p>
     * This will set the driver class for parsing.
     * </p>
     *
     * @param driverClass <code>String</code> name of parser class.
     */
    public void setDriverClass(String driverClass) {
        this.driverClass = driverClass;
    }

    /**
     * <p>
     * This returns the handlers the server should register.
     * </p>
     *
     * @return <code>Hashtable</code> of handlers.
     */
    public Hashtable getHandlers() {
        return handlers;
    }

    /**
     * <p>
     * This will set the handlers to register.
     * </p>
     *
     * @param handlers <code>Hashtable</code> of handler to register.
     */
    public void setHandlers(Hashtable handlers) {
        this.handlers = handlers;
    }

    /**
     * <p>
     * Parse the XML configuration information and
     *   make it available to clients.
     * </p>
     *
     * @throws <code>IOException</code> when errors occur.
     */
    private void parseConfiguration() throws IOException {
        try {
            // Request DOM Implementation and Xerces Parser
            DOMBuilder builder =
                new DOMBuilder("org.jdom.adapters.XercesDOMAdapter");

            // Get the Configuration Document, with validation
            doc = builder.build(in);
```

Example 12-1. Utility Class with Mutator Methods (continued)

```
            // Get the root element
            Element root = doc.getRootElement();

            // Get the JavaXML namespace
            Namespace ns = Namespace.getNamespace("JavaXML",
                           "http://www.oreilly.com/catalog/javaxml/");

            // Load the hostname, port, and handler class
            hostname =
                root.getChild("hostname", ns).getContent();
            driverClass =
                root.getChild("parserClass", ns).getContent();
            portNumber =
                    root.getChild("port", ns).getIntContent(0);

            // Get the handlers
            List handlerElements =
                root.getChild("xmlrpc-server", ns)
                    .getChild("handlers", ns)
                    .getChildren("handler", ns);

            Iterator i = handlerElements.iterator();
            while (i.hasNext()) {
                Element current = (Element)i.next();
                handlers.put(current.getChild("identifier", ns)
                                    .getContent(),
                             current.getChild("class", ns)
                                    .getContent());
            }
        } catch (JDOMException e) {
            // Log an error
            throw new IOException(e.getMessage());
        }
    }

    /**
     * <p>
     * This will save the current state out to the XML-RPC configuration
     *   file.
     * </p>
     *
     * @throws <code>IOException</code> - when errors occur in saving.
     */
    public synchronized void saveConfiguration(String filename)
        throws IOException {
```

Example 12-1. Utility Class with Mutator Methods (continued)

```
        saveConfiguration(new FileOutputStream(filename));
    }

    /**
     * <p>
     * This will save the current state out to the specified
     *   <code>OutputStream</code>.
     * </p>
     *
     * @throws <code>IOException</code> - when errors occur in saving.
     */
    public synchronized void saveConfiguration(OutputStream out)
        throws IOException {

        // To be implemented
    }

}
```

In addition to the new methods, you should notice that we create a `Document` member variable, `doc`, and use it in both the reading and the writing of the configuration document. It makes sense to store the reference to the JDOM `Document` object, rather than reloading it in the `saveConfiguration()` method. Our `parseConfiguration()` now loads the XML data into the `doc` member variable, which can then be reused in the `saveConfiguration()` method.

Displaying the Configuration

With the `XmlRpcConfiguration` class definition complete, we now need an interface for the user to view this configuration data and make changes. Using a Java servlet for this interface is a good idea, as it provides a simple request and response model without extensive network programming. This also makes remote administration possible through any Internet browser. We first need to code in the portion of the servlet that will respond to a simple browser request (which comes through the GET method) and display the current configuration information. All this requires is instantiating the `XmlRpcConfiguration` class and then outputting an HTML form with the information from the utility class filling the values within that form. Because this is basic Java and Java servlet code, Example 12-2 is provided without detailed explanation. If you are unfamiliar with the Java Servlet API, you should check out *Java Servlet Programming*, by Jason Hunter (O'Reilly & Associates).

Example 12-2. A Java Servlet to Display XML-RPC Configuration Information

```
import java.io.IOException;
import java.io.PrintWriter;
import java.util.Enumeration;
```

Example 12-2. A Java Servlet to Display XML-RPC Configuration Information (continued)

```
import java.util.Hashtable;
import javax.servlet.ServletException;
import javax.servlet.http.HttpServlet;
import javax.servlet.http.HttpServletRequest;
import javax.servlet.http.HttpServletResponse;

import com.oreilly.xml.XmlRpcConfiguration;

/**
 * <b><code>XmlRpcConfigurationServlet</code></b> is an
 *   administration tool that allows configuration changes
 *   to be saved to the XML configuration file.
 *
 * @version 1.0
 */
public class XmlRpcConfigurationServlet extends HttpServlet {

    /** Store the XML-RPC configuration file as a constant */
    private static final String CONFIG_FILENAME =
        "d:\\prod\\Java and XML\\WEB-INF\\conf\\xmlrpc.xml";

    /**
     * Point action back at this servlet (and the
     *   <code>{@link #doPost()}</code> method).
     *   In Servlet API 2.1 or 2.2, this can be done programmatically,
     *   but this example allows this to work in Servlet 2.0 as well
     */
    private static final String FORM_ACTION =
        "/javaxml/servlet/XmlRpcConfigurationServlet";

    /** Configuration object to work with */
    XmlRpcConfiguration config;

    /**
     * <p>
     * GET requests are received when the client wants to see the current
     *   configuration information. This provides a view-only look at
     *   the data. The generated HTML form then submits back to this
     *   servlet through POST, which causes the
     *   <code>{@link #doPost}</code> method to be invoked.
     * </p>
     */
    public void doGet(HttpServletRequest req,
                      HttpServletResponse res)
        throws ServletException, IOException {

        res.setContentType("text/html");
        PrintWriter out = res.getWriter();
```

Example 12-2. A Java Servlet to Display XML-RPC Configuration Information (continued)

```
        // Load the configuration information with our utility class
        config = new XmlRpcConfiguration(CONFIG_FILENAME);

        // Output HTML user interface
        out.println("<html><head>");
        out.println("<title>XML-RPC Configurations</title>");
        out.println("</head><body>");
        out.println("<h2 align=\"center\">XML-RPC Configuration</h2>");
        out.println("<form action=\"" + FORM_ACTION + "\" " +
                    "method=\"POST\">");
        out.println("<b>Hostname:</b> ");
        out.println("<input type=\"text\" " +
                    "name=\"hostname\" " +
                    "value=\"" + config.getHostname() +
                    "\" />");
        //out.println("<br />");
        out.println("    ");
        out.println("<b>Port Number:</b> ");
        out.println("<input type=\"text\" " +
                    "name=\"port\" " +
                    "value=\"" + config.getPortNumber() +
                    "\" />");
        out.println("<br />");
        out.println("<b>SAX Driver Class:</b> ");
        out.println("<input type=\"text\" " +
                    "name=\"driverClass\" size=\"50\"" +
                    "value=\"" + config.getDriverClass() +
                    "\" />");
        out.println("<br />");
        out.println("<br />");
        out.println("<h3 align=\"center\">XML-RPC handlers</h3>");

        // Display current handlers
        Hashtable handlers = config.getHandlers();
        Enumeration keys = handlers.keys();
        int index = 0;
        while (keys.hasMoreElements()) {
            String handlerID =
                (String)keys.nextElement();
            String handlerClass =
                (String)handlers.get(handlerID);
            out.println("<b>Identifier:</b> ");
            out.println("<input type=\"text\" " +
                        "value=\"" + handlerID + "\" " +
                        "name=\"handlerID\" />  ");
            out.println("<b>Class:</b> ");
            out.println("<input type=\"text\" " +
```

Example 12-2. A Java Servlet to Display XML-RPC Configuration Information (continued)

```
                    "value=\"" + handlerClass + "\" " +
                    "size=\"30\" " +
                    "name=\"handlerClass\" />  ");
            out.println("<br />");
            index++;
        }

        // Display empty boxes for additional handlers
        for (int i=0; i<3; i++) {
            out.println("<b>Identifier:</b> ");
            out.println("<input type=\"text\" " +
                        "name=\"handlerID\" />  ");
            out.println("<b>Class:</b> ");
            out.println("<input type=\"text\" " +
                        "size=\"30\" " +
                        "name=\"handlerClass\" />  ");
            out.println("<br />");
            index++;
        }

        out.println("<br /><center>");
        out.println("<input type=\"submit\" value=\"Save Changes\" />");
        out.println("</center>");
        out.println("</form></body></html>");

        out.close();
    }

    /**
     * <p>
     * This method receives requests for modification of the
     *   XML-RPC configuration information, all from the
     *   <code>{@link #doGet}</code> method.  This will again
     *   use the utility class to update the configuration
     *   file, letting the <code>{@link XmlRpcConfiguration}</code>
     *   object handle the actual writing to a file.
     * </p>
     */
    public void doPost(HttpServletRequest req,
                       HttpServletResponse res)
        throws ServletException, IOException {

        // Save the hostname
        String hostname =
          req.getParameterValues("hostname")[0];
        if ((hostname != null) && (!hostname.equals(""))) {
          config.setHostname(hostname);
        }
```

Example 12-2. A Java Servlet to Display XML-RPC Configuration Information (continued)

```
        // Save the port number
        int portNumber;
        try {
          portNumber =
            Integer.parseInt(
              req.getParameterValues("port")[0]);
        } catch (Exception e) {
          portNumber = 0;
        }
        if (portNumber > 0) {
          config.setPortNumber(portNumber);
        }

        // Save the SAX driver class
        String driverClass =
          req.getParameterValues("driverClass")[0];
        if ((driverClass != null) && (!driverClass.equals(""))) {
          config.setDriverClass(driverClass);
        }

        // Save the handlers
        String[] handlerIDs =
          req.getParameterValues("handlerID");
        String[] handlerClasses =
          req.getParameterValues("handlerClass");
        Hashtable handlers = new Hashtable();
        for (int i=0; i<handlerIDs.length; i++) {
          handlers.put(handlerIDs[i], handlerClasses[i]);
        }
        config.setHandlers(handlers);

        // Request the changes be written to the configuration store
        config.saveConfiguration(CONFIG_FILENAME);

        // Output a confirmation message
        res.setContentType("text/html");
        PrintWriter out = res.getWriter();

        out.println("Changes saved <br />");
        out.println("<a href=\"" + FORM_ACTION +
                    "\">Return to Configuration Administration" +
                    "</a>");
        out.close();

    }

}
```

We take advantage of knowing that initial requests come to the servlet through the GET method, while submitting our form can be done with the POST method. This allows us to display configuration information on the GET requests (with the `doGet()` method) and to update changes when POST requests are received (with the `doPost()` method). When requests come through GET requests, an HTML screen is rendered showing the current configuration information, as in Figure 12-1.

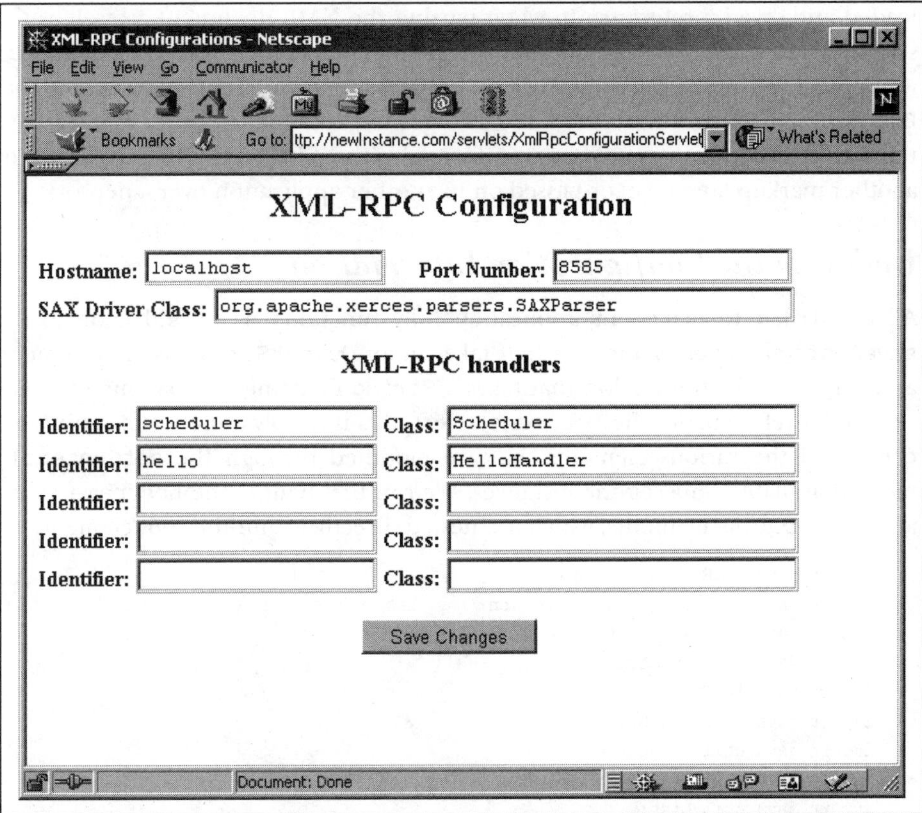

Figure 12-1. HTML user interface for viewing and modifying configuration information

When the button is clicked, the HTML form is submitted, and the same servlet receives the request, this time as a POST request. The `doPost()` method then reads each of the parameters from the submitted form and uses the mutator methods of the `XmlRpcConfiguration` class to update the configuration data. Finally, the `saveConfiguration()` method is called with the same filename as originally used. In the next section, we implement saving the updated data to the JDOM `Document` object and then the XML configuration file. Finally, our Java servlet displays an HTML hyperlink that (through another GET request) takes the user back to the configuration form. The updated data will then be displayed, and the process can be repeated.

Modifying the Data

At this point, we only need to implement code within the `saveConfiguration()` method to update the XML document with the modified member variable values. This can be done completely with the JDOM APIs, using the `Document` object we loaded and saved a reference to when parsing the XML document, as well as the supplied `OutputStream` (which, in our example, is actually a `FileOutputStream` wrapping a file on the filesystem). Once updates are made, we need to update that `Document` object, and then write the changes out to a file. In other applications, the modified `Document` could be transformed with XSLT and output as HTML or another markup language, or passed on to another application over a network.

Updating the Configuration Information

All that is left to make our application fully functional is to add code to the `saveConfiguration()` method that takes in an `OutputStream` as an argument, as this is called by the version that takes a `String` filename as a parameter. Since we saved a reference to the `Document` object, this is simply a matter of setting the content of the various elements that are modified through the `setContent()` method available on `Element` instances. We can first handle the `hostname`, `port`, and `parserClass` elements, which are nested directly within the root element:

```
import java.io.FileInputStream;
import java.io.FileNotFoundException;
import java.io.FileOutputStream;
import java.io.InputStream;
import java.io.IOException;
import java.io.OutputStream;
import java.util.Hashtable;
import java.util.Iterator;
import java.util.List;

import org.jdom.Document;
import org.jdom.Element;
import org.jdom.JDOMException;
import org.jdom.Namespace;
import org.jdom.input.DOMBuilder;
import org.jdom.output.XMLOutputter;
...
    /**
     * <p>
     * This will save the current state out to the specified
     *   <code>OutputStream</code>.
```

```
     * </p>
     *
     * @throws <code>IOException</code> - when errors occur in saving.
     */
    public synchronized void saveConfiguration(OutputStream out)
        throws IOException {

        try {
            Element root = doc.getRootElement();

            //Get the JavaXML namespace
            Namespace ns = Namespace.getNamespace("JavaXML",
                               "http://www.oreilly.com/catalog/javaxml/");

            // Update the hostname
            root.getChild("hostname", ns)
                .setContent(hostname);

            // Update the SAX driver class
            root.getChild("parserClass", ns)
                .setContent(driverClass);

            // Update the port number
            root.getChild("port", ns)
                .setContent(portNumber + "");

            // Easier to remove and re-add handlers
            Element handlersElement =
                root.getChild("xmlrpc-server", ns)
                    .getChild("handlers", ns);
            handlersElement.removeChildren("handler", ns);

            // Output the document, use standard formatter
            XMLOutputter fmt = new XMLOutputter();
            fmt.output(doc, out);

        } catch (JDOMException e) {
            // Log an error
            throw new IOException(e.getMessage());
        }
    }
```

As in our earlier examples, we use the version of `getChild()` that takes in both a `Namespace` and the local name of the element. We also perform a simple `String` concatenation with the port number to convert it to a `String`, the correct parameter type for `setContent()`. We finally write these changes to the supplied `OutputStream` using the `XMLOutputter` helper, ensuring that our changes are reflected in the configuration file on the local filesystem.

Adding in the handler information is a slightly different task. Rather than trying to iterate through current handler elements and replacing them, then adding or removing extra handlers so that the list matches that supplied by the user, it is simpler to remove all handlers and then create the user-requested ones. First we need to add in the Enumeration class to our import statements, which we use for handling the Hashtable of handlers to add:

```
import java.io.FileInputStream;
import java.io.FileNotFoundException;
import java.io.FileOutputStream;
import java.io.InputStream;
import java.io.IOException;
import java.io.OutputStream;
import java.util.Enumeration;
import java.util.Hashtable;
import java.util.Iterator;
import java.util.List;

import org.jdom.Document;
import org.jdom.Element;
import org.jdom.JDOMException;
import.org.jdom.Namespace
import org.jdom.input.DOMBuilder;
import org.jdom.output.XMLOutputter;
```

With this class available, we can remove all of the handler elements within the handlers element. It would be safe in this case to call removeChildren() with no arguments, causing all child elements to be removed, but again, it is clearer to explicitly remove the desired elements; if other types of elements were ever added within the handlers element, our code could run correctly without modification. Once those children are removed, we simply iterate through the user-defined handlers and add each to the JDOM Document object:

```
/**
 * <p>
 * This will save the current state out to the specified
 *   <code>OutputStream</code>.
 * </p>
 *
 * @throws <code>IOException</code> - when errors occur in saving.
 */
public synchronized void saveConfiguration(OutputStream out)
    throws IOException {

    try {
        Element root = doc.getRootElement();

        // Get the JavaXML namespace
```

```
Namespace ns = Namespace.getNamespace("JavaXML",
                "http://www.oreilly.com/catalog/javaxml/");

// Update the hostname
root.getChild("hostname", ns)
    .setContent(hostname);

// Update the SAX driver class
root.getChild("parserClass", ns)
    .setContent(driverClass);

// Update the port number
root.getChild("port", ns)
    .setContent(portNumber + "");

// Easier to remove and re-add handlers
Element handlersElement =
    root.getChild("xmlrpc-server", ns)
        .getChild("handlers", ns);
handlersElement.removeChildren("handler", ns);

// Add new handlers
Enumeration handlerIDs = handlers.keys();
while (handlerIDs.hasMoreElements()) {
    String handlerID =
        (String)handlerIDs.nextElement();

    // Ensure we don't register any blank string
    if (handlerID.trim().equals("")) {
        continue;
    }

    String handlerClass =
        (String)handlers.get(handlerID);

    handlersElement.addChild(
        new Element("handler", ns)
            .addChild(
                new Element("identifier", ns)
                    .setContent(handlerID))
            .addChild(
                new Element("class", ns)
                    .setContent(handlerClass))
            );
}

// Output the document, use standard formatter
XMLOutputter fmt = new XMLOutputter();
fmt.output(doc, out);
```

```
        } catch (JDOMException e) {
            // Log an error
            throw new IOException(e.getMessage());
        }
    }
```

With this change compiled into the `XmlRpcConfiguration` class, we are ready to test out our application. Figure 12-2 shows sample input being given to the `XmlRpcConfigurationServlet`.

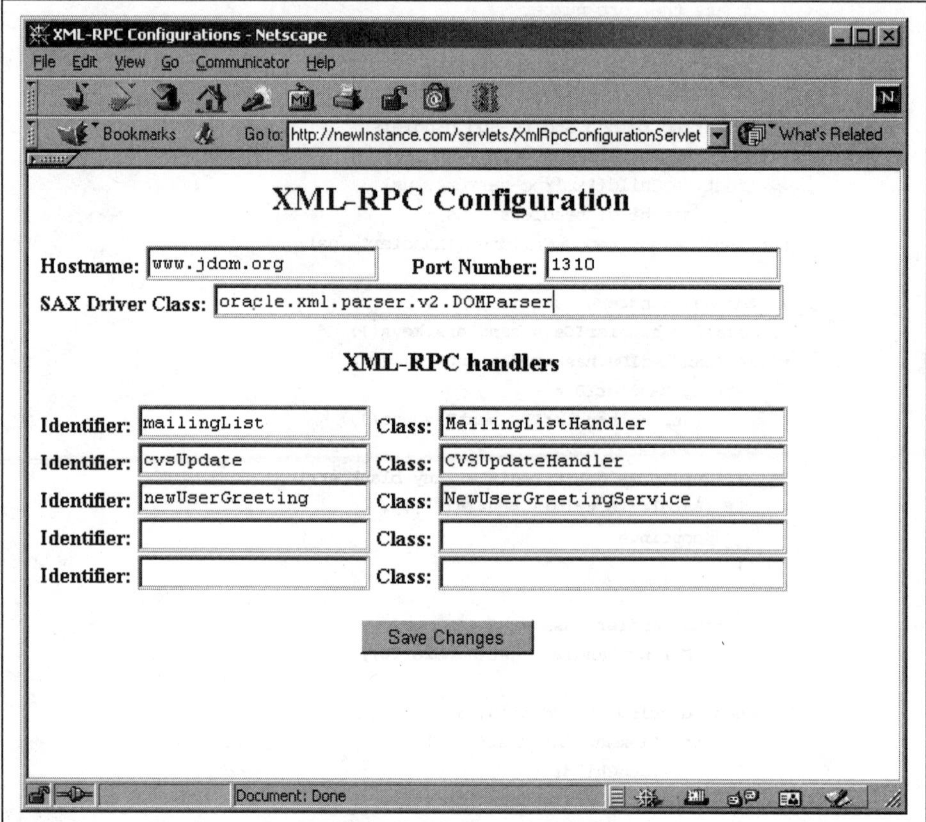

Figure 12-2. Sample input to the XmlRpcConfigurationServlet

With these changes submitted to the program, the updates are saved, and the resultant `xmlrpc.xml` file should look similar to Example 12-3.

Example 12-3. Modified XML-RPC Configuration File

```
<?xml version="1.0" encoding="UTF-8"?>
```

Example 12-3. Modified XML-RPC Configuration File (continued)

```
<JavaXML:xmlrpc-config
  xmlns:JavaXML="http://www.oreilly.com/catalog/javaxml/"
>
  <JavaXML:hostname>www.jdom.org</JavaXML:hostname>
  <JavaXML:port type="unprotected">1310</JavaXML:port>
  <JavaXML:parserClass>
    oracle.xml.parser.v2.DOMParser
  </JavaXML:parserClass>
  <JavaXML:xmlrpc-server>
    <JavaXML:handlers>
      <JavaXML:handler>
        <JavaXML:identifier>newUserGreeting</JavaXML:identifier>
        <JavaXML:class>NewUserGreetingService</JavaXML:class>
      </JavaXML:handler>
      <JavaXML:handler>
        <JavaXML:identifier>mailingList</JavaXML:identifier>
        <JavaXML:class>MailingListHandler</JavaXML:class>
      </JavaXML:handler>
      <JavaXML:handler>
        <JavaXML:identifier>cvsUpdate</JavaXML:identifier>
        <JavaXML:class>CVSUpdateHandler</JavaXML:class>
      </JavaXML:handler>
    </JavaXML:handlers>
  </JavaXML:xmlrpc-server>
</JavaXML:xmlrpc-config>
```

The `com.oreilly.xml.LightweightXmlRpcServer` class could now be started up with these new configuration changes, and assuming you have the Oracle parser and handler classes in your classpath (as well as access to *http://www.jdom.org*, which you probably don't!), you are ready to use the XML-RPC server and clients with the new information you entered.

XML from Scratch

One item we have not yet addressed is the idea of building up an XML document from scratch; this is common when either no original document exists, or the original document is so complex that it is easier to rebuild it than to modify it. Building a new XML document is also valuable when the output of an application should be XML suitable for another application component to use (such as in a business-to-business application, discussed in Chapter 13, *Business-to-Business*). In these cases, we need to create XML documents rather than just modify existing ones. Fortunately, this is not a large change for our JDOM code. Because JDOM relies on SAX and DOM (or any other implementation) only in the building of the initial JDOM `Document` object, all other interaction with the API is uncoupled from that building process; if a new XML document needs to be created, the `Builder` classes are simply not used. The JDOM `Document` is created with a new root element, added to and manipulated, and then output with a `Formatter` class. Seems a little simple, right? Example 12-4 shows the `saveConfiguration()` method we have been looking at modified to create a new `Document` to output as our XML-RPC configuration file.

Example 12-4. Building XML from Scratch

```
import java.io.FileInputStream;
import java.io.FileNotFoundException;
import java.io.FileOutputStream;
import java.io.InputStream;
import java.io.IOException;
import java.io.OutputStream;
import java.util.Enumeration;
import java.util.Hashtable;
import java.util.Iterator;
import java.util.List;

import org.jdom.DocType;
import org.jdom.Document;
import org.jdom.Element;
import org.jdom.JDOMException;
import org.jdom.Namespace;
import org.jdom.input.DOMBuilder;
import org.jdom.output.XMLOutputter;
...
    /**
     * <p>
     * This will save the current state out to the specified
     *   <code>OutputStream</code>.
     * </p>
     *
     * @throws <code>IOException</code> - when errors occur in saving.
     */
    public synchronized void saveConfiguration(OutputStream out)
        throws IOException {

        // Get the JavaXML namespace
        Namespace ns = Namespace.getNamespace("JavaXML",
                      "http://www.oreilly.com/catalog/javaxml/");
        // Create the root element
        Element root = new Element("xmlrpc-config", ns);
        Document doc = new Document(root);
        doc.setDocType(new DocType("JavaXML:xmlrpc-config",
                                   "DTD/XmlRpc.dtd"));

        root.addChild(new Element("hostname", ns)
                .setContent(hostname))
            .addChild(new Element("port", ns)
```

Example 12-4. Building XML from Scratch (continued)

```
                .addAttribute("type", "unprotected")
                .setContent(portNumber + ""))
            .addChild(new Element("parserClass", ns)
                .setContent(driverClass));

        Element handlersElement = new Element("handlers", ns);
        Enumeration e = handlers.keys();
        while (e.hasMoreElements()) {
            String handlerID = (String)e.nextElement();
            String handlerClass = (String)handlers.get(handlerID);

            handlersElement.addChild(new Element("handler", ns)
                .addChild(new Element("identifier", ns)
                    .setContent(handlerID))
                .addChild(new Element("class", ns)
                    .setContent(handlerClass))
                );
        }

        root.addChild(new Element("xmlrpc-server", ns)
                .addChild(handlersElement));

        // Output the document, use standard formatter
        XMLOutputter fmt = new XMLOutputter();
        fmt.output(doc, out);
    }
```

We first add an additional `import` statement for `org.jdom.DocType`. Because we are building the document from scratch, we need to add in the appropriate DTD reference. We also remove the entire block of code from the `try/catch` block it was previously in. The `JDOMException` we were previously catching was only thrown by our `Builder` classes; `XMLOutputter` throws an `IOException` when problems occur, and no other exceptions can occur. We then create our root `Element`, `JavaXML:xmlrpc-config`, and use that to generate a new JDOM `Document`. The textual elements (our hostname, port number, and SAX driver class variables) are then added to that root as additional `Elements`, and their textual content is set (as well as an attribute being added for `JavaXML:port`). Finally, we perform an iteration over the handlers entered by the user, similar to our original version of this method. Each handler is added as a `JavaXML:handler` `Element`, and that `Element` is in turn added to the `JavaXML:handlers` `Element`. This entire grouping is then added under `JavaXML:xmlrpc-server`, which in turn is added to the root of the document. Finally, the `Document` is output to the supplied `OutputStream`, and we are done!

Depending on the API used, the process of creating an XML document, either in memory or on a filesystem, can be as easy as modifying an XML document (as in this example). However, this is not always the case, as some APIs force factory creation of elements and attributes. We look at a comparison of the various Java APIs for creating XML in our final section, and we discuss other important issues concerning mutating XML from within Java.

The Real World

We finish this chapter up as we have finished our others: with a look at issues that affect using the tools in this chapter in a real-world situation. In this chapter, these include threading issues with writing XML data, alternatives to using JDOM for writing XML data, and handling lost references to the `XmlRpcConfiguration` utility class.

Threading, Writing, and Arithmetic

Although we sped through our look at the `saveConfiguration()` method and how it handled writing out XML, you may have noticed something key in the method declaration:

```
/**
 * <p>
 * This will save the current state out to the specified
 *   <code>OutputStream</code>.
 * </p>
 *
 * @throws <code>IOException</code> - when errors occur in saving.
 */
public synchronized void saveConfiguration(OutputStream out)
    throws IOException {

    // Method implementation
}
```

We use the `synchronized` keyword here to ensure that the lock for our `XmlRpcConfiguration` object is obtained before the configuration data is written. This is particularly important when using XML, as APIs like JDOM can be built on implementations that periodically reload the underlying data; in other words, changes by other programs to the XML data could cause serious errors or corrupted data if this method writes to the data as well.

Additionally, you should be very careful when multiple applications write to the same XML data source. Entire database systems have been written to handle pessimistic and optimistic locking, sharing data, and the other complex issues that surround concurrent access to data. While XML addressed portable data, it certainly does not address issues such as this. A good rule of thumb is to provide one single point of entry for writing to any single XML data source. Multiple entry points for mutability can cause tricky bugs and serious headaches.

JDOM, SAX, or DOM, Revisited

In Chapter 11, we discussed the alternatives to using JDOM for reading XML data. We now examine alternatives for writing and modifying XML. This provides you a complete look at the Java APIs, and should allow you to use any API you choose for your various projects.

For comparison, here is the `saveConfiguration()` method from the last chapter, which uses JDOM:

```
/**
 * <p>
 * This will save the current state out to the specified
 *   <code>OutputStream</code>.
 * </p>
 *
 * @throws <code>IOException</code> - when errors occur in saving.
 */
public synchronized void saveConfiguration(OutputStream out)
    throws IOException {

    // Get the JavaXML namespace
    Namespace ns = Namespace.getNamespace("JavaXML",
                   "http://www.oreilly.com/catalog/javaxml/");

    // Create the root element
    Element root = new Element("xmlrpc-config", ns);
    Document doc = new Document(root);
    doc.setDocType(new DocType("JavaXML:xmlrpc-config",
                               "DTD/XmlRpc.dtd"));

    root.addChild(new Element("hostname", ns)
            .setContent(hostname))
        .addChild(new Element("port", ns)
            .addAttribute("type", "unprotected")
            .setContent(portNumber + ""))
        .addChild(new Element("parserClass", ns)
            .setContent(driverClass));

    Element handlersElement = new Element("handlers", ns);
    Enumeration e = handlers.keys();
    while (e.hasMoreElements()) {
        String handlerID = (String)e.nextElement();
        String handlerClass = (String)handlers.get(handlerID);
```

```
            handlersElement.addChild(new Element("handler", ns)
                .addChild(new Element("identifier", ns)
                    .setContent(handlerID))
                .addChild(new Element("class", ns)
                    .setContent(handlerClass))
                );
        }

        root.addChild(new Element("xmlrpc-server", ns)
                .addChild(handlersElement));

        // Output the document, use standard formatter
        XMLOutputter fmt = new XMLOutputter();
        fmt.output(doc, out);
    }
```

Now we look at the SAX and DOM alternatives to this approach.

SAX

The discussion of SAX is short: simply put, you cannot modify XML with SAX. Because SAX is an event-based approach to XML data, it is only useful in parsing an XML document. The callbacks it defines are specifically designed for that purpose, and as SAX has no concept of an overall picture of an XML document, it also has no concept of changing that overall picture. It is this very fact that has caused much of the popularity of DOM; until recently, DOM has been the only means of creating XML from Java without having to write out XML directly using streams.

DOM

The Document Object Model does provide a means of creating and modifying XML from Java. However, it takes a more rigid view of the tree structure of an XML document. First, it considers everything in the DOM tree a `Node` (remember our discussions in Chapter 7, *Traversing XML*)? Because these `Node`s are all part of a tree, it is necessary to create a `Node` with an association to a particular DOM tree, represented by a DOM `Document` object. To ensure this model is adhered to, there is no facility for instantiating a DOM `Node` directly; instead, it is the `Document` interface within DOM that defines the `createElement()`, `createAttribute()`, and other `Node` creation operations. Another point to remember is that this rigid tree model considers everything in the tree a `Node`, including textual data. This means that there is no concept of an element's content in DOM; instead, a DOM `Element` has child `Node`s, some of which may be `Text` `Node`s. This means that setting the value of an `Element` requires using the `createTextNode()` method to create a `Text` `Node`, and then adding that new `Node` to the desired parent `Element`. Of course, the `createTextNode()` method itself is invoked on the overall DOM Document object, to ensure the correct association with the DOM tree.

NOTE This may feel a bit confusing to you: the creation of an XML element with text involves a DOM `Element` Node, a DOM `Text` Node, and a DOM `Document` object all working in concert. This has caused some newer XML developers to become frustrated, as they attempt to change an `Element`'s textual content with `setNodeValue()`, and get very different results than expected. Be careful when using DOM to keep thinking in a very strict tree model, and you will be able to avoid these types of problems.

With this in mind, let's look at building up an XML document from the data supplied by a user in the `XmlRpcConfigurationServlet` application.

You might be expecting us to repeat the process of finding each XML element with data and then changing the value of the textual nodes, as in our first `saveConfiguration()` method for JDOM. Although this is certainly possible (as DOM provides a `setValue()` method for textual `Nodes`), this is neither the easiest nor the quickest way to handle this task. Instead, we use the various `createXXX()` methods that are defined in the DOM `Document` interface. A method for each type of DOM `Node` is provided, such as `createElement()`, `createTextNode()`, and `createAttribute()`. As each of these is created, it is assigned to the `Document` object used to create it. This maintains an ownership between each created `Node` and the DOM tree they belong to.

In this way, all the needed elements and data can be created within our Java code. However, this is only half of the task; each element and its data then need to be inserted into the DOM tree and assembled into the correct hierarchy. The simplest way to insert a `Node` into the tree is to use the `appendChild()` method on the parent node.

WARNING Make sure you understand the difference between `createXXX()` and `appendNode()`. While `createXXX()` results in a `Node` that is associated with a DOM `Document` object, it does *not* insert that `Node` into the `Document`; the `appendNode()` method must still be invoked upon the desired parent of the new `Node`. Failure to distinguish between these two methods can result in a huge number of `Nodes` associated with a DOM `Document` object, but an empty DOM tree.

In this way, we can build up the complete document starting with the root element. Finally, we can replace the old root element with the new one, completing the update of our tree.

In addition to our not needing to perform complicated searching and retrieval of elements and data, building a tree this way is often much quicker. Searches through a DOM tree, particularly when the DOM tree becomes large, can take quite a lot of processing time; creating XML from the root element up is a much faster alternative to this extensive searching. The code to perform this task is included here:

```
/**
 * <p>
 * This will save the current state out to the specified
 *   <code>OutputStream</code>, using DOM
 * </p>
 *
 * @throws <code>IOException</code> - when errors occur in saving.
 */
public synchronized void saveConfiguration(OutputStream out)
    throws IOException {

    String NAMESPACE_URI = "http://www.oreilly.com/catalog/javaxml/";

    // We assume the DOM Document object was loaded in
    //   parseConfiguation() and is saved in a member variable called
    //   <code>doc</code>.
    Element oldRoot = doc.getDocumentElement();
    Element newRoot =
        doc.createElementNS(NAMESPACE_URI, "JavaXML:xmlrpc-config");

    // Handle hostname
    Element hostnameNode =
        doc.createElementNS(NAMESPACE_URI, "JavaXML:hostname");
    hostnameNode.appendChild(
        doc.createTextNode(hostname));
    newRoot.appendChild(hostnameNode);

    // Handle port number
    Element portNumberNode =
        doc.createElementNS(NAMESPACE_URI, "JavaXML:port");
    portNumberNode.appendChild(
        doc.createTextNode(portNumber + ""));
    portNumberNode.setValue("type", "unprotected");
    newRoot.appendChild(portNumberNode);

    // Handle SAX Driver class
    Element saxDriverNode =
        doc.createElementNS(NAMESPACE_URI, "JavaXML:parserClass");
    saxDriverNode.appendChild(
        doc.createTextNode(driverClass));
    newRoot.appendChild(saxDriverNode);

    Element serverNode =
        doc.createElementNS(NAMESPACE_URI, "JavaXML:xmlrpc-server");
```

```
        Element handlersNode =
            doc.createElementNS(NAMESPACE_URI, "JavaXML:handlers");

        // Handle handlers
        Enumeration handlerIDs = handlers.keys();
        while (handlerIDs.hasMoreElements()) {
          String handlerID = (String)handlerIDs.nextElement();
          String handlerClass = (String)handlers.get(handlerID);

          Element handlerIDNode =
              doc.createElementNS(NAMESPACE_URI, "JavaXML:identifier");
          handlerIDNode.appendChild(
              doc.createTextNode(handlerID));

          Element handlerClassNode =
              doc.createElementNS(NAMESPACE_URI, "JavaXML:class");
          handlerClassNode.appendChild(
              doc.createTextNode(handlerClass));

          Element handlerNode =
              doc.createElementNS(NAMESPACE_URI, "JavaXML:handler");
          handlerNode.appendChild(handlerIDNode);
          handlerNode.appendChild(handlerClassNode);

          handlersNode.appendChild(handlerNode);
        }

        serverNode.appendChild(handlersNode);
        newRoot.appendChild(serverNode);

        doc.replaceChild(newRoot, oldRoot);

        // Serialize the DOM tree
    }
```

We use the DOM Level 2 methods to create our XML document with namespace awareness. The `createElementNS()` method takes in the namespace URI and then the *full* name of the new element. The full name does include the namespace prefix; this allows the method to ensure that a namespace prefix and namespace URI are either both included, or both excluded, helping to ensure properly formed XML.

Serialization of a DOM tree is another task, like obtaining the DOM `Document` object, that is not outlined in the DOM specification. To achieve serialization, you need to see if your vendor provides a helper class that will handle that functionality for you. Once you have located your parser's serializer, you typically need only to import that class and pass it an `OutputStream` or `PrintWriter` instance. Using Apache Xerces, the class needed is the `org.apache.xml.serialize.`

XMLSerializer. We can use that class to write to the OutputStream that our saveConfiguration() method has supplied to it:

```
/**
 * <p>
 * This will save the current state out to the specified
 *   <code>OutputStream</code>, using DOM
 * </p>
 *
 * @throws <code>IOException</code> - when errors occur in saving.
 */
public synchronized void saveConfiguration(OutputStream out)
    throws IOException {

    // Modify Document object

    doc.replaceChild(newRoot, oldRoot);

    // Serialize the DOM tree
    org.apache.xml.serialize.XMLSerializer out =
        new org.apache.xml.serialize.XMLSerializer(out, null);
    out.serialize(doc);
}
```

The Apache XMLSerializer class has several different constructors; the one used here takes in an OutputStream and the format to use for output. We specify null to allow the default format to be used. The serialize() method takes as input the Document, Element, or DocumentFragment to serialize. We pass in the modified DOM tree Document, and the serialization occurs. At this point, we have emulated the functionality we created with JDOM to modify and output an XML document with user-supplied input.

Where Did That XmlRpcConfiguration Go?

When using a servlet or other web-based construct for providing a user interface, several issues must be handled that are not problems with thick or static clients. One of these is garbage collection and user lag. *User lag* refers to a user loading a servlet or piece of Java code on the Internet, and then taking a coffee break, attending three meetings, and eating a candy bar. What can happen is that object references in the servlet that was accessed may be garbage collected between the time of the original request and the user's (much later) action. When one servlet submits to another, this is not a problem; however, in our example, the XmlRpcConfigurationServlet submitted data to itself. The possible bug is that the config member variable, an instance of com.oreilly.xml.XmlRpcConfiguration, is only created in the doGet() method, but is then reused in the doPost() method:

```
public void doGet(HttpServletRequest req,
                  HttpServletResponse res)
    throws ServletException, IOException {

    res.setContentType("text/html");
    PrintWriter out = res.getWriter();

    // Load the configuration information with our utility class
    config = new XmlRpcConfiguration(CONFIG_FILENAME);

    // Rest of method
}

public void doPost(HttpServletRequest req,
                   HttpServletResponse res)
    throws ServletException, IOException {

    // Save the hostname
    String hostname =
      req.getParameterValues("hostname")[0];
    if ((hostname != null) && (!hostname.equals(""))) {
      config.setHostname(hostname);
    }

    // Rest of method
}
```

If sufficient time has passed between the initial GET request and the subsequent POST request, a `NullPointerException` can result when `config` is accessed in the `doPost()` method. This can also occur if the servlet code is changed and reloaded in the middle of a request, something the Jakarta Tomcat and other popular servlet engines support.

To avoid this problem, it makes sense to ensure that the `config` member variable is valid in both the `doGet()` and `doPost()` methods; however, there is a lot of overhead with instantiating the `XmlRpcConfiguration` class, as it must parse the supplied filename again. Instead of recreating the variable each time, we can take advantage of knowing the variables that are garbage-collected have their values set back to `null`.* Thus, we make a comparison to `null`, and only reinstantiate `config` when needed:

```
public void doPost(HttpServletRequest req,
                   HttpServletResponse res)
```

* This is a bit of an overstatement. However, in the case of a non-local variable, it will hold true, particularly when dealing with servlets. For more information on garbage collection and values of non-initialized or garbage-collected variables, you should consult *Java in a Nutshell*, by David Flanagan (O'Reilly & Associates).

```
        throws ServletException, IOException {

        // Update the configuration information
        if (config == null) {
            config = new XmlRpcConfiguration(CONFIG_FILENAME);
        }

        // Save the hostname
        String hostname =
          req.getParameterValues("hostname")[0];
        if ((hostname != null) && (!hostname.equals(""))) {
          config.setHostname(hostname);
        }

        // Rest of method
    }
```

This will ensure that if user lag occurs, it does not affect your program's operation.

What's Next?

By now we have managed to touch on many of the major subjects concerning using XML within Java code. Besides being able to create, parse, style, transform, constrain, and validate XML, we have looked at using XML within a publishing framework, using XML for remote procedure calls, storing configuration information within XML documents, and now creating XML "on the fly" from Java code. To round out this list of XML topics in Chapter 13, we look at using XML for business-to-business applications. This builds on what we have already seen with regard to XML as a solid solution for distributed applications as well as a standards-based data format. We apply this to some hypothetical companies and walk through the complete process of enabling inter- and intra-business communication for the companies.

In this chapter:
- *The Foobar Public Library*
- *mytechbooks.com*
- *Push Versus Pull*
- *The Real World*
- *What's Next?*

13

Business-to-Business

At this point, we've covered quite a bit of ground. We've examined the SAX, DOM, and JDOM APIs, and you should now feel familiar with web publishing frameworks and advanced transformations, XML-RPC, using XML for configuration information and as a data source, and creating XML from within your Java code. However, the one hot topic we have not yet spent time on is "business-to-business" applications. As companies have moved into the Internet era, communication has become the number one commodity for commerce. In fact, many companies thrive on their communication lines more than they do on their product offerings; aggressive online campaigns and e-business applications can overcome significant competition from other vendors. Spearheading this surge of business-to-business application development is XML. Because of the standard XML provides for data representation, companies have been able to communicate for the first time over disparate applications, systems, and programming languages.

In this chapter, we look at using XML to provide this sort of communication across application and company lines, using some companies invented for our purposes. Instead of focusing on XML for communication between application components or as a data source, we look at using XML to communicate between applications. To begin with, we examine the Foobar Public Library, a library that is allowing their suppliers to enter online new books being shipped to the library. These books are then added to the library's data store for later use. Unfortunately, the library is having a hard time finding good Java developers, so it has implemented a Perl-based CGI solution. New books are entered online and then stored by a Perl script.

We also look at another company, mytechbooks.com. Mytechbooks.com sells technical and computing books (such as this one) online through various partnerships with large bookstores. They have recently signed an agreement with the Foobar Public Library to obtain books from the library. They will pay for the shipping and inventory costs of the books, while the library agrees to order extra books at their discounted costs; these extra books are then sold by mytechbooks.com. Mytechbooks.com needs to be able to access the new books entered into the Foobar Public Library by suppliers to know when new offerings are available, and then advertise those new offerings. However, they have no idea how to interface with the Foobar Public Library's Perl-based system. Additionally, there are no protected network connections between the two organizations, so normal HTTP must be used for communication.

Finally, we look at customers of mytechbooks.com. The book store targets people who are active online, so wants to advertise on sites like Netscape Netcenter; they also want to allow people to easily obtain information from their site when new offerings are available. However, as in the situation with the Foobar Public Library, mytechbooks.com has no idea how to achieve this goal. In speaking with Netscape's Netcenter group, they have been told that Rich Site Summary (RSS) is a great solution for this sort of advertising, but are unsure of what RSS even is!

We tackle this common scenario by starting with the Foobar Public Library and examining their Perl system. Then, moving out to mytechbooks.com and then the customers of the bookstore, we enable this business-to-business (to-customer) application by using XML as a communication tool between each layer.

The Foobar Public Library

To start our creation of a business-to-business system, we look at the system currently in place at the Foobar Public Library. Before diving into their code, though, we need to examine the library's requirements so that we do not create a system they cannot support.

Evaluating the Requirements

All too often, good solutions to a problem are not appropriate solutions for the company with the problem. The Foobar Library is a perfect example of this: certainly a Java servlet that could communicate with servlets built by mytechbooks.com could quickly solve the two organizations' problems. However, this ignores the library's requirements. Before creating a solution, they have detailed what these requirements are:

- The solution must be Perl-based; no Java engineers are on staff.
- The solution must not involve new software or library installations.
- The solution must not impact the existing order-entry system (no interface changes).

While these are not extremely stringent requirements, they force us to rethink our problem. We must avoid using Java as a solution. Of course, as this is a book on XML, you should be thinking that storing the data about new books in an XML format could allow us to then supply that XML to clients through an HTTP request, thus enabling those clients to use the data in any way they wish. In fact, this is a much better solution than servlet-to-servlet communication, as the XML can be used by any company or client in their applications, rather than tying the library (and their books) to a specific company. This then defines our goal for updating the Foobar Public Library's system: save the entered information as XML data, and then provide HTTP access to that XML data for clients and customers.

Entering Books

First, we need to examine the existing HTML interface for suppliers entering new books into the system. Example 13-1 shows the static HTML used to generate this form.

Example 13-1. Static HTML for Foobar Public Library User Interface

```
<html>

<head>
  <title>Foobar Public Library: Add Books</title>
  <style>
<!--
body          { font-family: Arial }
h1            { color: #000080 }
-->
  </style>
</head>

<body link="#FFFF00" vlink="#FFFF00" alink="#FFFF00">
 <table border="0" width="100%" cellpadding="0" cellspacing="0">
  <tr>
   <td width="15%" bgcolor="#000080" valign="top" align="center">
    <b><i>
     <font color="#FFFFFF" size="4">Options</font>
    </i></b>
   <p><b>
     <font color="#FFFFFF">
      <a href="/javaxml/foobar">Main Menu</a>
     </font>
   </p></b>
   <p><b>
    <font color="#FFFFFF">
     <a href="/javaxml/foobar/catalog.html">Catalog</a>
    </font>
```

Example 13-1. Static HTML for Foobar Public Library User Interface (continued)

```
  </b></p>
  <p><b>
   <i><font color="#FFFF00">Add Books</font></i>
  </b></p>
  <p><b>
   <font color="#FFFFFF">
    <a href="/javaxml/foobar/logout.html">Log Out</a>
   </font>
  </p></td>
  <td width="*" valign="top" align="center">
   <h1 align="center">The Foobar Public Library</h1>
   <h3 align="center"><i>- Add Books -</i></h3>

<!-- This will need to point at your CGI directory and script, which
     we look at next -->
   <form method="POST" action="/cgi/addBook.pl">

    <table border="0" cellpadding="5" width="100%">
     <tr>
      <td width="100%" valign="top" align="center" colspan="2">
       Title 
       <input type="text" name="title" size="20">
       <hr width="85%" />
      </td>
     </tr>
     <tr>
      <td width="50%" valign="top" align="right">Author 
       <input type="text" name="author" size="20">
      </td>
      <td width="50%" valign="top" align="left">Subject 
       <select size="1" name="subject">
        <option>Fiction</option>
        <option>Biography</option>
        <option>Science</option>
        <option>Industry</option>
        <option>Computers</option>
       </select></td>
      </tr>
      <tr>
       <td width="50%" valign="top" align="right">Publisher 
        <input type="text" name="publisher" size="20">
       </td>
       <td width="50%" valign="top" align="left">ISBN 
        <input type="text" name="isbn" size="20">
       </td>
      </tr>
      <tr>
       <td width="50%" valign="top" align="right">Price 
```

Example 13-1. Static HTML for Foobar Public Library User Interface (continued)

```
          <input type="text" name="price" size="20">
         </td>
         <td width="50%" valign="top" align="left">Pages 
          <input type="text" name="numPages" size="20">
         </td>
        </tr>
        <tr>
         <td width="100%" valign="top" align="center" colspan="2">
          Description 
          <textarea rows="2" name="description" cols="20"></textarea>
         </td>
        </tr>
       </table>
       <p>
        <input type="submit" value="Add this Book" name="addBook">
        <input type="reset" value="Reset Form" name="reset">
        <input type="button" value="Cancel" name="cancel">
       </p>
     </form>
    </td>
   </tr>
  </table>
</body>
</html>
```

This file, saved as *addBooks.html*, provides the portion of the library application allowing suppliers to add new books they are sending to the library.

NOTE In Example 13-1 and throughout the rest of the chapter, complete code and HTML listings will be given so that you can create the sample applications, and walk through the process of enabling XML communication across the applications. If you instead wish to see a working copy of the examples, they are available online at *http://www.newInstance.com*, and can be downloaded from there and from *http://www.oreilly.com/catalog/javaxml/*. Additionally, the code samples in this chapter assume you are using the filenames supplied in the text; you will need to change the code and examples if you use your own filenames. Code that may need to be changed to reference different filenames or scripts is emphasized in the listings to help you walk through the examples.

The HTML in Example 13-1, when accessed through a web server, results in the output shown in Figure 13-1. Although we do not look at the other menu options, the supplier can also view the library's catalog, go to the application's main menu, and log out of the application by using the menu on the left of the screen.

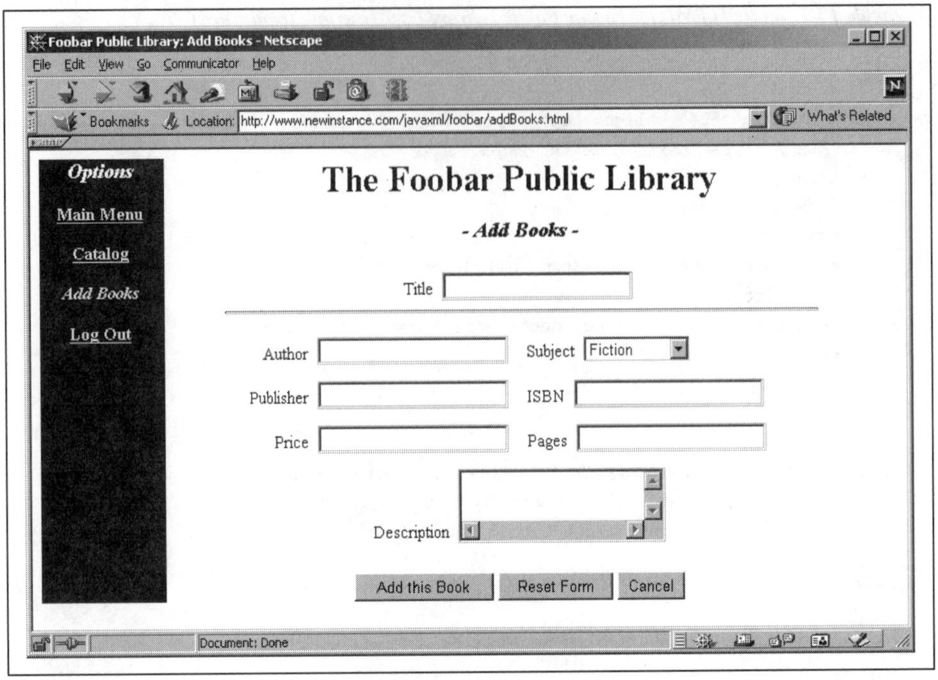

Figure 13-1. HTML user interface for Foobar Public Library

This form allows the supplier to enter the details about each book it is sending to the library. The supplier enters the book's essentials (title, author, publisher, pages, and a description), as well as a subject to categorize the book and sales details, which include the price and ISBN number.

Once this information has been entered, it is submitted to a Perl CGI script:

```
<form method="POST" action="/cgi/addBook.pl">
```

This script, then, must produce XML output. The easiest solution would be to download a Perl library that handled XML parsing, such as Xerces-Perl; however, remember that one requirement of the library was that no libraries or software could be added. While this may seem silly and frustrating, keep in mind that many companies have very strict lock-downs on their production systems. In this case, the Foobar Public Library is just beginning to introduce applications on the Internet, and they do not have resources to support additional software.

Luckily, we only have to output XML; this is done fairly easily by generating a file with information on the entered books by brute force. Because we need to keep any existing books, each new entry is appended to an existing file, instead of creating as a new file. As we are Java coders, writing Perl is almost trivial for us, and the complete Perl program to read the request parameters and append the information to an existing file is shown in its entirety in Example 13-2.

Example 13-2. Perl CGI Script to Generate XML Entries from Entered Books

```
#!/usr/local/bin/perl

# This should be the directory you wish to write files to
$baseDir = "/home/bmclaugh/javaxml/foobar/books/";

# This should be the filename to use
$filename = "books.txt";

$bookFile = $baseDir . $filename;

# Get the user's input
use CGI;
$query = new CGI;

$title = $query->param('title');
$author = $query->param('author');
$subject = $query->param('subject');
$publisher = $query->param('publisher');
$isbn = $query->param('isbn');
$price = $query->param('price');
$numPages = $query->param('numPages');
$description = $query->param('description');

# Save the book to a file in XML
if (open(FILE, ">>" . $bookFile)) {
  print FILE "<book subject=\"" . $subject . "\">\n";
  print FILE " <title><![CDATA[" . $title . "]]></title>\n";
  print FILE " <author><![CDATA[" . $author . "]]></author>\n";
  print FILE " <publisher><![CDATA[" . $publisher . "]]></publisher>\n";
  print FILE " <numPages>" . $numPages . "</numPages>\n";
  print FILE " <saleDetails>\n";
  print FILE "  <isbn>" . $isbn . "</isbn>\n";
  print FILE "  <price>" . $price . "</price>\n";
  print FILE " </saleDetails>\n";
  print FILE " <description>";
  print FILE "<![CDATA[" . $description . "]]>";
  print FILE "</description>\n";
  print FILE "</book>\n\n";

  # Give the user a confirmation
  print <<"EOF";
Content-type: text/html

  <html>
   <head>
    <title>Foobar Public Library: Confirmation</title>
   </head>
   <body>
```

Example 13-2. Perl CGI Script to Generate XML Entries from Entered Books (continued)

```
    <h1 align="center">Book Added</h1>
    <p align="center">
     Thank you.  The book you submitted has been added to the Library.
    </p>
   </body>
  </html>
EOF

} else {
  print <<"EOF";
Content-type: text/html

  <html>
   <head>
    <title>Foobar Public Library: Error</title>
   </head>
   <body>
    <h1 align="center">Error in Adding Book</h1>
    <p align="center">
     We're sorry.  The book you submitted has <i>not</i> been added to
     the Library.
    </p>
   </body>
  </html>
EOF
}
close (FILE);
```

This program, saved as *addBook.pl*, is invoked by a form submittal when the supplier enters a new book. The script defines the file to write to, and then assigns the request parameter values to local variables:

```
$title = $query->param('title');
$author = $query->param('author');
$subject = $query->param('subject');
$publisher = $query->param('publisher');
$isbn = $query->param('isbn');
$price = $query->param('price');
$numPages = $query->param('numPages');
$description = $query->param('description');
```

Once these values are easily accessible, the script opens the file defined earlier in append mode (signified by >> preceding the filename) and writes raw XML-formatted information about the entered book to the end of the file:

```
print FILE "<book subject=\"" . $subject . "\">\n";
print FILE " <title><![CDATA[" . $title . "]]></title>\n";
print FILE " <author><![CDATA[" . $author . "]]></author>\n";
print FILE " <publisher><![CDATA[" . $publisher . "]]></publisher>\n";
```

```
print FILE " <numPages>" . $numPages . "</numPages>\n";
print FILE " <saleDetails>\n";
print FILE "  <isbn>" . $isbn . "</isbn>\n";
print FILE "  <price>" . $price . "</price>\n";
print FILE " </saleDetails>\n";
print FILE " <description>";
print FILE "<![CDATA[" . $description . "]]>";
print FILE "</description>\n";
print FILE "</book>\n\n";
```

The subject is used as an attribute on the enclosing element, book, and the rest of the information is entered in as elements. Because a book's title, author, description, and publisher may include quotation marks, apostrophes, ampersands, and other characters that would have to be escaped, we enclose that data within a CDATA section so as not to have to worry about escaping the data.

Additionally, you should notice that no XML declaration or root element is created, as multiple books will exist in a single file. Because it is a bit difficult to check if the file exists, write the declaration and root element if the file is new, and then write out the ending element (which has to be overwritten at each new entry), we leave the file as an XML document fragment. For example, here is a sample of what the file might look like after two books have been entered:

```
<book subject="Computers">
 <title><![CDATA[Java Servlet Programming]]></title>
 <author><![CDATA[Jason Hunter]]></author>
 <publisher><![CDATA[O'Reilly & Associates]]></publisher>
 <numPages>528</numPages>
 <saleDetails>
  <isbn>156592391X</isbn>
  <price>36.95</price>
 </saleDetails>
 <description><![CDATA[This book is a superb introduction to Java
  servlets and their various communications mechanisms.]]></description>
</book>

<book subject="Fiction">
 <title><![CDATA[Second Foundation]]></title>
 <author><![CDATA[Isaac Asimov]]></author>
 <publisher><![CDATA[Bantam Books]]></publisher>
 <numPages>279</numPages>
 <saleDetails>
  <isbn>0553293362</isbn>
  <price>5.59</price>
 </saleDetails>
 <description><![CDATA[fter the First Foundation was taken over by the
  Mule, only the Second Foundation stood between order and the utter
  destruction the Mule would bring.]]></description>
</book>
```

Although not a complete XML document, this fragment is well-formed and could be inserted into an XML document with the header and root element already set. In fact, when we look at providing a listing of books in the next section, that is precisely how we handle output of the fragment.

The rest of the script outputs HTML indicating whether the book was successfully added or if errors occurred. Once a book has been added to the XML storage, the supplier would receive the simple confirmation message shown in Figure 13-2.

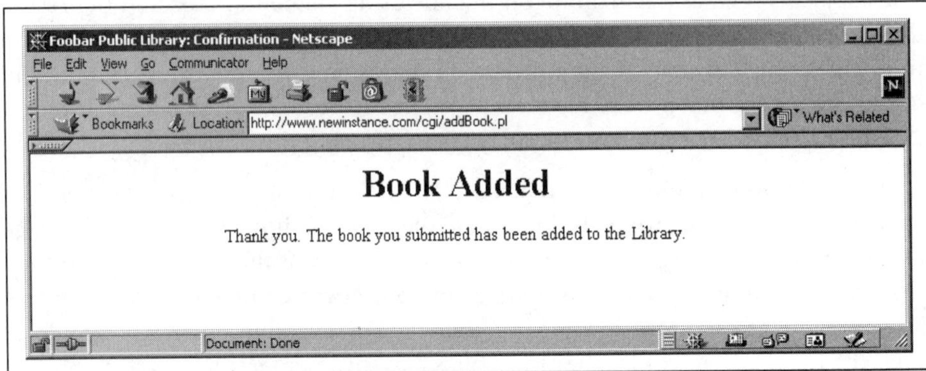

Figure 13-2. Confirmation message when a book is added

Now that we have an XML document fragment with information about new books, we need to take that file and provide it to requestors.

Providing a Listing of Available Books

We again can use Perl as a mechanism to provide clients and customers with an XML listing of new books. We make the assumption that some other portion of the library's application periodically reads the XML data and updates the library's catalog; at this point, that application component would be responsible for removing the entries within the file (or the file itself) so that the books within it are no longer regarded as new entries. With this assumption, all our second Perl script has to do is read the XML fragment and add all the data within it to an XML document that is output to the screen. As we already mentioned, the script also needs to add an XML declaration and a root element to surround the content within the new books file. This new script, shown in Example 13-3, reads the file created by the *addBook.pl* script and outputs the content within an XML document when it is requested over HTTP.

Example 13-3. Perl CGI Script to Output XML Document with New Book Listings

```
#!/usr/local/bin/perl

# This should be the directory you wish to write files to
```

Example 13-3. Perl CGI Script to Output XML Document with New Book Listings (continued)

```
$baseDir = "/home/bmclaugh/javaxml/foobar/books/";

# This should be the filename to use
$filename = "books.txt";

$bookFile = $baseDir . $filename;

# First open the file
open(FILE, $bookFile) || die "Could not open $bookFile.\n";

# Let browser know what is coming
print "Content-type: text/plain\n\n";

# Print out XML header and root element
print "<?xml version=\"1.0\"?>\n";
print "<books>\n";

# Print out books
while (<FILE>) {
  print "$_";
}


# Close root element
print "</books>\n";

close(FILE);
```

This script, saved as *supplyBooks.pl*, will accept a request, read the file created by *addBook.pl*, and output XML upon an HTTP request. The result of requesting this script in a web browser (with several books added) is shown in Figure 13-3.

As you can see, we have easily turned the library's simple Perl-based application into a component capable of supplying useful information to its clients, including the mytechbooks.com technical bookstore. Additionally, we were able to accomplish this without installing new software, changing the architecture of their system or application, or even writing a line of Java!

mytechbooks.com

With the Foobar Public Library allowing access to an XML listing of their new books, mytechbooks.com is moving closer to their goal of providing up-to-date content to their customers. In addition, mytechbooks.com already has an established standard for using Java for application development. This makes the process of accessing and using the XML from the library even easier, as Java has the excellent support for XML we have been looking at throughout this book. We

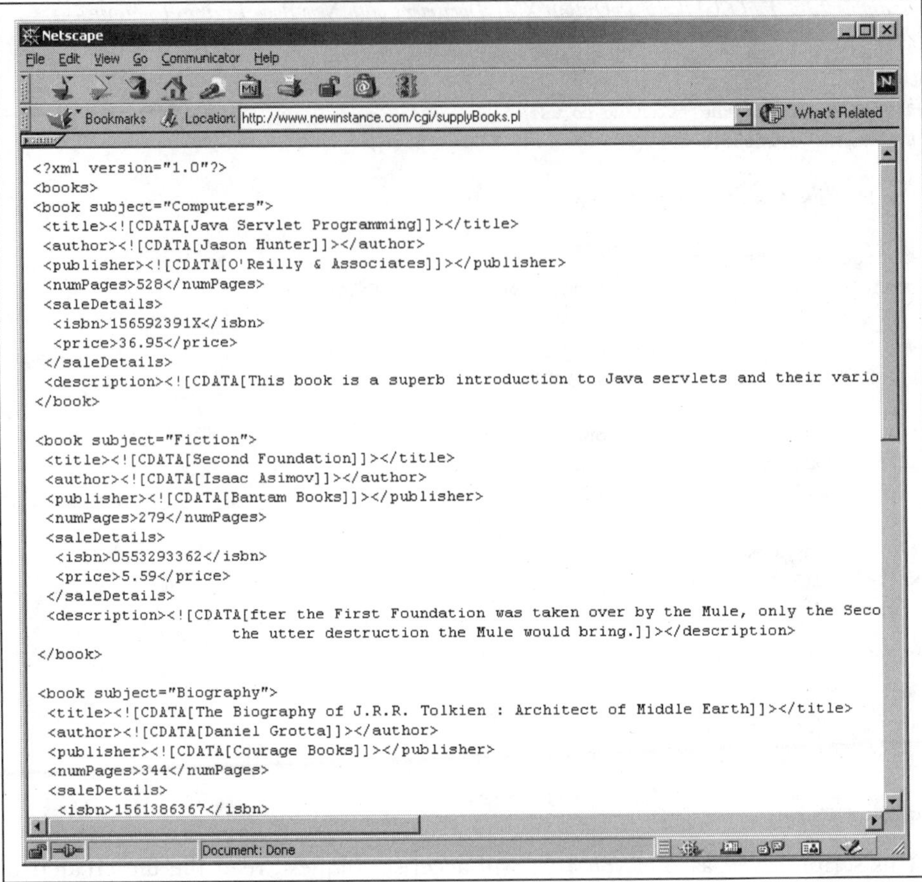

Figure 13-3. XML output from supplyBooks.pl

need to allow mytechbooks.com to provide an online listing of new books first, and then look at how to get this information out to their customers automatically.

Filtering the XML Data

Mytechbooks.com wants to ensure that only technical books are shown on their web site. If you remember, the Foobar Public Library allowed books on several different subjects to be entered into their system; mytechbooks.com wants only the books about computer-related subjects. Fortunately, the library captured this information in the `subject` attribute of the `book` element for each book in their XML data. Our first task, then, is to filter out all books whose subject is not "Computers." Once the technical books have been obtained, they should be formatted into an HTML page that can be shown to customers visiting mytechbooks.com.

For this company and application, there is no static HTML, since the page showing new listings must be generated each time it is accessed. Of course, we use a servlet here for handling these responses. Although Apache Cocoon would be an excellent choice for converting the XML data from the library into an HTML response, mytechbooks.com is under a tremendous time pressure to make these book listings available, and does not want to introduce such a large change into their system immediately; instead, they would prefer to use XML parsers and processors and then add Cocoon in as a second-phase addition. This means that we have to handle conversion from XML to HTML as well as the filtering of the data and the addition of other presentation-specific items, such as a company logo and menu bar.

However, taking all the information at your disposal about XML and XSL, you remember that even without Cocoon we can use XSL to transform an XML document into HTML. Applying a transformation would also allow us to filter out the books that do not have the subject criteria that mytechbooks.com desires. With this in mind, we can create an XSL stylesheet that can be applied to the XML response from the Foobar Public Library. Example 13-4 shows the beginning of this stylesheet, which handles generation of the HTML specific to the mytechbooks.com web site.

Example 13-4. XSL Stylesheet for Foobar Public Library Book Listings

```
<?xml version="1.0"?>

<xsl:stylesheet xmlns:xsl="http://www.w3.org/1999/XSL/Transform"
                version="1.0"
>

  <xsl:template match="books">
   <html>
    <head>
     <title>mytechbooks.com - Your Computer Bookstore</title>
    </head>
    <body background="/javaxml/techbooks/images/background.gif"
          link="#FFFFFF" vlink="#FFFFFF" alink="#FFFFFF">
     <h1 align="center">
      <font face="Arial" color="#00659C">
       &lt;mytechbooks.com&gt;
      </font>
     </h1>
     <p align="center">
      <i><b>
       Your source on the Web for computing and technical books.
      </b></i>
     </p>
     <p align="center">
```

Example 13-4. XSL Stylesheet for Foobar Public Library Book Listings (continued)

```
    <b><font size="4" color="#00659C">
     <u>New Listings</u>
    </font></b>
   </p>
   <table border="0" cellpadding="5" cellspacing="5">
    <tr>
     <td valign="top" align="center" nowrap="nowrap" width="115">
      <p align="center">
       <font color="#FFFFFF"><b>
        <a href="/javaxml/techbooks/">Home</a>
       </b></font>
      </p>
      <p align="center">
       <font color="#FFFFFF"><b>
        <a href="/javaxml/techbooks/current.html">Current Listings</a>
       </b></font>
      </p>
      <p align="center">
       <b><font color="#FFFFFF">
        <i>New Listings</i>
       </font></b>
      </p>
      <p align="center">
       <font color="#FFFFFF"><b>
        <a href="/javaxml/techbooks/contact.html">Contact Us</a>
       </b></font>
      </p>
     </td>
     <td valign="top" align="left">
      <table border="0" cellpadding="5" cellspacing="5">
       <tr>
        <td width="450" align="left" valign="top">
         <p>
          <b>
           Welcome to <font face="courier">mytechbooks.com</font>,
           your source on the Web for computing and technical books.
           Our newest offerings are listed on the left.  To purchase
           any of these fine books, simply click on the
           &quot;Buy this Book!&quot; link, and you will be taken to
           the shopping cart for our store.  Enjoy!
          </b>
         </p>
         <p>
          <b>
           You should also check out our current listings, information
           about the store, and you can call us with your questions.
           Use the links on the menu to the left to access this
           information.  Thanks for shopping!
```

Example 13-4. XSL Stylesheet for Foobar Public Library Book Listings (continued)

```
          </b>
         </p>
        </td>
        <td align="left">

      <!-- Handle creation of content for each new *computer* book -->

        </td>
       </tr>
      </table>
     </td>
    </tr>
   </table>
  </body>
 </html>
</xsl:template>

</xsl:stylesheet>
```

While this doesn't yet filter the incoming XML data or transform that data, it does take care of the HTML interface for the user. Often it is much easier to take care of these presentation details first, and then add the transformation-specific logic afterwards.

NOTE When developing XSL stylesheets, particularly for web applications, you should test the results out with your XSLT Processor using its command-line capabilities. This can help you ensure that the stylesheet is transforming your document as you expect at each step of its development; trying to debug a large stylesheet's problems once it is complete is much more difficult. Using Apache Xalan from the command line is covered in Chapter 7, *Traversing XML*. For this example, you could access the *supplyBooks.pl* script in a web browser, save the results to an XML file, and test that and the stylesheet as you follow the examples.

Similar to the Foobar Public Library's application, this provides a menu on the left with hyperlinks to other portions of the application, some text about the company and their offerings, and then leaves a right column open for the addition of new book listings.

Before filtering our content, we need to add a template for outputting HTML content from a single book element's entry. As you recall, an entry will look like this:

```
<book subject="Computers">
 <title><![CDATA[Running Linux]]></title>
 <author><![CDATA[Matt Welsh]]></author>
 <publisher><![CDATA[O'Reilly & Associates]]></publisher>
```

```
  <numPages>630</numPages>
  <saleDetails>
   <isbn>1565921518</isbn>
   <price>29.95</price>
  </saleDetails>
  <description><![CDATA[In the tradition of all O'Reilly books, Running
   Linux features clear, step-by-step instructions that always seem to
   provide just the right amount of information.]]></description>
</book>
```

We can then convert this to HTML with the following XSL template:

```
<?xml version="1.0"?>

<xsl:stylesheet xmlns:xsl="http://www.w3.org/1999/XSL/Transform"
                version="1.0"
>

 <xsl:template match="books">
   <!-- Presentation of User Interface -->
 </xsl:template>

 <xsl:template match="book">
  <table border="0" cellspacing="1" bgcolor="#000000">
   <tr>
    <td>
     <table border="0" cellpadding="3" cellspacing="0">
      <tr>
       <td width="100%" bgcolor="#00659C" nowrap="nowrap" align="center">
        <b><font color="#FFFFFF">
         <xsl:value-of select="title" />
        </font></b>
       </td>
      </tr>
      <tr>
       <td width="100%" align="center" nowrap="nowrap" bgcolor="#FFFFFF">
        <font color="#000000"><b>
         Author: <xsl:value-of select="author" /><br />
         Publisher: <xsl:value-of select="publisher" /><br />
         Pages: <xsl:value-of select="numPages" /><br />
         Price: <xsl:value-of select="saleDetails/price" /><br />
         <br />
        </b></font>
        <xsl:element name="a">
         <xsl:attribute name="href">/servlets/BuyBookServlet?isbn=
          <xsl:value-of select="saleDetails/isbn" />
         </xsl:attribute>
         <font color="#00659C">Buy the Book!</font>
        </xsl:element>
       </td>
```

```
          </tr>
         </table>
        </td>
       </tr>
      </table>
      <br />
    </xsl:template>

  </xsl:stylesheet>
```

This template matches the book element, and then creates a table with a heading in one row, and contents in the second row. The entire table is within another table with a black background, which results in the appearance of the table being surrounded by a beveled black border. The title is inserted into the header of the table, and the information about the book (author, publisher, pages, and price) is added to the content of the table. Finally, a link to a Java servlet, `BuyBookServlet`, is provided to allow easy access to purchasing the book. The value of the book's `isbn` element is supplied as an argument to this servlet, which enables it to load the book being purchased.

WARNING In your XSL stylesheet, you should ensure that the line indicating the use of `BuyBookServlet` and the line with the `xsl:value-of` element selecting the book's ISBN number is actually one single line. If not, spaces and a carriage return could be inserted into the resultant URL, causing incorrect information to be passed to the servlet. The example stylesheet has this information broken into two lines because of the space constraints of the printed page.

The last addition we need to make to our stylesheet is to ensure that our new template is applied, and that only books whose subject is "Computers" are passed to the new template. We can reference the value of the subject attribute with the `@` symbol in our stylesheet, and filter our requests with the `select` attribute on the `xsl:apply-templates` element:

```
       </td>
       <td align="left">

        <!-- Handle creation of content for each new *computer* book -->
       <xsl:apply-templates select="book[@subject='Computers']" />

       </td>
      </tr>
     </table>
```

We reference the value of the attribute and compare it to a literal, enclosed within single quotes because the entire XPath expression is enclosed within double quotes. Because we are accessing an attribute of a nested element, we reference the element by name, and surround the expression on the element's attribute with brackets. This will ensure that only books with a subject of "Computers" have templates applied, and are therefore included in the HTML output. Once the stylesheet is complete, it can be saved as *computerBooks.xsl* and referenced programmatically by a Java servlet, which we write next.

XSLT from a Servlet

With our stylesheet ready for use, we need to add Java code to apply it to the XML data from the Foobar Public Library. This data is accessed easily by using Java's URL class to make an HTTP request to the library's system. Once we have this set up, all that is left is to actually apply the XSL transformation programmatically. Example 13-5 shows the Java servlet code that loads the XML data from the library, and indicates where our transformation code would be inserted.

Example 13-5. Java Servlet for Transforming Book Listings into HTML

```
package com.techbooks;

import java.io.FileInputStream;
import java.io.InputStream;
import java.io.IOException;
import java.io.PrintWriter;
import java.net.URL;
import javax.servlet.*;
import javax.servlet.http.*;

public class ListBooksServlet extends HttpServlet {

    /** Host to connect to for books list */
    private static final String hostname = "newInstance.com";
    /** Port number to connect to for books list */
    private static final int portNumber = 80;
    /** File to request (URI path) for books list */
    private static final String file = "/cgi/supplyBooks.pl";

    /** Stylesheet to apply to XML */
    private static final String stylesheet =
        "/home/bmclaugh/javaxml/techbooks/XSL/computerBooks.xsl";

    public void service(HttpServletRequest req, HttpServletResponse res)
        throws ServletException, IOException {

        res.setContentType("text/html");

        // Connect and get XML listing of books
        URL getBooksURL = new URL("http", hostname, portNumber, file);
        InputStream in = getBooksURL.openStream();
```

Example 13-5. Java Servlet for Transforming Book Listings into HTML (continued)

```
        // Transform XML for InputStream into HTML output
    }

}
```

This simple servlet requests the Foobar Public Library's application through an HTTP request, and gets the XML response in an `InputStream`.* This stream should then be used as a parameter to the XSLT processor, as well as the XSL stylesheet defined as a constant in the servlet.

There is currently no Java API that specifies how XSLT transformations can occur programmatically; however, each processor vendor should have classes that allow a transformation to be invoked from your Java code. We continue to look at using the Apache Xalan processor here; you should consult your processor's vendor for the method or methods to invoke in your own programs.

For Apache Xalan, the `XSLTProcessor` class is provided in the `org.apache.xalan.xslt` package for just this purpose. It takes as parameters an `XSLTInputSource` wrapping the XML file to process, an `XSLTInputSource` wrapping the XSL stylesheet to apply, and an `XSLTResultTarget` to use for output of the transformation. All three of these helper classes are in the `org.apache.xalan.xslt` package as well. Each of these classes can conveniently be created by passing in an `InputStream` (to `XSLInputSource`) or an `OutputStream` (to `XSLTResultTarget`). We have our XML document as an `InputStream`, we can wrap our XSL stylesheet within a `FileInputStream`, and the servlet API provides us easy access to the `ServletOutputStream` object through the `getOutputStream()` method on the `HttpServletResponse` object. The last detail we need to address is obtaining an instance of `XSLTProcessor`. Because there are several underlying mechanisms that can be used for processing, this class is not instantiated directly, but rather obtained through the `XSLTProcessorFactory` class, also in the `org.apache.xalan.xslt` package. We are familiar with factory classes by now, so all that is left is to import the classes we need and add the processing method calls to our servlet:

```
package com.techbooks;

import java.io.FileInputStream;
import java.io.InputStream;
import java.io.IOException;
import java.io.PrintWriter;
import java.net.URL;
```

* For more information on the `URL` class and Java I/O, see *Java I/O*, by Elliotte Rusty Harold (O'Reilly & Associates).

```
import javax.servlet.*;
import javax.servlet.http.*;

// Import Xalan XSLT Processor components
import org.apache.xalan.xslt.XSLTInputSource;
import org.apache.xalan.xslt.XSLTProcessor;
import org.apache.xalan.xslt.XSLTProcessorFactory;
import org.apache.xalan.xslt.XSLTResultTarget;

public class ListBooksServlet extends HttpServlet {

    /** Host to connect to for books list */
    private static final String hostname = "newInstance.com";
    /** Port number to connect to for books list */
    private static final int portNumber = 80;
    /** File to request (URI path) for books list */
    private static final String file = "/cgi/supplyBooks.pl";

    /** Stylesheet to apply to XML */
    private static final String stylesheet =
        "/home/bmclaugh/javaxml/techbooks/XSL/computerBooks.xsl";

    public void service(HttpServletRequest req, HttpServletResponse res)
        throws ServletException, IOException {

        res.setContentType("text/html");

        // Connect and get XML listing of books
        URL getBooksURL = new URL("http", hostname, portNumber, file);
        InputStream in = getBooksURL.openStream();

        // Transform XML for InputStream into HTML output
        try {
            XSLTProcessor processor = XSLTProcessorFactory.getProcessor();

            // Transform XML with XSL stylesheet
            processor.process(new XSLTInputSource(in),
                              new XSLTInputSource(
                                  new FileInputStream(stylesheet)),
                              new XSLTResultTarget(
                                  res.getOutputStream()));

        } catch (Exception e) {
            PrintWriter out = res.getWriter();
            out.println("Error: " + e.getMessage());
            out.close();
        }
    }

}
```

With the processor outputting to our `ServletOutputStream`, we don't even need to add any output of our own, except in the case of errors! Saving this servlet as *ListBooksServlet.java* and compiling it will make it accessible through your servlet engine in a web browser.

NOTE If you are following along with the examples, you should take several steps before accessing the servlet. First, ensure that you are connected to the Internet, or that both the Foobar example and the mytechbooks.com example are running locally; the mytechbooks.com servlet must be able to access the XML data from the Foobar Public Library. Second, you should enter several books into the Foobar Public Library system through the HTML user interface. Entering books on a variety of subjects is the most effective way to see exactly what these applications do and how they interact. Once you have data in the library and access to that data, you can access the `ListBooksServlet`.

When this new servlet is requested, it in turn requests the XML data from the Foobar Public Library. This data (a listing of the newly available books) is then transformed and output to the screen as HTML. The response from the servlet should look similar to Figure 13-4.

Along with the menu links on the left (not implemented in this example), the newest book listings are printed in a very nice format, all with up-to-date information (thanks to our changes at the Foobar Public Library!) as well as links to buy the book with a few mouse clicks. Now mytechbooks.com customers can easily browse the new book listings online; all that is left is to push this information out to these customers, so they don't even have to type in a URL. We look at solving this difficult problem next.

Push Versus Pull

So far, we have looked at building our applications assuming that the application clients would always *pull* data and content. In other words, a user had to type a URL into their browser (in the case of the mytechhbooks.com new book listings), or an application like the mytechbooks.com servlet had to make an HTTP request for XML data (in the case of the Foobar Public Library). While this is not a problem, it is not always the best way for a company like mytechbooks.com to sell books. Clients pulling data have to remember to visit sites they would buy items from, and often don't revisit those sites for days, weeks, or even months. While those clients may often purchase goods and services when they do remember, on average, those purchases do not result in as much revenue as if small purchases were made more frequently.

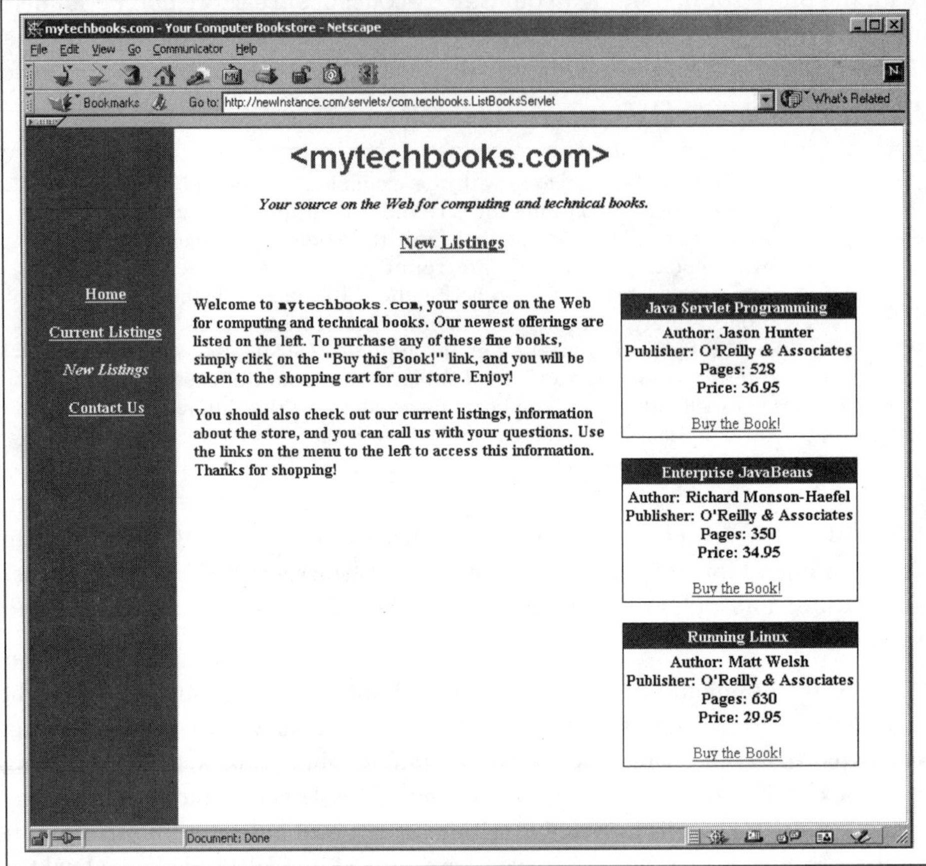

Figure 13-4. HTML output from mytechbooks.com new book listing

Realizing this trend, mytechbooks.com wants to be able to *push* data to its clients. Pushing data involves letting the client know (without any client action) that new items are available, or that specials are being run. This in turn allows the client to make more frequent purchases without having to remember to visit a web page. However, pushing data to clients is difficult in a web medium, as the Internet does not behave as a thick client: it is harder to send pop-up messages or generate alerts for users. What mytechbooks.com has discovered, though, is the popularity of personalized "start pages" like Netscape's My Netscape and Yahoo's My Yahoo pages. In talking with Netscape, mytechbooks.com has been hearing about a technology called Rich Site Summary (RSS), and thinks it may be the answer to their need to push data out to clients.

Rich Site Summary

Rich Site Summary (RSS) is a particular flavor of XML. It has its own DTD, and defines what is called a *channel*. A channel is a way to represent data about a specific subject, and provides for a title and description for the channel, an image or logo, and then several *items* within the channel. Each item, then, is something of particular interest about the channel, or a product or service available. Because the allowed elements of an item are fairly generic (title, description, hyperlink), almost anything can be represented as an item of a channel. An RSS channel is not intended to provide a complete site's content, but rather a short blurb about a company or service, suitable for display in a portal-style framework, or as a sidebar on a web site. In fact, the different "widgets" at Netscape's Netcenter are all RSS channels, and Netscape allows the creation of new RSS channels that can be registered with Netcenter. Netscape also has a built-in system for displaying RSS channels in an HTML format, which of course fits into their Netcenter start pages.

At this point, you may be a little concerned that RSS is to Netscape as Microsoft's XML parser is to Microsoft: almost completely useless when used with other tools or vendors. Although originally developed by Netscape specifically for Netcenter, the XML structure of RSS has made it usable by any application that can read a DTD. In fact, many portal-style web sites and applications are beginning to use RSS, such as the Apache Jetspeed project (*http://java.apache.org/jetspeed*), an open source Enterprise Information Portal system. Jetspeed takes the same RSS format that Netscape uses, and renders it in a completely different manner. Because of the concise grammar of RSS, this is easily done.

As many users have start pages, or home pages, or similar places on the Web that they frequent, mytechbooks.com would like to create an RSS channel that provides new book listings, and then allows interested clients to jump straight to buying an item that catches their eye. This is an effective means to push data, as products like Netcenter will automatically update RSS channel content as often as the user desires.

Creating an RSS XML Document

The first thing we need to do to use RSS is create an RSS file. This is almost too simple to be believed: other than referencing the correct DTD and following that DTD, there is nothing at all complicated about creating an RSS document. Example 13-6 shows a sample RSS file that mytechbooks.com has modeled.

Example 13-6. Sample RSS Channel Document for mytechbooks.com

```
<?xml version="1.0" encoding="UTF-8"?>

<!DOCTYPE rss PUBLIC "-//Netscape Communications//DTD RSS 0.91//EN"
```

Example 13-6. Sample RSS Channel Document for mytechbooks.com (continued)

```
             "http://my.netscape.com/publish/formats/rss-0.91.dtd">

<rss version="0.91">
 <channel>
  <title>mytechbooks.com New Listings</title>
  <link>http://www.newInstance.com/javaxml/techbooks</link>
  <description>
   Your online source for technical material, computers,
   and computing books!
  </description>
  <language>en-us</language>

  <image>
   <title>mytechbooks.com</title>
   <url>
    http://newInstance.com/javaxml/techbooks/images/techbooksLogo.gif
   </url>
   <link>http://newInstance.com/javaxml/techbooks</link>
   <width>140</width>
   <height>23</height>
   <description>
    Your source on the Web for technical books.
   </description>
  </image>

  <item>
   <title>Java Servlet Programming</title>
   <link>
    http://newInstance.com/javaxml/techbooks/buy.xsp?isbn=156592391X
   </link>
   <description>
    This book is a superb introduction to Java servlets
    and their various communications mechanisms.
   </description>
  </item>

 </channel>
</rss>
```

The root element must be `rss`, and the `version` attribute must be defined; additionally, this attribute's value must match up with the version of the DTD referenced. Within the root element, one single `channel` element must appear. This has elements that describe the channel (`title`, `link`, `description`, and `language`), an optional image that can be associated with the channel (as well as information about that image), and then as many as fifteen `item` elements, each detailing one item related to the channel. Each item has a `title`, `link`, and `description` element, all of which are self-explanatory.

WARNING As in previous examples, actual RSS channel documents should avoid having whitespace within the `link` and `url` elements, but rather have all information on a single line. Again, the formatting in the example does not reflect this due to printing and sizing constraints.

An optional text box and button to submit the information in the book can be added as well, although these are not included in the example. For a complete detail of allowed elements and attributes, visit *http://my.netscape.com/publish/help/mnn20/quickstart.html* online.

It is simple enough to create RSS files programmatically; the procedure is similar to how we generated the HTML for the mytechbooks.com web site. Half of the RSS file (the information about the channel as well as the image information) is static content; only the `item` elements must be generated dynamically. However, just as you were getting ready to open up vi and start creating another XSL stylesheet, another requirement was dropped into your lap: the machine that will house the RSS channel is a different server than that used in our last example, and only has very outdated versions of the Apache Xalan libraries available. Because of some of the high-availability applications that also run on that machine, such as the billing system, mytechbooks.com does not want to update those libraries until change control can be stepped through, a week-long process. However, they do have newer versions of the Xerces libraries available (as XML parsing is used in the billing system), so Java APIs for handling XML are available.* While SAX and DOM are both viable alternatives, JDOM again would seem to be the simplest way to convert the XML from the Foobar Public Library into an RSS channel format. Example 13-7 does just this.

Example 13-7. Java Servlet to Convert New Book Listings into an RSS Channel Document

```
package com.techbooks;

import java.io.FileInputStream;
import java.io.InputStream;
import java.io.IOException;
import java.io.PrintWriter;
import java.net.URL;
import java.util.Iterator;
import java.util.List;
```

* Yes, this is a bit of a silly case, and perhaps not so likely to really occur. However, it does afford us the opportunity to look at another alternative for creating XML programmatically. Don't sneer too much at the absurdity of the example; all of the examples in this book, including the silly ones, stem from actual experiences consulting for real-world companies; laughing at this scenario might mean your next project has the same silly requirements!

Example 13-7. Java Servlet to Convert New Book Listings into an RSS Channel Document (continued)

```
import javax.servlet.*;
import javax.servlet.http.*;

// JDOM
import org.jdom.Document;
import org.jdom.Element;
import org.jdom.JDOMException;
import org.jdom.input.SAXBuilder;

public class GetRSSChannelServlet extends HttpServlet {

    /** Host to connect to for books list */
    private static final String hostname = "newInstance.com";
    /** Port number to connect to for books list */
    private static final int portNumber = 80;
    /** File to request (URI path) for books list */
    private static final String file = "/cgi/supplyBooks.pl";

    public void service(HttpServletRequest req, HttpServletResponse res)
        throws ServletException, IOException {

        res.setContentType("text/plain");
        PrintWriter out = res.getWriter();

        // Connect and get XML listing of books
        URL getBooksURL = new URL("http", hostname, portNumber, file);
        InputStream in = getBooksURL.openStream();

        try {
            // Request SAX Implementation and use default parser
            SAXBuilder builder = new SAXBuilder();

            // Create the document
            Document doc = builder.build(in);

            // Output XML
            out.println(generateRSSContent(doc));

        } catch (JDOMException e) {
            out.println("Error: " + e.getMessage());
        } finally {
            out.close();
        }
    }

    /**
```

Example 13-7. Java Servlet to Convert New Book Listings into an RSS Channel Document (continued)

```
     * <p>
     * This will generate an RSS XML document using the supplied
     *   JDOM <code>Document</code>.
     * </p.
     *
     * @param doc <code>Document</code> to use for input.
     * @return <code>String</code> - RSS file to output.
     * @throws <code>JDOMException</code> when errors occur.
     */
    private String generateRSSContent(Document doc) throws JDOMException {
        StringBuffer rss = new StringBuffer();

        rss.append("<?xml version=\"1.0\"?>\n")
           .append("<!DOCTYPE rss PUBLIC ")
           .append("\"-//Netscape Communications//DTD RSS 0.91//EN\" ")
           .append("\"http://my.netscape.com/publish/formats")
           .append("/rss-0.91.dtd\">\n")
           .append("<rss version=\"0.91\">\n")
           .append(" <channel>\n")
           .append("  <title>Technical Books</title>\n")
           .append("  <link>")
           .append("http://newInstance.com/javaxml/techbooks</link>\n")
           .append("  <description>\n")
           .append("   Your online source for technical materials, ")
           .append("computers, and computing books!\n")
           .append("  </description>\n")
           .append("  <language>en-us</language>\n")
           .append("  <image>\n")
           .append("   <title>mytechbooks.com</title>\n")
           .append("   <url>")
           .append("http://newInstance.com/javaxml/techbooks/")
           .append("images/techbooksLogo.gif")
           .append("</url>\n")
           .append("   <link>")
           .append("http://newInstance.com/javaxml/techbooks</link>\n")
           .append("   <width>140</width>\n")
           .append("   <height>23</height>\n")
           .append("   <description>\n")
           .append("    Your source on the Web for technical books.\n")
           .append("   </description>\n")
           .append("  </image>\n");

        // Add an item for each new title with Computers as subject
        List books = doc.getRootElement().getChildren("book");
        for (Iterator i = books.iterator(); i.hasNext(); ) {
            Element book = (Element)i.next();
            if (book.getAttribute("subject")
```

Example 13-7. Java Servlet to Convert New Book Listings into an RSS Channel Document (continued)

```
                    .getValue()
                     .equals("Computers")) {
                // Output an item
                rss.append("<item>\n")
                    // Add title
                   .append(" <title>")
                   .append(book.getChild("title").getContent())
                   .append("</title>\n")
                    // Add link to buy book
                   .append(" <link>")
                   .append("http://newInstance.com/javaxml")
                   .append("/techbooks/buy.xsp?isbn=")
                   .append(book.getChild("saleDetails")
                               .getChild("isbn")
                               .getContent())
                   .append("</link>\n")
                   .append(" <description>")
                    // Add description
                   .append(book.getChild("description").getContent())
                   .append("</description>\n")
                   .append("</item>\n");

            }
        }

        rss.append(" </channel>\n")
           .append("</rss>");

        return rss.toString();
    }

}
```

By this time, nothing in this code should be the least bit surprising to you; we import the JDOM and I/O classes we need, and access the Foobar Public Library application as in the `ListBooksServlet`. The resulting `InputStream` is used to create a JDOM `Document`, with the default parser (Apache Xerces in JDOM 1.0) and the JDOM implementation built on SAX doing the work for us:

```
// Request SAX Implementation and use default parser
SAXBuilder builder = new SAXBuilder();

// Create the document
Document doc = builder.build(in);
```

We then hand off the JDOM `Document` to the `generateRSSContentMethod()`, which prints out all of the static content for the RSS channel. This method then obtains the book elements within the XML from the library, and iterates through them, ignoring those without a `subject` attribute equal to "Computers":

```
// Add an item for each new title with Computers as subject
List books = doc.getRootElement().getChildren("book");
for (Iterator i = books.iterator(); i.hasNext(); ) {
    Element book = (Element)books.elementAt(i);
    if (book.getAttribute("subject")
            .getValue().equals("Computers")) {
        // Output as an item element
    }
}
```

Finally, each element that makes it through the comparison is added to the RSS channel. Nothing very exciting here, right? Figure 13-5 shows a sample output from accessing this servlet, saved as `GetRSSChannelServlet.java`, through a web browser.

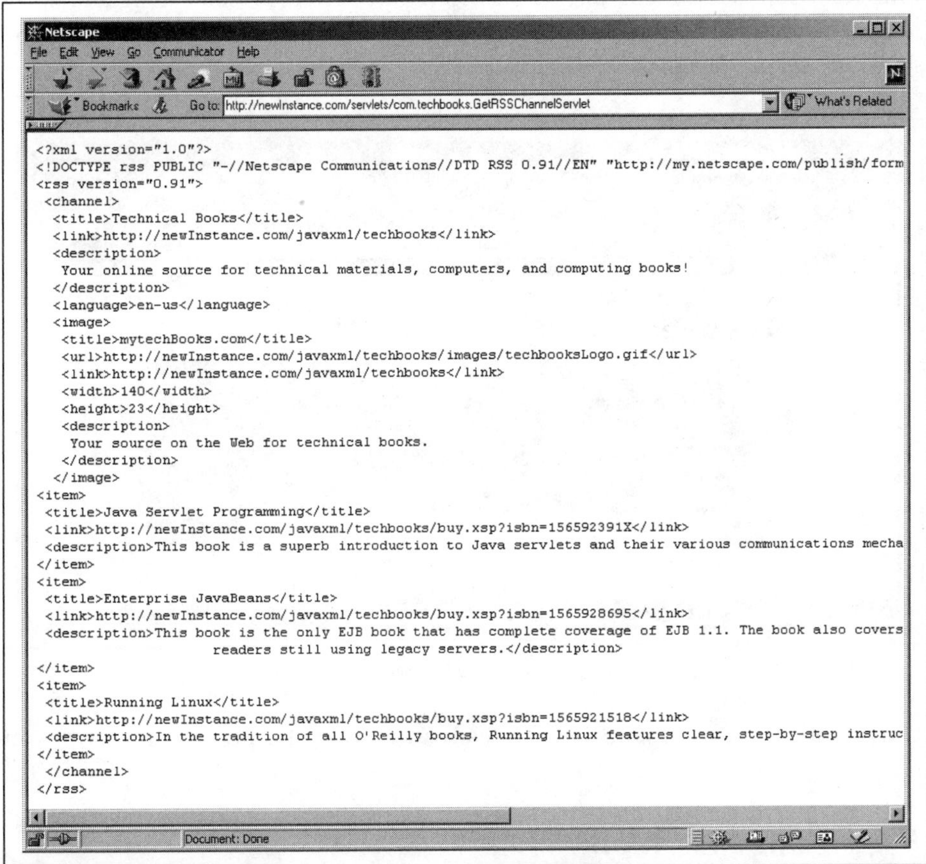

Figure 13-5. RSS channel generated by the GetRSSChannelServlet

With this RSS channel ready for use, mytechbooks.com has made their content available by any service provider that supports RSS! To get the ball rolling on allowing clients to use their channel, mytechbooks.com would like to register their channel with Netscape Netcenter and see it in action (and so would we!).

Validating the RSS Channel

Once the channel is created, it should be validated. In addition to ensuring that the document meets the constraints laid out by the RSS DTD, there are limitations that Netscape lays out that the DTD cannot enforce (although XML Schema could rectify this in the future). In order to ensure that channels are properly formed and usable, Netscape provides an online validation mechanism, located at *http://my.netscape.com/publish/help/validate.tmpl*. Visiting this site and entering in the URL to your RSS channel (which can be a servlet, CGI script, or static file) allows the Netscape program to ensure you are generating a usable RSS channel. Figure 13-6 shows the output of a successful validation run.

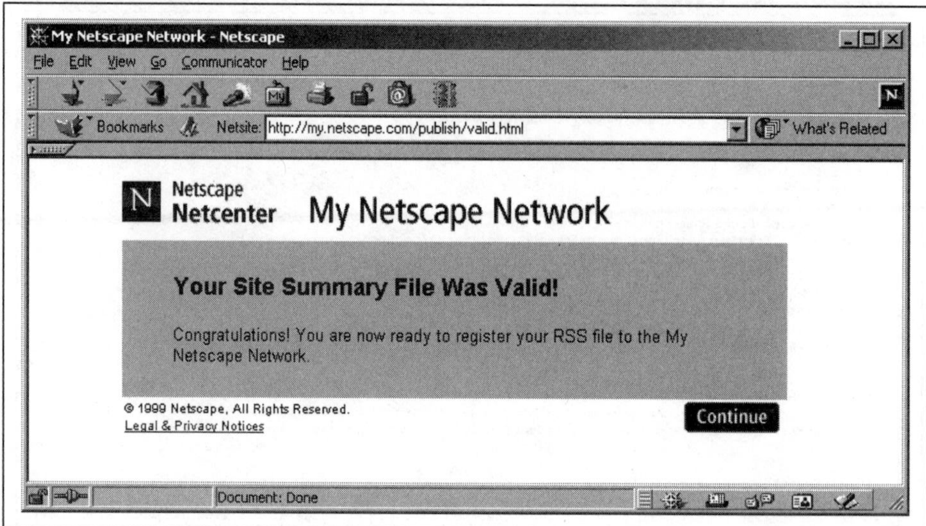

Figure 13-6. Validation confirmation from an RSS channel

Once validation is complete, we are ready to register the RSS channel with Netcenter.

Registering the Channel

Once the RSS channel has been validated, we need to publish the channel to Netcenter (or whatever other service provider is being used). This can be done through accessing *http://my.netscape.com/publish*. Walking through the steps, you have to supply a Netcenter account name, as a confirmation email is sent to the address attached to that account. Once the valid RSS channel URL has been accepted, Netcenter adds the channel to its system and sends an email. Figure 13-7 shows this email, which includes instructions on adding links to the RSS channel from a web site (like mytechbooks.com, which we look at next), as well as how to add the channel to a Netcenter start page.

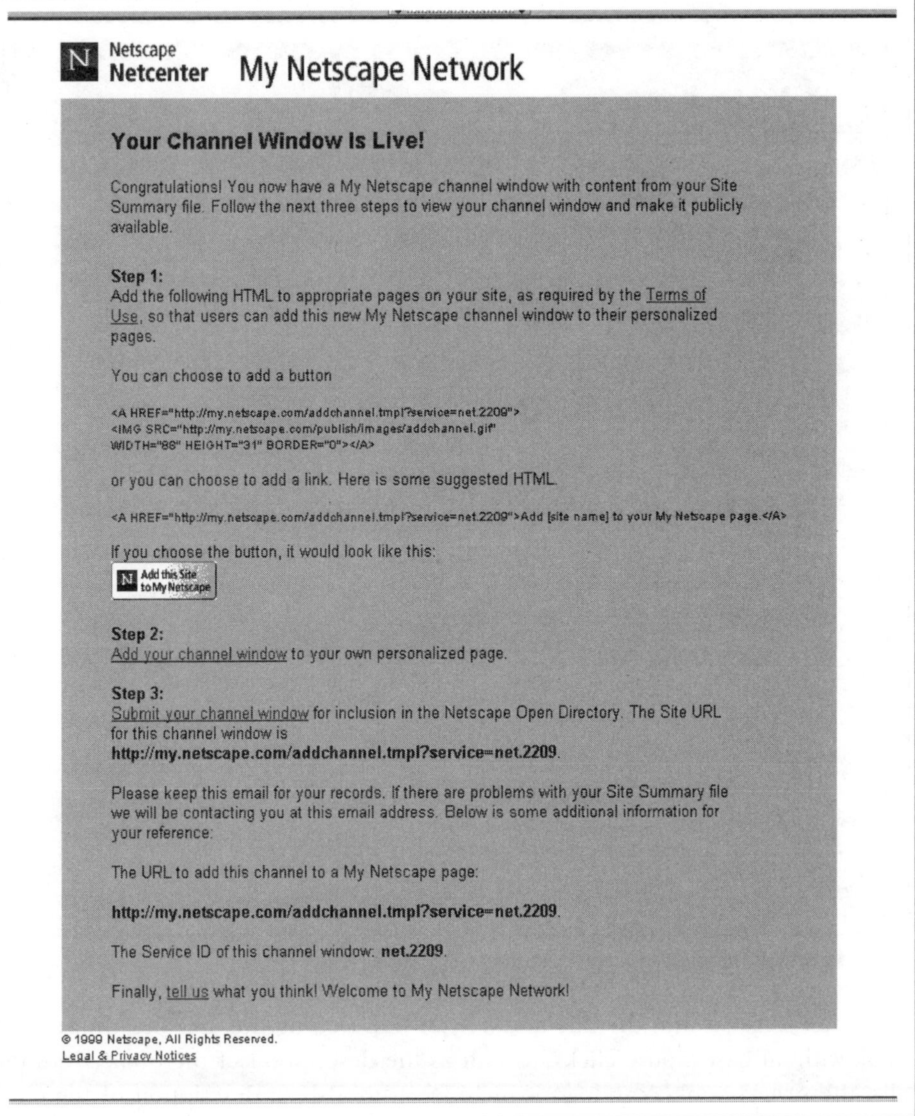

Netscape Netcenter **My Netscape Network**

Your Channel Window Is Live!

Congratulations! You now have a My Netscape channel window with content from your Site Summary file. Follow the next three steps to view your channel window and make it publicly available.

Step 1:
Add the following HTML to appropriate pages on your site, as required by the Terms of Use, so that users can add this new My Netscape channel window to their personalized pages.

You can choose to add a button

```
<A HREF="http://my.netscape.com/addchannel.tmpl?service=net.2209">
<IMG SRC="http://my.netscape.com/publish/images/addchannel.gif"
WIDTH="88" HEIGHT="31" BORDER="0"></A>
```

or you can choose to add a link. Here is some suggested HTML.

```
<A HREF="http://my.netscape.com/addchannel.tmpl?service=net.2209">Add [site name] to your My Netscape page.</A>
```

If you choose the button, it would look like this:

Add this Site to My Netscape

Step 2:
Add your channel window to your own personalized page.

Step 3:
Submit your channel window for inclusion in the Netscape Open Directory. The Site URL for this channel window is **http://my.netscape.com/addchannel.tmpl?service=net.2209**.

Please keep this email for your records. If there are problems with your Site Summary file we will be contacting you at this email address. Below is some additional information for your reference:

The URL to add this channel to a My Netscape page:

http://my.netscape.com/addchannel.tmpl?service=net.2209.

The Service ID of this channel window: **net.2209**.

Finally, tell us what you think! Welcome to My Netscape Network!

Figure 13-7. Netscape RSS channel confirmation email

Using the Channel

Validating and registering the channel has been a breeze! Additionally, the email that Netscape generates even makes adding the channel to a start page simple. Following the hyperlink provided, it takes two mouse clicks to make this channel visible. Figure 13-8 shows the RSS channel within a Netcenter start page, displayed in the left column, with all of our XML converted into formatted HTML.

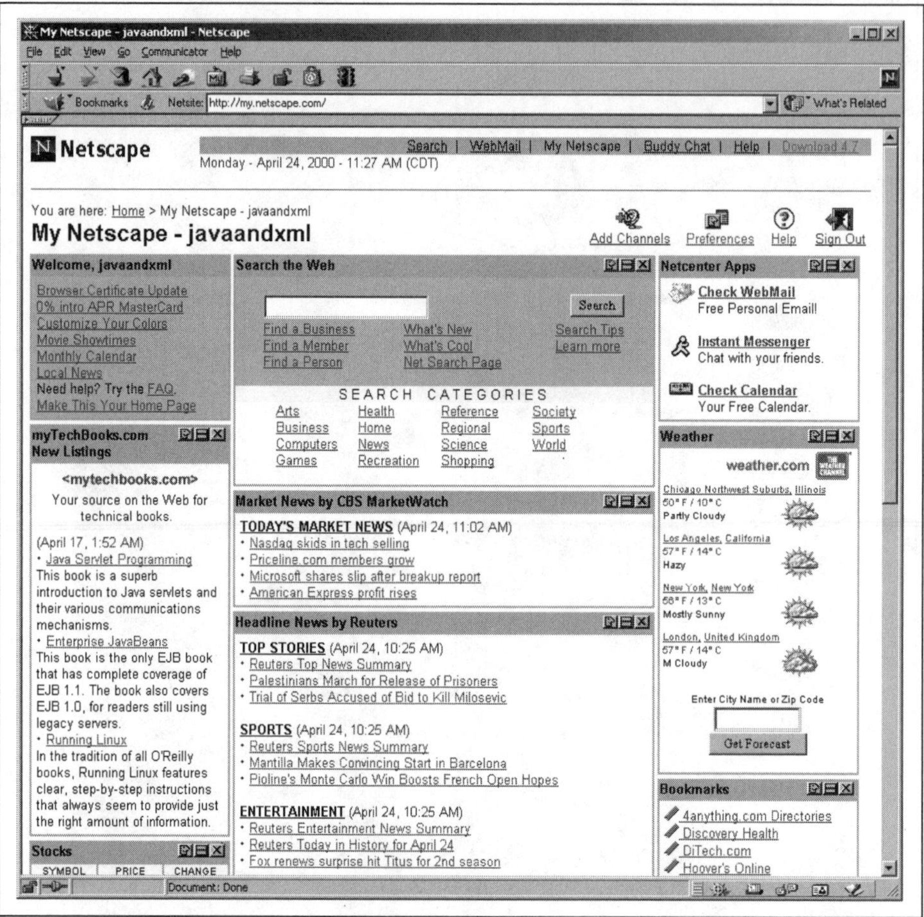

Figure 13-8. Netcenter with custom RSS channel

Each item is listed with the title and a hyperlink (letting the user buy the selected book with an easy mouse click), as well as the description of the book. Additionally, the mytechbooks.com logo is included with a short description of the channel. Every time a user opens her start page, this channel can inform her of new books available through mytechbooks.com, potentially doubling or tripling the income of the company.

Finally, as a means of advertising the availability of this channel to other customers, we can update the XSL stylesheet we created for mytechbooks.com to include a link that will automatically add the channel to a customer's own start page. This means that a single pull of data from mytechbooks.com can result in the client having data pushed to them daily! Add in the following HTML to our XSL stylesheet:

```
    <p align="center">
     <font color="#FFFFFF"><b>
      <a href="/javaxml/techbooks/contact.html">Contact Us</a>
     </b></font>
    </p>
  <br />
  <p align="center">
   <A HREF="http://my.netscape.com/addchannel.tmpl?service=net.2209">
   <IMG SRC="http://my.netscape.com/publish/images/addchannel.gif"
    WIDTH="88" HEIGHT="31" BORDER="0" /></A>
  </p>
   </td>
   <td valign="top" align="left">
    <table border="0" cellpadding="5" cellspacing="5">
     <tr>
      <td width="450" align="left" valign="top">
       <p>
        <b>
         Welcome to <font face="courier">mytechbooks.com</font>,
         your source on the Web for computing and technical books.
         Our newest offerings are listed on the left.  To purchase
         any of these fine books, simply click on the
         &quot;Buy this Book!&quot; link, and you will be taken to
         the shopping cart for our store.  Enjoy!
        </b>
       </p>
```

This change (included in the email that Netscape generates and sends to you when registering an RSS channel) will add a button with a Netscape graphic taking the user straight to the web site that adds the custom channel to his start page. The formatted HTML that results from this change is shown in Figure 13-9.

At this point, we have completed our business-to-business case study. We have taken an organization that had one language and no XML capabilities (the Foobar Public Library with their Perl scripts) and allowed that organization to communicate with a company that uses an entirely different technology (Java servlets). The two companies are completely uncoupled, meaning that there is no code in either application that is tied to code in the other application. Because of the standard XML data used as a communication medium, either company can change applications, technologies, and even architectures without affecting the operation of the

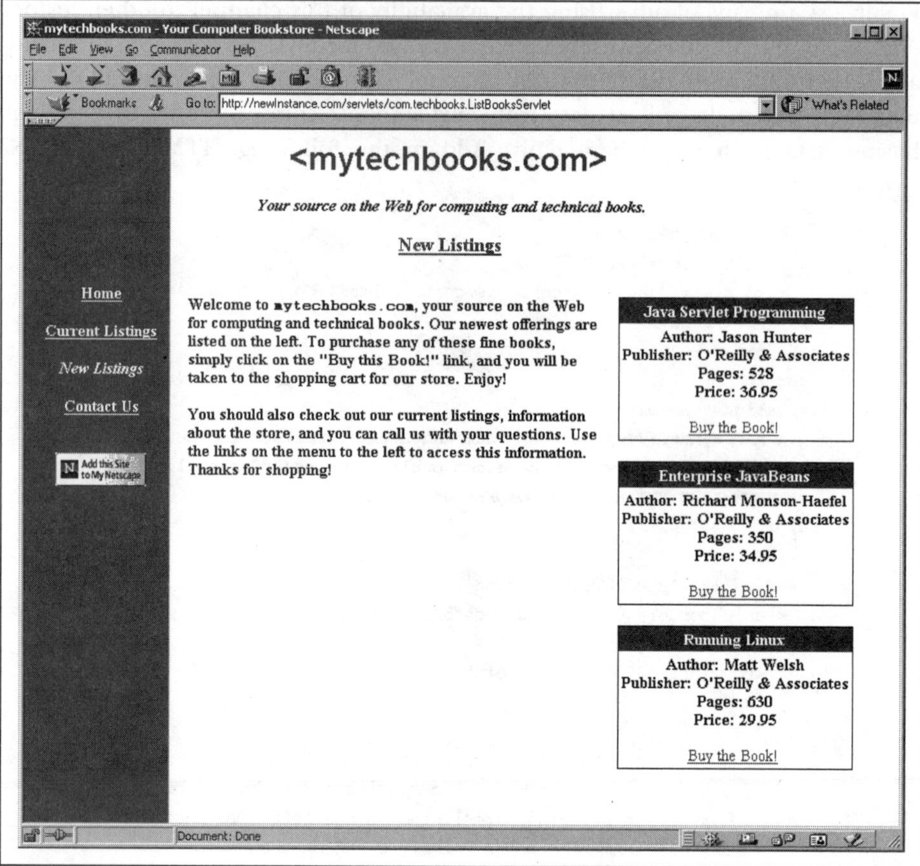

Figure 13-9. HTML output with Netscape RSS channel link

other. We then looked at how this communication could be used to present HTML content to users (in a totally different fashion for each application), and how to push that content out to customers in yet *another* HTML format through the use of RSS channels. Underneath all this interaction and communication, XML drove the communication and interoperability of these very different businesses.

The Real World

There is very little to say in regard to business-to-business that we have not covered. Our examples in this chapter were pulled right out of the project deliverables and mission statements of today's top companies, and may solve problems you are faced with in your current job! We will now look briefly at how this XML-centric approach differs from Electronic Data Interchange (EDI), as well as other uses of RSS channels.

XML Versus EDI

With the increasing need for communication between companies, Electronic Data Interchange (EDI) has become a hot topic. Expensive products and heavy-duty solutions have had "EDI" slapped on their label, and are selling like mad. However, these expensive solutions may quickly fall out of favor with companies that do not have deep pockets. In fact, with the rise of XML, even companies that can afford enterprise-level EDI solutions are deciding to go with an XML-based approach instead. While this is certainly due in part to the standardization that XML provides, it is also a testament to the ease of use of XML. In a single chapter, you have acquired the skills to enable disparate systems to communicate in complex ways, something that ten years ago would have required an entire team of developers and still would have resulted in a proprietary solution.

In fact, it is arguable that XML totally replaces the need for EDI. Legacy systems, proprietary applications, massive databases, and tightly secured products can all interchange data by using XML as a data format. With APIs like SAX and DOM, and now JDOM, developing complete XML solutions is practical, and building XML layers over existing data in different formats is a matter of weeks and months instead of years. Expect to see EDI system sales slow to a crawl, and e-business offerings based on XML and Java rocket in the years to come.

RSS Channels: Here to Stay?

One of the common questions regarding using XML formats such as RSS is "Are they here to stay?" This most often stems from an assumption that because the format is used in a particular way (such as Netscape using RSS for their Netcenter page), the format must always be used in that particular way. This is true in the case of RSS, as early supporters were dismissed, and RSS was considered something "that Netscape did." However, with XML as the underpinnings, RSS and other XML-based formats can be used just as any other XML document can. The styling of the document is totally arbitrary, and a stylesheet to transform an RSS channel into WML for a wireless phone is trivial to write. In fact, as we mentioned, the Apache Jetspeed project uses RSS, and the O'Reilly Network (*http://www.oreillynet.com*) is using RSS channels on sites like XML.com (*http://www.xml.com*).

Even more important than understanding that RSS is a viable technology for years to come is realizing that XML-based solutions, by their nature, are non-proprietary. Any XML document can be manipulated in any way the content author or developer can imagine. Don't be surprised to see most presentation layers migrate to XML in the coming years, or move to a particular flavor of XML such as RSS, as they seek to increase their applications' dynamic content without having to keep a fleet of web developers on staff just to update that content.

What's Next?

By now we have managed to touch on the major subjects concerning using XML within Java code. Besides being able to create, parse, style, transform, constrain, and validate XML, we have looked at using XML within a publishing framework, using XML for remote procedure calls, storing configuration information within XML documents, and now creating XML "on the fly" from Java code. This rounds out our XML and Java skills, and should prepare you for nearly any XML-related application programming you could be tasked with. In our next chapter, we wrap up our look at XML and this book with another look at XML Schema. Although we have discussed using XML Schema for constraining documents, we will take a look at some of the new and innovative directions XML Schema is moving in which, and how this affects using XML. Although this is slightly tangential to using XML from Java, it does bear on how XML is used in your applications.

In this chapter:

- *To DTD or Not To DTD*
- *Java Parallels*
- *What's Next?*

14

XML Schema

As a final look at XML, and, in particular, XML topics that are particularly hot right now, we'll spend a bit of time discussing XML Schema. Although the last several chapters have focused specifically on using Java to manipulate XML, in this chapter we look at XML Schema as a whole. In fact, XML Schema is still relatively new and the support for specific Java classes and interfaces to manipulate XML Schema has been slow in surfacing.

Despite the difficulty in using XML Schema directly through Java, the specification for XML Schema is important enough to warrant further discussion. In this chapter, we first spend time discussing whether using XML Schema is a stable and good choice, particularly as compared to continuing to use DTDs. We then spend a bit of time discussing how XML Schema closely maps to Java, and how that relationship may cause some significant changes to the way XML content is stored.

To DTD or Not To DTD

Although nearly every XML content author and developer has been hearing about XML Schema for almost a year, there is still quite a bit of uncertainty as to whether XML Schema is ready to be used in "prime time." While some of this concern is based on the changes and immaturity of the XML Schema specification, the majority seems to be based on a familiarity with DTDs. Many XML developers still use only DTDs for document constraints, despite the wave of publicity that XML Schema has received. There are quite a few reasons for this resistance to change, and all are important in deciding for yourself if you need to use XML Schema.

Stability of the XML Schema Specification

One of the largest problems that XML Schema is still attempting to overcome is the rapid change in its own specification (which can be read online at *http://www.w3.org/TR/xmlschema-1/* and *http://www.w3.org/TR/xmlschema-2/*). Within six months (from August of 1999 to March of 2000), three revisions of this specification were released; while this in itself is neither unusual nor problematic, the significant changes introduced through the revisions are. Each revision basically made schemas corresponding to previous revisions obsolete and therefore useless. This generated a lot of frustration and discontent in the XML community. In addition, the complexity of the specification has only seemed to increase over the lifecycle of XML Schema, and this complexity has compounded the community's uncertain feelings towards XML Schema.

Despite all this "negative press," XML Schema still promises to be at least as significant as the XML namespaces specification, and arguably as important as the original XML 1.0 specification itself. While the unhappiness at writing schemas that later become useless is understandable, the XML Schema specification and working group have always maintained that until the specification is complete and final at the W3C, changes are unavoidable. In fact, many of the authors frustrated at the changes are the same voices that made suggestions and criticisms about items that *should be* changed; in other words, not using XML Schema because it has changed a lot is simply a poor idea. Almost every change, including minor ones, by the XML Schema working group has assisted in the clarity and usability of the specification.

Enhanced Document Constraints

It would be almost impossible to even briefly discuss schemas without emphasizing (not for the first time in this book) the ease of constraining data through their use. You would be hard-pressed to find anyone, even those dead-set on continuing to use DTDs, who would deny the flexibility and ease of setting data constraints with XML Schema. In fact, the arguably more important uses of XML Schema that we discuss later in this chapter have been overshadowed by this fact! The truth is that any application that seeks to enforce strict data type and range constraints with an XML-based medium *must* elect to use XML Schema. Days if not weeks of time and effort can be saved.

In addition to traditional constraints, XML Schema allows content model constraints for generic data formats to be built. These constraints can then be shared and referenced from other schemas by using XLink and XPointer. DTDs, not being XML themselves, are extremely limited in this respect. It would not be unusual to see large applications using DTDs that are thousands of lines long. This is hardly an object-oriented approach to data, let alone a maintainable approach to data validation.

Namespace Issues with DTDs

We've already looked at how parsing an XML document that uses namespaces and needs to be validated can cause significant problems for DTDs. Remember this code:

```
DOMParser parser = new DOMParser();

// Turn on namespace support
parser.setFeature("http://xml.org/sax/features/namespaces", true);

// Turn on validation
parser.setFeature("http://xml.org/sax/features/validation", true);

// Parse
parser.parse();

// Get results
Document doc = parser.getDocument();
```

When this code is compiled within an application, running the application generates the following fatal error (this example is the specific verbiage from Apache Xerces, but your results should be similar):

```
org.xml.sax.SAXParseException: Document root element "JavaXML:Book", must
 match DOCTYPE root "JavaXML:Book".
        at org.apache.xerces.framework.XMLParser.reportError
            (XMLParser.java:1318)
        at org.apache.xerces.validators.dtd.DTDValidator
            .reportRecoverableXMLError(DTDValidator.java:1602)
        at org.apache.xerces.validators.dtd
            .DTDValidator.rootElementSpecified(DTDValidator.java:576)
        at org.apache.xerces.framework.XMLParser
            .scanAttributeName(XMLParser.java:2076)
        at org.apache.xerces.framework.XMLDocumentScanner
            .scanElement(XMLDocumentScanner.java, Compiled Code)
        at org.apache.xerces.framework
            .XMLDocumentScanner$ContentDispatcher.dispatch
            (XMLDocumentScanner.java, Compiled Code)
        at org.apache.xerces.framework.XMLDocumentScanner
            .parseSome(XMLDocumentScanner.java, Compiled Code)
        at org.apache.xerces.framework
            .XMLParser.parse(XMLParser.java:1208)
        at org.apache.xerces.framework
            .XMLParser.parse(XMLParser.java:1247)
```

This is because DTDs are ignorant of namespaces, but the mechanism handling the root element as well as the constructs nested within it is not. This difference in functionality causes conflicts between validation and namespace processing. XML documents often require both, making XML Schema an even more attractive solution for document constraints. Additionally, XML Schema's close parallels to Java and the possibility of future integration are extremely promising.

Java Parallels

As the XML Schema specification has solidified, the similarity between XML Schema and Java class and interface definitions has only increased. Although still strictly only a set of constraints, an XML Schema closely models the code you write in Java when creating a class or interface definition. The schema defines the set of allowed data that is contained within an XML document; this is similar to the way a Java class or interface defines the allowed methods and variables that an instance of the class may represent. Just as a Java program only needs to know this definition to use the instance (without having to know specific details about the instance implementation, such as its memory address or contents), an XML-aware application only needs to understand a document's constraints (defined in the XML Schema) to use the XML document.

The importance of this parallel might not seem obvious to you; however, this facet of XML Schema is particularly critical to how XML may be used in new types of applications, and new implementations of old techniques. We look at just a few of these important applications here, but you should be able to extend these concepts to many more uses, perhaps pushing the envelope of your own applications' functionality.

Equivalence

One important concept that XML Schema introduces is *element equivalence.* In XML 1.0 and DTDs, one element type must be mapped to one element. In other words, if two elements shared identical content, both elements had to have an explicit definition:

```
<!ELEMENT element1 (element2, element3*)>
<!ATTLIST element1
    atttribute1 CDATA #REQUIRED
    attrribute2 (foo|bar) "foo"
>

<!ELEMENT sameAsElement1 (element2, element3*)>
<!ATTLIST sameAsElement1
    atttribute1 CDATA #REQUIRED
    attrribute2 (foo|bar) "foo"
>
```

This is obviously redundant, and can introduce errors if one element's definition is changed while the other definition is left untouched. By allowing types, XML Schema can remedy this:

```
<complexType name="sameAsType">
  <attribute name="attribute1" type="string" minOccurs="1" />
  <attribute name="attribute2" default="foo">
    <simpleType base="string">
      <enumeration value="foo" />
      <enumeration value="bar" />
    </simpleType>
  </attribute>
</complexType>

<element name="element1" type="sameAsType" />
<element name="sameAsElement1" type="sameAsType" />
```

Through this mechanism, a single element type can be defined and then applied to multiple elements. This is similar to a Java model, where a class is defined and then several instances are created. However, XML Schema adds even more functionality. Consider the following XML document fragment, representing a shipper's manifest:

```
<shipperManifest>
  <item>
    <name>Ceramic Vase</name>
    <quantity>400</quantity>
    <quality>excellent</quality>
  </item>

  <item>
    <name>Crystal Candy Dish</name>
    <quantity>150</quantity>
    <quality>fine</quality>
  </item>
</shipperManifest>
```

Either the shipper or manufacturer may want to add additional information regarding the items in the manifest, such as why two of the vases are cracked or where the candy dishes were acquired:

```
<shipperManifest>
  <item>
    <name>Ceramic Vase</name>
    <quantity>400</quantity>
    <quality>excellent</quality>
    <comment>2 vases broken in transit</comment>
  </item>
```

```
  <item>
    <name>Crystal Candy Dish</name>
    <quantity>150</quantity>
    <quality>fine</quality>
    <comment>These dishes were acquired in Venice, Italy</comment>
  </item>
</shipperManifest>
```

The problem now is that the source of the comments is ambiguous; are they from the shipper who delivered this cargo, or the manufacturer of the items, or a retailer who bought and then resold the items? It is impossible to tell. Changing the element names can help this:

```
<shipperManifest>
  <item>
    <name>Ceramic Vase</name>
    <quantity>400</quantity>
    <quality>excellent</quality>
    <shipperComment>2 vases broken in transit</shipperComment>
  </item>

  <item>
    <name>Crystal Candy Dish</name>
    <quantity>150</quantity>
    <quality>fine</quality>
    <retailerComment>
      These dishes were acquired in Venice, Italy
    </retailerComment>
  </item>
</shipperManifest>
```

While this aids in clarity, now our schema starts to look a little strange:

```
<element name="retailerComment" type="string" />
<element name="shipperComment" type="string" />
<element name="manufacturerComment" type="string" />

<element name="shipperManifest">
  <complexType>
    <element name="item" maxOccurs="*">
      <complexType>
        <element name="name" type="string" />
        <element name="quantity" type="integer" />
        <element name="quality" type="string" />
        <element ref="retailerComment" minOccurs="0" />
        <element ref="shipperComment" minOccurs="0" />
        <element ref="manufacturerComment" minOccurs="0" />
      </complexType>
    </element>
  </complexType>
</element>
```

Here the three different comment elements are defined, and each one is allowed to appear zero or more times within the `item` element. While this is correct, it seems a bit silly to have to allow each of the three comment elements to appear, as they are all intrinsically the same data type; the comment is handled as pure textual data in each case. In Java, this could be accomplished by defining a `Comment` class and then extending that class to `RetailerComment`, `ShipperComment`, and `ManufacturerComment`. We could then allow one or more `Comment` types, or `comment` elements in XML-speak, to appear within the `item` element. Fortunately, the XML Schema working group thought of this as well, and added the `equivClass` keyword. This allows an element to be defined, and for other elements to declare themselves equivalent with that element. These equivalent elements are then able to be substituted for the base element, called an *exemplar*. Using this construct, we can simplify our schema:

```
<element name="comment" type="string" />
<element name="retailerComment" type="string" equivClass="comment" />
<element name="shipperComment" type="string" equivClass="comment" />
<element name="manufacturerComment" type="string" equivClass="comment" />

<element name="shipperManifest">
  <complexType>
    <element name="item" maxOccurs="*">
      <complexType>
        <element name="name" type="string" />
        <element name="quantity" type="integer" />
        <element name="quality" type="string" />
        <element ref="comment" minOccurs="0" />
      </complexType>
    </element>
  </complexType>
</element>
```

This new schema more accurately reflects the intent of the constraints, as well as offering a more Java-centric look at our XML elements and how they relate to each other. Any of the `comment`-based elements can appear within an item element, and the schema validation will handle determining the relationship and equivalence between the different element types for us. We can extend this functionality even further as we begin to apply these constructs to data used within Java applications, which we look at next.

Complementing Java with XML Schema

Consider a Java class as a set of constraints, and an instance of that class as data that adheres to those constraints. The data in this case is binary data; in other words, bytecode. The constraints define the variables that can be filled with data, the methods that can be implemented, and acceptable inputs and outputs. However, the actual values of the variables and method calls are unknown, and undetermined until runtime. Much as a content author populates an XML document with data that conforms to a schema, an application populates a Java instance with values for the specific task at hand. This concept can then be layered upon itself when you consider a Java interface as another set of constraints, this time on the class definition. The interface defines the actual method signatures, what inputs and outputs are acceptable, and what contract classes that implement the interface must follow. In this way, an interface constrains class definitions, which in turn constrain class instances.

While this chain of constraints makes for highly effective modeling and object-oriented design, the data that is used to set values within the class instance is not constrained except by type. As long as the variable is, for example, an `int`, any range is accepted. Implementing further constraints requires code within the class or method implementation. In addition, the return values of methods are similarly unconstrained. The application client then must enforce validation of its own if the return value of the invoked method must fall within a certain range. This makes for quite a bit of extra coding, and also can result in ambiguity to those using classes you may have written. The values you may be returning may not be in the range of values the client expects; if validation is not explicitly coded, serious and unexpected behavior can result from miscommunication.

The perfect solution and complement to Java in this case is XML Schema. By using XML Schema to constrain the data acceptable for member variables in a Java class instance, much tighter controls can be enforced that enable application clients to know exactly what ranges of data may be returned from method calls. XML Schema can also be used to define values acceptable for class instance use. For example, let's look back at some of the member variables used by our `XmlRpcConfigurationHandler` class:

```
private String uri;

private String hostname;
private int portNumber = 0;
private Hashtable handlers;
```

The problem here is that the hostname may need to be a limited number of characters in length; the port number should be a positive integer less than 64,000; and the handlers may have additional constraints. The XML-RPC clients are able to set these values with any appropriate type, forcing the handler to perform validation within code. However, along with the Java class definition, we could add the following schema (fragment), which defines the allowed data parameters:

```
<attribute name="hostname">
  <simpleType baseType="string">
```

```
      <minLength value="2" />
      <maxLength value="20" />
    </simpleType>
  </attribute>

  <attribute name="portNumber">
    <simpleType baseType="integer">
      <minExclusive value="0" />
      <maxExclusive value="64000" />
    </simpleType>
  </attribute>
```

Here, each member variable is treated as an attribute of the class itself. With this XML Schema as a counterpart to your Java code, validation can occur outside of the code with a standard mechanism, and can also allow the client to act more intelligently, understanding the allowed ranges and constraints on allowed data types.

While this integration at the Java Virtual Machine (JVM) level is still a long way from reality, the promise of integration is important enough to warrant thinking about how validation is currently occurring. If you can convert your data constraints from DTDs to schemas, you are ahead of the game if and when XML Schema is integrated more tightly with the Java language. Additionally, you may find ways to integrate XML Schema constraints into your application logic in the process of constraint conversion.

Pattern Matching

Extending our look at XML Schema in light of how it can constrain data and integrate with Java even further, we look at XML Schema's pattern matching capabilities. In the last section, we talked about using XML Schema to avoid complicated validation within Java code. This is only applicable, though, if XML Schema can do more than just determine simple numeric ranges and `String` lengths. For example, ensuring that a monetary value is entered with allowed formatting applied is more complicated than requiring a data type and length. Instead, pattern matching must occur, as a dollar value can be entered in a number of ways:

```
$4.50
$45.96
$54
$45.6
```

These types of scenarios must be handled for schemas to be useful for data validation. XML Schema provides the ability to perform pattern matching through the `pattern` attribute on an element or attribute. A money type could be represented with the following definition, which requires any of the above examples (as long as they start with a dollar sign):

```
<simpleType name="money" base="string">
  <pattern value="\$[0-9]+(\.[0-9]{1,2})?
</simpleType>
```

Here, the dollar sign is required (`$`). Then a sequence of digits can follow, occurring an unlimited number of times (`[0-9]+`). Then, as signified by the question mark around the entire parenthesized group, an optional cents qualifier can be given ($4.*50*). Again, digits can appear, but this time only singly or in a pair (`{1,2}`), and they must be preceded by a decimal (`.`).

While this is a simple example, as Perl and regular expression aficionados will let you know, it does show that XML Schema provides for pattern matching constraints. You should consult the XML Specification for more information about the supported regular expression constructs. Using these expressions can result in very complex validation occurring in your schema, which reduces the responsibility of your Java code to perform this validation in complicated code.

XML-RPC and Distributed Systems

A particularly important application of using data constraints to complement Java code is in the case of XML-RPC, which we have already looked at briefly. Currently, XML-RPC libraries have a predefined set of variable types that can be passed between server and client. These constraints on what can be transferred across the network allow the client to have only a general idea of the handlers on the server and still interact with them. However, there is no knowledge of the ranges of values accepted as input and returned as output; although this may seem a minor issue, a handler being able to set these constraints and allow the client to recognize them can save significant processing time in validation and greatly increase its usability.

With a schema defining the ranges and specifics of data input and output for XML-RPC handlers, a complete map of a handler's functionality is available to clients. This also applies for developers seeking to use another developer's classes. Not only is the input known, but specific details about useful input are available; exceptions thrown as a result of invalid data can be almost completely eliminated. This more complete mapping of XML-RPC handlers could easily be extended to other distributed systems; a prime candidate for this is EJB. In addition to the remote interface, imagine an XML Schema contract of the allowable data that is input and output from the methods in the remote interface. This additional information could greatly enhance the usability and reliability of distributed systems, particularly when the developers of the beans and handlers are not able to directly communicate with developers of application clients.

Databases and XML

Another revolution that could be brought on by additional data constraints and mappings is XML involvement in database use. First, it should be pointed out that we are not talking about pure XML databases here. Although complete XML database systems are being developed, they are very young technologies, and will most likely encounter a lot of resistance among traditionalists in management and application development. Additionally, there has yet to be a compelling reason for converting existing relational databases to this new format. What is worth taking a long look at, however, is using XML to map data from Java (or any other programming language) to a relational or object-oriented database.

Again, the key is that while mappings occur today, these mappings do not reflect the physical constraints that may exist on a database. Thus, complex validation and range checking has to occur in application code before database inserts and updates can occur, and even then rigorous error checking has to be performed to ensure that errors do not occur from database constraint violation. Let's look at a sample database table, shown in Figure 14-1, complete with some physical constraints.

Column	Type	Size	Can be Null
username	VARCHAR	12	no
firstName	VARCHAR	20	no
lastName	VARCHAR	30	no
salary	NUMBER	8,2	yes

Figure 14-1. Database table with physical constraints

The equivalent SQL for this table is shown as well:

```
CREATE TABLE users
 (
  username              VARCHAR(12) NOT NULL,
  firstName             VARCHAR(20) NOT NULL,
  lastName              VARCHAR(30) NOT NULL,
  salary                NUMBER(8,2)
 )
```

Now suppose that an EJB or JDBC application must insert and update this table. A tight coupling must exist between the code and the table, as checks must be made to ensure the lengths of fields do not exceed the storage capacity of the table, and that the salary column is set with a valid monetary value. Changes to the database can result in needing to make changes to database code; this is certainly neither a maintainable nor a robust design.

This is another case where XML Schema can complement Java code to form a more complete picture of data mappings. Consider a schema that defines the allowable values that can be inserted into the database table. In this example, a table is considered an element of a schema, and each field is considered an attribute of the table:

```
<schema>

  <element name="users">
    <complexType>
      <attribute name="username">
        <simpleType baseType="string">
          <minLength value="1" />
          <maxLength value="12" />
        </simpleType>
      </attribute>

      <attribute name="firstName">
        <simpleType baseType="string">
          <minLength value="1" />
          <maxLength value="20" />
        </simpleType>
      </attribute>

      <attribute name="lastName">
        <simpleType baseType="string">
          <minLength value="1" />
          <maxLength value="30" />
        </simpleType>
      </attribute>

      <attribute name="salary">
        <simpleType baseType="decimal">
          <precision value="8" />
          <scale value="2" />
        </simpleType>
      </attribute>
    </complexType>
  </element>

</schema>
```

With this schema in place, application code can be slimmed down and requires only a loose coupling to the underlying database. Changes to the physical database constraints only require changes to the schema, rather than changes to the compiled code. Extend this concept to a database with included or third party tools that can generate this schema from existing tables, and a complete data mapping is possible without ever modifying Java code.

These are just a few of the possibilities that a close marriage between XML Schema and Java code suggest. Only time will tell how far the envelope will be pushed; in the future, XML Schema almost certainly will hold as important a place in Java programming as XML itself promises to. Beginning to use XML Schema now for validation and data constraints will prepare you for this future, and may in fact allow you be involved in creating it.

What's Next?

Appendixes. The index. And then some information about me (the author), and a colophon. And then probably some advertising for the other great O'Reilly books.

Seriously, though, we've covered quite a bit of information at this point. Taking a few days to let the material sink in, and then trying to apply your new XML skills on a project for work, or maybe something personal, should help you polish your XML knowledge. Soon you'll be an XML wizard, and find your applications' value increasing as they are more flexible, configurable, and productive. Finally, you'll see your value to your boss (and lots of potential bosses at other companies!) dramatically rise as you code maintainable and performance-driven applications. Have fun, and stay extensible.

API Reference

This appendix is a quick reference to the major Java and XML APIs, SAX and DOM. It also includes a complete API reference for JDOM, covered in Chapter 8, *JDOM*, and the rest of the book. It is broken down into sections based on the API being documented.

SAX 2.0

SAX 2.0 provides a sequential look into an XML document. Detailed in Chapter 3, *Parsing XML*, and Chapter 5, *Validating XML*, SAX defines a set of interfaces that can be implemented and will be invoked as callbacks during the XML parsing process. The SAX packages are detailed here, with the classes and interfaces listed alphabetically. In the `org.xml.sax.helpers` package, a large percentage of the available methods in the helper classes are implementations of interfaces already defined in the core SAX package (`org.xml.sax`). For the sake of brevity, these duplicate method definitions will be omitted in the helper classes, and instead a comment will be included noting that an interface's methods are implemented.

Package: org.xml.sax

This package contains the core interfaces and classes for SAX 2.0. Most of the interfaces defined are intended to be implemented by you, the Java developer, with the exception of the actual `XMLReader` and `Attributes` implementation. These interfaces should be implemented by your vendor's XML parsing software. In addition, several exceptions that SAX methods are allowed to throw are defined. Several of the interfaces defined here are part of the SAX 1.0 and 2.0 alpha distributions, and are now deprecated.

AttributeList

This interface was defined in SAX 1.0, and is now deprecated. The `Attributes` interface should be used instead of `AttributeList` for SAX 2.0 implementations.

```
public interface AttributeList {
    public abstract int getLength ();
    public abstract String getName (int i);
    public abstract String getType (int i);
    public abstract String getValue (int i);
    public abstract String getType (String name);
    public abstract String getValue (String name);
}
```

Attributes

This interface represents a listing of XML attributes. It is reported to the callbacks associated with the start of element (`startElement()` in `ContentHandler`), and is somewhat analogous to a Java `Vector`. The number of attributes represented can be obtained, as well as various views of the attributes' names (local, namespace prefix and URI, and raw) and values. Additionally, methods are available for locating the index of an attribute given its name. The primary difference between this interface and its predecessor, `AttributeList`, is that this interface is namespace-aware.

```
public interface Attributes {
    public abstract int getLength ();
    public abstract String getURI (int index);
    public abstract String getLocalName (int index);
    public abstract String getQName (int index);
    public abstract String getType (int index);
    public abstract String getValue (int index);
    public int getIndex (String uri, String localPart);
    public int getIndex (String qName);
    public abstract String getType (String uri, String localName);
    public abstract String getType (String qName);
    public abstract String getValue (String uri, String localName);
    public abstract String getValue (String qName);
}
```

ContentHandler

This interface defines the callback methods available to an application that deal with the content of the XML document being parsed. These include notification of the start and end of parsing (which precede and follow all other handler callbacks, respectively), processing instructions, and entities that may be skipped by non-validating parsers. Element callbacks, complete with namespace mappings, are also made available. Complete coverage of this interface is included in Chapter 3.

```
public interface ContentHandler {
    public void setDocumentLocator (Locator locator);
    public void startDocument ()throws SAXException;
    public void endDocument() throws SAXException;
    public void startPrefixMapping (String prefix, String uri)
        throws SAXException;
    public void endPrefixMapping (String prefix)
        throws SAXException;
    public void startElement (String namespaceURI, String localName,
                    String qName, Attributes atts)
        throws SAXException;
    public void endElement (String namespaceURI, String localName,
                    String qName)
        throws SAXException;
    public void characters (char ch[], int start, int length)
        throws SAXException;
    public void ignorableWhitespace (char ch[], int start, int length)
        throws SAXException;
    public void processingInstruction (String target, String data)
        throws SAXException;
    public void skippedEntity (String name)
        throws SAXException;
}
```

DocumentHandler

This interface was defined in SAX 1.0, and is now deprecated. The ContentHandler interface should be used instead of DocumentHandler for SAX 2.0 implementations.

```
public interface DocumentHandler {
    public abstract void setDocumentLocator (Locator locator);
    public abstract void startDocument () throws SAXException;
    public abstract void endDocument () throws SAXException;
    public abstract void startElement (String name, AttributeList atts)
        throws SAXException;
    public abstract void endElement (String name)
        throws SAXException;
    public abstract void characters (char ch[], int start, int length)
        throws SAXException;
    public abstract void ignorableWhitespace (char ch[], int start,
                                                   int length)
        throws SAXException;
    public abstract void processingInstruction (String target,
                                                String data)
        throws SAXException;
}
```

DTDHandler

This interface defines callbacks that are invoked in the process of parsing a DTD. Note that this interface does not provide information about the constraints within the DTD, but instead about references to unparsed entities and NOTATION declarations, indicating items that are generally unparsed data. Complete coverage of this interface is included in Chapter 5.

```
public interface DTDHandler {
    public abstract void notationDecl (String name, String publicId,
                                       String systemId)
        throws SAXException;
    public abstract void unparsedEntityDecl (String name, String publicId,
                                             String systemId,
                                             String notationName)
        throws SAXException;
}
```

EntityResolver

This interface allows applications to intervene in the process of referencing external entities, such as an XML document that references a DTD or stylesheet. By implementing this interface, a modified or even completely different SAX InputSource can be returned to the calling program. Additionally, null can be returned to indicate that a normal URI connection should be opened to the specified system ID.

```
public interface EntityResolver {
    public abstract InputSource resolveEntity (String publicId,
                                               String systemId)
        throws SAXException, IOException;
}
```

ErrorHandler

This interface allows custom behavior to be attached to the three types of problem conditions that can occur within the lifecycle of XML parsing. Each receives the SAXParseException indicating what problem initiated the callback. The SAXException is provided to allow a means of throwing an exception that could stop parsing altogether. Complete coverage of this interface is included in Chapters 3 and 5.

```
public interface ErrorHandler {
    public abstract void warning (SAXParseException exception)
        throws SAXException;
    public abstract void error (SAXParseException exception)
        throws SAXException;
    public abstract void fatalError (SAXParseException exception)
```

```
        throws SAXException;
}
```

HandlerBase

This helper class provides empty implementations of all the SAX 1.0 core handler interfaces, and can be extended to allow the quick addition of handlers by overriding methods with application-defined behavior. This class was defined in SAX 1.0, and is now deprecated. The `org.xml.sax.helpers.DefaultHandler` class should be used instead of `HandlerBase` for SAX 2.0 implementations.

```
public class HandlerBase implements EntityResolver, DTDHandler,
                                    DocumentHandler, ErrorHandler {

    // EntityResolver implementation
    public InputSource resolveEntity (String publicId, String systemId);

    // DTDHandler implementation
    public void notationDecl (String name, String publicId,
                              String systemId);
    public void unparsedEntityDecl (String name, String publicId,
                            String systemId, String notationName);

    // DocumentHandler implementation
    public void setDocumentLocator (Locator locator);
    public abstract void startDocument () throws SAXException;
    public abstract void endDocument () throws SAXException;
    public abstract void startElement (String name, AttributeList atts)
        throws SAXException;
    public abstract void endElement (String name)
        throws SAXException;
    public abstract void characters (char ch[], int start, int length)
        throws SAXException;
    public abstract void ignorableWhitespace (char ch[], int start,
                                              int length)
        throws SAXException;
    public abstract void processingInstruction (String target,
                                                String data)
        throws SAXException;

    // ErrorHandler implementation
    public abstract void warning (SAXParseException exception)
        throws SAXException;
    public abstract void error (SAXParseException exception)
        throws SAXException;
    public abstract void fatalError (SAXParseException exception)
        throws SAXException;
}
```

InputSource

This class encapsulates all information about a resource used in XML processing. This can be as little as a `String` or `InputStream` used for locating input, or as complex as an entity with a public ID and system ID as well as a URI reference (such as a DTD publicly defined). This class is the preferred wrapper for passing input into a SAX parser.

```
public class InputSource {
    public InputSource ();
    public InputSource (String systemId);
    public InputSource (InputStream byteStream);
    public InputSource (Reader characterStream);
    public void setPublicId (String publicId);
    public String getPublicId ();
    public void setSystemId (String systemId);
    public String getSystemId ();
    public void setByteStream (InputStream byteStream);
    public InputStream getByteStream ();
    public void setEncoding (String encoding);
    public String getEncoding ();
    public void setCharacterStream (Reader characterStream);
    public Reader getCharacterStream ();
}
```

Locator

This class is a complement to an XML document or other parsed construct, as it provides the document's system ID and public ID as well as information about the location within the file being processed. This is particularly helpful for use in IDE applications and for identifying where errors occur in parsing. Complete coverage of this interface is included in Chapter 3.

```
public interface Locator {
    public abstract String getPublicId ();
    public abstract String getSystemId ();
    public abstract int getLineNumber ();
    public abstract int getColumnNumber ();
}
```

Parser

This interface was defined in SAX 1.0, and is now deprecated. The `XMLReader` interface should be used instead of this one for SAX 2.0 implementations.

```
public interface Parser {
    public abstract void setLocale (Locale locale) throws SAXException;
    public abstract void setEntityResolver (EntityResolver resolver);
    public abstract void setDTDHandler (DTDHandler handler);
```

```
    public abstract void setDocumentHandler (DocumentHandler handler);
    public abstract void setErrorHandler (ErrorHandler handler);
    public abstract void parse (InputSource source)
        throws SAXException, IOException;
    public abstract void parse (String systemId)
        throws SAXException, IOException;
}
```

SAXException

This is the core exception thrown by SAX callbacks and parser implementations. Because it is often thrown as a result of other exceptions, it has a constructor that allows the passing in of a lower-level `Exception` as well as an accessor method to retrieve the originating `Exception`. It is also the base class for all other SAX `Exception` classes.

```
public class SAXException extends Exception {
    public SAXException (String message);
    public SAXException (Exception e);
    public SAXException (String message, Exception e);
    public String getMessage ();
    public Exception getException ();
    public String toString ();
}
```

SAXNotRecognizedException

This class provides a means for an `XMLReader` implementation to throw an error when an unrecognized identifier is received. This is most common in the `setProperty()` and `setFeature()` methods (as well as their accessor counterparts) when a URI is supplied about which the parser has no information.

```
public class SAXNotRecognizedException extends SAXException {
    public SAXNotRecognizedException (String message);
}
```

SAXNotSupportedException

This class provides a means for an `XMLReader` implementation to throw an error when an unsupported (but recognized) identifier is received. This is most common in the `setProperty()` and `setFeature()` methods (as well as their accessor counterparts) when a URI is supplied for which the parser has no supporting code.

```
public class SAXNotSupportedException extends SAXException {
    public SAXNotSupportedException (String message)
}
```

SAXParseException

This class represents exceptions that can occur during the parsing process. Information about the location of the error within the XML document is available through this class's accessor methods. The preferred means of supplying this information to the class is through a `Locator`, but the line and column number where problems occurred can be supplied directly through overloaded constructors. The system and public ID of the document with the problem are also made available to the class through various means in the constructors.

```
public class SAXParseException extends SAXException {
    public SAXParseException (String message, Locator locator);
    public SAXParseException (String message, Locator locator,
                    Exception e);
    public SAXParseException (String message, String publicId,
                   String systemId, int lineNumber,
                   int columnNumber);
    public SAXParseException (String message, String publicId,
                         String systemId, int lineNumber,
                         int columnNumber, Exception e);
    public String getPublicId ();
    public String getSystemId ();
    public int getColumnNumber ();
}
```

XMLFilter

This class is analogous to an `XMLReader`, but it obtains its events from another `XMLReader` rather than a static document or network resource. These filters can also be chained on each other. Their primary use is in modifying the output from a lower-level `XMLReader` in the chain, providing filtering of the data reported to callback methods before the final application receives notification of the data.

```
public interface XMLFilter extends XMLReader {
    public abstract void setParent (XMLReader parent);
    public abstract XMLReader getParent ();
}
```

XMLReader

This is the core interface that defines parsing behavior in SAX 2.0. Each vendor's XML parsing software package must include at least one implementation of this interface. It replaces the SAX 1.0 `Parser` interface by adding support for namespaces in a document's elements and attributes. In addition to providing an entry into parsing (with either a system ID or `InputSource` as input), it allows registering of the various handler interfaces that SAX 2.0 provides. The features and properties available to a SAX parser implementation are also set through this interface. Complete coverage of this interface is included in Chapter 3, and a complete list of SAX core features and properties is contained in Appendix B, *SAX 2.0 Features and Properties.*

```
public interface XMLReader {
    public boolean getFeature (String name)
        throws SAXNotRecognizedException, SAXNotSupportedException;
    public void setFeature (String name, boolean value)
        throws SAXNotRecognizedException, SAXNotSupportedException;
    public Object getProperty (String name)
        throws SAXNotRecognizedException, SAXNotSupportedException;
    public void setProperty (String name, Object value)
        throws SAXNotRecognizedException, SAXNotSupportedException;
    public void setEntityResolver (EntityResolver resolver);
    public EntityResolver getEntityResolver ();
    public void setDTDHandler (DTDHandler handler);
    public DTDHandler getDTDHandler ();
    public void setContentHandler (ContentHandler handler);
    public ContentHandler getContentHandler ();
    public void setErrorHandler (ErrorHandler handler);
    public ErrorHandler getErrorHandler ();
    public void parse (InputSource input)
        throws IOException, SAXException;
    public void parse (String systemId)
        throws IOException, SAXException;
}
```

Package: org.xml.sax.ext

This package provides extensions to the SAX core classes and interfaces. Specifically, additional handlers are defined for less common processing within the SAX parsing process. `XMLReader` implementations are not required to support these extension handlers.

DeclHandler

This interface defines callbacks that give specific information about DTD declarations. Element and attribute definitions invoke the appropriate callback with their names (and the element names for attributes) as well as constraint information. While this is a fairly rigid set of data for attributes, elements only receive a `String` with the constrained model as pure text. Additionally, internal and external entity reference notifications are defined.

```
public interface DeclHandler {
    public abstract void elementDecl (String name, String model)
        throws SAXException;
    public abstract void attributeDecl (String eName, String aName,
                                        String type, String valueDefault,
```

```
                                                String value)
        throws SAXException;
    public abstract void internalEntityDecl (String name, String value)
        throws SAXException;
    public abstract void externalEntityDecl (String name, String publicId,
                                             String systemId)
        throws SAXException;
}
```

LexicalHandler

This interface defines callbacks for various events that are at a document level in terms of processing, but do not affect the resulting data within the XML document. For example, the handling of a DTD declaration, comments, and entity references would invoke callbacks in implementations of this interface. Additionally, a callback is defined to signal when a CDATA section is started and ended (although the reported data will always remain the same).

```
public interface LexicalHandler {
    public abstract void startDTD (String name, String publicId,
                          String systemId)
        throws SAXException;
    public abstract void endDTD ()
        throws SAXException;
    public abstract void startEntity (String name)
        throws SAXException;
    public abstract void endEntity (String name)
        throws SAXException;
    public abstract void startCDATA ()
        throws SAXException;
    public abstract void endCDATA ()
        throws SAXException;
    public abstract void comment (char ch[], int start, int length)
        throws SAXException;
}
```

Package: org.xml.sax.helpers

This package provides extensions to the SAX core classes and interfaces. Specifically, additional handlers are defined for less common processing within the SAX parsing process. `XMLReader` implementations are not required to support these extension handlers.

AttributeListImpl

This class provides a default implementation of the `org.xml.sax.AttributeList` interface, and is deprecated in SAX 2.0. It allows addition and removal of attributes as well as a clearing of the list.

```
public class AttributeListImpl implements AttributeList {
    public AttributeListImpl ();
    public AttributeListImpl (AttributeList atts);

    // Implementation of AttributeList interface

    // Additional methods
    public void setAttributeList (AttributeList atts);
    public void addAttribute (String name, String type, String value);
    public void removeAttribute (String name);
    public void clear ();

}
```

AttributesImpl

This class provides a default implementation of the `org.xml.sax.Attributes` interface. It allows addition and removal of attributes as well as a clearing of the list.

```
public class AttributesImpl implements Attributes {
    public AttributesImpl ();
    public AttributesImpl (Attributes atts);

    // Implementation of Attributes interface

    // Additional methods
    public void addAttribute (String uri, String localName,
                              String rawName, String type, String value);
    public void setAttribute (int index, String uri, String localName,
                  String rawName, String type, String value);
    public void clear ();
}
```

DefaultHandler

This helper class provides empty implementations of all the SAX 2.0 core handler interfaces, and can be extended to allow for quick addition of handlers by only overriding methods with application-defined behavior. This replaces the SAX 1.0 `org.xml.sax.HandlerBase` class.

```
public class DefaultHandler implements EntityResolver, DTDHandler,
                                       ContentHandler, ErrorHandler {
```

```
    // (Empty) Implementation of EntityResolver interface

    // (Empty) Implementation of DTDHandler interface

    // (Empty) Implementation of ContentHandler interface

    // (Empty) Implementation of ErrorHandler interface
}
```

LocatorImpl

This class provides a default implementation of the `org.xml.sax.Locator` interface. It also provides a means of directly setting the line and column numbers.

```
public class LocatorImpl implements Locator {
    public LocatorImpl ();
    public LocatorImpl (Locator locator);

    // Implementation of Locator interface

    // Additional methods
    public void setPublicId (String publicId);
    public void setSystemId (String systemId);
    public void setLineNumber (int lineNumber);
    public void setColumnNumber (int columnNumber);
}
```

NamespaceSupport

This encapsulates namespace behavior, allowing applications to not have to implement the behavior on their own (unless desired for performance reasons). It allows handling of namespace contexts in a stack fashion, and also provides the ability to process XML 1.0 names, retrieving their "namespace-aware" counterparts.

```
public class NamespaceSupport {
    public NamespaceSuport ();
    public void reset ();
    public void pushContext ();
    public void popContext ();
    public boolean declarePrefix (String prefix, String uri);
    public String [] processName (String rawName, String parts[],
                                  boolean isAttribute);
    public String getURI (String prefix);
    public Enumeration getPrefixes ();
    public Enumeration getDeclaredPrefixes ();
}
```

ParserAdapter

This helper class wraps a SAX 1.0 `Parser` implementation and makes it behave like a 2.0 `XMLReader` implementation (making namespace support available). The only callback that will not behave normally is `skippedEntity()` in the `ContentHandler` interface; it will never be invoked.

```
public class ParserAdapter implements XMLReader, DocumentHandler {
    public ParserAdapter () throws SAXException;
    public ParserAdapter (Parser parser);

    // Implementation of XMLReader interface

    // Implementation of DocumentHandler interface
}
```

ParserFactory

This class contains methods that dynamically create an instance of a `Parser` implementation from a specified class name, or if none is supplied, from a system property named "org.xml.sax.driver".

```
public class ParserFactory {
    public static Parser makeParser () throws ClassNotFoundException,
                IllegalAccessException, InstantiationException,
                NullPointerException, ClassCastException;
    public static Parser makeParser (String className)
                throws ClassNotFoundException, IllegalAccessException,
                InstantiationException, ClassCastException;
}
```

XMLFilterImpl

This class provides a default implementation of the `org.xml.sax.XMLFilter` interface.

```
public class XMLFilterImpl implements XMLFilter, EntityResolver,
                                      DTDHandler, ContentHandler,
                                      ErrorHandler {
    public XMLFilterImpl ();
    public XMLFilterImpl (XMLReader parent);

    // Implementation of XMLFilter interface

    // Implementation of XMLReader interface

    // Implementation of EntityResolver interface
    // Implementation of DTDHandler interface
```

```
        // Implementation of ContentHandler interface

        // Implementation of ErrorHandler interface
    }
```

XMLReaderAdapter

This helper class wraps a SAX 2.0 `XMLReader` implementation and makes it behave like a 1.0 `Parser` implementation (making namespace support unavailable). The namespaces feature (*http://xml.org/sax/features/namespaces*) must be supported or errors in parsing will occur.

```
public class XMLReaderAdapter implements Parser, ContentHandler {
    public XMLReaderAdapter () throws SAXException;
    public XMLReaderAdapter (XMLReader xmlReader);

// Implementation of Parser interface

    // Implementation of ContentHandler interface
}
```

XMLReaderFactory

This class contains methods that dynamically create an instance of an `XMLReader` implementation from a specified class name, or if none is supplied, from a system property named "org.xml.sax.driver".

```
final public class XMLReaderFactory {
    public static XMLReader createXMLReader () throws SAXException;
    public static XMLReader createXMLReader (String className)
        throws SAXException;
}
```

DOM Level 2

DOM provides a complete, in-memory representation of an XML document. Developed by the W3C, DOM provides detail about the structure of a document *after* it has been completely parsed. While DOM Level 3 is rumored to specify an API for getting the DOM `Document` object, there is currently nothing in DOM that defines this behavior. Like SAX, most of the core DOM package is made up of interfaces that define structures within an XML document, and map those structures to the Java language (these same mappings apply to CORBA, JavaScript, and other languages, as well).

Package: org.w3c.dom

This package contains the core interfaces and classes for DOM Level 2. Typically a vendor's parsing software provides an implementation of those interfaces that are implicitly used by your application software.

Attr

This interface represents an XML attribute (on an element) within Java. It provides access to the name and value of the attribute, and allows the setting of the value (for mutability).* The `getSpecified()` method indicates if the attribute (and its value) was explicitly noted in the XML document, or if a value was not specified but the document's DTD assigned a default value to the attribute. Finally, the "owning" element can be obtained from this interface.

```
public interface Attr extends Node {
    public String getName();
    public boolean getSpecified();
    public String getValue();
    public void setValue(String value) throws DOMException;
    public Element getOwnerElement();
}
```

CDATASection

This interface does not define any methods of its own; instead it inherits all of the `Text` interface's methods. However, by having its own interface (and thus its own node type), a distinction can be drawn between text within XML `CDATA` sections and simple text (not in a `CDATA` section) within an element.

```
public interface CDATASection extends Text {
}
```

CharacterData

This interface is the "super" interface for all textual `Node` types in DOM (`Text`, `Comment`, and indirectly `CDATASection`). It defines methods for accessing and setting the data within a textual node, as well as a set of methods for dealing with the textual data directly as characters; obtaining the length, appending, inserting, and deleting data, and replacing all or part of the data. All of these methods throw `DOMExceptions` when the node is read-only.

```
public interface CharacterData extends Node {
    public String getData() throws DOMException;
```

* In this and other `setXXX()` methods in DOM, a `DOMException` results when a modification is attempted on a node that is read-only.

```
    public void setData(String data) throws DOMException;
    public int getLength();
    public String substringData(int offset, int count)
        throws DOMException;
    public void appendData(String arg) throws DOMException;
    public void insertData(int offset, String arg) throws DOMException;
    public void deleteData(int offset, int count) throws DOMException;
    public void replaceData(int offset, int count, String arg)
        throws DOMException;
}
```

Comment

This interface provides a Java representation for an XML comment. Similar to `CDATASection`, it adds no methods of its own but does allow a distinction (based on the type of the interface) to distinguish between text and comments in an XML document.

```
public interface Comment extends CharacterData {
}
```

Document

This interface is the DOM representation of a complete XML document. It is also the key for creating new XML elements, attributes, PIs, and other constructs. In addition to allowing retrieval of the DTD declaration (`getDocType()`) and root element (`getDocumentElement()`), this allows searching through the tree in a pre-order fashion for a specific element (`getElementsByTagName()`). Because the DOM model requires that all `Node` implementations be tied to a DOM `Document` object, this provides methods for creating the various types of DOM `Node`s. Each `createXXX()` method has a complement that supports namespaces through `createXXXNS()`. Additionally, `Node`s can be imported into this `Document` through `importNode()`; the `boolean` value indicates if the children of the imported `Node` should be recursively imported as well.

```
public interface Document extends Node {
    public DocumentType getDoctype();
    public DOMImplementation getImplementation();
    public Element getDocumentElement();
    public Element createElement(String tagName) throws DOMException;
    public DocumentFragment createDocumentFragment();
    public Text createTextNode(String data);
    public Comment createComment(String data);
    public CDATASection createCDATASection(String data)
        throws DOMException;
    public ProcessingInstruction
        createProcessingInstruction(String target, String data)
        throws DOMException;
```

```
    public Attr createAttribute(String name) throws DOMException;
    public EntityReference createEntityReference(String name)
        throws DOMException;
    public NodeList getElementsByTagName(String tagname);
    public Node importNode(Node importedNode, boolean deep)
        throws DOMException;
    public Element createElementNS(String namespaceURI,
                                   String qualifiedName)
        throws DOMException;
    public Attr createAttributeNS(String namespaceURI,
                                  String qualifiedName)
        throws DOMException;
    public NodeList getElementsByTagNameNS(String namespaceURI,
                                           String localName);
    public Element getElementById(String elementId);
}
```

DocumentFragment

This interface provides for dealing with only a portion of a complete `Document` object at one time. It is useful for manipulating portions of a DOM tree without having to store the entire tree in memory.

```
public interface DocumentFragment extends Node {
}
```

DocumentType

This interface represents an XML document's `DOCTYPE` declaration. The name is the element name immediately following `<!DOCTYPE`, and the system ID and public ID of any referenced DTD are available as well. Additionally, if any inline entities or notations are present, they can be obtained through the appropriate `getXXX()` methods.

```
public interface DocumentType extends Node {
    public String getName();
    public NamedNodeMap getEntities();
    public NamedNodeMap getNotations();
    public String getPublicId();
    public String getSystemId();
    public String getInternalSubset();
}
```

DOMException

This class provides an `Exception` for DOM interfaces to throw when problems occur. It also provides a set of error codes that represent the various problems that occur using DOM and might result in the `Exception` being thrown.

```
public class DOMException extends RuntimeException {
    public DOMException(short code, String message);

    // Exception codes
    public static final short INDEX_SIZE_ERR;
    public static final short DOMSTRING_SIZE_ERR;
    public static final short HIERARCHY_REQUEST_ERR;
    public static final short WRONG_DOCUMENT_ERR;
    public static final short INVALID_CHARACTER_ERR;
    public static final short NO_DATA_ALLOWED_ERR;
    public static final short NO_MODIFICATION_ALLOWED_ERR;
    public static final short NOT_FOUND_ERR;
    public static final short NOT_SUPPORTED_ERR;
    public static final short INUSE_ATTRIBUTE_ERR;
    public static final short INVALID_STATE_ERR;
    public static final short SYNTAX_ERR;
    public static final short INVALID_MODIFICATION_ERR;
    public static final short NAMESPACE_ERR;
    public static final short INVALID_ACCESS_ERR;
}
```

DOMImplementation

This interface attempts to provide a standard entry point for accessing vendor-specific DOM implementations, and allowing the creation of a `DocumentType` and `Document` within those vendor implementations.* It also provides a method (`hasFeature()`) for querying the implementation for a specific feature support.

```
public interface DOMImplementation {
    public boolean hasFeature(String feature, String version);
    public DocumentType createDocumentType(String qualifiedName,
                                           String publicId,
                                           String systemId)
        throws DOMException;
    public Document createDocument(String namespaceURI,
                                   String qualifiedName,
                                   DocumentType doctype)
        throws DOMException;
}
```

Element

This interface provides a Java representation of an XML element. It provides methods to get its name and attributes, as well as to set these values. It also

* Unfortunately, to obtain an instance of a `DOMImplementation`, you must have a `Document` object and use `getDOMImplementation()`, or directly load the vendor's classes. This tends to result in a chicken-and-egg scenario; see JDOM (in Chapter 8, and later in this appendix) for alternatives to this approach to creating XML documents.

provides several flavors of access to the XML attributes, including namespace-aware versions of the `getXXX()` and `setXXX()` methods.

```
public interface Element extends Node {
    public String getTagName();
    public String getAttribute(String name);
    public void setAttribute(String name, String value)
        throws DOMException;
    public void removeAttribute(String name) throws DOMException;
    public Attr getAttributeNode(String name);
    public Attr setAttributeNode(Attr newAttr) throws DOMException;
    public Attr removeAttributeNode(Attr oldAttr) throws DOMException;
    public NodeList getElementsByTagName(String name);
    public String getAttributeNS(String namespaceURI, String localName);
    public void setAttributeNS(String namespaceURI, String qualifiedName,
                               String value)
        throws DOMException;
    public void removeAttributeNS(String namespaceURI, String localName)
                                  throws DOMException;
    public Attr getAttributeNodeNS(String namespaceURI, String localName);
    public Attr setAttributeNodeNS(Attr newAttr) throws DOMException;
    public NodeList getElementsByTagNameNS(String namespaceURI,
                                           String localName);
}
```

Entity

This provides a Java representation of an entity (parsed or unparsed) in an XML document. Access to the system ID and public ID as well as the notation for the entity (from the DTD) is provided through accessor methods.

```
public interface Entity extends Node {
    public String getPublicId();
    public String getSystemId();
    public String getNotationName();
}
```

EntityReference

This interface represents the resulting value from an entity reference, once the entity has been resolved. This interface assumes that character and predefined entity references have already occurred when this interface is exposed to the application client.

```
public interface EntityReference extends Node {
}
```

NamedNodeMap

This interface defines a list, much like `NodeList`, but requires that each `Node` in the list be a named `Node` (such as an `Element` or `Attr`). Because of this requirement, methods can be provided to access members of the list by their name (with or without namespace support). The list also provides for removal and modification of its members. These methods all throw `DOMExceptions` when the referenced `Node` is read-only.

```
public interface NamedNodeMap {
    public Node getNamedItem(String name);
    public Node setNamedItem(Node arg) throws DOMException;
    public Node removeNamedItem(String name) throws DOMException;
    public Node item(int index);
    public int getLength();
    public Node getNamedItemNS(String namespaceURI, String localName);
    public Node setNamedItemNS(Node arg) throws DOMException;
    public Node removeNamedItemNS(String namespaceURI, String localName)
        throws DOMException;
}
```

Node

This is the central interface for all DOM objects. It provides a robust set of methods for accessing information about a `Node` in the DOM tree. It also allows for handling of a `Node`'s children (if they exist). While most of the methods are self-explanatory, there are several methods worth noting: `getAttributes()` only returns non-`null` data if the `Node` is an `Element`; `cloneNode()` provides for a shallow or deep copy of a `Node`; `normalize()` moves all text into non-adjacent `Text` nodes (no two `Text` nodes are adjacent, and all resolved textual entity references are consolidated into `Text` nodes); and `supports()` provides information about the feature set of the `Node`. Namespace-aware methods are also provided (`getNamespaceURI()`, `getPrefix()`, and `getLocalName()`). Finally, a set of constants is provided for identifying the type of a `Node` by comparing the constants against the result of `getNodeType()`.

```
public interface Node {
    public String getNodeName();
    public String getNodeValue() throws DOMException;
    public void setNodeValue(String nodeValue) throws DOMException;
    public short getNodeType();
    public Node getParentNode();
    public NodeList getChildNodes();
    public Node getFirstChild();
    public Node getLastChild();
    public Node getPreviousSibling();
    public Node getNextSibling();
```

```
    public NamedNodeMap getAttributes();
    public Document getOwnerDocument();
    public Node insertBefore(Node newChild,  Node refChild)
        throws DOMException;
    public Node replaceChild(Node newChild, Node oldChild)
                             throws DOMException;
    public Node removeChild(Node oldChild) throws DOMException;
    public Node appendChild(Node newChild) throws DOMException;
    public boolean hasChildNodes();
    public Node cloneNode(boolean deep);
    public void normalize();
    public boolean supports(String feature, String version);
    public String getNamespaceURI();
    public String getPrefix();
    public void setPrefix(String prefix) throws DOMException;
    public String getLocalName();

    // Node Type Constants
    public static final short ELEMENT_NODE;
    public static final short ATTRIBUTE_NODE;
    public static final short TEXT_NODE;
    public static final short CDATA_SECTION_NODE;
    public static final short ENTITY_REFERENCE_NODE;
    public static final short ENTITY_NODE;
    public static final short PROCESSING_INSTRUCTION_NODE;
    public static final short COMMENT_NODE;
    public static final short DOCUMENT_NODE;
    public static final short DOCUMENT_TYPE_NODE;
    public static final short DOCUMENT_FRAGMENT_NODE;
    public static final short NOTATION_NODE;
}
```

NodeList

This interface is a DOM structure analogous to a Java `Vector` or `List`. It is the return value of any method that supports multiple `Node` implementations as a result. This allows iteration through the items as well as providing the ability to get a `Node` at a specific index.

```
public interface NodeList {
    public Node item(int index);
    public int getLength();
}
```

Notation

This interface represents a `NOTATION` construct in a DTD, used to declare the format of an unparsed entity or for declaration of PIs. This provides access to both the system ID and public ID within the declaration. Both return `null` if they are not present.

```
public interface Notation extends Node {
    public String getPublicId();
    public String getSystemId();
}
```

ProcessingInstruction

This interface represents an XML processing instruction (PI). It provides methods for getting the target and the data of the PI. Note that there is no means of accessing the name/value pairs within the PI individually. The data can also be set for the PI.

```
public interface ProcessingInstruction extends Node {
    public String getTarget();
    public String getData();
    public void setData(String data) throws DOMException;
}
```

Text

This interface provides a Java representation of an XML element's textual data. The only method it adds to those defined in `CharacterData` is one that will split the node into two nodes. The original `Text` node will contain text up to the specified offset, and the method returns a new `Text` node with the text after the offset. Like other mutability methods, a `DOMException` is thrown when the node is read-only.

```
public interface Text extends CharacterData {
    public Text splitText(int offset) throws DOMException;
}
```

JAXP 1.0

JAXP provides an abstraction layer over the process of getting a vendor's implementation of a SAX or DOM parser. Currently, JAXP supports SAX 1.0 and DOM Level 1 parser implementations only.

Package: javax.xml.parsers

This is the single package used in JAXP, and details the classes needed for the JAXP abstraction and pluggability layer.

DocumentBuilder

This class is the wrapper over an underlying parser implementation class. It allows parsing to occur in a vendor-neutral way.

```
public abstract class DocumentBuilder {
    public Document parse(InputStream stream)
        throws SAXException, IOException, IllegalArgumentException;
    public Document parse(String uri)
        throws SAXException, IOException, IllegalArgumentException;
    public Document parse(File file)
        throws SAXException, IOException, IllegalArgumentException;
    public abstract Document parse(InputSource source)
        throws SAXException, IOException, IllegalArgumentException;
    public abstract Document newDocument();
    public abstract boolean isNamespaceAware();
    public abstract boolean isValidating();
    public abstract void setEntityResolver(EntityResolver er);
    public abstract void setErrorHandler(ErrorHandler eh);
}
```

DocumentBuilderFactory

This class is the factory used to create instances of the `DocumentBuilder` class, and allows namespace and validation features to be set for the production of those instances.

```
public abstract class DocumentBuilderFactory {
    protected DocumentBuilderFactory();
    public static DocumentBuilderFactory newInstance();
    public abstract DocumentBuilder newDocumentBuilder()
        throws ParserConfigurationException;
    public void setNamespaceAware(boolean aware);
    public void setValidating(boolean validating);
    public boolean isNamespaceAware();
    public boolean isValidating();
}
```

FactoryConfigurationException

This defines an `Error` that is thrown if a factory instance cannot be created.

```
public class FactoryConfigurationException extends Error {
    public FactoryConfigurationError();
    public FactoryConfigurationError(String msg);
    public FactoryConfigurationError(Exception e);
    public FactoryConfigurationError(Exception e, String msg);
    public Exception getException();
}
```

ParserConfigurationException

This defines an `Exception` that is thrown if a parser is requested but cannot be constructed with the specified validation and namespace-awareness settings.

```
public class ParserConfigurationException extends Exception {
    public ParserConfigurationException();
    public ParserConfigurationException(String msg);
}
```

SAXParser

This class is the wrapper over an underlying SAX 1.0 parser implementation class, and allows parsing to occur in a vendor-neutral way.

```
public abstract class SAXParser {
    public void parse(InputStream stream, HandlerBase base)
        throws SAXException, IOException, IllegalArgumentException;
    public void parse(String uri, HandlerBase base)
        throws SAXException, IOException, IllegalArgumentException;
    public void parse(File file, HandlerBase base)
        throws SAXException, IOException, IllegalArgumentException;
    public void parse(InputSource source, HandlerBase base)
        throws SAXException, IOException, IllegalArgumentException;
    public abstract Parser getParser() throws SAXException;
    public abstract boolean isNamespaceAware();
    public abstract boolean isValidating();
}
```

SAXParserFactory

This class is the factory used to create instances of the `SAXParser` class, and allows namespace and validation features to be set for the production of those instances.

```
public abstract class SAXParserFactory {
    public static SAXParserFactory newInstance();
    public SAXParser newSAXParser()
        throws ParserConfigurationException, SAXException;
    public void setNamespaceAware(boolean aware);
    public void setValidating(boolean validating);
    public boolean isNamespaceAware();
    public boolean isValidating();
}
```

JDOM 1.0

JDOM 1.0, introduced in Chapter 8, provides a complete view of an XML document within a tree model. Although this model is similar to DOM, it is not as rigid a representation; this allows the content of an `Element`, for example, to be set directly, instead of setting the value of the child of that `Element`. Additionally, JDOM provides concrete classes rather than interfaces, allowing direct instantiation of objects rather than through the use of a factory. SAX and DOM are only used in JDOM for the construction of a JDOM `Document` object from existing XML data, and are detailed in the `org.jdom.input` package.

*Package: org.jdom**

This package contains the core classes for JDOM 1.0. These consist of XML objects modeled in Java and a set of `Exceptions` that can be thrown when errors occur.

Attribute

`Attribute` defines behavior for an XML attribute, modeled in Java. Methods allow the user to obtain the value of the attribute as well as namespace information about the `Attribute`. An instance can be created with the name of the attribute and its value, or the `Namespace` and local name, as well as the value, of the attribute. Several convenience methods are also provided for automatic data conversion of the attribute's value.

```
public class Attribute {
    public Attribute(String name, String value);
    public Attribute(String name, String prefix, String uri, String value);
    public Attribute(String name, Namespace ns, String value);
    public String getName();
    public String getQualifiedName();
    public String getNamespacePrefix();
    public String getNamespaceURI();
    public String getValue();
    public void setValue(String value);

    // Convenience Methods for Data Conversion
    public String get StringValue(String default Value);
    public int getIntValue(int defaultValue);
    public int getIntValue() throws DataConversionException;
    public long getLongValue(long defaultValue);
    public long getLongValue() throws DataConversionException;
    public float getFloatValue(float defaultValue);
    public float getFloatValue() throws DataConversionException;
    public double getDoubleValue(double defaultValue);
    public double getDoubleValue() throws DataConversionException;
    public boolean getBooleanValue(boolean defaultValue);
    public boolean getBooleanValue() throws DataConversionException;
```

* Please note that while the JDOM API is fairly stable, it is at the time of this writing still in beta. Minor changes may occur during the production and shelf-life of this book. Please consult *http://www.jdom.org* for the latest JDOM classes.

```
    public char getCharValue()throws DataConversionException;
    public char getCharValue(char defaultValue);
    public byte getByteValue(byte defaultValue);
    public byte getByteValue() throws DataConversionException;
}
```

Comment

`Comment` is a simple representation of an XML comment, and contains the text within the XML comment.

```
public class Comment {
    public Comment(String text);
    public String getText();
    public void setText(String text);
    public String toString();
}
```

DataConversionException

This `Exception` is thrown when a conversion from an `Attribute`'s or `Element`'s value to a specified data type occurs. The message that results specifies the name of the `Attribute` whose value was requested as well as the data type to which conversion is requested. It is provided as a subclass of `JDOMException` so that an application using JDOM can catch that single `Exception` and receive all error notifications.

```
public class DataConversionException extends JDOMException {
    public DataConversionException(String name, String dataType);
}
```

DocType

`DocType` represents a `DOCTYPE` declaration within an XML document. It includes information about the element name being constrained, as well as the public ID and system ID of the external DTD reference, if one is present.

```
public class DocType {
    public DocType(String elementName, String publicID, String systemID);
    public DocType(String elementName, String systemID);
    public DocType(String elementName);
    public String getElementName();
    public String getPublicID();
    public DocType setPublicID(String publicID);
    public String getSystemID();
    public DocType setSystemID(String systemID);
}
```

Document

Document models an XML Document in Java. It requires that it be created with a root Element, although that Element can be replaced with setRootElement(). It also allows the setting of a DocType and a List of ProcessingInstructions, and the retrieval of those same objects. Convenience methods are provided to allow inline addition of PIs to the Document. The getContent() method returns all the content of the Document, which includes the root Element and any Comments that may exist at the document level in the XML document.

```
public class Document {
    public Document(Element rootElement, DocType docType);
    public Document(Element rootElement);
    public Element getRootElement() throws NoSuchElementException;
    public Document setRootElement(Element rootElement);
    public DocType getDocType();
    public Document setDocType(DocType docType);
    public List getProcessingInstructions();
    public List getProcessingInstructions(String target);
    public ProcessingInstruction getProcessingInstruction(String target)
        throws NoSuchProcessingInstructionException;
    public Document addProcessingInstruction(ProcessingInstruction pi);
    public Document addProcessingInstruction(String target, String data);
    public Document addProcessingInstruction(String target, Map data);
    public Document setProcessingInstructions(
        List processingInstructions);
    public boolean removeProcessingInstruction(
        ProcessingInstruction processingInstruction);
    public boolean removeProcessingInstruction(String target);
    public boolean removeProcessingInstructions(String target);
    public Document addComment(Comment comment);
    public List getMixedContent();
}
```

Element

Element is a Java representation of an XML element. It is completely namespace-aware, so all methods take in a single element name as an argument, as well as optional namespace information. The result of calls to getContent() is always a String, either the textual content of the XML element, or an empty String. An Element is considered to have mixed content when it has a combination of textual data and nested elements, as well as optional comments, entities, and processing instructions. This complete List of content can be obtained with getMixedContent(), and the results in the List evaluated through instanceof against a String, Element, or Comment.

The addXXX() methods are designed to be chained together, and therefore return the modified Element:

```
Element element = new Element("root");
element.addChild(new Element("child")
    .addChild(new Element("grandchild")
        .addAttribute("name", "value")
        .setContent("Hello World!"))
    .addChild(new Element("anotherChild"))
);
```

This would result in the following XML document fragment:

```
<root>
  <child>
    <grandchild name="value">
      Hello World!
    </grandchild>
  </child>
  <anotherChild />
</root>
```

There are also convenience methods to allow inline adding of Attributes to an Element, through setAttribute(String name, String value). The removal methods work in the same fashion, and provide namespace-aware versions as well.

```
public class Element {
    public Element(String name);
    public Element(String name, String uri);
    public Element(String name, String prefix, String uri);
    public Element(String name, Namespace ns);
    public String getName();
    public String getNamespacePrefix();
    public String getNamespaceURI();
    public String getQualifiedName();
    public String getContent();
    public Element setContent(String textContent);
    public boolean hasMixedContent();
    public List getMixedContent();
    public Element setMixedContent(List mixedContent);
    public List getChildren();
    public Element setChildren(List children);
    public List getChildren(String name);
    public List getChildren(String name, Namespace ns);
    public Element getChild(String name) throws NoSuchElementException;
    public Element getChild(String name, Namespace ns)
        throws NoSuchElementException;
    public Element addChild(Element element);
    public Element addChild(ProcessingInstruction pi);
    public Element addChild(Comment comment);
```

```
        public Element addChild(String s);
        public boolean removeChild(Element element);
        public boolean removeChild(Comment comment);
        public boolean removeChild(String name);
        public boolean removeChild(String name, Namespace ns);
        public boolean removeChildren(String name);
        public boolean removeChildren(String name, Namespace ns);
        public boolean removeChildren();
        public List getAttributes();
        public Attribute getAttribute(String name)
            throws NoSuchAttributeException;
        public Attribute getAttribute(String name, Namespace ns)
            throws NoSuchAttributeException;
        public Element setAttributes(List attributes);
        public Element addAttribute(Attribute attribute);
        public Element addAttribute(String name, String value);
        public Element addAttribute(String name, Namespace ns, String value);
        public void removeAttribute(String name);
        public void removeAttribute(String name, Namespace ns);
    }
```

JDOMException

This is the core JDOM `Exception` that other JDOM `Exception` classes subclass. It provides for error messages as well as the wrapping of a root cause `Exception`, in the case that a `JDOMException` needs to wrap a lower-level `Exception`.

```
    public class JDOMException extends Exception {
        public JDOMException();
        public JDOMException(String message);
        public JDOMException(String message, Throwable rootCause);
        public Throwable getRootCause();
    }
```

Namespace

The `Namespace` class handles namespace mappings used in JDOM `Document` objects.

```
    public class Namespace {
        public static Namespace getNamespace(String uri);
        public static Namespace getNamespace(String prefix, String uri);
        public String getPrefix();
        public String getURI();
        public boolean isDefault();
    }
```

NoSuchAttributeException

This Exception is thrown when a specific Attribute is searched for and not found. The message that results contains the name of the Attribute that was searched upon.

```
public class NoSuchAttributeException extends JDOMException {
    public NoSuchAttributeException(String attributeName);
}
```

NoSuchElementException

This Exception is thrown when a specific Element is searched for and not found. The message that results contains the name of the Element that was searched upon.

```
public class NoSuchElementException extends JDOMException {
    public NoSuchElementException(String elementName);
}
```

NoSuchProcessingInstructionException

This Exception is thrown when a specific ProcessingInstruction is searched for and not found. The message that results contains the target of the ProcessingInstruction that was searched upon.

```
public class NoSuchProcessingInstructionException extends JDOMException {
    public NoSuchProcessingInstructionException(String target)
}
```

ProcessingInstruction

ProcessingInstruction defines behavior for an XML processing instruction, modeled in Java. It allows specific handling for the target as well as the raw data for the target. Additionally, as many PIs use data in the form of name/value pairs (much like attributes), this allows retrieval and addition of name/value pairs. For example, in the <?cocoon-process type="xslt"?> processing instruction, invoking getValue("type") on the ProcessingInstruction representing that XML PI would return xslt.

```
public class ProcessingInstruction {
    public ProcessingInstruction(String target, Map data);
    public ProcessingInstruction(String target, String data);
    public String getTarget();
    public String getData();
    public ProcessingInstruction setData(String data);
    public ProcessingInstruction setData(Map data);
    public String getValue(String name);
    public ProcessingInstruction setValue(String name, String value);
```

```
    public boolean removeValue(String name);
}
```

Package: org.jdom.adapters

This package contains adapters that allow a standard interface for obtaining a DOM Document object from any DOM parser (including DOM Level 1 parsers). Adapters can be easily added for any parser that desires to have JDOM support.

AbstractDOMAdapter

This class provides default behavior for the version of getDocument() that takes in a filename by wrapping the file in a FileOutputStream and delegating invocation to getDocument(InputStream).

```
public abstract class AbstractDOMAdapter implements DOMAdapter {
    public Document getDocument(String filename, boolean validate)
        throws IOException;
    public abstract Document getDocument(InputStream in,boolean validate)
        throws IOException;
    public abstract Document createDocument() throws IOException;
}
```

DOMAdapter

This class defines the interface that adapters must implement. This includes a means to produce a DOM Document from a filename or an InputStream, as well as a means of obtaining a new, empty DOM Document object.

```
public interface DOMAdapter {
    public Document getDocument(String filename, boolean validate)
        throws IOException;
    public Document getDocument(InputStream in, boolean validate)
        throws IOException;
    public Document createDocument() throws IOException;
}
```

Specific adapter classes are not detailed here, as additions and modifications may be made during publication of the book. As of this writing, functional adapters are provided for the following parsers:

- Oracle Version 1 XML Parser
- Oracle Version 2 XML Parser
- Sun Project X Parser
- Apache Xerces Parser
- IBM XML4J Parser

Package: org.jdom.input

This package defines the interface for building a JDOM `Document` object. Additional `Builder` implementations can be added for new implementations on other XML APIs, or for a new parsing implementation, such as deferring complete document reading until a user requests it.

AbstractBuilder

This base implementation of `Builder` provides routing for the `build()` methods that take in a `File` or `URL`, and convert them to streams to pass to the `build()` method that takes in an `InputStream`.

```
public abstract class AbstractBuilder implements Builder {
    public abstract Document build(InputStream in) throws JDOMException;
    public Document build(File file) throws JDOMException;
    public Document build(URL url) throws JDOMException;
}
```

Builder

This base interface defines behavior for all `Document` builders. Each `Builder` implementation must provide a mechanism to create a JDOM Document object from an `InputStream`, `File`, or `URL`. All throw `JDOMExceptions`, which will hold information about well-formedness or validity errors (when appropriate) if errors in `Document` building occur.

```
public interface Builder {
    public Document build(InputStream in) throws JDOMException;
    public Document build(File file) throws JDOMException;
    public Document build(URL url) throws JDOMException;
}
```

DOMBuilder

This class provides the ability to create a JDOM `Document` object from an XML input source using a parser that supports DOM, the Document Object Model. It uses the various adapters in `org.jdom.adapters`, so if a parser is requested for which there is no adapter, errors will occur. Additionally, a method is provided for building a JDOM `Document` object from an existing DOM tree (`org.w3c.dom.Document`). When the `DOMBuilder` is constructed, validation can be requested, as can the class name of the adapter to use. If neither is supplied, the default behavior occurs: no validation takes place and the Apache Xerces parser is used.

```
public class DOMBuilder extends AbstractBuilder {
    public DOMBuilder(String adapterClass, boolean validate);
    public DOMBuilder(String adapterClass);
```

```
        public DOMBuilder(boolean validate);
        public DOMBuilder();
        public Document build(InputStream in) throws JDOMException;
        public Document build(org.w3c.dom.Document domDocument);
    }
```

SAXBuilder

This class provides the ability to create a JDOM `Document` object from an XML input source using a parser that supports SAX, the Simple API for XML. It can use any SAX parser implementation that is SAX 2.0–compliant.* When the `SAXBuilder` is constructed, validation can be requested, as well as the class name of the SAX driver to use. If neither is supplied, the default behavior occurs: no validation takes place and the Apache Xerces parser is used.

```
    public class SAXBuilder extends AbstractBuilder {
        public SAXBuilder(String saxDriverClass, boolean validate);
        public SAXBuilder(String saxDriverClass);
        public SAXBuilder(boolean validate);
        public SAXBuilder();
        public Document build(InputStream in) throws JDOMException;
    }
```

Package: org.jdom.output

This package defines behavior for output of JDOM `Document` objects. The only offering currently is the `XMLOutputter`, which provides for output of a JDOM `Document` to a stream, but additional output classes are being added, with several expected to be included in the JDOM 1.0 final release. Of particular note is the `SAXOutputter` class (not included here), which will allow a JDOM `Document` to fire SAX events off to an application expecting SAX behavior.

XMLOutputter

This class handles output of a `Document` to a supplied `OutputStream` in XML format. Various constructors are provided for setting the level of indention that should occur, as well as determining if new line feeds should be added to the output. The default behavior is "pretty-printing," which uses two spaces for each indention level and outputs new line feeds. Once the instance is created, the `output()` method will output the supplied `Document` to the specified `OutputStream`.

```
    public class XMLOutputter {
        public XMLOutputter();
```

* Depending on user demand, support for SAX 1.0 parsers may be added in later versions of JDOM.

```
    public XMLOutputter(String indent);
    public XMLOutputter(String indent, boolean newlines);
    public void output(Document doc, OutputStream out)
        throws IOException;
}
```

B

SAX 2.0 Features and Properties

This appendix details the SAX 2.0 standard features and properties. Although a vendor's parsing software can add additional features and properties for vendor-specific functionality, this list represents the core set of functionality that any SAX 2.0–compliant parser implementation should support.

Core Features

The core set of features supported by SAX 2.0 `XMLReader` implementations is listed here. These features can be set through `setFeature()`, and the value of a feature can be obtained through `getFeature()`. Any feature can be read-only, or read and write; features also may be modifiable only when parsing is occurring, or only when parsing is not occurring.

Namespace Processing

This feature instructs a parser to perform namespace processing, which will cause namespace prefixes, namespace URIs, and element local names to be available through the SAX namespace callbacks (`startPrefixMapping()` and `endPrefixMapping()`, as well as certain parameters supplied to `startElement()` and `endElement()`). When this feature is `true`, this processing will occur. When `false`, namespace processing will not occur (this implies that the namespace prefix reporting feature is on).

URI: *http://xml.org/sax/features/namespaces*
Access: Read-only when parsing; read/write when not parsing

Namespace Prefix Reporting

This feature instructs a parser to report the attributes used in namespace declarations, such as the `xmlns:[namespace prefix]` attributes. When this feature is not on (`false`), namespace-related attributes are not reported, as the parser consumes them in order to discover a namespace prefix to URI mappings, and they are generally not of value to the wrapping application in that context. In addition, when namespace processing is turned on, generally namespace prefix mapping is turned off.

URI: *http://xml.org/sax/features/namespace-prefixes*
Access: Read-only when parsing, read/write when not parsing

String Interning

This feature dictates that all element raw and local names, namespace prefixes, and namespace URIs are interned using `java.lang.String.intern()`. When not on (`false`), all XML components are left as is.

URI: *http://xml.org/sax/features/string-interning*
Access: Read-only when parsing, read/write when not parsing

Validation

This feature requests that validation occur and that any errors as a result of broken constraints be reported through the SAX `ErrorHandler` interface (if an implementation is registered). When set to `false`, no validation occurs.

URI: *http://xml.org/sax/features/validation*
Access: Read-only when parsing, read/write when not parsing

Process External Entities (General)

This feature requests that all general (textual) entities be processed within an XML document.

URI: *http://xml.org/sax/features/external-general-entities*
Access: Read-only when parsing, read/write when not parsing

Process External Entities (Parameter)

This feature requests that all external parameters be parsed, including those in any external DTD's subset.

URI: *http://xml.org/sax/features/external-parameter-entities*
Access: Read-only when parsing, read/write when not parsing

Core Properties

Properties provide a way to deal with objects used in the parsing process, particularly when dealing with handlers such as `LexicalHandler` and `DeclHandler` that are not in the core set of SAX 2.0 handlers (`EntityResolver`, `DTDHandler`, `ContentHandler`, and `ErrorHandler`). Any property can be read-only, or read and write; features also may be modifiable only when parsing is occurring, or only when parsing is not occurring.

Lexical Handler

This property allows the setting and retrieval of a `LexicalHandler` implementation to be used for handling of comments and DTD references within an XML document.

URI: *http://xml.org/sax/properties/lexical-handler*
Data type: `org.xml.sax.ext.LexicalHandler`
Access: Read/write when parsing, read/write when not parsing

Declaration Handler

This property allows the setting and retrieval of a `DeclHandler` implementation to be used for handling of constraints within a DTD.

URI: *http://xml.org/sax/properties/declaration-handler*
Data type: `org.xml.sax.ext.DeclHandler`
Access: Read/write when parsing, read/write when not parsing

DOM Node

When parsing is occurring, this will retrieve the current DOM node (if a DOM iterator is being used). When parsing is not occurring, this retrieves the root DOM node.

URI: *http://xml.org/sax/properties/dom-node*
Data type: `org.w3c.dom.Node`
Access: Read-only when parsing, read/write when not parsing

Literal (XML) String

This retrieves the literal characters in the XML document that triggered the event in process when this property is used.

URI: *http://xml.org/sax/properties/xml-string*
Data type: `java.lang.String`
Access: Read-only when parsing, read-only when not parsing

Index

Symbols

[ ] brackets, 156
<!-- --> comments, 220
& ampersand, 43
* asterisk, 156
: colon, 38
:: double colon, 157
/ forward slash, 40
- hyphen, 40
. period, 40
| pipe operator, 102
* recurrence operator, 101
+ recurrence operator, 101
? recurrence operator, 101
; semicolon, 44
@ sign, 161
_ underscore, 40

A

AbstractBuilder (JDOM), 460
AbstractDOMAdapter (JDOM), 459
addAttribute(Attribute attribute), 220
addAttribute(String name, String value), 220
addChild(Comment), 221
addChild(Element), 217
addChild(String content), 218
addComment(Comment), 221
addEvent( ), 295, 297
addHandler( ), 287
Adobe Acrobat, 245
ampersand (&) in entity references, 43
Ant tool, 237
  generating documentation or Javadoc, 239
ANY keyword, 96
Apache Cocoon (see Cocoon)
Apache Xalan (see Xalan processor)
Apache Xerces (see Xerces parser)
API reference, 429–462
APIs for XML, 12–14
application clients, 143
application portability, 128
applications
  transforming information between, 17–19
  XML used in, 15–22
asterisk (*) indicating value, 156
ATTLIST construct, 104
Attribute constructor, 220
attribute element, 120
Attribute (JDOM), 453
AttributeList interface (SAX), 430
AttributeListImpl class (SAX), 439
attributes, 42
  creating, 163–166
  defining, 103–108
    in XML Schema, 119–123

attributes (*continued*)
elements and, 219
ordering of, 66
types of, 104
when to use vs. elements, 42
Attributes interface (SAX), 65, 430
AttributesImpl class (SAX), 439

B

base keyword, 122
binary data, unparsed entities and, 136
brackets [ ] ending selection criteria, 156
browsers (see web browsers)
Builder interface (JDOM), 209, 460
business-to-business communication, 20, 379–414
evaluating requirements, 380
validation and, 93

C

card element, 252
cards, 252
Cascading Style Sheets (CSS), 233
case sensitivity, element names, 40
case statement, 186
Castor project, 340, 341
CDATA keyword, 104
CDATA section, 44
whitespace and, 69
CDATASection interface (DOM), 443
channels, 401, 408–412
future trends, 413
Character Data (see CDATA)
CharacterData interface (DOM), 443
characters( ), 67
character arrays and, 87
whitespace reported by, 68
Clark, James, 285
clients, 143
types of, 17
updating, 337–339
closing opened elements, 40
Cocoon
building, 238–240
installing, 236–243
making logicsheets available to, 269
project, 28
publishing framework, 193
Release 1.x.dev, obtaining, 237
Release 2.0+, 272–276
cocoon-format, 255
cocoon.jar, 239
cocoon.properties file, 239, 241, 242
colon (:) with namespaces/elements, 38
Comment class, 220
Comment constructor, 221
Comment interface (DOM), 444
Comment (JDOM), 454
Comment object, 220
comments (<!-- -->), 220
com.oreilly.xml package, 303
complex data types, 113
complexType element, 114
components, 145–149
Concurrent Versioning System (CVS), 236
configuration data
displaying, 356–362
LDAP and, 340
loading, 350–362
modifying, 362–367
XML and, 317–348
configuration files
creating, 321–328
design decisions for, 327
information contained in, 322
organization and, 320
reading, 328–339
getting configuration information, 328–331
loading configuration information, 331–334
using configuration information, 334–339
XML-RPC server, 302–309
configuration repositories, 26–27
configuration, XML for, 21
conformity to XML specification, parsers and, 23
constants, 43
constraining XML documents, 89–124

constraints, 319
 configuration files and, 326
 ease of with schemas, 416
constructors, invoking, 207
content, 36–45
 vs. presentation, 16
 separated from presentation, 259
content attribute, 120
content handlers, 54–74
ContentHandler instance, 86
ContentHandler interface (SAX), 54–59, 430
control structures, 155–163
core DOM object interfaces, 183
count( ) function, 149
createAttribute( ), 373
createElement( ), 373
createElementNS( ), 375
createTextNode( ), 372, 373
creating
 configuration files, 321–328
 XML documents, 32–45
 XML from scratch, 367–370
 XSP pages, 259–266
cross-platform portability, 36
CSS (Cascading Style Sheets), 233
CVS (Concurrent Versioning System), 236

D

data
 contained in elements, 67–69
 parsed, 98
 specifying elements as, 166–170
 textual, 67
data constraints, ease of with schemas, 416
data elements (see elements)
data types
 complex, 113
 user-defined, 112, 114–116
 XML Schema, 112
database queries, represented by XQL, 11
databases
 XML and, 339, 425–427
DataConversionException (JDOM), 219, 454
Davidson, James Duncan, 205, 237
DECHandler interface (SAX), 437
decks, 253
declaration handler property (SAX), 465
default attribute, 122
default keyword (Java), 162
default namespace, 110
DefaultHandler helper class, 439
deployment descriptors
 EJB, 318–321
 XML and, 21
directory services vs. XML, 340
distributed systems, 424
docs target, 239
DOCTYPE declaration, 36
DocType (JDOM), 212, 454
Document interface (DOM), 185, 444
Document (JDOM), 455
document locator, 59
Document node, 187
Document object (JDOM), 183, 207, 208, 334
 building from scratch, sample code, 224–231
 firing off SAX events, 223
Document Object Model (see DOM)
Document Type Definitions (see DTDs)
documentation
 generating with Ant, 239
 online, for DOC, 186
 self-, 90–92
DocumentBuilder class (JAXP), 451
DocumentBuilderFactory class (JAXP), 451
DocumentFragment interface (DOM), 445
DocumentHandler interface (SAX), 431
documents, start/end of, 60
DocumentType interface (DOM), 195, 445
doGet( ), 361, 377
DOM (Document Object Model), 13, 178–197
 as alternative for accessing XML, 345–348
 as alternative to JDOM for writing or modifying XML, 372–376

DOM (*continued*)
caution when using with large data, 197
elements, 187–189
importance for XSLT processors, 196
Level 2, 442–450
node types, 186–196
online documentation, 186
parsers (see DOM parsers)
tree
mutability of, 196
serializing, 375
using, 183–186
DOM node property (SAX), 465
DOM Nodes, 372
DOM parsers
building, 179–181
output, 181–183
formatting, 190–193
throwing SAX exceptions, 198
DOMAdapter (JDOM), 459
DOMBuilder class (JDOM), 210, 334, 460
DOMException class, 445
DOMImplementation interface, 446
DOMOutputter class, 223
DOMParser class, 181
doPost( ), 361, 377
double colon (::) separating keywords and elements, 157
downloads
com.oreilly.xml, 303
JDOM, 206
UP.SDK software, 253
DTD references, 195
DTDHandler interface (SAX), 136–139, 432
registering, 137
DTDs (Document Type Definitions), 5, 36, 93–108, 195
constraining XML Schema, 109
handling, 139–140
namespaces and, 417
non-fatal errors and, 135
RSS and, 401
vs. XML Schema, 415–418
(see also XML Schema)
dynamic content generation, 233

E

EDI vs. XML, 413
EJB deployment descriptors, 318–321
EJB (Enterprise JavaBeans)
distributed systems and, 424
enterprise-beans element, 321
XML and, 21
ejb-jar root element, 319
element attributes (see attributes)
Element class, 215
element element, 112
element equivalence, 418–421
Element interface (DOM), 446
Element (JDOM), 455
element names, case sensitivity and, 40
elements, 40–41, 215–220
child vs. parent, 68
choosing which to process, 160–163
closing opened, 40
creating, 163–166
data contained in, 67–69
empty, 98
nesting, 97
primitive, 113
SAX callbacks, 64–67
specifying, 95
data as, 166–170
in XML Schema, 112–119
when to use vs. attributes, 42
embedded spaces, 40
empty content, 116
empty data type, removed from XML Schema specification, 117
empty elements, 41, 98
EMPTY keyword, 98
end of document, 60
end users, 143
endDocument( ), 60
endElement( ), 66
Enterprise JavaBeans (see EJB)
enterprise-beans element, 321
entities
skipped (see skipped entities)
unparsed, 136
Entity (DOM), 447

entity references, 43, 99, 195
EntityReference interface (DOM), 195, 447
EntityResolver interface (SAX), 432
enumeration element, 122
enumerations, 105, 122
equivalence, 418–421
error handlers, 74–81
error testing, 229
ErrorHandler interface (SAX), 74, 432
  adding to import statement, 75
errors
  document not well-formed, 80
  during parsing, 60
  fatal, 78, 135
  finding with Xalan processor, 175
  non-fatal, 78, 134
  syntax, 135
  version of XML and, 79
events
  adding/removing, 295–297
  returning list of, 297
  sorting, 298–302
events vector variable, 298
exclude-result-prefixes attribute, 255
execute( ), 291, 292
exemplar, 421
ExoLab, 340
explicit types, 116
Extensible Markup Language (see XML)
Extensible Server Pages (see XSP)
Extensible Stylesheet Language (see XSL)
Extensible Stylesheet Language Transformation (see XSLT)

F

FactoryConfigurationException (JAXP), 451
FAQs, Cocoon, 236
fatal errors, 78, 135
features, setting (parser configuration), 126
#FIXED keyword, 105
focus attribute, 106, 122, 161
FOP (Formatting Objects Processor), 171, 245
formatting model, 147
formatting objects, 7, 147
formatting processors, 171, 245
forward slash (/) in ending element tags, 40
frameworks (see web publishing frameworks)

G

GET method, 356, 361
GET requests, 361
getAttributes( ), 188
getAttribute(String name), 219
getBooleanValue( ), 219
getByteValue( ), 219
getChild( ), 331, 363
getChildNodes( ), 187
getChildren( ), 217, 331, 334
getColumnNumber( ), 59
getContent( ), 217, 220, 331
getDocumentElement( ), 187
getDraftDate( ), tag libraries and, 269
getException( ), 61
getFeature( ), 126, 463
getFloatValue( ), 219
getHandlers( ), 334
getInstance( ), 314
getIntValue( ), 219
getLineNumber( ), 59
getLocalName(int index), 65
getMixedContent( ), 217, 220
getNodeName( ), 187, 189
getNodeType( ), 185
getNodeValue( ), 189
  textual data, printing, 193
getProperty( ), 126
getTitle( ), tag libraries and, 269
getURI(int index), 65
grouping elements, 101

H

handler classes, XML-RPC server configuration file, 302–309
handler elements, 324
  configuration data and, 364
handler information, 323
HandlerBase helper class, 202, 433
handlers (see content handlers; error handlers; response handlers; XML-RPC handlers)
Hashtable, 295, 307
header, 34–36
helma.xmlrpc.WebServer class, 284
helma.xmlrpc.XmlRpcClient class, 289
helma.xmlrpc.XmlRpcServer class, 283
hierarchy of elements, 97
HTML
  leaving unprocessed, 166–170
  outputting XML document to, 149
  XML converted to, viewing, 243
HTTP transport protocol
  RPC with, 279
  used for business-to-business communication, 380
Hunter, Jason, 205
hyphen (-) in element names, 40

I

ignorableWhitespace( ), 68, 69, 132
images
  formatting objects for, 147
  unparsed entities and, 136
implicit types, 116
#IMPLIED keyword, 105
import statements, 52, 54
include (Java), 268
InputSource class (SAX), 53, 434
installing Cocoon, 236–243
IOException, 198
items, 401
iteration, 158–160

J

Jakarta Tomcat servlet engine, 240
jar files, 48
  placing logicsheets in, 270
Java
  code, using XML-RPC, 281–294
  complementing with XML Schema, 421–423
  creating XML with, 349–378
  DOM and, 179
  JDOM and, 207
  parallels with XML Schema, 418–427
  perfect match with XML, 15
  portability and, 92
  properties files, 317
  servlet, displaying configuration data, 356
Java API for XML Parsing (see JAXP)
Java Development Kit (JDK), 317
Java language bindings, 179
Java Naming and Directory Interface (JNDI), 279
Java Server Pages (JSP), 233, 257
Java Servlet API, resources for further information, 356
Javadoc, generating with Ant, 239
java.io.IOException, 292
java.net.MalformedURLException, 290
java.text.SimpleDateFormat class, 297
java.util.Properties class, 317
javax.xml.parsers package, 201, 450–452
JAXP (Java API for XML Parsing), 14, 200–205
  Release 1.0, 450–452
  using with DOM, 203
  using with SAX, 201–203
  which parser to use, 204
JDK (Java Development Kit), 317
JDOM Document object (see Document object)
JDOM documents, 207–231
  obtaining, 207–212
    building from XML, 208–212
    from scratch, 207
  outputting, 221–231
  using, 212–221

JDOM 200, 205–231
  accessing XML, 341
  alternatives to for writing/modifying XML, 371–376
  documents (see JDOM documents)
  download, 206
  later releases and implementations, 348
  Release 1.0, 452–462
JDOMException, 457
JDOMTest class, 227
JNDI (Java Naming and Directory Interface), 279
JSP (Java Server Pages), 233, 257

K

keywords for web browsers, 250

L

language bindings, 179
LDAP (Lightweight Directory Access Protocol), 279
  vs. XML, 340
legacy data, 339
levels of DOM, 178
lexical handler property (SAX), 465
LexicalHandler interface (SAX), 438
Lightweight Directory Access Protocol (see LDAP)
literal (XML) string (SAX), 465
Locator class (SAX), 59, 434
Locator instance, 86
LocatorImpl class (SAX), 440
logicsheets, 267
  making available to Cocoon, 269
  placing in jar files, 270
looping, 158–160

M

mailing lists
  Cocoon, 236, 275
  Xerces parser, 47
  XSL, advanced, 163
maxOccurs attribute, 118
McLaughlin, Brett, 205
media files, unparsed entities and, 136
memory, DOM and, 197
methods
  making available in RPC/RMI, 287
  mutator, 350, 361
Microsoft Word documents, formatting objects for, 147
minOccurs attribute, 118, 121
mixed content, 217
MSXML parser, caution with, 24
mutability of DOM tree, 196
mutator methods, 350, 361
MySQL, 339

N

name attribute, 164
NamedNodeMap interface (DOM), 448
nameless types, 116
names of elements, 65
Namespace class (JDOM), 457
namespace definitions, omitting with XML Schema, 119
namespace prefix reporting (SAX), 464
namespace processing (SAX), 463
namespaces, 6
  for configuration files, 322
  DTDs and, 417
  elements and, 219
  identifying XML with, 37–39
  JDOM and, 229
  multiple, caution with, 38
  root elements and, 320
  SAX callbacks, 62–64
  support for with SAX, 130
  XML Schema, 110–111
NamespaceSupport (SAX), 440
NDATA keyword, 137
nested tags, 40
networks, XML and, 17, 19
Node central interface (DOM), 448
Node implementation, 188
Node interface, 183, 185
node sets, 149
node types, DOM, 186–196
nodes, 9, 372
  determining type of, 185
  textual, 193

non-fatal errors, 78, 134
non-validating parsers, 69
  skipped entities, 70
NoSuchAttributeException (JDOM), 458
NoSuchElementException (JDOM), 458
NoSuchProcessingInstructionException (JDOM), 458
not( ) function, 149, 156
NOTATION construct, 137
notation declaration, 137
Notation interface (DOM), 449
notation names, 136
notationDecl( ), 137
NoteList interface (DOM), 449

O

OODBMS (object-oriented database management systems), 339
Open Source Software (OSS), 25
"or" function/operator, 102
Oracle, 339
ordering of attributes, 66
organization, configuration files and, 320, 323
org.jdom package, 453–459
org.jdom.adapters package, 210, 459
org.jdom.input package, 208, 460
org.jdom.input.DOMBuilder class, 210
org.jdom.input.SAXBuilder class, 209
org.jdom.output package, 221, 461
org.jdom.output.XMLOutputter class, 222
org.jdom.SAXOutputter class, 223
org.w3c.dom package, 443–450
org.xml.sax package, 429–437
org.xml.sax.Attributes instance, 64
org.xml.sax.ContentHandler, 54
org.xml.sax.DTDHandler, 54
org.xml.sax.EntityResolver., 54
org.xml.sax.ErrorHandler, 54
org.xml.sax.ext package, 437
org.xml.sax.helpers package, 438–442
org.xml.sax.helpers.ParserAdapter class, 85
OSS (Open Source Software), 25
output
  from XSLT processors, 174
  standard XML, 222–223
OutputStream, 222

P

parentheses used in grouping, 102
parse( ), 181
Parse interface (SAX), 434
parseConfiguration( )
  using DOM, 346
  using SAX, 342
Parsed Character Data (#PCDATA), 98
parsed data, 98
ParserAdapter helper class (SAX), 441
ParserConfigurationException (JAXP), 452
ParserFactory class (SAX), 441
parsers, 23
  configuring, 125–130
  non-validating (see non-validating parsers)
  not reentrant, 86
  obtaining, 47
  portability and, 81–84
  SAX 2.0 not supported, 85
  schema validation and, 109
  setting validation feature, 139
  validating (see validating parsers)
  XML Schema not supported/partially supported, 109
parsing XML documents, 52
pattern matching, 423
#PCDATA keyword, 98
PDF (Portable Document Format), 170
  formatting objects for, 147
  viewing from XML, 245–248
period (.) in element names, 40
pipe operator (|), 102
PIs (processing instructions), 5, 35, 214
  DOM and, 193–194
  DTDs and, 108
  SAX and, 61
pluggability, 201

portability, 1
  application, 128
  constraining XML and, 92
  cross-platform, 36
  DTDs and, 6, 108
  EJB and, 21
Portable Document Format (see PDF)
position( ), 254
POST method, 361
POST requests, 361
prefix mapping, 62
presentation vs. content, 16
primitive elements, 113
process external entities (SAX), 464
processing instructions (see PIs)
ProcessingInstruction class, 213
ProcessingInstruction interface (DOM), 193–194, 450
ProcessingInstruction (JDOM), 458
processors, 24, 144, 276
producers, 276
properties files (Java), 317
properties parameter, 242
properties. setting (parser configuration), 126
public ID, 195
publishing frameworks (see web publishing frameworks)
push vs. pull, 399–412

R

RDF (Resource Description Framework), 11
recurrence, 100–103
  XML Schema and, 117
recurrence operators, 100
  applied to groups, 102
ref attribute, 115
relational databases vs. XML, 339
relative paths, 148
Remote Method Invocation (RMI), 19
Remote Procedure Calls (RPC), 277
removeChildren( ), 364
removeEvent( ), 295, 297
repositories, configuration, 26–27
request variable (XSP), 264
#REQUIRED keyword, 105
Resource Description Framework (RDF), 11
resource-ref element, 321
resources for further information
  formatting objects, 147
  RMI, 278
  servlets, 315
  sorting algorithms, 298
  WAP, 256
  WML, 256
  XML, 33
    transformations, 142
  XSL, advanced, 163
response handlers, 282
Rich Site Summary (see RSS)
RMI (Remote Method Invocation), 19, 277, 278
  making methods available, 287
  vs. RPC, 278–281
Rocha, Ricardo, 28
root element, 37, 215
  for configuration file, 322
RPC (Remote Procedure Calls), 19, 277, 279
  making methods available, 287
  vs. RMI, 278–281
  (see also XML-RPC), 19
RSS (Rich Site Summary), 380, 401–412
  channels, 401, 408–412
    future trends, 413

S

saveConfiguration( ), 361
SAX (Simple API for XML), 12
  as alternative for accessing XML, 342–345
  as alternative to JDOM for writing/modifying XML, 372
  API Javadocs, 48
  classes, 48
  events, firing off, 223
  exceptions, thrown by DOM parsers, 198

SAX (*continued*)
  namespace support, 130
  parsers, 49–54
  reasons for using, 177
  Release 2.0, 429–442
    features, 463
    not supported by parsers, 85
    properties, 465
  sequential model, 176
  siblings and, 177
SAXBuilder class (JDOM), 461
SAXBuilder constructor (JDOM), 209
SAXException class, 61
SAXExceptions, 61, 435
SAXNotRecognizedException, 435
SAXNotSupportedException, 435
SAXParseException class, 436
  adding to import statement, 75
SAXParseExceptions, 74
SAXParser class (JAXP), 452
SAXParser class (JDOM), 201
SAXParserFactory class (JAXP), 452
SAXParserFactory class (JDOM), 201
SAXTest class, 222
Scheduler class, 295
schema root element, 110
schema validation, 109
schema-valid documents, 109
select attribute, 154, 156, 159
selecting axes, 156
self keyword, 157
self-documentation, 90–92
semicolon (;) in entity references, 44
serialize( ), 376
server, updating, 334–337
servlet configuration, XML and, 22
servlet engine, configuring for Cocoon, 240–243
servlet mapping, 274
servlets, 315
  XSLT from, 396–399
setContent( ), 362
setContentHandler( ), 71
setContent(String content), 218
setDocumentLocator( ), Locator instance, 86
setDriver( ), 285, 289
setDTDHandler( ), 137
setErrorHandler( ), 76
setFeature( ), 126, 463
setNodeValue( ), 373
setProperty( ), 126
shared information, 323, 324
shared instances, 314
Simple API for XML (see SAX)
simpleType element, 122
single tag, 41
singletons, 314
sitemap, 274
skeletons, 278
skipped entities, 70
  SAX and, 85
sorting algorithms, 298
spaces, embedded, 40
specifying elements (see elements, specifying)
speed
  parsers, 23
  processors, 24
standard XML output, 222–223
start of document, 60
startDocument( ), 60
startElement( ), 64
startPrefixMapping( ), 63
static content generation, 233
string interning (SAX), 464
stubs, 278
stylesheets
  CSS, 233
  using with WAP devices, 251–256
support for XML, 22–25
switch construct (Java), 185
switch statement (Java), 162
synchronized keyword, 370
syntax errors, 135
system ID, 195
system resources, DOM and, 197

T

tag libraries
  using, 266–272
tags, nested, 40
target namespace, 112, 114
targetNamespace attribute, 111
targets, 239
telecommunications, XML and, 20
template element, 151
test attribute, 161, 162
testing cycles, validation and, 128
text editors, 25
Text interface (DOM), 450
textual data, 67
textual nodes, 193
threads, 301, 370
Tomcat servlet engine, 240
tools (see web publishing frameworks)
tree model, 372
tree structure
  DOM, 183–186
  XSL and, 146
try-catch block, 309

U

underscore (_) in element names, 40
Uniform Resource Indicator (URI), 36
Uniform Resource Locators (see URLs)
unparsed data, 44
unparsed entities, 136
unparsed entity declarations, 136
unparsedEntityDecl( ), 136
UP.SDK software, 253
URI (Uniform Resource Indicator), 36
URLs
  Adobe Acrobat, 245
  Ant tool, 237
  Apache Jetspeed project, 401
  Apache XML Group, 171
  API Javadocs, 48
  Castor project, 340
  Cocoon, 236
  code for business-to-business applications, 383
  CVS, 236
  DOM, 14
    documentation, 186
    Level One/Level Two, 178
  JAXP, 14
  JDOM, 206, 348
  namespaces, 7
  Netscape channel validation mechanism, 408
  processors, 24
  publishing frameworks, 25
  SAX, 13
  W3C, 4
  WML, 253
  Xalan processor, 174
  Xerces parser, 47
  XML 1.0 Specification, 4
  XML editors, 25
  XML Schema, 10, 109, 416
  XML-RPC, 19, 281
  XPath, 10
  XQL, 11
  XSL, 9
    advanced, 163
  XSP, 30
user agents (see web browsers)
user lag, 376–378
user-defined data types, 112, 114–116

V

valid documents, 41
validating parsers, 23, 69
validating XML, 92
  handling, 139–140
  turning on, 127–130
  when to/not to, 140
validation (SAX), 464
Vector, 295
version attribute, 151

W

W3C (World Wide Web Consortium), 4
WAP (Wireless Application Protocol), 256
  devices, WML and, 251–256
warnings, 77
  validation and, 133

web browsers, media-specific XML transformations, 249–252
web publishing frameworks, 24, 232–276
  selecting, 234–236
    list of software, 234
  using, 242–256
WebServer class, 284, 287
well-formed documents, 40
whitespace
  ignored during parsing, 67
  reporting, 68
  RSS and, 403
  treatment during validation, 132
Wireless Application Protocol (see WAP)
wireless devices (see WAP, devices)
Wireless Markup Language (see WML)
wml element, 252
WML (Wireless Markup Language), 16
  resources for further information, 256
  software for testing pages, 253
  WAP and, 251–256
WORA (Write Once Run Anywhere), 319
Word (Microsoft), formatting objects for, 147
World Wide Web Consortium (W3C), 4
Write Once Run Anywhere (WORA), 319

X

Xalan processor, 174, 397
  supplied with Cocoon, 238
Xerces parser, 47
  supplied with Cocoon, 238
  used with Xalan, 174
XHTML, 11
XLink, 11
XLL (XML Link Language), 11
XML declaration, 187
XML documents
  constraining, 89–124
    reasons for, 89–93
  creating, 32–45
  locator, 59
  outputting in HTML format, 149
  parsing, 52
  well-formed vs. valid, 40
XML editors, 25
XML (Extensible Markup Language), 1–31
  1.0 Specification, 4
  APIs for, 12–14
  for configuration, 21
  configuration data and, 317–348
  configuration files (see configuration files)
  converted to HTML, viewing, 243
  creating
    from scratch, 367–370
    with Java, 349–378
  as data, 31
  databases and, 339, 425–427
  vs. directory services, 340
  documents (see XML documents)
  vs. EDI, 413
  errors involving version of, 79
  future trends, 25–31
  how it is used today in applications, 15–22
    for communication, 17–21
    for configuration, 21
    for presentation, 16
  identifying with namespaces, 37–39
  vs. LDAP, 340
  perfect match with Java, 15
  reasons for using, 14–30
  RSS, future trends and, 413
  support for, 22–25
  transformations
    media-specific, 249–252
    (see also XML transformations)
  validating, 92
  viewing PDFs from, 245–248
XML instructions, 35
XML Link Language (XLL), 11
XML parser classes, 47
XML parsers, DOM and, 179
XML Path Language (see XPath)
XML Schema, 10, 38–39, 108–123, 415–427
  complementing Java with, 421–423
  constrained DTDs, 109
  data types, 112

vs. DTDs, 415–418
namespace, 110–111
omitting namespace definitions, 119
parallels with Java, 418–427
specification revisions, 416
XML transformations
purpose of, 143–145
syntax for, 149–171
with Xalan processor, 174
xml-cocoon directory, 238
XMLFilter class (SAX), 436
XMLFilterImpl class (SAX), 441
xmlns attribute, 104, 120
default namespace and, 110
xmlns:[Namespace] attribute, 119
xmlns:[namespace prefix] attribute, 219
xmlns:xs attribute, 120
XMLOutputter class (JDOM), 461
XMLReader interface (SAX), 125, 128, 436
XMLReaderAdapter helper class (SAX), 442
XMLReaderFactory class (SAX), 442
XML-RPC, 19, 277–316, 424
client, 289–293, 309–312
code using, 281–294
handlers, 282–284, 294–302, 324–325
libraries, obtaining, 281
server, 284–289, 294–313
configuration file, 302–309
supported Java types, 283
XmlRpcClient class, 290
XmlRpcConfiguration utility class, 376–378
XmlRpcException class, 292
XMLSerializer class, 376
XPath expressions, 156
XPath (XML Path Language), 9, 148
using for filtering, 156–157
XPointer, 11
XQL, 11
xsi:schemaLocation attribute, 120
XSL (Extensible Stylesheet Language), 7–9, 145–147
stylesheets
in business-to-business communication, 391–396
using with XSLT processors, 175
templates, 151–155
in business-to-business communication, 394
XSL transformations, 147
xsl:apply-templates construct, 177
xsl:attribute construct, 164
<xsl:attribute> tag, 164
xsl:choose construct, 161
xsl:copy-of construct, 167
xsl:element construct, 164
xsl:for-each construct, 158, 159
xsl:if construct, 160
xsl:number element, 254
xsl:otherwise construct, 162
XSLT (Extensible Stylesheet Language Transformation), 7–9
in business-to-business communication, 396–399
processors, 174
importance of DOM for, 196
xsl:when construct, 162
XSP (Extensible Server Pages), 28–30, 257–272
creating pages, 259–266
tag libraries, using, 266–272
<xsp:expr> tag, 269
xsp:include, 268
xsp:logic element, 258
xsp:structure, 268

About the Author

Brett McLaughlin has been working in computers since the Logo days (remember the little triangle?). He currently specializes in building application infrastructure using Java and Java-related technologies. He has spent the last several years implementing these infrastructures at Nextel Communications and Allegiance Telecom, Inc. Brett is one of the cofounders of the Java Apache project Turbine, which builds a reusable component architecture for web application development using Java servlets. He is also a contributor to the EJBoss project, an open source EJB application server, and Cocoon, an open source XML web-publishing engine. His projects all focus on using XML and the J2EE platform in mission-critical, high-performance, distributed systems. Together with Jason Hunter, he has defined the JDOM API for manipulating XML in Java programs. When he's not bathed in the glow of a computer screen, Brett can usually be found playing the guitar or being dragged around the block by his five dogs.

Colophon

Our look is the result of reader comments, our own experimentation, and feedback from distribution channels. Distinctive covers complement our distinctive approach to technical topics, breathing personality and life into potentially dry subjects.

Madeleine Newell was the production editor, and Jane Ellin was the copyeditor for *Java and XML*. Emily Quill, Jane Ellin, and Nancy Kotary provided quality control. Darren Kelly, Mary Sheehan, and Emily Quill provided production assistance. Brenda Miller wrote the index.

Hanna Dyer designed the cover of this book, based on a series design by Edie Freedman. The image of the Tupperware SHAPE-O® was photographed by Kevin Thomas and manipulated in Adobe Photoshop by Michael Snow. Emma Colby produced the cover layout with QuarkXPress 3.3 using the Bodoni Black font from URW Software and the Bodoni Bold Italic font from Bitstream.

Alicia Cech and David Futato designed the interior layout based on a series design by Nancy Priest. Mike Sierra and David Futato implemented the design in FrameMaker 5.5.6 and provided technical support. The illustrations that appear in the book were produced by Robert Romano and Rhon Porter using Macromedia FreeHand 8 and Adobe Photoshop 5.

Whenever possible, our books use a durable and flexible lay-flat binding. If the page count exceeds the lay-flat binding limit, perfect binding is used.

More Titles from O'Reilly

In a Nutshell Quick References

Java Enterprise in a Nutshell

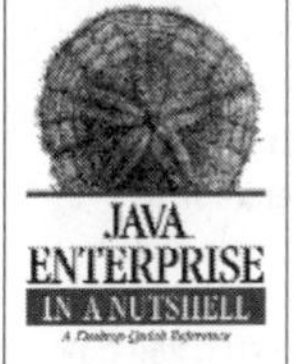

By David Flanagan, Jim Farley, William Crawford & Kris Magnusson
1st Edition September 1999
622 pages, ISBN 1-56592-483-5

The Java Enterprise APIs are essential building blocks for creating enterprise-wide distributed applications in Java. *Java Enterprise in a Nutshell* covers the RMI, Java IDL, JDBC, JNDI, Java Servlet, and Enterprise JavaBeans APIs, providing a fast-paced tutorial and compact reference material on each of the technologies. Covers Java 2.

Jini in a Nutshell

By Scott Oaks & Henry Wong
1st Edition March 2000
416 pages, ISBN 1-56592-759-1

Jini is a simple set of Java classes and services that allows devices (i.e., printers) and services (i.e., printing) to seamlessly interact with each other. *Jini in a Nutshell* is an O'Reilly-style quick reference guide to developing these services and clients using Jini. It covers everything an experienced Java programmer needs to know about Jini, including tutorial chapters to get you up to speed quickly and reference chapters that analyze and explain every Java package related to Jini.

Java Examples in a Nutshell

By David Flanagan
1st Edition September 1997
414 pages, ISBN 1-56592-371-5

From the author of *Java in a Nutshell*, this companion book is chock full of practical real-world programming examples to help novice Java programmers and experts alike explore what's possible with Java 1.1. If you learn best by example, this is the book for you.

Java in a Nutshell, 3rd Edition

By David Flanagan
3rd Edition November 1999
668 pages, ISBN 1-56592-487-8

The third edition of this bestselling book covers Java 1.2 and 1.3. It contains an advanced introduction to Java and its key APIs and provides quick-reference material on all the classes and interfaces in the following APIs: java.lang, java.io, java.beans, java.math, java.net, java.security, java.text, java.util, and javax.crypto.

Java Foundation Classes in a Nutshell

By David Flanagan
1st Edition September 1999
748 pages, ISBN 1-56592-488-6

Java Foundation Classes in a Nutshell provides an in-depth overview of the important pieces of the (JFC), such as the Swing components and Java 2D. It also includes compact reference material on all the GUI- and graphics-related classes in the numerous javax.swing and java.awt packages. Covers Java 2.

Java

Developing Java Beans

By Robert Englander
1st Edition June 1997
316 pages, ISBN 1-56592-289-1

Developing Java Beans is a complete introduction to Java's component architecture. It describes how to write Beans, which are software components that can be used in visual programming environments. This book discusses event adapters, serialization, introspection, property editors, and customizers, and shows how to use Beans within ActiveX controls.

Java

Java Servlet Programming

By Jason Hunter with William Crawford
1st Edition November 1998
528 pages, ISBN 1-56592-391-X

Java servlets offer a fast, powerful, portable replacement for CGI scripts. *Java Servlet Programming* covers everything you need to know to write effective servlets. Topics include: serving dynamic Web content, maintaining state information, session tracking, database connectivity using JDBC, and applet-servlet communication.

Java Swing

By Robert Eckstein, Marc Loy & Dave Wood
1st Edition September 1998
1252 pages, ISBN 1-56592-455-X

The Swing classes eliminate Java's biggest weakness: its relatively primitive user interface toolkit. *Java Swing* helps you to take full advantage of the Swing classes, providing detailed descriptions of every class and interface in the key Swing packages. It shows you how to use all of the new components, allowing you to build state-of-the-art user interfaces and giving you the context you need to understand what you're doing. It's more than documentation; *Java Swing* helps you develop code quickly and effectively.

Java Power Reference

By David Flanagan
1st Edition March 1999
64 pages, Features CD-ROM
ISBN 1-56592-589-0

Java Power Reference is a searchable, browser-based resource that documents all the packages and classes of the Java 2™ platform on a single CD-ROM. Based on the clear, concise quick-reference style of the bestselling *Java in a Nutshell*, the *Java Power Reference* provides a unique view of the functionality of the Java APIs. In addition to the CD-ROM, the package contains a concise printed overview of the newly released Java 2 platform.

Enterprise JavaBeans

By Richard Monson-Haefel
1st Edition June 1999
336 pages, ISBN 1-56592-605-6

Enterprise JavaBeans is a thorough introduction to EJB for the enterprise software developer. It shows how to get started developing enterprise Beans, how to deploy those Beans in a server, and how to use those Beans to create applications that do useful tasks. The end result is a highly flexible system built from components that can easily be reused and that can be changed to suit your needs without upsetting other parts of the system.

Java 2D Graphics

By Jonathan Knudsen
1st Edition May 1999
366 pages, ISBN 1-56592-484-3

Java 2D Graphics describes the 2D API from top to bottom, demonstrating how to set line styles and pattern fills as well as more advanced techniques of image processing and font handling. You'll see how to create and manipulate the three types of graphics objects: shapes, text, and images. Other topics include image data storage, color management, font glyphs, and printing.

Java I/O

By Elliotte Rusty Harold
1st Edition March 1999
596 pages, ISBN 1-56592-485-1

All of Java's Input/Output (I/O) facilities are based on streams, which provide simple ways to read and write data of different types. Java I/O tells you all you need to know about the four main categories of streams and uncovers less-known features to help make your I/O operations more efficient. Plus, it shows you how to control number formatting, use characters aside from the standard ASCII character set, and get a head start on writing truly multilingual software.

Java

Java Cryptography

By Jonathan B. Knudsen
1st Edition May 1998
362 pages, ISBN 1-56592-402-9

Java Cryptography teaches you how to write secure programs using Java's cryptographic tools. It includes thorough discussions of the java.security package and the Java Cryptography Extensions (JCE), showing you how to use security providers and even implement your own provider. It discusses authentication, key management, public and private key encryption, and includes a secure talk application that encrypts all data sent over the network. If you work with sensitive data, you'll find this book indispensable.

Java Distributed Computing

By Jim Farley
1st Edition January 1998
384 pages, ISBN 1-56592-206-9

Java Distributed Computing offers a general introduction to distributed computing, meaning programs that run on two or more systems. It focuses primarily on how to structure and write distributed applications and discusses issues like designing protocols, security, working with databases, and dealing with low bandwidth situations.

Java Network Programming

By Elliotte Rusty Harold
1st Edition February 1997
442 pages, ISBN 1-56592-227-1

The network is the soul of Java. Most of what is new and exciting about Java centers around the potential for new kinds of dynamic networked applications. *Java Network Programming* teaches you to work with Sockets, write network clients and servers, and gives you an advanced look at the new areas like multicasting, using the server API, and RMI. Covers Java 1.1.

Java Security

By Scott Oaks
1st Edition May 1998
474 pages, ISBN 1-56592-403-7

This essential Java 2 book covers Java's security mechanisms and teaches you how to work with them. It discusses class loaders, security managers, access lists, digital signatures, and authentication and shows how to use these to create and enforce your own security policy.

Java Threads, 2nd Edition

By Scott Oaks & Henry Wong
2nd Edition January 1999
336 pages, ISBN 1-56592-418-5

Revised and expanded to cover Java 2, *Java Threads, 2nd Edition* shows you how to take full advantage of Java's thread facilities: where to use threads to increase efficiency, how to use them effectively, and how to avoid common mistakes. It thoroughly covers the Thread and ThreadGroup classes, the Runnable interface, and the language's synchronized operator. The book pays special attention to threading issues with Swing, as well as problems like deadlock, race condition, and starvation to help you write code without hidden bugs.

Web Programming

ASP in a Nutshell

By A. Keyton Weissinger
1st Edition February 1999
426 pages, ISBN 1-56592-490-8

This detailed reference contains all the information Web developers need to create effective Active Server Pages (ASP) applications. It focuses on how features are used in a real application and highlights little-known or undocumented aspects, enabling even experienced developers to advance their ASP applications to new levels.

Web Programming

CGI Programming with Perl, 2nd Edition

By Shishir Gundavaram
2nd Edition July 2000
470 pages , ISBN 1-56592-419-3

Completely rewritten, this comprehensive explanation of CGI for those who want to provide their own Web servers features Perl 5 techniques and shows how to use two popular Perl modules, CGI.pm and CGI_lite. It also covers speed-up techniques, such as FastCGI and mod_perl, and new material on searching and indexing, security, generating graphics through ImageMagick, database access through DBI, Apache configuration, and combining CGI with JavaScript.

Dynamic HTML: The Definitive Reference

By Danny Goodman
1st Edition July 1998
1088 pages, ISBN 1-56592-494-0

Dynamic HTML: The Definitive Reference is an indispensable compendium for Web content developers. It contains complete reference material for all of the HTML tags, CSS style attributes, browser document objects, and JavaScript objects supported by the various standards and the latest versions of Netscape Navigator and Microsoft Internet Explorer.

PHP Pocket Reference

By Rasmus Lerdorf
1st Edition January 2000
120 pages, ISBN 1-56592-769-9

The *PHP Pocket Reference* is a handy quick reference for PHP, an open-source, HTML-embedded scripting language that can be used to develop web applications. This small book acts both as a perfect tutorial for learning the basics of PHP syntax and as a reference to the vast array of functions provided by PHP.

JavaScript: The Definitive Guide, 3rd Edition

By David Flanagan
3rd Edition June 1998
800 pages, ISBN 1-56592-392-8

This third edition of the definitive reference to JavaScript covers the latest version of the language, JavaScript 1.2, as supported by Netscape Navigator 4 and Internet Explorer 4. JavaScript, which is being standardized under the name ECMAScript, is a scripting language that can be embedded directly in HTML to give Web pages programming-language capabilities.

Learning VBScript

By Paul Lomax
1st Edition July 1997
616 pages, Includes CD-ROM
ISBN 1-56592-247-6

This definitive guide shows Web developers how to take full advantage of client-side scripting with the VBScript language. In addition to basic language features, it covers the Internet Explorer object model and discusses techniques for client-side scripting, like adding ActiveX controls to a Web page or validating data before sending it to the server. Includes CD-ROM with over 170 code samples.

XML

XML Pocket Reference

By Robert Eckstein
1st Edition October 1999
112 pages, ISBN 1-56592-709-5

The *XML Pocket Reference* is both a handy introduction to XML terminology and syntax, and a quick reference to XML instructions, attributes, entities, and datatypes. This small book acts both as a perfect tutorial for learning the basics of XML and as a reference to the XML and XSL specifications.

XML

DocBook: The Definitive Guide

By Norman Walsh & Leonard Muellner
1st Edition October 1999
652 pages, Includes CD-ROM
ISBN 1-56592-580-7

DocBook is a Document Type Definition (DTD) for use with XML (the Extensible Markup Language) and SGML (the Standard Generalized Markup Language). DocBook lets authors in technical groups exchange and reuse technical information. This book contains an introduction to SGML, XML, and the DocBook DTD, plus the complete reference information for DocBook.

Hand-held Computing

PalmPilot: The Ultimate Guide, 2nd Edition

By David Pogue
2nd Edition June 1999
624 pages, Includes CD-ROM
ISBN 1-56592-600-5

This new edition of O'Reilly's runaway bestseller is densely packed with previously undocumented information. The bible for users of Palm VII and all other Palm models, it contains hundreds of timesaving tips and surprising tricks, plus an all-new CD-ROM (for Windows 9x, NT, or Macintosh) containing over 3,100 PalmPilot programs from the collection of palmcentral.com, the Internet's largest Palm software site.

Hand-held Computing

Palm Programming: The Developer's Guide

By Neil Rhodes & Julie McKeehan
1st Edition December 1998
482 pages, Includes CD-ROM
ISBN 1-56592-525-4

Emerging as the bestselling hand-held computers of all time, PalmPilots have spawned intense developer activity and a fanatical following. Used by Palm in their developer training, this tutorial-style book shows intermediate to experienced C programmers how to build a Palm application from the ground up. Includes a CD-ROM with source code and third-party developer tools.

How to stay in touch with O'Reilly

1. Visit Our Award-Winning Web Site

http://www.oreilly.com/

★"Top 100 Sites on the Web" —*PC Magazine*
★"Top 5% Web sites" —*Point Communications*
★"3-Star site" —*The McKinley Group*

Our web site contains a library of comprehensive product information (including book excerpts and tables of contents), downloadable software, background articles, interviews with technology leaders, links to relevant sites, book cover art, and more. File us in your Bookmarks or Hotlist!

2. Join Our Email Mailing Lists

New Product Releases

To receive automatic email with brief descriptions of all new O'Reilly products as they are released, send email to:
listproc@online.oreilly.com
Put the following information in the first line of your message (*not* in the Subject field):
subscribe oreilly-news

O'Reilly Events

If you'd also like us to send information about trade show events, special promotions, and other O'Reilly events, send email to:
listproc@online.oreilly.com
Put the following information in the first line of your message (*not* in the Subject field):
subscribe oreilly-events

3. Get Examples from Our Books via FTP

There are two ways to access an archive of example files from our books:

Regular FTP

- ftp to:
  ftp.oreilly.com
  (login: anonymous
  password: your email address)
- Point your web browser to:
  ftp://ftp.oreilly.com/

FTPMAIL

- Send an email message to:
  ftpmail@online.oreilly.com
  (Write "help" in the message body)

4. Contact Us via Email

order@oreilly.com
To place a book or software order online. Good for North American and international customers.

subscriptions@oreilly.com
To place an order for any of our newsletters or periodicals.

books@oreilly.com
General questions about any of our books.

software@oreilly.com
For general questions and product information about our software. Check out O'Reilly Software Online at **http://software.oreilly.com/** for software and technical support information. Registered O'Reilly software users send your questions to: **website-support@oreilly.com**

cs@oreilly.com
For answers to problems regarding your order or our products.

booktech@oreilly.com
For book content technical questions or corrections.

proposals@oreilly.com
To submit new book or software proposals to our editors and product managers.

international@oreilly.com
For information about our international distributors or translation queries. For a list of our distributors outside of North America check out:
http://www.oreilly.com/www/order/country.html

5. Work with Us

Check out our website for current employment opportunites:
www.jobs@oreilly.com
Click on "Work with Us"

O'Reilly & Associates, Inc.
101 Morris Street, Sebastopol, CA 95472 USA
TEL 707-829-0515 or 800-998-9938
(6am to 5pm PST)
FAX 707-829-0104

International Distributors

UK, Europe, Middle East and Africa (except France, Germany, Austria, Switzerland, Luxembourg, Liechtenstein, and Eastern Europe)

INQUIRIES
O'Reilly UK Limited
4 Castle Street
Farnham
Surrey, GU9 7HS
United Kingdom
Telephone: 44-1252-711776
Fax: 44-1252-734211
Email: information@oreilly.co.uk

ORDERS
Wiley Distribution Services Ltd.
1 Oldlands Way
Bognor Regis
West Sussex PO22 9SA
United Kingdom
Telephone: 44-1243-779777
Fax: 44-1243-820250
Email: cs-books@wiley.co.uk

France

INQUIRIES
Éditions O'Reilly
18 rue Séguier
75006 Paris, France
Tel: 33-1-40-51-52-30
Fax: 33-1-40-51-52-31
Email: france@editions-oreilly.fr

ORDERS
GEODIF
61, Bd Saint-Germain
75240 Paris Cedex 05, France
Tel: 33-1-44-41-46-16 (French books)
Tel: 33-1-44-41-11-87 (English books)
Fax: 33-1-44-41-11-44
Email: distribution@eyrolles.com

Germany, Switzerland, Austria, Eastern Europe, Luxembourg, and Liechtenstein

INQUIRIES & ORDERS
O'Reilly Verlag
Balthasarstr. 81
D-50670 Köln
Germany
Telephone: 49-221-973160-91
Fax: 49-221-973160-8
Email: anfragen@oreilly.de (inquiries)
Email: order@oreilly.de (orders)

Canada (French language books)

Les Éditions Flammarion ltée
375, Avenue Laurier Ouest
Montréal (Québec) H2V 2K3
Tel: 00-1-514-277-8807
Fax: 00-1-514-278-2085
Email: info@flammarion.qc.ca

Hong Kong

City Discount Subscription Service, Ltd.
Unit D, 3rd Floor, Yan's Tower
27 Wong Chuk Hang Road
Aberdeen, Hong Kong
Tel: 852-2580-3539
Fax: 852-2580-6463
Email: citydis@ppn.com.hk

Korea

Hanbit Media, Inc.
Chungmu Bldg. 201
Yonnam-dong 568-33
Mapo-gu
Seoul, Korea
Tel: 822-325-0397
Fax: 822-325-9697
Email: hant93@chollian.dacom.co.kr

Philippines

Global Publishing
G/F Benavides Garden
1186 Benavides Street
Manila, Philippines
Tel: 632-254-8949/637-252-2582
Fax: 632-734-5060/632-252-2733
Email: globalp@pacific.net.ph

Taiwan

O'Reilly Taiwan
No. 3, Lane 131
Hang-Chow South Road
Section 1, Taipei, Taiwan
Tel: 886-2-23968990
Fax: 886-2-23968916
Email: taiwan@oreilly.com

China

O'Reilly Beijing
Room 2410
160, FuXingMenNeiDaJie
XiCheng District
Beijing, China PR 100031
Tel: 86-10-66412305
Fax: 86-10-86631007
Email: beijing@oreilly.com

India

Computer Bookshop (India) Pvt. Ltd.
190 Dr. D.N. Road, Fort
Bombay 400 001 India
Tel: 91-22-207-0989
Fax: 91-22-262-3551
Email: cbsbom@giasbm01.vsnl.net.in

Japan

O'Reilly Japan, Inc.
Yotsuya Y's Building
7 Banch 6, Honshio-cho
Shinjuku-ku
Tokyo 160-0003 Japan
Tel: 81-3-3356-5227
Fax: 81-3-3356-5261
Email: japan@oreilly.com

All Other Asian Countries

O'Reilly & Associates, Inc.
101 Morris Street
Sebastopol, CA 95472 USA
Tel: 707-829-0515
Fax: 707-829-0104
Email: order@oreilly.com

Australia

Woodslane Pty., Ltd.
7/5 Vuko Place
Warriewood NSW 2102
Australia
Tel: 61-2-9970-5111
Fax: 61-2-9970-5002
Email: info@woodslane.com.au

New Zealand

Woodslane New Zealand, Ltd.
21 Cooks Street (P.O. Box 575)
Waganui, New Zealand
Tel: 64-6-347-6543
Fax: 64-6-345-4840
Email: info@woodslane.com.au

Latin America

McGraw-Hill Interamericana
Editores, S.A. de C.V.
Cedro No. 512
Col. Atlampa
06450, Mexico, D.F.
Tel: 52-5-547-6777
Fax: 52-5-547-3336
Email: mcgraw-hill@infosel.net.mx